SUBMARINES
OF WORLD WAR TWO

ERMINIO BAGNASCO

CASSELL&CO

Cassell & Co
Wellington House, 125 Strand
London WC2R OBB

First published in English by Arms and Armour 1977
This edition 2000
Reprinted 2000

British Library Cataloguing-in-Publication Data:
A catalogue record for this book is available from the British Library

ISBN 1-85409-532-3

Distributed in the USA by
Sterling Publishing Co. Inc.
387 Park Avenue South
New York
NY 10016-8810

Half-title illustration: the German *U 625* under attack from Canadian aircraft off the coast
of Ireland on 10 March 1944.
Title spread illustration: the United States submarine *SS. 168 Nautilus* off the west coast of
the USA in August 1943.

The publishers wish to express their special thanks to David Lyon, who undertook the
revisions necessary for the production of this English-language edition, and to Antony
Preston, for his invaluable assistance with the photographs.
Edited by Michael Boxall; designed by David Gibbons; diagram artwork A. A. Evans.
Printed in Great Britain by The Bath Press

Contents

Data key/abbreviations/bibliography

This book deals with the submarines of the navies engaged in the Second World War and includes those boats or classes which had been laid down, but which never entered service, or which had not been completed until after hostilities had ceased.

Mention of vessels which did not progress beyond the design stage is made, only if the design had special importance in the technical evolution of the boats of a given navy. In addition to data relating to submarines proper, the principal technical and operational data of the so-called 'midgets' and the more important type of 'human' torpedoes is given.

The book commences with the technical and operational evolution of the submarine from its origins until the end of the Second World War. It deals with the birth and development of underwater craft from the seventeenth century until our time, with particular emphasis on the First World War and the inter-war years. The Second World War—dealt with in a more detailed manner in the main body of the book—is here analysed only in relation to general operational aspects and the development of anti-submarine equipment and weapons.

The main part of the book concentrates on the eight major and ten minor navies which participated in the war. Each chapter deals with one of the major navies and is divided into two sections. The first treats of naval policy, preparations for undersea warfare, types of wartime operations undertaken and the characteristics of the submarines in question: equipment, construction, performance and weapons. The second section of each chapter gives a detailed description of the various classes of submarines, beginning with the oldest, and lists the names of the boats, description, principal technical characteristics, a brief history of their wartime careers and the fate of each member of the class.

The following explanation will enable the reader to easily understand the data presented throughout the book.

Units of measurement: Both metric and imperial measurements are used in this book; equivalents should be taken as a guide, rather than as an absolutely precise conversion, especially in the case of torpedo ranges, etc.

Type-class-series: The term *type* is used when a specific and known designation of the design exists (e.g. the German boats, whose designs were numbered progressively from I to XXXVI): within each type, the different *variants* have been indicated (e.g. VII B, VII C, etc.). The term *class* is used when, to indicate a specific group of similar vessels, recourse has had to be made to the name of one of these boats, generally the first to have entered service, or to a standard term such as, a displacement, the initial letter of the names of the boats (e.g. *Balilla* Class, *600* Class, *I* Class, etc.). Within the classes, it has been necessary at times, to break down the boats into different *series* or *groups* of boats (e.g. *600* Class, *Acciaio* Series).

Number of vessels: This indicates the total number of boats belonging to a given type, class or series: where two figures are separated by a plus sign (e.g. 175 + 3), the first indicates the number of vessels that entered service, the second, that of boats laid down or launched, but whose construction was not completed. Boats ordered, but whose contract was cancelled before they were laid down, are excluded from this count.

Name or number: The names, numbers or groups of identifying letters and numbers of the various boats are given. For those that changed their name or number, the name or number prior to the final one are indicated in brackets. For US submarines, the recognition number which, in the US Navy, is an integral part of the name of the boat, is also indicated (e.g. SS.220 *Barb*).

Builder: Vessels are grouped by the name of the building yard, the location of which, is also given.

Date: For each group of boats built by a given yard, three dates are indicated (e.g. 1942–1943/44). The first and second indicate, respectively, the year of laying down and of commissioning of the first boat of the group: the third indicates the date of commissioning of the last unit.

Displacement: This, as in all other cases where it is necessary to differentiate underwater from surface characteristics, is represented by two figures or sets of figures, separated by an oblique stroke (e.g. 480/530). The first number indicates the *normal load displacement* of the boat on the surface; the second indicates the displacement, always in normal load, completely submerged. The English ton (1,016kg) has been selected as the unit of measurement, as it is generally used by all navies.

Dimensions: The first figure represents overall length; the second, maximum breadth (moulded) and the third, maximum draught at normal load. Measurements are given in imperial and metric units.

Maximum speed: This is expressed in knots (nautical miles per hour) and is the maximum operational speed with the boat at normal load, both on the surface and submerged.

Range: This is the maximum (in sea miles) attainable with a normal fuel load at the speed indicated (e.g. 4,500 at 12; 6,200 at 8). Range submerged (given speed) is that given by the maximum capacity of the storage batteries. It should be noted that the figures given for British submarines are actual figures achieved in practice: the other figures are the theoretical results of calculations based on short endurance trials. To compare the British figures with those of other navies, approximately 30 per cent extra should be added.

Armament: As a general rule, the size of guns and torpedoes are given both in inches and millimetres. However, these measurements have been presented with more regard to general convention than to logic, for there is little point in describing the well-known Bofors and Oerlikon anti-aircraft cannon as 1.6in and 0.8in respectively, when 40mm and 20mm are the generally accepted descriptions. For the same reason, British and American weapons are quoted in inches only, as per their original designations.

For automatic cannon, the twin, triple or quadruple mounts are indicated by the formula 2 x 1, 3 x 1, 4 x 1, where the first figure represents the number of barrels per mount, and the second, the number of mounts.

The number of torpedo tubes is qualified by their location, forward and aft. The number of torpedoes shown represents the total number of torpedoes capable of being stowed in the boat—those contained in the tubes plus those in reserve.

The particulars of speed, running distance and warhead weight of the various types of torpedoes, are given in tables in the Introduction, or in the part that precedes, for each major navy, the chapter dedicated to the various classes of submarine.

Maximum operational depth: This means the maximum depth that can be reached under operational conditions. It generally represents two-thirds of the theoretical 'crushing' depth and is less than the maximum test depth. It is given, when known, in the section describing the boats.

Maximum fuel load: This is expressed in tons, and is diesel oil unless otherwise indicated.

Minimum crash-dive time: This is expressed in seconds, and indicates the minimum time needed for a trained crew to completely submerge a boat from being on the surface with conning tower hatch open and a watch on deck.

Complement: The total number of officers, NCOs and ratings normally aboard in wartime.

Fate of boats: This is reported at the end of the description of each type, class or series. The abbreviations used to indicate cause of loss are shown in the following list. Where the loss can be attributed to a number of causes, the letters are combined (e.g. n–a, n–sb, etc.).

n = naval action by surface ship/s (depth-charges, guns torpedoes, ramming, etc.).

s = action by submarine/s.

a = aircraft; m = mine/s; c = capture (during the war).

sb = sabotaged, scuttled, abandoned in non-operational state.

uc = unknown causes.

v = accident (shipwreck, grounding, accidental explosion, technical accident, collision, etc.).

b = bombed in port or in building or fitting-out yard.

r = reserve, stricken, scrapped, employed for other purposes (battery-charging station, fuel depot, etc.), interned in neutral country, ceded to another country.

e = error of identification, sunk by 'friendly' forces.

x = surrendered (at cessation of hostilities).

The various losses are sub-divided according to the year of loss (or of leaving service) and, within this sub-division, by operational theatre, where all the boats lost to the same causes are grouped together. By exclusion, all boats that do not appear as lost or out of service before the end of hostilities were still in service then.

Drawings: In view of the significant difference in dimensions between the various types of boats, the drawings have not been made to a constant scale, but each has its own scale shown.

S.43 *(SS.154)* in January 1944 off San Francisco.

Bibliography

In the original Italian edition of this book, the author did not furnish a bibliography. The following list of books, however, may be of value to the reader who wishes to pursue specific subjects further.

Colledge, J. J. *Ships of the Royal Navy,* Newton Abbot, 1969.

Colledge, J. J. and Dittmar, F. J. *British Warships 1914–1919,* London, 1972.

Couhat, J. Labayle. *French Warships of World War I,* London, 1974.

Couhat, J. Labayle. *French Warships of World War II,* London, 1971.

Fraccaroli, A. *Italian Warships of World War I,* London, 1970.

Fraccaroli, A. *Italian Warships of World War II,* London, 1968.

Jentschura, H., Jung, D., Mickel, P. *Warships of the Imperial Japanese Navy 1869–1945,* London, 1977.

Lenton, H. T. *Royal Netherlands Navy,* London, 196?

Lenton, H. T. *British Submarines,* London, 1972.

Lenton, H. T. *American Submarines,* London, 1973.

Lenton, H. T. *German Warships of the Second World War,* London, 1975.

Lenton, H. T. and Colledge, J. J. *Warships of World War II,* 2nd edn., London, 1973.

Lipscomb, F. W. *The British Submarine, 2nd edn.,* London, 1975.

Le Masson, H. *The French Navy, vol. 1,* London, 1969.

Preston, A. M. *The First Submarines,* London, 1973.

Preston, A. M. *Submarines since 1919,* London, 1974.

Showell, J. P. M. *U-boats under the Swastika,* London, 1973.

Silverstone, P. *U.S. Warships of World War I,* London, 1970.

Silverstone, P. *U.S. Warships of World War II,* London, 1969.

Taylor, J. C. *German Warships of World War I,* London, 1969.

Taylor, J. C. *German Warships of World War II,* London, 1966.

Watts, A. J. *Japanese Warships of World War II,* London, 1966.

Also, of course, *Jane's Fighting Ships.* There are many good books about submarines in action, but a good starting point for the student of the Second World War at sea is the British official history, *The War at Sea,* by S. W. Roskill, published in four parts by H.M.S.O., London, 1954–1961. The American naval history by S. E. Morison is equally informative and readable. Finally, there is a penetrating analysis of submarine warfare in Hezlett's *The Submarine and Seapower.*

Preface

Submarines played a major role in the war at sea between 1939 and 1945, and achieved their best results against merchant ships, vital alike to the economy of nations at war and to the conduct of warlike operations overseas. Of an approximate total of 33,000,000 tons of merchant shipping lost by all parties in the conflict, more than 23,000,000 tons were sunk by submarines. Undoubtedly, the German and US Navies gained the greatest advantage from the employment of the submarine, sinking respectively, in the Atlantic and in the Pacific Oceans, 14 million and 4.8 million tons gross. In both cases, the submarine was employed on a large scale and fully confirmed its value as a strategic weapon.

Towards the end of the war, however, well-organised defences had become technically superior to the submarine. The closely integrated use of carrier- and land-based aircraft and surface escorts, and the unwearying and intelligent application of science had decisively defeated the conventional submarine. With the end of hostilities, this situation began to change as new developments tended to restore much of the submarine's original invulnerability. Today, the submarine can be considered the new capital ship, thanks to nuclear propulsion and the atomic warheads of the missiles carried, which make these 'boats' a major part of the strategic deterrent of the great powers.

This book deals with the more than 2,500 submarines of 18 countries, that operated in all the seas during the Second World War, and I have endeavoured to gather the principal technical and operational information relating to their design, construction and employment during the war. While particular attention has been paid to those that actually entered service, I have examined, also, those boats—several hundreds in number—whose construction was not completed in time to take part in the war or which, for

various reasons, remained in the design stage. Above all, the book aims to illustrate the 'make up' of these submarines, to show which boats constituted the various classes, what their technical characteristics were and what the boats looked like. As the wartime activities of submarines decisively influenced their technical evolution, brief mention has been made of the principal operations carried out during the war.

Most of the many books about submarines of the Second World War have confined themselves to the boats of one particular navy or another. I have endeavoured to furnish the reader with the overall picture and to supply enough material for him to compare the technical and operational histories of all the submarines that took part in the war. In order to achieve this, it has not always been possible to go into exhaustive detail.

I have made the drawings and selected the photographs with the intention of illustrating the majority of the boats mentioned. Wherever possible, I have depicted pre-war vessels in their wartime guise and have shown major wartime modifications. For the benefit of the less expert reader, the working of submarines has been illustrated by diagrams with explanatory text, in the introduction to the section dealing with technical and operational evolution.

I should like to end this brief introduction by thanking all those who have helped me in the preparation of this book; and particularly my dear friends Giorgio Giorgerini and Augusto Nani, whose assistance has proved invaluable, and Elio Occhini and Arrigo Barilli, who generously allowed me free access to their vast and precious collection of photographs.

Erminio Bagnasco

Introduction
The evolution of the submarine

Right: The Italian submarine *Smeraldo* in 1939.

According to some recent theorists, the first humans may have evolved in the shallows of lakes. Man may have been accustomed to gather his food under water before he learnt to walk. Certainly, various forms of skin-diving have been practised since recorded history began. Pearl divers and gallant underwater saboteurs have been known since the very dawn of history.

The capacity of human lungs is small: the numerous legends of men living under the sea indicate a deep-seated and long-lasting desire to extend the time and range of diving activities. The technical, physiological and psychological barriers were great, but not insuperable. The medieval story of Alexander's descent in a diving-bell is probably mythical, but, by the seventeenth century, crude forms of this device were in use for salvage purposes. At the same time, other ideas were being put forward which would lead first to the helmeted diver, then, to the self-contained set used today.

These developments do not particularly concern us here, for they had little to do with the evolution of the self-propelled vessel, capable of submerging and returning to the surface independently. It is generally agreed that the first semi-practicable idea for a submarine was published by the Englishman William Bourne during the reign of Queen Elizabeth I. His proposal was for a vessel having primitive ballast tanks within the hull, the moving walls of which would admit or expel water, causing the craft to sink or rise at will. No attempt seems to have been made to build such a vessel at the time.

Some years later, Cornelius van Drebbel, a Dutch doctor at the Court of King James I, built an oar-propelled submarine which apparently submerged, moved underwater and surfaced in the River Thames. Apparently the king witnessed this event and may have inspected the boat, but the story that he himself made a descent in it is almost certainly untrue.

During the next century, various attempts were made to produce working submarines. In 1653, the Frenchman de Son, working in Holland, produced a twin-hulled, clockwork-powered vessel. The motor, alas, was not powerful enough to move the boat. Henceforward, a number of designs were produced in England, one of which made successful shallow dives but was then lost in Plymouth Sound during a more ambitious trial.

In 1776, an extraordinary and surprisingly successful design was produced by the American David Bushnell. His was the first practicable submarine to be used in war and merits detailed description. During the early years of the American War of Independence, British warships blockaded the Atlantic coast and the patriot Bushnell thought that the blockade might be broken by underwater attack. He invented what may be considered the first naval mines, but his most interesting project was the submarine, *Turtle*. Its hull was in the form of two turtle-shells joined at the edge, and contained a ballast tank. Lead ballast was also carried and contemporary correspondence indicates that two screw propellers were fitted, one horizontal and one vertical, remarkably similar to the propulsion device, supposedly not invented until several

years later. These propellers were to be hand-operated by the one-man crew, from a miniature brass conning tower, with glass ports, at the top of the craft. Air was supplied by a primitive schnorkel. The armament consisted of what a later generation would call a limpet mine. It was made of oak, hollowed to contain powder, and was carried outside the submarine. It was intended to fasten this device to the hull of a ship by means of a wood screw. When detached from the submarine, the bomb, being lighter than the water it displaced, would float up against the ship and explode. All this machinery was to be operated by one man in cramped and dangerous surroundings.

Astonishingly, an attack was actually carried out by the extremely brave Sergeant Ezra Lee. On the night of 6 September 1776 he endeavoured to fix the bomb to the underside of the 64-gun *Eagle*, flagship of Lord Howe, which was lying off Governor's Island. He was unsuccessful because he had no means of holding the submarine firmly against the target hull. It was thought that Lee was defeated by the coppered hull of the British ship. This is not true: *Eagle* had not been coppered at that time. Anyone who has worked underwater knows how difficult it is to exert any force unless firmly anchored.

After this, Bushnell seems to have abandoned the development of his design, but the idea of submarine warfare was taken up by another American inventor. Robert Fulton offered a design to the French government in 1797. Despite their need of attacking British sea supremacy by any means, the French gave Fulton little encouragement, but in 1800 he was granted financial aid to build his *Nautilus*. Of copper on iron frames, she looked more like a modern submarine than *Turtle*, having an elongated hull, a propeller aft, a raised hemispherical conning tower and diving planes. She was larger than *Turtle* and the efforts of her three-man crew could be supplemented on the surface by a collapsible sail. Again, her weapon was a floating charge to be attached to the hull of a target. It was tried successfully in August 1801, when an anchored shallop was blown up, the first vessel to be sunk by submarine attack. In September 1800, Fulton claimed to have attacked two British brigs off the Normandy coast, but he was foiled by the lack of mobility of his vessel and the French rapidly lost interest. Soon afterwards, Fulton offered his idea to the Royal Navy who, sensibly, rejected it.

Thereafter, Fulton devoted his inventiveness to steam navigation. It is interesting to note that both French and British naval authorities had grave doubts about the ethics of employing submarines in war, as well as about their practicality; as to the latter, they were justified at that time. Not until advancing industry and science could provide lightweight engines for surface propulsion, electric power for submerged propulsion and the Whitehead 'fish' torpedo for attack, and gather these into a steel hull strong enough to resist pressure at depth, would the submarine become a workable weapon of war.

Meanwhile, a number of interesting designs appeared, all of which contributed to the development of a practical submarine. After Fulton, the next serious step was taken by the Bavarian Wilhelm Bauer. In 1850 the Danish Fleet was blockading the German coast and Bauer produced a submarine *Le Plongeur Marin* which, despite her limitations, succeeded in keeping the Danes at a distance. She was built of sheet iron and resembled an oblong tank. On 1851 she sank in Kiel harbour when her plates buckled under pressure. Bauer saved his own life and those of his two-man crew by insisting that more water be admitted to the vessel until the pressure was equal and the hatches burst open. This was the first escape from a submerged submarine. After an unsuccessful visit to England, Bauer persuaded the Russians

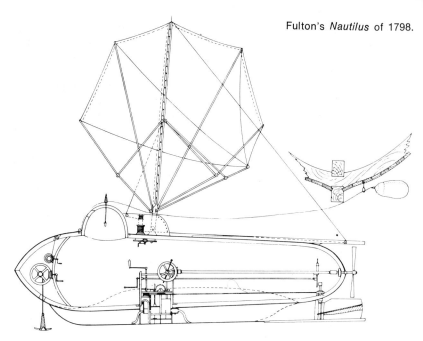

Fulton's *Nautilus* of 1798.

to build his *Le Diable Marin*, but little is known of this vessel save that he took her beneath the surface of Kronstadt harbour during the coronation of Tsar Alexander II and during the royal salute, several musicians in the submarine struck up *God Preserve The Tsar*.

The English and Americans were also producing submarine designs during the middle years of the nineteenth century, but the next significant step was taken by the French Navy with the launching of *Plongeur* at Rochefort in 1863. She was designed by Charles Brun from an idea conceived by Captain Siméon Bourgois. Powered by compressed air which could also be used to blow the ballast tanks free of water, she was clumsy, with hydroplanes aft only, and her range was minimal. Her armament consisted of a 'spar' torpedo, an explosive charge on the end of a long pole projecting from the bow. This was an improvement on previous ideas for attack, but still required a close approach to the enemy and the explosion presented danger of swamping or sinking to the parent craft. The French did not develop the design of *Plongeur* though she represented an advance on all that had appeared hitherto.

The spar torpedo was used in action by both sides during the American Civil War. The North carried them in steam boats only, but the South, without a navy and blockaded by the North, was prepared to try submarines. These were small steam-powered boats called 'Davids' (the Confederate forces were up against a large fleet and saw themselves as giant-killers) and although they trimmed right down until only funnel and conning tower showed, they could not submerge completely and cannot really be thought of as submarines. Meanwhile, a hand-powered design was being developed by H. L. Hunley. After two failures, his third boat, powered by an eight-man crew with a commander conning from forward, showed promise. She sank on trials, drowning her designer but was raised, named after him and dispatched with a volunteer crew against the Northern warship, *Housatonic*. On 17 February 1864, *H. L. Hunley*'s spar torpedo exploded against the side of *Housatonic,* sinking both vessels. The first successful wartime attack had also demonstrated that, as yet, the submarine was virtually a suicide weapon. The Yankee North's answer to the Confederate Davids was *Intelligent Whale*. Like *H. L. Hunley*, she was hand-propelled but was hard to manoeuvre and lacked a suitable weapon. The end of the Civil War robbed her of targets and she was never used.

In 1879, George Garrett, a clergyman from Liverpool launched his submarine, *Resurgam*. She was steam-powered on the surface, but when submerged, her fires were extinguished and she relied on steam stored in an extra-large boiler. *Resurgam* was wrecked during trials off the Welsh coast, but Garrett had attracted the attention of the Swedish industrialist and inventor; Thorsten Nordenfelt who backed Garrett to build an improved version in Sweden. Trials of *Nordenfelt No. 1* in 1885 proved her to be extremely difficult to control under water, but she was sold to the Greek Navy in 1886. Her main significance was that she carried a torpedo tube for a Whitehead 'fish' torpedo and a Nordenfelt machine-gun mounted on deck, and these heralded the standard armament of later submarines. Subsequent Nordenfelts were built in England for Turkey and Russia, and two were built in Germany for the Germans but none was much more successful than the first with regard to depth-keeping.

An apparently unsuccessful electrically-driven submarine was built in England (Campbell and Ash's *Nautilus II* of 1885), but the first successful attempt to utilise what was to become the standard underwater propulsion method for submarines, was made in Spain. In 1886, a Spanish naval officer, Lieutenant Peral built a boat for the Spanish Navy. Named after himself, his boat was the first to use an underwater propulsion system entirely independent of the atmosphere. She was powered by 420 batteries driving two 30hp main motors and three 5hp auxiliary motors for pumping out ballast tanks. Peral created problems for himself by using the same unsatisfactory system of vertical screws for depth-keeping as the *Nordenfelt*s. Although a generally sound design, Peral's submarine came to nothing owing to lack of official support.

It was left to the French to develop what proved to be the first effective modern submarine. The great French naval architect, Dupuy de Lôme, started work on the design of a submersible and when he died in 1885, his disciple, Gustave Zedé, carried on with the work. In 1886, a small electrically-powered boat, to his designs, was ordered for the French Navy. In 1888, she was launched as *Gymnote*. She too, was fitted with the pernicious vertical screws and was not particularly successful at first, but she showed enough promise for a much larger vessel, *Gustave Zedé* to be ordered. Again, her initial trials were not entirely satisfactory but a prolonged period of experiment and alteration finally produced workable submarines in both cases. Hydroplanes made the boats more controllable and casings were added to make running on the surface safer. While these alterations were being made, a third vessel, *Morse* was ordered. Her main distinction was that she introduced the periscope.

Even while *Morse* was building, another submarine had been laid down by the French Navy. This was the epoch-making *Narval*. Her designer, Maxime Laubeuf had won an open competition for the design of a submarine displacing 200 tons with a range of 100 miles surfaced and 100 miles submerged. The crucial features of Laubeuf's remarkable boat were the separate propulsion systems (steam for surface and electricity for underwater) and a double hull for water and fuel. These set the pattern for future submarines, nearly all of which were to have a dual propulsion system until the Walter turbine and the atomic engine were realised. With the completion of this boat in 1899, the submarine had become a practicable weapon of war,

suitable for regular employment by navies. The French were not slow to order *Narval's* successors and became the first naval power to have an appreciable submarine force.

Other nations were not far behind. In 1892, the Italians had built a small electrically-powered boat. Named *Delfino,* she was extensively modernised a number of times and survived until 1919. But it was the US Navy, after the French, that played the most important part in introducing the submarine into naval service. This was brought about largely through the efforts of the Irish-American inventor, John P. Holland. He, like Bushnell and Fulton before him, had been trying to produce a weapon for use against the British Royal Navy, and had made several designs before he launched *Plunger* for the US Navy in 1897. He had already realised the importance of a dual propulsion system and sensibly, adopted the internal combustion engine for power on the surface and to recharge the batteries of the electric motor— which would give a much quicker diving time than the steam engine in *Narval*. Unfortunately, there were delays in placing an order and far too many design changes while building so that the boat was a failure, but Holland had already severed his connections with her and, privately, had begun to build a craft which was to be called *Holland No. 8*. This proved successful and was purchased by the US Navy in 1900. Soon, similar vessels were building, not only for America but, ironically, given Holland's Fenianism, for the Royal Navy.

Simon Lake was another original and important American inventor who had been developing submarine designs, though he did not succeed in obtaining orders until much later. Peculiar features of his early designs were the addition of wheels for mobility on the sea bottom and air locks for divers.

From *Narval* to the First World War

Perhaps the most important aspect of Laubeuf's thinking when he designed *Narval* was his concept of a submersible torpedo-boat. Previous submarines had been quite incapable of remaining at sea because their electric motors severely limited their range and because their narrow hulls, scarcely appearing above the surface, made navigation hazardous in the extreme. *Narval* with her length of 111ft 6in (34m), beam of 13ft 0in (3.8m) and displacing 117 tons surfaced and 202 tons submerged, was capable of operating offensively as well as defensively. She could remain surfaced until forced to dive for attack or concealment.

In other words, *Narval,* like nearly all submarines up to the latter years of the Second World War, was basically a surface ship which could also submerge, not a true 'submarine' which operates under water most of the time. Attempts to achieve this ideal in previous designs had been thwarted by the inadequte technology of the day.

Laubeuf realised the importance of a strong hull and in *Narval,* both outer and inner hulls were—for that time—heavily plated. The inner hull was cylindrical and this caused an early commander to think of her as "a torpedo-boat which carried a submarine inside". She carried a crew of thirteen and was armed with four 'drop-collars' for 18in (450mm) torpedoes. The drop-collar was invented by the Russian, Drzewiecki and consisted of a sling that held the torpedo at any desired angle before launching. It was preferred to torpedo tubes by the French at that time.

Narval's 220ihp steam engine gave a maximum surface speed of 9.88 knots, and could recharge the batteries on the surface, using the 80ehp electric motor coupled to the same shaft as a generator. The

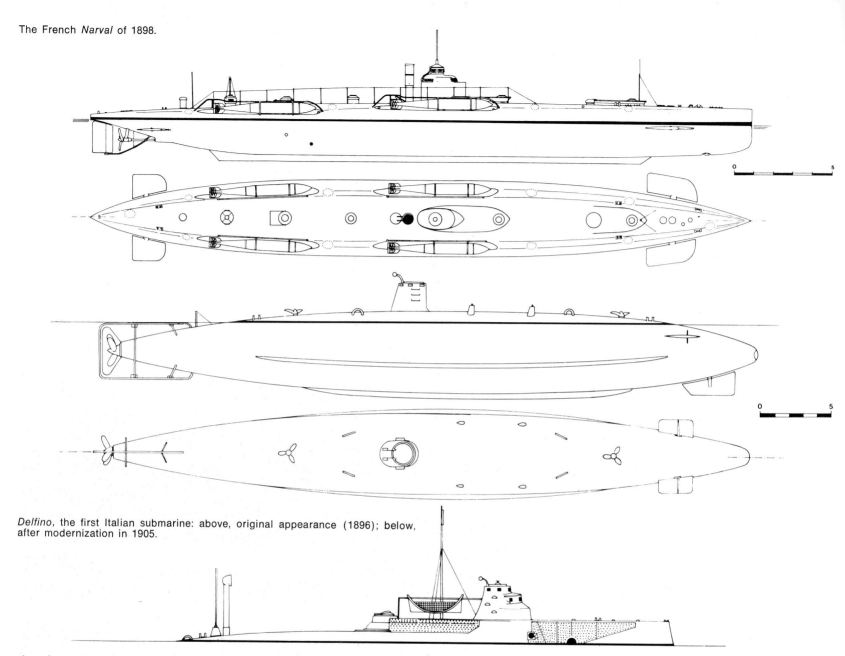

The French *Narval* of 1898.

Delfino, the first Italian submarine: above, original appearance (1896); below, after modernization in 1905.

electric motor gave a maximum submerged speed of 5.3 knots. Her endurance was 58 miles at 2.2 knots submerged, 345 miles at 8.8 knots surfaced. The worst feature was her diving time (10–15 minutes) because of the necessity of shutting down the boiler and steam engine. The first operational trials confirmed her as a practicable weapon. Remaining at sea between Cherbourg (where she was built) and Brest for forty-eight hours; she made several dives, the longest of which lasted twelve hours.

At the beginning of the twentieth century, therefore, France was the most advanced naval power in the theory and practice of building submarines. By the end of 1901, she had eleven boats on order or in service, some operational, others purely experimental. At the same time, the United States had one boat in service and seven building. The Italians were still experimenting with the little *Delfino,* which was one of the first submarines to be equipped with a periscope.

The Royal Navy was still biding its time. On 13 May 1900, Lord Goschen, First Lord of The Admiralty, stated in the House of Commons that the Admiralty were not ready to take the initiative with regard to the submarine. It was a weapon for weaker navies. Were this weapon to become operationally practicable, however, the threat to Britain, as possessor of the largest navy and mercantile marine, would be greater than to any other nation.

This was a sensible attitude, and not the unthinking conservatism seen by so many commentators. The submarine was an obvious danger to Britain and there was little point in encouraging its development while its powers as yet, were potential rather than actual. It were better to allow others to suffer the expense and trouble of development. The concomitant of this attitude was the quick and decisive reaction to proven success. This the Royal Navy showed, by ordering five submarines to be built to Holland's designs by Vickers at

British *Holland*-type submarine
of 1901.

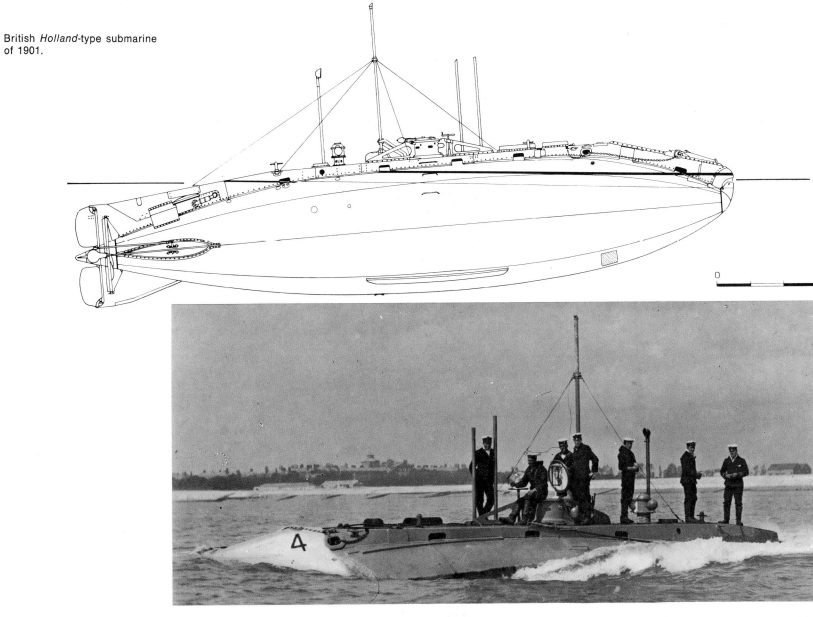

British *Holland No. 4* and *B 1*
(bottom) of the 1900s, seen
in the Solent.

Barrow in 1901, becoming thereby the third navy to order effective submarines in quantity. In this way, Britain took full advantage of foreign developments while utilising the resources of her own ship-building industry, which was not only the world's largest by a huge margin but, in many respects, the most efficient.

The thorny question of the submarine's status in international law had already been discussed at the Hague Conference in 1899. During the session on 31 May, the Russians had proposed that construction of submarines be prohibited. The British, Danish, German, Italian and Japanese representatives were in favour of a ban if it were accepted by all nations. As France was (understandably) opposed to the ban and the United States and Austria-Hungary were not prepared to surrender their future freedom of action regarding underwater warfare, nothing was done. The question was not even discussed during the second Hague Conference in 1907, so that when the First World War began, no valid international agreement about the use of submarines in war had been reached.

Meanwhile, the submarine developed rapidly. The early American and British models, whose short hulls had been designed with little or no thought to surface seaworthiness, were followed by other designs, closer to *Narval*, with appreciably raised casings, longer hulls and built-up conning towers. The British *A*-Class boats were home-designed and tended to stick to the 'single hull with saddle tanks' formula. The Americans tried developments of both Holland and Lake designs. The French continued to build large numbers of boats, some of single-hull design, but the majority of the twin-hull *Laubeuf* type.

In 1902, Russia ordered her first effective submarine, though she had already purchased a fair number of experimental types, of little or no value, during the preceding years. In 1903, Italy ordered the first of a class of submarines—first that is, if one disregards the experimental *Delfino*. In 1904, Japan ordered her first submarines (more Holland designs) from the United States. Surprisingly, in view of later developments, Germany was the last of the naval powers to acquire a modern submarine. This was *Unterseeboot 1 (U 1)*, built by Krupp in 1906 to a French design modified from that of three submarines already built for Russia at the same yard.

During the immediate pre-war years, there was a profusion of hull designs: the Italian Laurenti, the British Hay-Denny (used by the Dutch but not in its country of origin), the Krupp partial double hull and the Laubeuf double hull. Lake continued to develop his designs and throughout the world, shipbuilders purchased licences to build the most successful boats. Thus, Scott's of Greenock purchased the right to build Laurenti's designs, and the Laubeuf design became associated with the great French armament firm of Schneider.

A series of technical developments rapidly became common property, used in all submarines and making them safer and more efficient. The use of pairs of hydroplanes, forward and aft, had early been seen as the best way to gain more precise control of diving and surfacing than was possible from flooding or blowing the main ballast tanks. However, trim tanks were introduced at either end of the hull to supplement this control and to adjust the attitude of the submerged boat, even when at rest. The negative tank, generally placed at the centre of the boat, inside or outside the pressure hull, had a volume which corresponded to that of the conning tower. When the boat was trimmed down, with main tanks flooded and only the conning tower above the surface, its flooding would cause a crash dive. Conversely, if this were the only tank to be blown, it would put

the conning tower back on the surface. Torpedo compensating tanks, close to the torpedo tubes at bow and stern, were so arranged as to flood at the instant of firing torpedoes. If this were not done, or were done badly, the bow or stern of the boat was liable to rise suddenly to the surface, having lost the weight of the torpedo or torpedoes. This effect was known as 'porpoising' and submarines at periscope depth, only a few feet below the surface, were very prone to it.

The fuel tanks were normally contained in the space between the pressure hull and the casing (external hull). Openings in the bottom were fitted with adjustable valves which allowed sea water to enter as fuel was consumed. There was no danger of the fuel mixing with the water because oil has a lower specific weight and floats on top. The ballast tanks, or double hulls, were fitted with valves, adjustable from the inside. For diving, air vents at the top allowed air in the ballast tanks to escape while water entered through gates at the bottom. For surfacing, the vents were closed and water was blown from the tanks by compressed air piped from tanks inside the boat. The floodable compartments were normally situated in the mid-section of the hull. At the extremities of the hull, open to the free flow of water, casings imparted a more seaworthy shape to the forward and after sections of the boat.

Neither the steam engines used by the French, nor the petrol (gasoline) engines adopted initially by the Americans and British, were particularly suitable for submarine propulsion. Steam engines and their boilers were bulky, required large uptakes which represented points of weakness in a submerged hull and required a long shutting-off and starting period at either end of a dive. The volatile and inflammable fuel of the petrol engine was a constant source of danger. The answer lay in the diesel engine, which combined the compactness of the petrol engine with less dangerous fuel. The French were the first to adopt it in *Aigrette* of 1904. Curiously, though the diesel was a German invention, the first U-boat was not fitted with one of these engines until 1912, some time after the other major navies had adopted it. Instead, the Germans had been using the Korting heavy oil engine.

Until the invention of the gyro-compass (1910–11), submarines had had to mount their magnetic compasses on the conning tower where they were less affected by the surrounding metal of the hull. Submerged, the helmsman used a system of prisms and mirrors to see the compass dial. The gyro-compass, uninfluenced by the magnetism of the hull, could be mounted inside, which made accurate steering a lot easier.

The first periscopes of the 1890s were crude, but they were rapidly improved and by 1914 most submarines had a large 'search' periscope and a smaller 'attack' periscope which left a much less conspicuous wake on the surface.

By 1914, most submarines had been fitted with a small calibre gun for surface use, but their main weapon was the torpedo, itself a miniature submarine. Without this deadly underwater weapon, the submarine would have proved of little use in warfare. It is possible, though not proven, that Robert Whitehead, its inventor, was influenced in the early stages of its development by *Plongeur* of 1863. The crude device that Whitehead produced in 1868 had undergone a continuous process of development, and during the early years of the twentieth century great strides were made in speed and range, thanks to the introduction of air heating. The almost simultaneous introduction of the gyroscope, improved its accuracy, so that the submarines of 1914 were armed with a formidable weapon.

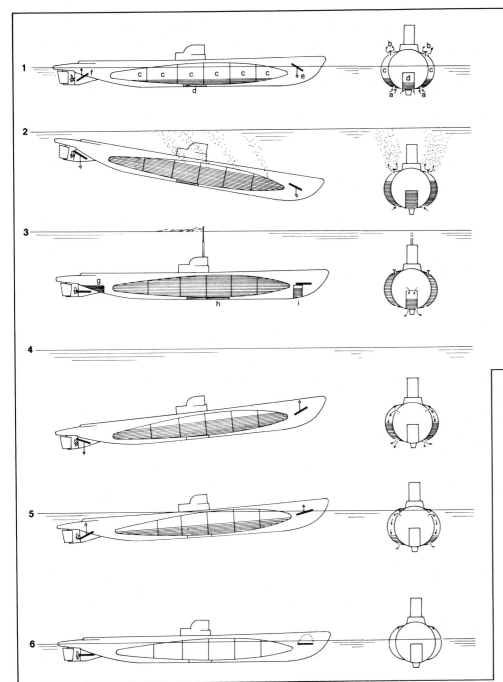

Phases of diving and surfacing a submarine.

1. Boat moving on surface: beginning of dive.
The lower valves (a) and the air vents (b) of the ballast tanks (c) and of the crash-dive (or negative) tank (d) are opened; the bow planes (e) are angled to the 'down' position and the tail planes (f) to an 'up' position, so as to cause the boat, powered by the diesel engines, to assume a 'bow down' attitude and hasten the dive.
2. Boat submerged with ballast tanks still not completely flooded.
Diesels replaced by electric motors for powering the boat and tail planes are angled to the 'down' position to impart a horizontal attitude to the boat.
3. Boat submerged and moving at periscope depth.
Ballast tanks are completely flooded and negative tank is emptied. Depth and trim of boat are controlled by minor movements of horizontal planes and by transfer of water in trim tanks (g/h/i).
4. Boat moving at great depth: beginning of surfacing.
Air vents of ballast tanks are closed and the water is blown out of them by compressed air from containers inside pressure hull; at the same time, bow planes are angled to 'up' and tail planes to 'down' causing boat to assume 'stern down' attitude to hasten operation.
5. Boat moving while surfacing.
Tail planes angled to 'down' causing boat to assume horizontal attitude; pumps are started which draw air from conning-tower hatch and pump it to dive tanks, completing their evacuation.
6. Boat moving on surface.
Dive tanks are emptied completely and diesel engines started, replacing electric engines for powering boat.

Midships sections of submarines of the period 1900–1910.

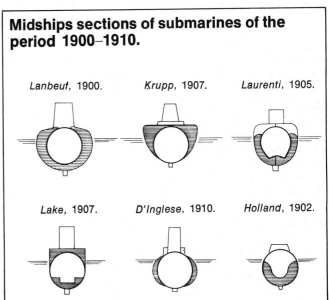

Lanbeuf, 1900. *Krupp, 1907.* *Laurenti, 1905.*

Lake, 1907. *D'Inglese, 1910.* *Holland, 1902.*

The progressive improvement in the performance of torpedoes can be seen in Table 1. There were variations in the performance of different nation's torpedoes, but they were not great. Although for a time the French had favoured the unreliable externally mounted drop-collar, the standard method of firing torpedoes from submarines was, and remains, the torpedo tube. The torpedo is loaded from inside the boat with the tube's outer door closed. The inner door is then closed, and when the torpedo is ready for firing the outer door is opened and the torpedo is pushed out by a blast of compressed air. The outer door is then closed and the tube is emptied of water, ready for the reload.

Table 1: Torpedoes, 1867 to 1914

Year:	Diameter: (inches)	Length:	Charge: (lb)	Speed: (knots)	Range: (yards)
1867	14	11ft 7in	40	5.7	200
1872	16	?	?	12	600
1876	14	14ft 6in	32	18	600
1887	14	15	70	27	600
1890	18	16ft 7in	198	30	800
1905	18	17	220	29	2,190
1914	21	—	225	29	10,000

Another type of underwater weapon available to the world's navies was the mine. The Americans were the first to use submerged mines during the War of Independence and the War of 1812, but the first effective use of moored mines was made by the Russians during the Crimean War. Since then, they have specialised in mine warfare and, appropriately, ordered the first minelaying submarine, *Krab*, in 1912. She was not completed until 1915, by which time the Germans were bringing their own minelaying submarines into service. *Krab*'s sixty mines were stowed in two fore-and-aft rows, inside the casing but above the pressure hull, exposed alike to deterioration and danger. They were laid from two side by side ports in the stern. *Krab* was not very successful but she and her later, improved sisters were to be usefully employed in the shallow waters of the Baltic, a sea, ideally suited to mine warfare.

The submarines of the early years of the twentieth century were not particularly safe to operate. Between 1904 and 1914, fifteen boats were lost to collisions, internal explosions and other causes. The British lost seven, the French four, the Russians two and the Germans and Japanese, one each. Several of these boats were subsequently recovered and returned to service, but the loss of life was considerable. Few effective safety devices had been fitted, apart from the telephone buoys which marked the position of a sunken boat and enabled the trapped crew to communicate with the surface. As yet, there existed no workable device that would enable survivors to escape from a sunken submarine.

At the outbreak of war in 1914, the major submarine fleets were made up as shown in Table 2.

Table 2: The major submarine fleets of the world in 1914

Country:	Number in service:	Building or on order:
Austria-Hungary	6	6
France	45	25
Germany	29	19
Great Britain	77	32
Italy	18	2
Japan	13	2
Russia	28	2
United States	35	6

British submarines in this period can be separated, for convenience, into four groups. The early, small submarines of the *A* and *B* Classes (1903–5); the thirty-eight obsolescent *C* Class of 1906–10, suited only to harbour defence or coastal work; the larger *D* Class (1910–12) and the excellent *E* Class which was coming into service in 1914. In addition, an enormous programme of orders had begun in 1913, including experimental designs and foreign types building under licence.

Primarily, Britain's submarines were intended for use in the North Sea, as were the Germans', though the German Navy was a late starter and most of her boats were comparatively large and modern. The *U 23–U 6* Series of 1913–14 were of 669–864ts compared to the 668–810ts of their British contemporaries of the *E* Class.

The French had a large submarine fleet, but seem to have devoted little thought to its employment since their old enemy, Britain, had become an ally. There were suggestions of using submarines in conjunction with the fleet; a concept which appealed also to the British, but the submarine was unsuitable for the proposed role.

Other powers had submarines thought to be suitable for particular theatres of operations. For Italy and Austria, it was the Aegean; for the Russians, the Baltic and Black Sea, though they also had one submarine based in the Arctic. The United States, believing in an isolationist policy, had a fleet of comparatively small boats, suitable for coastal defence. Japan, as yet, relied on foreign designs.

The submarine in the First World War

On 8 August 1914, six days after the war with France had begun and three days after the opening of hostilities against Great Britain, the first torpedo of the war was fired at a capital ship. The German *U 15*, patrolling with nine others in northern Scottish waters, attacked the British battleship *Monarch* without success. At dawn the next day, *U 15*, apparently immobilised by engine trouble, was rammed and sunk by the British cruiser *Birmingham*. When the U-boats returned to Heligoland, *U 13* was also missing and is thought to have been mined on 12 August. These were the first of approximately 278 submarines lost in action during the First World War.

The first success registered by a submarine, was the sinking of the British light cruiser *Pathfinder*. She was torpedoed off Edinburgh on 5 September 1914 by *U 21* (Leutnant Hersing) a boat later to become famous for her exploits in the Mediterranean and off the Dardanelles. The effect of this first sinking was immediate; on the same day, the British Grand Fleet abandoned its base in the North Sea and transferred to Loch Ewe, on the western coast of Scotland. This move

North Sea, 22 September 1914. Sinking of the British armoured cruisers *Aboukir*, *Hogue* and *Cressy* by U9 (Lt. Weddigen).

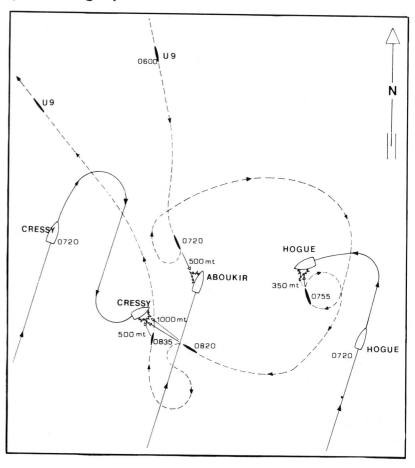

Table 3: Selected examples of submarines in service in 1914

Country:	Class:	Year entered service:	Displacement (tons)	Maximum speed (knots): surfaced/subm	Range (miles at knots): surfaced	Range (miles at knots): submerged	Armament: Drop-collar torpedo mounting	Torpedo tubes	Gun
Austria-Hungary	U 5–6	1909	233/270	11.4/10	1,000 at 10	50 at 5		2 x 18in (457mm)	
France	Sirène	1902	157/213	9.75/5.8	430 at 7.75	55 at 3.75	4 x 18in (457mm)		
	Archimède	1911	598/810.5	14.92/10.95	1,160 at 10	100 at 4.5	4 x 18in (457mm)	1	
Germany	U 1	1906	238/283	10.8/8.7	1,500 at 10	50 at 5		1 x 18in (457mm)	
	U 31–U 41	1915–15	685/867	16.75/10.3	7,800 at 9	80 at 5		4 x 20in (530mm)	2 x 88mm
Great Britain	A	1903–5	165/180	11/7	320 at 10	30 at 5		2 x 18in (457mm)	
	D	1908–12	550/620	14/10	2,500 at 10	45 at 5		3 x 18in (457mm)	1 x 12pdr
Italy	Pullino	1913	355/405	14/10	2,700 at 8	170 at 2.5		6 x 18in (457mm)	
Japan	Ha 3–Ha 5 British-built	1911	291/326	12/8.5	660 at 12	60 at 4		2 x 18in (457mm)	
Russia	Morsch	1914	650/780	18/10	2,500 at 12	30 at 8	8	4	1 x 76mm
U.S.A.	H Class	1914	358/467	14/10.5	2,300 at XX	100 at X		4 x 18in (457mm)	

did not bother Kapitän-Leutnant Otto Weddigen, the first of the U-boat aces. Commanding *U 9* off the Dutch coast, between the hours of 07.20 and 08.20 on 22 September 1914, he attacked and sank the British 12,000-ton armoured cruisers *Aboukir, Hogue* and *Cressy*. Weddigen's success confirmed unequivocally the great operational possibilities of the submarine which hitherto had been purely theoretical. The attack had been carried out with determination and skill. The tubes had been reloaded while submerged and advantage had been taken of the confusion of the British who, thinking that the first casualty had struck a mine, stopped to pick up survivors.

Historians accord the same degree of importance to this action, as to the battle at Hampton Roads on 8 March 1862, when armoured ships faced each other for the first time. A new era of naval warfare had begun. Henceforward, the submarine would prove a key element of naval power to the point where, with the appearance of the first strategic missile submarines, it would be considered the new capital ship.

Following the successes against warships came the first sinking of a merchant ship: the British collier *Glitra* was sunk by *U 17* on 20 October 1914, off the coast of Norway.

Thus began the warfare that would be waged by German submarines against enemy merchant shipping until 1918, warfare which would result in the loss of 18,716,982 GRT (more than 10,000,000 of which were under the British flag) and bring Great Britain to the brink of defeat.

Before the war, Germany had given little thought to the employment of the submarine against enemy shipping and, internationally, the methods and limitations of this type of warfare—sinking without warning in certain areas, attitude towards neutrals, etc.—had not been fully defined. Increasingly, the practical difficulties of commerce raiding by traditional methods and the gradual improvement of Allied defensive measures drove the Germans to adopt a more ruthless stance. Early in 1916, they tentatively adopted unrestricted submarine warfare, employing 'sink on sight' methods in the war zone. The pressure of neutral opinion, led by the United States, caused a temporary relaxation, but the attraction of strangling British commerce was too great and on 1 February 1917, Germany again declared unrestricted submarine warfare. By now, the Allied defensive measures were becoming increasingly effective, but the German boats achieved notable successes, sinking in 1917 (the crucial year of the war), nearly

9,000,000 GRT. These were enemy ships and neutral ships in the service of the enemy, torpedoed or sunk by mines laid by submarines.

Having entered the war with only 29 boats, Germany ordered another 800 during the war. Of these, 343 entered service and 178 were lost in action. At the armistice, 207 boats were still building. The maximum size of the submarine fleet was reached in October 1917 with 140 operational boats of which, 55 were at sea, 39 temporarily in base and 46 undergoing refit. German losses were rather heavy but can be considered to have been acceptable when measured against sinkings effected: one submarine lost for approximately 31 ships sunk. This ratio was to be far less favourable during the Second World War.

Between 1914 and 1918, U-boats were present in all the major theatres of operations: in the North Sea, in the Atlantic, in the Baltic and in the Mediterranean which they reached via the Straits of Gibraltar, and where they used the facilities of Austrian bases in the Adriatic, and Turkish bases in the Dardanelles. Some smaller boats were delivered in sections, by train to the Austrian bases and there assembled.

The major of these theatres was, undoubtedly, the North Sea and the waters to the west of Great Britain but, from mid 1917, with the entry into service of the first long-range 'U-cruisers', even the central Atlantic and the waters off the eastern coast of North America became a hunting ground for the German boats.

When the war ended, the German submarine fleet numbered 121 boats which were taken over by the Allies and divided among the navies of the victors.

Allied submarines were employed chiefly against enemy submarines and warships: enemy merchantmen were scarce. The British boats were mainly deployed patrolling the German bases in the North Sea, and scored a number of successes against surface warships and U-boats. Some pentrated the Skaggerak and operated in the Baltic, where they sank several German merchantmen as well as warships. Eventually, the seven surviving British boats were scuttled at their Russian base because of the October Revolution. A number of daring penetrations of the Dardanelles caused losses to the Turks at the expense of heavy casualties.

The French deployed their submarines mainly along their Atlantic coastline, in the English Channel, in the North Sea and in the Mediterranean. Like the British, they operated mainly against enemy boats.

French boats also operated alongside Italian boats in the Adriatic with some degree of success, and took part in the forcing of the Dardanelles.

During the first two years of the war, the few Austro-Hungarian submarines ventured into the central Mediterranean and the Tyrrhenian Sea where they operated against Allied shipping, supported by numerous German boats, based mainly at Cattaro (now Kotor in Yugoslavia). Nearly all of them were later bottled up in the Adriatic by the increasingly effective barrier across the Straits of Otranto (the Otranto Barrage consisted of a line of mined nets which descended to a great depth) and by a patrol line of small anti-submarine vessels.

American and Japanese submarines had no opportunity to carry out any major operation.

Russian submarines operated chiefly in the Baltic against the Germans, but ceased all activity (as did the rest of her fleet) with the outbreak of the Revolution in 1917.

The U-boat played the major role in undersea operations during the First World War. Its characteristics were continuously improved and its tactics revised in the light of technical development and experience gained. But at the same time, the Allied navies—particularly the Royal Navy—were developing the first anti-submarine weapons. These, though of rudimentary design, were the forerunners of those which, twenty-five years hence, would defeat the 'conventional' submarine in the Battle of the Atlantic. In 1914, the only weapons that surface units could employ against submarines were the gun and the torpedo for use against boats surprised on the surface, and the ramming of boats caught at periscope depth or beginning to dive.

The most famous ramming was, undoubtedly, that of *U 29* (commanded by Otto Weddigen) by the British battleship *Dreadnought* on 18 March 1915. It is ironical that Weddigen, to whom must be credited the first great demonstration of the submarine's capabilities (action of *U 9* on 22 September 1914) should have been lost as the result of an action by a ship which, herself, was the very epitome of a class of vessel the supremacy of which was most threatened by the submarine.

The first truly anti-submarine weapon was the depth-charge, which appeared in British ships in 1916. Basically, the depth-charge was a bomb dropped into the sea above the presumed position of the submerged boat, and which exploded at a predetermined depth by means of a time fuze or, later, a hydrostatic device. The first depth-charges contained from 90lb (41kg) to 300lb (136kg) of explosive. Because of the limited number carried and the lack of accuracy with which they were launched, they had little practical effect. The ships launching them had no instrument capable of detecting a submerged submarine, so that an attack with depth-charges was of necessity a haphazard affair, carried out only after a submarine had attacked or revealed herself or her periscope.

From 1917, the number of depth-charges aboard British ships was considerably increased and the first depth-charge throwers with a range of 60–100 yards (55–91m), were fitted. A great step forward in anti-submarine operations was made with the development of the hydrophone. This was a submerged microphone which could detect at a distance, the noise of a boat's propellers and trim-tank pumps. Progressively modified and improved in performance, the hydrophone became the basic instrument for hunting submarines during the First World War. Because of the great distances over which sound waves propagate themselves in water, hydrophones were of value to sub-marines, enabling them, while submerged, to detect moving surface vessels beyond visual range.

During this period, adopting the principle of the Fessenden apparatus for the transmission of signals between submerged submarines, the British, in great secrecy, developed ASDIC (the initials of the Anti-Submarine Detection Investigation Committee). This instrument was based on the directional propagation and reflection of ultrasonic waves in water. Not only could it detect the presence of a submerged boat (by the reflection of sound waves emitted by an underwater transmitter) but also, its course (by orientation of the transmitter) and its distance (based on the time that elapsed between the transmission of the ultrasonic impulse and the reception of the echo: the speed of propagation of sound in water being more or less constant and equal to some 1,500 yards (1,372m) per second). ASDIC could have greatly reduced the operational possibilities of the submarine, but it was never employed operationally during the war, and retained its experimental status for some time afterwards.

In a desperate attempt to hit back at the undersea aggressor, the British, Germans, Italians and French all tried the idea of decoy ships. The British, by far the chief employers of the craft, called theirs 'Q-ships'. They were merchant vessels of various kinds, tramps, colliers and schooners, fitted with concealed guns and, sometimes, torpedoes and bomb-throwers. Casks in the hold and similar measures, gave extra buoyancy in the event of torpedo hits. The submarine, lured to the surface to sink an apparently helpless target by gunfire, was suddenly confronted by the unmasked weapons.

So fond were the British of this idea, that they altered numbers of small warships to look like merchantmen and converted many merchantmen to Q-ships. At first, these vessels scored some heartening successes, but when the secret leaked out Q-ships became less and less useful. Early in 1915, two U-boats were sunk by an ingenious variant of the Q-ship idea, the trawler-submarine trap. A trawler towed a *C* Class submarine instead of a trawl, and when attacked by a U-boat's deck gun, notified the towed submarine via a telephone cable attached to the tow line.

These were but temporary expedients: airships and aeroplanes were to prove infinitely more valuable as anti-submarine weapons.

Convoy of 20 ships with an escort of 6 destroyers zigzagging at high speed (1917).

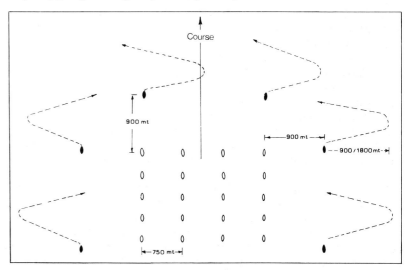

They and the balloons and kites that were also used, were more successful in detecting and frightening off submarines than in actually sinking them. Submarines were sunk by air attack, however, during this war. The first, was the British *B 10*, hit by Austrian bombers at her moorings in Venice in August ,1916. She was quickly raised. Austria also achieved the first sinking of a submarine at sea. This was the French *Foucault*, a month after their success against the British boat.

In order to protect their submarines in the port of Bruges in Flanders, the Germans built the first reinforced concrete shelters in 1917. These were to serve as models for the much larger and more numerous 'pens' built by the *Todt* Organisation, twenty-five years later.

The Allies made several attempts to limit the scope of German submarine action. The Otranto Barrage has already been mentioned: It was a copy of the elaborate net, mine and patrol-vessel barrier across the Straits of Dover, which was finally made submarine-proof in 1918. At the end of the war, the British and Americans were still laying an enormous and nearly useless mine barrier between Norway and the Orkneys.

The mine seems to have been the most effective anti-submarine weapon of the war, in terms of actual sinkings, especially when laid offensively in the channels used by the boats on passage to and from their bases. Thus, one undersea weapon was used against another.

Convoy, that ancient defence against sea raiders, was by far the most useful counter to submarine attack. Not only did convoy constitute a defensive measure enabling a small number of escorts to protect a large number of merchantmen, but, paradoxically, it was an offensive ploy. In attacking the convoy, submarines were lured to the chosen battlegrounds of the escorts. Here was a far more sensible use of anti-submarine vessels than the largely pointless patrols and sweeps of the early years of the war. Convoy made the job of the submariner much more difficult. The constant stream of individual ships, easy enough to pick off, was replaced by a vast assemblage that swept by, leaving the sea empty until the next convoy convened. At best, only a few ships would be sunk. A possible answer, the 'wolf pack' was only in its infancy at the end of the war. It is extraordinary that the British failed to adopt the convoy tactic until it was nearly too late.

Despite the check administered by the adoption of convoy, the submarine emerged as an unbeaten weapon in 1918. But the rapidly rising total of U-boat losses during the last year of the war, and the rapid development of new anti-submarine weapons indicated that new tactics and technical developments were required, if the submarine were to remain the powerful menace it had proved to be. The U-boats might have won the war for Germany in 1917, had their enemies persisted in their rejection of the convoy system. The testing time for the Allies might have come earlier, had the Germans adopted unrestricted submarine warfare nearer the beginning of the war, or built more boats, earlier. By 1918, the submarine had reverted to being a great menace, tying up many times its own value in defensive measures, but it was no longer a potential war-winning weapon unless improved.

As well as attacking warships and armed merchantmen with torpedoes from periscope depth, surfaced boats could use guns to stop and destroy unarmed merchant ships, trawlers and small coasters. At the beginning of the war, however, few boats were fitted with surface armament. The need, especially for the Germans, of sinking suitable targets by gunfire, to save torpedoes, necessitated the fitting of one or two guns of small calibre (37mm or 57mm). The calibre increased progressively, stabilizing around 3in (76mm), 3.4in (88mm) and 4in (102mm). The Germans did, however, build large submarines which relied as much on heavy guns—5.9in (152mm)—as on their torpedo tubes. These were the 'U-cruisers', most of which were fitted with two of these guns, though some had only one.

Although most submarines continued to be fitted with 18in (457mm) torpedo tubes, some of the later British boats had 21in (533mm) tubes, and the Germans had 20in (530mm) tubes in their later, large boats. Apart from increasing size, there were no very significant improvements to the performance of the torpedoes, but the effectiveness of a boat's patrol was increased, because of the greater number of torpedoes carried. Minelaying submarines were built in numbers, especially in Germany: between 1917 and 1918, 116 minelaying boats entered service in the German Navy. Most of these were of the *UC* Class, in three successive variants: *UC 1* (1915), *UC II* (1916) and *UC III* (1918). They carried, respectively, 12, 18 and 14 mines, in six semi-vertical tubes. Their displacement ranged from the 168/183 tons of *UC 1* to the 434/511 of *UC II*, reaching 491/571 in *UC III*, with resulting improvements in seakeeping and range. The first type were fitted for minelaying only, but the other two types were also fitted with three torpedo tubes: their mines laid, they became normal torpedo-launching submarines.

In addition to the *UC* Class, which were primarily for coastal use, especially in the first variant, Germany also built the *UE* Class, ocean-going submarines in two variants, *UE 1* and *UE II*. These boats were also armed with torpedo tubes and could carry, respectively, 32 and 42–48 mines, laid from two special launching tubes. The displacement of the first variant was 755/830 tons and that of the second, 1,164/1,512 tons, with a significant increase in size and range, which reached 13,900 miles at 8 knots, enabling them to operate in American waters.

The activities of the *UC* and *UE* Classes formed an important part of the U-boat campaign and, in the case of the latter type, ranged far afield. The overall minelaying operations by German boats resulted in the sinking of some 2,980,000 GRT of merchant shipping and the destruction of numerous warships.

In other navies, the development of the minelayer was rather more modest, because the naval forces of the Central Powers were blocked within the North Sea and the Adriatic, and their commercial traffic was paralyzed. The British, however, made use of submarines for offensive minelaying, close to enemy bases, especially as part of their anti-submarine measures, and several torpedo-equipped boats of the *E*, *H* and *L* Classes were equipped for minelaying. France built only four submarine minelayers: Italy put three into service (*X* Class) whose prototype was a salvaged German boat of the *UC* Class, which had been sunk off Taranto.

The design of the torpedo-launching boats—which constituted the great majority of submarines—was considerably improved during the war. From the small and lightly armed coastal boats of 1914, little more than three years of war produced larger, more powerfully armed boats, able to operate independently and for protracted periods, far from their bases.

Most of the submarines employed during the war had a surface displacement of between 450 and 900 tons. Surface propulsion was generally by diesel, and maximum surface speed was about 15–16 knots. Maximum submerged speed did not exceed an average of 10 knots, and that only for the very brief period allowed by the limited capacity of the storage batteries of the day. Submerged speed was

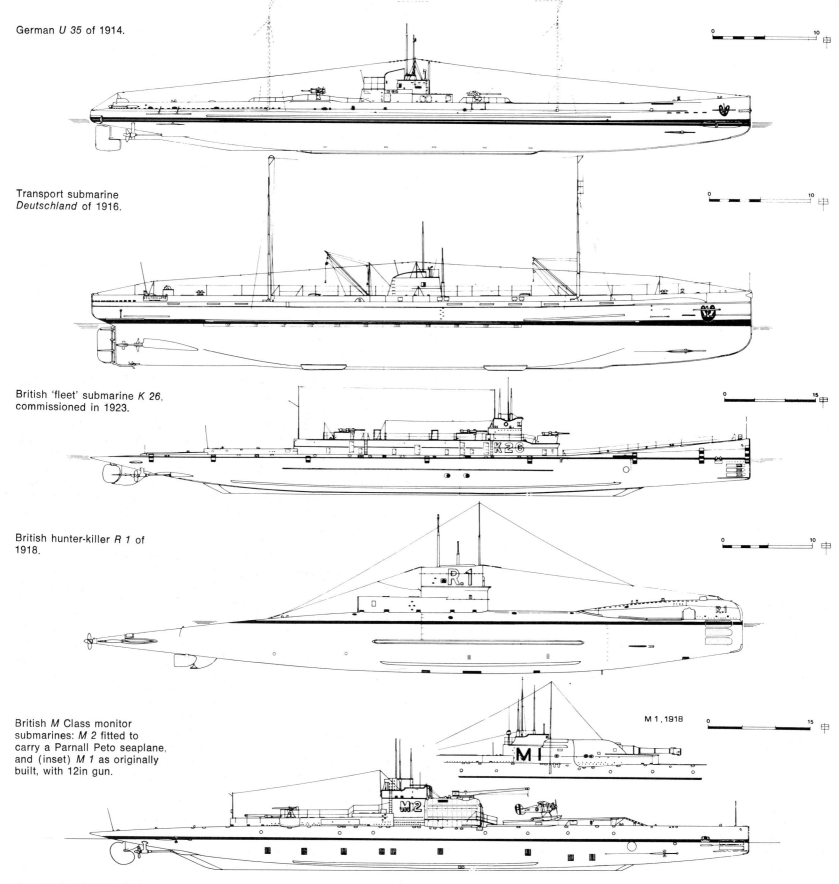

German *U 35* of 1914.

Transport submarine *Deutschland* of 1916.

British 'fleet' submarine *K 26*, commissioned in 1923.

British hunter-killer *R 1* of 1918.

British *M* Class monitor submarines: *M 2* fitted to carry a Parnall Peto seaplane, and (inset) *M 1* as originally built, with 12in gun.

M 1, 1918

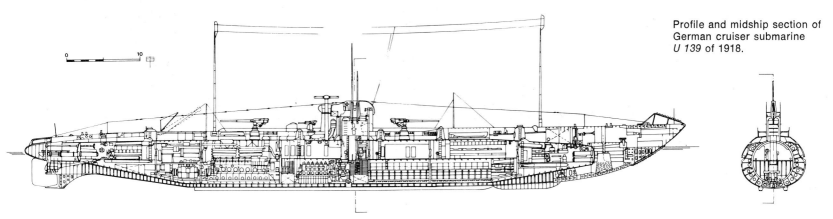

generally limited to about 4–5 knots, with a range of 40–50 miles maximum.

The considerable reduction obtained (especially by German boats) in the time needed to crash dive represented a significant development. The normal two to three minutes of 1914 was reduced to forty to thirty seconds for the last series of medium displacement boats of 1918.

Above all, range was increased. In the spring of 1915, *U 21* made a non-stop voyage from Wilhelmshaven to Cattaro (Kotor) in the Adriatic and in 1916, a slightly larger boat, *U 53* crossed the Atlantic, both ways, without refuelling, remaining at sea for 42 days and logging 7,550 miles.

Although Britain, France, Italy and the United States produced good classes of submarines during the course of the war, the best boats were produced, inevitably, by Germany. This stemmed from the unquestionable capacities of their shipbuilding industry, the widespread use of submarines by that country, the importance given to the design of new types and the improvements made to those already in service. But of course, the most important of these factors was the circumstance of the war, providing German boats with infinitely more targets. Their submarines were Germany's best naval weapon: the Allied boats were merely a useful part of the Allied naval effort.

The German torpedo-armed submarines, built during the First World War, were of three main types: Mittel-U or medium displacement boats (the most widespread type), U-Kreuzer or cruiser submarines and UB or coastal submarines. The *UB* Class, the first examples of which were laid down in the autumn of 1914, were initially of very limited displacement (*UB I* Series, 127/142 tons) and were only 88ft 6in (27m) long. They could be quickly dismantled and transported in sections, by rail. Many of them were transferred overland to Pola (Pula) to assist the small Austrian Fleet. In the second series (*UB II*), displacement was increased considerably, but did not reach the 520/650 tons of the third series (*UB III*) of 1917–18. This type lost many of the coastal characteristics and was so successful that, fifteen years later, it served as the prototype for the development of the design of the famous Type *V II* of the Second World War.

The U-Kreuzer were boats of great displacement and range, with a powerful gun armament, and were intended for use against ocean-going shipping. The creation and development of cruiser submarines was a direct result of the invention of another special type of underwater boat, the transport submarine. The prototype, *Deutschland* (1,512/1,875 tons) was rated as an unarmed merchant ship and was sent, as a blockade-runner, to the still neutral United States to embark a cargo of high-value materials, vital to Germany. She was later converted to U-carrier *U 155*.

The second transport submarine, *Bremen,* left Germany on 17 September 1916 but never reached her destination, being lost during the voyage, cause unknown. A third boat, *Oldenburg*, was not completed in time to make any transport trips and, converted to a cruiser submarine, became *U 151*.

With the entry of the United States into the war, merchant submarines lost their raison d'être and, with two guns and torpedo tubes added, became the first cruiser submarines. The modified transport submarines were later followed by other large submarines, expressly designed as 'cruisers'; in these, speed, armament and seakeeping qualities were improved.

Special-purpose boats also appeared in the Royal Navy: the *K*-Class Fleet submarines, *M*-Class monitor submarines and *R*-Class killer submarines. The *K* Class were large boats, characterised by a high surface speed of 24 knots. This was achieved by the adoption of 10,000shp steam turbines. The fourteen units of the class were built so as to have a uniform group of boats that would be capable, because of their speed, of direct cooperation with the surface units of the Grand Fleet.

However, various difficulties, such as lack of effective means of communication with surface ships, caused the project to be abandoned. The considerable length of these boats (338ft (103m)) made them very difficult to manoeuvre when submerged. Consequently, it was very risky to take advantage of the high underwater speeds that could be achieved during the first fifteen minutes of submersion, using residual boiler pressure. The British *K* Class were an unfortunate attempt to return to steam power for submarines. Steam had been abandoned virtually everywhere after 1910, except in France, where it continued to be used for several years. Not until the arrival of the atomic pile, which created a self-contained source of heat, would steam turbines again be used in submarines.

The monitor submarines of the British *M* Class were designed in 1917 for the purpose of surprise attack, using their single 12in (305mm) gun. The guns, which came from old battleships, could be elevated, but not traversed. Aiming was achieved through the periscope, and to fire the gun, the boat was surfaced sufficiently to raise the muzzle clear of the water, but the technique was never used in action. Of the three boats (*M 1, M 2* and *M 3*), one was subsequently deprived of her gun and fitted with a hangar and catapult for a seaplane, and one was converted to a minelayer.

The *R* Class killer submarines represented a true innovation. Their design was prompted by the fact that a significant number of German

Table 4: Selected examples of submarines in service in 1918

Country:	Class:	Year entered service:	Displacement: (tons) surfaced/subm	Speed (knots): surfaced/subm	Range (miles at knots): surfaced/subm	Armament: Torpedo tubes	Guns:
France	*Lagrange*	1918	920/1,318	16.5/10	4,300 at 10/125 at 5	8 x 18in (457mm)	2 x 3in (76mm)
Germany	U 81	1916	808/946	16.8/9.1	8,100 at 8/56 at 5	6 x 20in (530mm)	1 x 4.1in (105mm), 1 x 3.4in (88mm)
	U 139[1]	1918	1,930/2,483	15.8/7.6	12,630 at 8/53 at 4.5	6 x 20in (530mm)	2 x 5.9in (152mm)
	Deutschland[2]	1916	1,575/1,860	10/6.7	12,000 at 10/65 at 3	unarmed: 750 tons of cargo	
	UB III	1918	512/643	13.9/7.6	7,280 at 6/55 at 4	5 x 20in (530mm)	1 x 4.1in (105mm)
	UC III	1918	491/571	11.5/6.6	9,850 at 7/40 at 4.5	3 x 20in (530mm)	1 x 3.4in (88mm), 6 mine tubes, 14 mines
Great Britain	E (first group)	1913	660/800	16/10	3,000 at 10/35 at 5	5 x 18in (457mm)	1 x 3in (76mm) 12pdr
	L (second group)	1917	890/1,080	17.5/10.5	3,800 at 10/45 at 6	6 x 21in (533mm)	1 x 4in (102mm)
	K[3]	1917	1,880/2,560	24.5/9	3,000 at 13/50 at 5	10 x 18in (457mm)	2 x 4in (102mm), 1 x 3in (76mm)
	M 1[4]	1918	1,600/1,950	15.5/9.5	3,840 at 10/60 at 5	4 x 18in (457mm)	1 x 12in (305mm), 1 x 3in (76mm)
	R[5]	1918	420/500	9.5/15	2,000 at 8/10 at 15	6 x 18in (457mm)	
Italy	A[6]	1915	21/37	6.8/5	12 at 6/8.5 at 4	2 x 18in (457mm)	
	B[6]	1916	40/46	6.9/5	128 at 6.9/9 at 5	2 x 18in (457mm)	
	F	1916	262/319	12.5/8	1,300 at 8/120 at 2.5	2 x 18in (457mm)	1 x 3in (76mm)

1: monitor submarine type.
2: 'cruiser' submarine type.
3: 'Fleet submarine' type.
4: 'killer' type.
5: transport submarine type.
6: 'pocket' submarine type.

boats had been destroyed by normal submarines. Twelve of the class were completed in 1918. Having a single screw, their surface power of 240hp was decidedly inferior to their submerged power (1,200hp) which was achieved by a large number of storage batteries and a powerful electric motor. Consequently, their maximum surface speed was only 9 knots, but submerged, they reached 15 knots, which was exceptional for the time. Their hull shape was designed for high underwater speed. They were fitted with six 18in (457mm) torpedo tubes, all disposed forward.

Their role was to lie in ambush at periscope depth until a surfaced boat was sighted, when entire salvoes of torpedoes would be launched in a series of lightning close-range attacks. Despite their late entry into service, the R Class achieved several successes against German boats. However, these remarkable submarines were very clumsy on the surface and they were quickly abandoned after the war.

Other special-purpose boats were the Italian 'pocket' submarines of the A and B types, respectively of 31/37 and 40/46 tons. They were armed with only two torpedo tubes, external on the first type and internal on the second. They were small boats, of very limited performance, built for the defence of naval bases, but their design led to later developments in the Italian and other navies during the Second World War.

United States Navy submarine *S.9 (SS.114)* during March 1929.

To better illustrate the improvement of technical characteristics of the submarine during the First World War, Table 4 gives details of several types of boats in service in 1918.

Development between the wars
By 1918, the submarine had come of age—technically and operationally. During the war it had become a weapon to be feared, strategically and tactically and its employment by Germany, in large numbers against shipping had proved its importance as an element of sea power.

Technically, submarine design had reached a very high level and during the twenty years between the wars, few substantial technical innovations were made other than increasing the structural strength of hulls, which allowed greater operating depths (from the 150–250ft (50–80m) of 1918 to 300–350ft (100–120m) in 1939); more effective escape and salvage apparatus (radio-telephone buoys, watertight bells, underwater respirators, etc.) and, in about 1930, the adoption of hydraulic systems for rapid and remote control of valves, air vents and rudders. Until then, when diving and surfacing, a good half of the crew had to be stationed at various valves and controls throughout the boat: with the introduction of remote control all these functions could be controlled by a single operator in the central compartment.

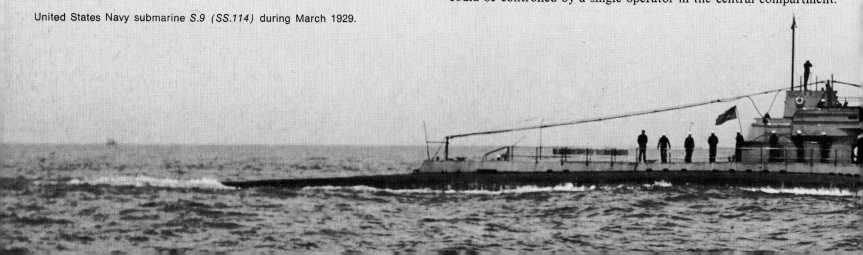

Diplomatic debates regarding the future of the submarine continued during the inter-war period. Proposals to limit its proliferation and operational capabilities had no practical results. In fact, the policy of armaments reduction pursued at the conferences of Washington in 1921 and London in 1930 had no significant influence on the development of the submarine.

At the Washington Conference, as at the Hague twenty years earlier, Britain (from obvious motives) proposed the abolition of the submarine and prohibition of their construction, but this was rejected and the Conference closed with the approval of four Articles designed to limit their use. These Articles, however, were very difficult to implement because of the problem of reconciling treaty limits with the operational characteristics of submarines.

During the Conference of London which followed, the problem of the submarine was raised again, but despite the fact that limitations were approved, no practical results were achieved in limitation of numbers or operational restrictions. The problem remained unsolved, but it was decided that no submarine could displace more than 2,000 tons surfaced and could not mount guns larger than 5.25in (130mm).

It was also decided to divide underwater craft into two categories: coastal submarines of up to 600 tons displacement and ocean-going submarines of more than 600 tons. The first category were to be exempt from any limitation as to numbers: for ocean-going boats, however, an agreement was reached between the United States, Britain and Japan, not to exceed an overall displacement of 52,700 tons standard surface displacement.[1]

Two decisions made during the Conference demonstrate the lack of any real desire to establish valid limitations to submarines—or at least, the lack of intelligent analysis of the war. It seems strange that the calibre of guns mounted, rather than the size and number of torpedo tubes should be taken as the measure of offensive power of an underwater weapon. Undoubtedly, contemporary interest in the German U-cruisers and the British *M* Class played a part in this odd decision. The second concerns the definition 'coastal' applied to 600-ton boats which had already been used with success by the Germans in the Atlantic. In other words, a convenient formula had been found which allowed all interested nations to continue to build long-range submarines without any limitations. In addition, it should be noted that only four years later, in 1934, Japan repudiated the Treaty, declaring herself free of all naval limitations. Germany, shackled by the Treaty of Versailles which prohibited her possessing submarines, was free to begin their construction only in 1935, the year in which she repudiated the Treaty and signed the subsequent Anglo-German Naval Agreement. This allowed her to build an underwater fleet equal to 45 per cent of the total displacement of the British submarine force, with the option of reaching parity by forfeiting a corresponding amount of surface tonnage.

Despite the scrapping of the majority of surface ships building at the end of the First World War, submarine programmes of the Allies were, for the most part, completed during the immediate post-war period. At the same time, several prototypes were built, based on recent combat experience. These had displacements of about 1,000–1,500 tons, speed in the order of 16–18 knots surfaced, 8–9 knots submerged, and an armament of 6 to 8 × 21in (533m) torpedo tubes plus 1 or 2 × 4—4.7in (100–120mm) guns. Many boats were built to this pattern but there were exceptions, the most significant of which, was the British *X 1*. Laid down in 1921 and commissioned in 1923, this boat had a normal load displacement of 2,780/3,600 tons. She was armed with only six 21in (533mm) torpedo tubes but had two 5.25in (133mm) twin mountings. She was a true cruiser submarine, inspired by the earlier German boats. *X 1* was unlucky, however. Her diesel engines, of considerable power, never worked perfectly, and despite her otherwise surprisingly good performance—for so large a submarine —she was stricken in 1931, after only seven years of service. She was the longest submarine yet built.

Broadly speaking, the ocean-going navies preferred those types of boats that could operate for long periods, far from their bases: consequently, surface displacement figures soon exceeded 1,000 tons. In particular, the United States and Japan, which at the end of the war had large programmes in progress for strengthening their navies, built most of the submarines that had been scheduled until the time of the conclusion of the Washington Conference (1922).

The United States built some forty boats of 850/1,090 tons (*S* Class), characterised by long surface range and a good burst speed underwater—in the order of 11 knots. Following the Washington Conference, the US Navy tended to order boats with displacements between 1,300 and 1,500 tons. The boats were called Fleet submarines because they were to operate under the command of the headquarters of various fleets in different operational theatres. They had a high surface speed (17–18 knots) and considerable range (about 10,000 miles), obviously suited to ocean-going employment. The type was successively improved and became standard in the US Navy.

There were, of course, several exceptions which were never developed: the six large boats, planned for in the War Programme, whose construction was not completed until between 1924 and 1930: the three *Barracuda* Class of 2,000/2,620 tons; the two *Narwhal* types, of 2,730/4,050 tons, armed with 6in (152mm) guns—all of the cruiser-submarine type, and a minelayer, *Argonaut*, of 2,710/4,080 tons.

The Japanese Navy initially followed the same criteria as the Americans, laying down or completing ten boats of the coastal type between 1919 and 1922, with surface displacements slightly in excess of 1,000 tons. They derived from earlier types, in turn inspired by the British *L* Class and by the French *Schneider-Laubeuf* types. Following the Washington Conference, where Japan had been assigned a battleship tonnage, less than her expectations (especially in relation to the United States), the Japanese Navy began to consider a new strategy, the war of attrition, with the submarine attacking surface forces en masse in the open sea and it was necessary to build boats suited for the role, with great range, high surface speed and considerable displacement.

Basing their designs on British Fleet submarines and German cruiser submarines which the Allies had taken at the end of the war, the Japanese built numerous long-range and cruiser-type boats between 1924 and 1940. They had surface displacements of between 1,300 and 2,200 tons, with great range (between 10,000 and 17,000 miles), high surface speed (20–23 knots) and a powerful gun armament of one or two 4.7–5.5in (120–140mm) guns. They were intended chiefly for use in conjunction with surface units and were to have operated in squadrons and flotillas directly subordinate to the fleet. They were also intended to replace—in part—the cruiser in the sighting and reporting of enemy forces, by sailing in advance of their own surface formations and by patrolling focal areas. Several of the boats carried a small reconnaissance floatplane for this purpose.

In addition to these large boats which formed the backbone of the Japanese undersea fleet, four ocean-going minelayers were built. They were copies of similar German boats, one example of which had been assigned to Japan in 1919. Several coastal submarines were built for patrolling the Inland Sea and the China coast.

The Japanese Navy conceived its submarine fleet essentially as a complement to its surface fleet, and did not consider at all, the possibility of using boats against merchant shipping, despite the lessons of the war. Those lessons, however, were to prove very profitable to other navies, including the American but, above all to the new German Navy.

Following *X 1*'s lack of success, the British Navy returned to more traditional types. Between 1924 and 1927, the nine units of the *O* Class were laid down. These were of about 1,400/2,000 tons, with a speed of 17/9 knots and a surface range of 6,500 miles at 10 knots, which suited them for employment in the Pacific. The subsequent *P* and *R* Classes (nine units) of 1929–30 represented an improved version of the *O* Class.

There was a return to the Fleet submarine in 1932, with the launching of the first of three boats of the *Thames* Class of 1,850/ 2,710 tons and 22.5/10 knots, and a considerable range of approximately 10,000 miles. Although they were not developed, the experience gained from and the problems presented by these units, induced the Royal Navy to standardize construction on two basic types of boat: one, of limited displacement, for operations in restricted waters such as the North Sea and the Mediterranean, and the other, larger and scheduled to replace the *O*, *P* and *R* Classes in oceanic warfare. The first type was represented by the *S* Class: eight boats, launched between 1932 and 1937, with a displacement of 735/935 tons, a speed of 14/10 knots and an armament of six 21in (533mm) bow torpedo tubes and a 3in (76mm) gun. They were highly successful and their building was resumed in 1940, with a second series of 50 boats.

The second type was represented by the *T* Class, the first example of which was commissioned in 1938. They had a displacement of 1,325/1,573 tons, a speed of 15.25/8.75 knots and were armed with ten 21in (533mm) torpedo tubes and a 4in (102mm) gun. Approximately fifty examples of the design (with minor modifications) were built between 1938 and 1945.

Meanwhile, the British Navy also devoted attention to the building of minelaying boats, completing between 1933 and 1939, the six boats of the *Porpoise* Class, of 1,772/2,117 tons, carrying fifty mines and armed with six 21in (533mm) torpedo tubes and a gun.

In 1937, the Royal Navy launched the first boat of a new class that was to be reproduced, without substantial changes in the design, in more than seventy examples until 1944. Classified as coastal submarines, the *U* Class and the very similar *V* Class which followed, were slightly smaller than the *S* Class and were armed with four to six 21in (533mm) torpedo tubes. Their underwater characteristics were excellent and they were easy and quick to build and maintain.

Manoeuvrability, simplicity and speed of construction and maintenance, together with strength and operational safety, were characteristics fundamental to all British boats during the inter-war period and throughout the Second World War. The British attached great importance to these factors in order to limit construction costs, build rapidly in numbers and, above all, to increase operational effectiveness. British submarine warfare between 1939 and 1945, in all the oceans of the world, fully demonstrated the value of this philosophy.

The French Navy built a large submarine fleet between the wars: on 1 September 1939, seventy-seven boats were in service and twenty-five under construction. They belonged to three basic types: 1500-tonnes type, long-range *Requin* Class and coastal (600–630 tonnes types). There were also six coastal minelaying submarines of 761/925 tons (*Saphir* Class) and a cruiser submarine, *Surcouf*, launched in 1929. She was an experimental boat of 3,250/4.304 tons, armed, in

addition to her torpedo tubes, with an 8in (204mm) twin turret, and was designed as an ocean-going 'corsair'.

All in all, France equipped her navy with an excellent underwater fleet, composed of a good number of boats of standard construction, though they did not have exceptional characteristics. All French torpedo-launching submarines had a large number of torpedo tubes (some of which were of the external traversing type), generally 10–11 on the ocean-going and sea-going boats and 7–8 on the coastal types.

It was not until about 1930 that the Soviet Navy began strengthening her underwater fleet. The first boats (*D* Class) were of medium displacement and gave rise to numerous problems which were eliminated in the subsequent series (*L, P* and *S* Classes of medium displacement and *Shch,* coastal) built between 1929 and 1939. In 1939, construction of boats of limited displacement (161/202 tons) was begun. These were the *M* Class, suitable for employment in restricted waters, and built in numbers during the war, making widespread use of prefabrication techniques. The type was later slightly enlarged and perfected until it was probably the most successful Soviet submarine built before 1945.

In Italy, the construction of submarines received such great emphasis between 1923 and 1939 that, when she entered the war in June 1940, her 115 boats in service represented one of the largest underwater fleets in the world. The development of Italian submarines was undertaken with two basic types in mind: long-range ocean-going and medium-range coastal.

Following the period 1923–26, during which prototypes of both kinds of vessels were built in limited series, improvements were made to the existing boats and this led to the development of even more classes. The medium-range type stabilized at about 600/700 tons surface displacement (*600* Class), and the ocean-going type at about 1,000/1,100 tons (*Marcello, Liuzzi, Marconi* Classes, etc.), with the exception of several boats exceeding 1,500 tons (*Calvi* and *Saint Bon* Classes). From 1938 to 1940, only ocean-going submarines were laid down, with the intention of strengthening that sector of the submarine fleet, because of the political situation at the time.

The Italian Navy generally built good boats, strong and safe; many were ordered from Italian shipyards by other navies too. But serious shortcomings in the areas of training and of auxiliary systems (fire-control centres, etc.) and the special features of the Mediterranean theatre, denied the Italian submarine service the successes that had been expected, in view of its size and the attention that had been lavished on it.

As we have seen, Germany had been unable to resume construction until 1935, but for some years before then, German technicians had been working on submarines, developing and improving the designs of the most successful boats of the war. Their studies led to the building of several boats for other navies, under German direction in foreign yards. When it was able to begin construction of its own boats, the Kriegsmarine, after several experimental craft, developed an underwater arm which, by 1939, was already fifty units strong, centring series production on three basic types: coastal type (Type II) of 254/381 tons, for use in the Baltic and the North Sea; ocean-going type of medium displacement (Type VII) of 626/915 tons, for employment in the Atlantic; ocean-going type of large displacement (Type IX) of 1,032/1,408 tons, with long-range characteristics for prolonged employment in the Atlantic and more distant areas.

Characteristic of German boats were their uniformity and simplicity of construction, plus their exceptional strength and underwater manoeuvrability. The Type VII was especially successful, and more than 700 examples, progressively improved, were built between 1935 and 1945. Together with the Type IX, which, though less popular was also built in numbers during the war, Type VII, formed the backbone of the German submarine service during the Second World War and was possibly the best conventional boat ever built.

The German boats, especially the medium displacement ocean-going type, were selected following the development of strategic and tactical concepts by the Submarine Command, headed by the then Captain Doenitz, which called for the employment of large numbers of submarines against merchant shipping. In order to make the most efficient use of available industrial resources and to juggle those clauses of the Anglo-German Naval Agreement which limited not the number but the overall displacement of submarines, Doenitz preferred to build the greatest possible number of medium-displacement boats rather than a lesser number of units of greater displacement and better performance.

An important characteristic of German submarines, particularly of the Type VII, was the reduced bulk of the conning tower and the speed with which they could crash dive (about 30 seconds). It was planned to employ these boats in great numbers, chiefly for high-speed night attacks on the surface, against enemy convoys, adopting the 'wolf pack' tactics conceived by Doenitz, which later, were to be used successfully by the Americans in the Pacific. Another feature was the adoption of a mechanical computer for the calculation of torpedo firing data, based on input relative to the course and speed of the target. The British and Americans called their equivalent devices, 'fruit machines'.

By this time, the various types of construction had narrowed to two: single hull submarines with external tanks, and double hull

A Type VII C boat leaving her Atlantic base in France.

submarines, partial or full. Fuel tanks were generally located inside the pressure hull on the single hull types, and in the space between the hulls on the double hull boats. Structural strength was much increased, so as to allow greater depths to be reached, and to ensure greater safety for the boats.

With regard to safety, despite numerous technical improvements, the number of boats lost in accidents of various kinds from 1919 to 1939 was quite high: seventeen boats, six of which were American, six British, three French, one German and one Italian. Many were salvaged and returned to service, but loss of life was considerable.

In all boats, diesel engines provided surface propulsion, and electric motors powered by batteries, underwater propulsion. In several types, the diesels were not coupled directly to the propeller shafts, but to a dynamo; on the surface, these acted as diesel generators, furnishing current to the electric motors.

In order to give an idea of the importance, in terms of weight, of the structural components, weapons and the various on-board equipment, Table 6 shows the dead weight tonnages, i.e. the percentage breakdown of displacement, in its various components, of a 'typical' coastal submarine of the 1937–38 period.

The increasing menace of air attack meant that, by 1939, virtually all submarines had been fitted with one or more small or medium calibre machine-guns. Some were in retractable or 'disappearing' mounts, others had to be unshipped before every dive and placed in watertight containers, yet others were left exposed. Most were mounted on or just aft of the conning tower. Calibres ranged from

Table 5: The world's submarine fleets in August 1939

Country:	Boats:	Country:	Boats:
Denmark	11	Japan	65
Estonia	2	Latvia	2
Finland	5	Netherlands	24
France	77	Norway	9
Germany	65	Poland	5
Great Britain	69	Rumania	1
Greece	6	United States	100[2]
Italy	107[1]	U.S.S.R.	150[3] (approx)

1: 218 in August 1941.   2: 112 on 7 December 1941.   3: 115 on 10 June 1940.

Table 6: Deadweight tonnages of a 'typical' coastal submarine

Weights:	Percentage of whole:
Bare hull	38.4
Hull fittings	4.7
Auxiliary machinery	9.8
Surface propulsion gear	11.7
Underwater propulsion gear and storage batteries	14.2
Guns and ammunition	0.4
Underwater armament (torpedoes and tubes)	3.0
Fixed ballast	5.8
Crew, outfit, etc.	10.7
Various	1.3

Table 7: Torpedoes in service in 1939

Calibre:	Torpedo weight:	Warhead weight:	Speed:	Run:
21in	3,000–3,300lb	550–660lb	48–50 knots	4,376yds (4,000m)
(533mm)	(1,400–1,500kg)	(250–300kg)	30–35 knots	10,940yds (10,000m)
18in	1,750–2,200lb	440lb	45–47 knots	2,188yds (2,000m)
(457mm)	(800–1,000kg)	(200kg)	28–30 knots	8,752yds (8,000m)

0.303in to 0.5in up to 20mm and even 40mm cannon. Occasionally the smaller guns were fitted in twin mounts. Normally, torpedoes were still of the standard 21in (533mm) and 18in (457mm) sizes, though the French Navy and several smaller navies (under French influence) such as the Yugoslav and Polish, adopted 21.7in (550mm) and 15.7in (400mm) torpedoes.

Performance characteristics—weight of warhead, speed, length of run and accuracy—were considerably improved during the inter-war period. In 1939, the characteristics of normal ('steam') i.e. heated torpedoes issued to the various navies were as shown in Table 7.

In addition to the normal torpedoes in service in all navies, special types had been developed. The electric torpedo was designed and built in Germany, with batteries and a super-light electric motor. This 21in (533mm) weapon, of approximately the same weight as a normal torpedo of the same calibre, had the advantage of leaving no wake at all, because there were no exhaust gases, but was unable to develop more than 28 knots with a run of only 3,829 yards (3,500m).

The oxygen torpedo was developed in France and Japan. In France it was still in the experimental stage in 1940, but in Japan it had been distributed to submarine units (Type 95) and to surface units (Type 93) before she entered the war. The Type 95 was a 21in (533mm) torpedo, powered by oxygen, showing no wake and capable of a run of fully 21,880 yards (20,000m) at 50 knots, or of 40,478 yards (37,000m) at 36 knots. Britain had experimented with oxygen torpedoes in the 1920s, but had abandoned the idea. Wartime experience would soon prove the lack of practical value of long range for submarine-launched torpedoes, because of the limitations imposed by periscope observations and submarine instruments, with the inevitable inaccuracy at long range. Great importance, however, would be attached to speed over short distances, allied to initial accuracy of aim, and to the absence of wake, providing the element of surprise.

In 1939, most service torpedoes were fitted with impact fuzes, which caused the torpedo to explode at the instant of direct contact with the target hull. The Germans, British and Americans, however, were perfecting a new fuze which, utilizing the variations of the earth's magnetic field—recorded by a device sensitive to the torpedo's passage under the metal hull of the target—caused the warhead to explode with considerably greater destructive effect than was obtained by explosion against a ship's side.

Torpedoes were normally fired from fixed launching tubes (located forward or aft) which could be reloaded from inside the pressure hull. A few types of German (VII A) and British boats were fitted with fixed tubes located externally (generally aft) and thus not reloadable while submerged. Many French boats had fixed internal and external tubes; some fitted on the broadside and some in external, traversable mounts, both single and twin types. The Dutch also had external traversing tubes in some of their boats.

The Second World War

During the night of 1 September 1939, the German Army invaded Poland: three days later, Britain and France were at war with Germany. Italy, though tied by an alliance to Germany, temporized with a declaration of non-belligerency that was to last until 10 June 1940, the day she entered the war alongside Germany. On 22 June 1941, Germany attacked the Soviet Union, and on 7 December in the same year, Japan attacked the American base of Pearl Harbor, in the Hawaiian Islands. This provoked the entry into the war of the United States, who until that time, had remained neutral, while

Bordeaux, 1941: an Italian ocean-going boat loading torpedoes before a patrol.

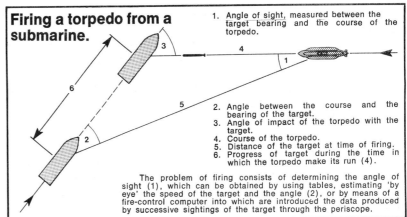

Firing a torpedo from a submarine.

1. Angle of sight, measured between the target bearing and the course of the torpedo.
2. Angle between the course and the bearing of the target.
3. Angle of impact of the torpedo with the target.
4. Course of the torpedo.
5. Distance of the target at time of firing.
6. Progress of target during the time in which the torpedo make its run (4).

The problem of firing consists of determining the angle of sight (1), which can be obtained by using tables, estimating 'by eye' the speed of the target and the angle (2), or by means of a fire-control computer into which are introduced the data produced by successive sightings of the target through the periscope.

openly supporting Great Britain who alone had continued to resist the Axis powers.

During this war, the submarine played a much more important role than during the First World War, inasmuch as the 1939–45 conflict was a truly inter-continental struggle, during which, the maintenance or destruction of maritime lines of communication was an object of primary importance for all the belligerents. Germany committed all her resources in an endeavour to isolate Great Britain, cutting the 'bridge of ships' which supplied the United Kingdom. Between Europe and Africa, the Mediterranean served as a passageway for the Axis forces in Libya, and for Allied convoys bound for Malta and Egypt. From August 1941 until the end of the war, more than 4,000,000 tons of materials were sent by the Anglo-Americans to the Soviet ports of Murmansk and Arkhangelsk. In the Pacific, Japan could not survive without the products of the conquered territories (rice, oil, rubber and minerals), and had to supply her armies which were operating overseas.

The United States immediately began unrestricted submarine warfare against Japan. Germany used the maritime communications around Europe as much as possible, so as to ease the burden on rail and road networks.

Submarines were widely used in all these theatres, and the bitter battle of the supply lines led to the destruction of approximately half of the merchant shipping tonnage that existed in 1939. More than 21,000,000 GRT were lost by the Allies and about 12,000,000 by the Axis; twice the total tonnage sunk between 1914 and 1918.

The methods of attacking merchant shipping were varied: submarines, aircraft, mines, major surface ships, disguised raiders, torpedo-boats and air attacks on ports. Of all these, the submarine scored the greatest results; about 70 per cent of the tonnage sunk.

The most violent and bloodiest series of operations for control of the lines of communications was that which on 6 March 1941, Winston Churchill defined as the Battle of the Atlantic. This gargantuan battle taxed the energies of all concerned. Science and technology applied to weapons and tactics brought about important changes in the development of the submarine.

At first, German operations were severely limited by the small number of boats available and by political restrictions imposed on the attacking of British and French merchant shipping. In the spring of 1940, the number of merchant-ship sinkings declined sharply, following the almost complete withdrawal of submarines from the Atlantic for use in support of the invasion of Norway, and because of serious defects in their torpedoes. When these had been remedied, and the invasion completed, the boats resumed their activity in the Atlantic, making use of French ports in the Bay of Biscay, occupied after the French defeat. In the summer of 1940, the first Italian ocean-going boats also began to operate in the Atlantic, but their contribution was less than had been anticipated, chiefly because of their different technical characteristics and crew training. The Italian boats, numbering 80 by the end of 1940, began to be used for wolf-pack tactics which had been studied before the war. Large groups of boats (coordinated and directed by radio from Submarine Command) were 'homed' on a convoy, attacking by night en masse at high speed and on the surface–acting, in fact, as surface torpedo-boats. The attack completed, the pack re-assembled over the horizon and attacked again, the following night.

Doenitz manoeuvred his boats so as to achieve the greatest possible success in terms of overall tonnage sunk, regardless of where these successes were obtained. This was in keeping with the overall strategic aim of striking at merchant shipping as heavily as possible and with minimum losses. His strategy, however, collided on a number of occasions with the immediate needs of the German High Command who shifted boats to heavily contested areas where there was little chance of success, and thereby significantly limited their effectiveness. Doenitz was aware of the vast Anglo-American industrial potential, and he wished to keep Allied losses above the level of new construction, which would lead to the slow strangulation of enemy maritime communications. He knew also, that time was not on his side and he sought to obtain the greatest possible number of boats as quickly as possible, before the Allies devised tactics and equipment to counter them. The entry of the United States into the war, coincided with a notable increase in sinkings by the U-boats, but America's contribution to the construction of merchant and warships, aircraft and electronic apparatus soon tipped the scales, and early in 1943, the ratio between Allied merchant tonnage sunk, and new construction underwent a sharp reversal. For the first time since the war began, the Allies managed to launch more merchant ships than the Axis were able to destroy. Doenitz's overall strategy was beginning to fail and he realised that unless substantial remedies were found, Germany would lose the Battle of the Atlantic, and the war.

In December 1942, the Germans had 397 operational submarines, only two-thirds of which, however, were deployed in the Atlantic. They

The veteran *U 47* (which sank the British battleship *Royal Oak* in Scapa Flow), with crew mustered, passes the German battlecruiser *Scharnhorst*.

A *Marcello* Class ocean-going boat, *Barbarigo,* leaving the Gironde estuary for an Atlantic patrol.

The Italian *Calvi* meets a German Type IX boat in the Atlantic in 1941.

The Italian destroyer escort *Alcione,* escorting two ships off the northern coast of Crete, is torpedoed by the British submarine *Truant* on 11 December 1941.

Rendezvous in the central Atlantic on 19 June 1941.

Grand Admiral Karl Doenitz, head of the German submarine arm and, from 30 January 1943, Commander in Chief of the German Navy.

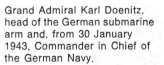

capture of *Bronzo* by the British minesweeper *Seaham* yracuse on 12 July 1943. The Italian boat, unaware e fall of the fortresses of Augusta and Syracuse, ced near Allied naval units, thinking them to be n. After being subjected to intense fire, she was ded, captured, and subsequently ceded to the French , in which she served as *Narval* until 1946.

The Type VII C boat, *U 243*, attacked and sunk by British aircraft in the Bay of Biscay on 8 July 1944.

were mostly variants of the Type VII and Type IX, but the first 'supply' boats had entered service, increasing significantly the operational duration of these types by replenishing diesel fuel and torpedoes. Type VII were normally used for large-scale attacks against convoys in the Central Atlantic, while Type IX usually operated along the coastlines of the United States, Africa and South America. In December 1942, they were joined by ten Italian boats. These were based at Bordeaux and because of their particular characteristics, were employed singly in the Central and Southern Atlantic and along the coastline of the United States.

By December 1942, Allied merchant tonnage sunk by the U-boats since the beginning of that year had reached the record figure of 5,819,065 GRT, to which should be added the approximately 300,000 GRT sunk by Italian boats. The Allies had sunk 60 German boats in the Atlantic of the 88 lost in all theatres, and two of 23 Italian boats.

The U-boats were supported by several groups of aircraft, mainly Focke-Wulf 200 Condor four-engined reconnaissance/bombers based in France and Norway. Employed for long-range attacks against convoys and spotting for the U-boats, they destroyed numerous Allied ships including the 42,000-ton liner *Empress of Britain,* which was set ablaze off the coast of Ireland on 27 October 1940, and subsequently torpedoed by a U-boat.

The use of the Focke-Wulf 200 in the Atlantic began to diminish in 1942, however, and later ceased completely thanks to the countermeasures adopted by the Allies. Catapults for fighter aircraft began to be fitted in merchant ships ('CAM' ships), and later, there was the ever present threat from long-range fighters aboard escort carriers. It is difficult to state the exact size of the Allied air and naval force employed at any one time. It is known, however, that the number of escort vessels (destroyers, corvettes, frigates, etc.) employed in the Atlantic by the end of 1942, greatly exceeded 500 ships, and the number of aircraft based on the ground and on the early escort carriers, was slightly less than 1,000.

The weapons available to the Allied naval units consisted of the normal equipment of guns and automatic weapons and the various types of depth-charges.

Corvettes—the escort vessels built in great numbers by the British, early in the war—soon proved too slow to catch a surfaced U-boat, but increasing numbers of larger and faster escorts were entering service and more old destroyers were becoming available for conversion to escort vessels. In addition, the continuing improvement of radar, enabled anti-submarine units to detect surfaced boats, locate them precisely and speedily adopt effective countermeasures.

By the end of 1942, British ships, whose depth-charges in 1939, were of a First World War type, were beginning to be equipped with a new weapon. This was the 'hedgehog', a spigot mortar, capable of firing 24 projectiles 200 yards ahead of the attacking ship, forming an elliptical or circular pattern over the presumed position of the submerged boat. Unlike the normal depth-charges, hedgehog bombs (they carried a smaller charge) did not explode at a pre-determined depth, but only on contact with a submerged boat. The great advantage of firing the pattern ahead, was that sonar contact was not lost during the critical last moments of an attack.

The basic instrument for detecting and locating submerged boats was the echo-detection apparatus known to the British as asdic, and to the Americans as sonar. It was perfected in great secrecy by the British and American Navies between the wars and by 1939 had already become very effective. Still further improved, it was fitted

Relationship between sinkings of Allied merchant shipping and losses of German submarines during the Battle of the Atlantic.

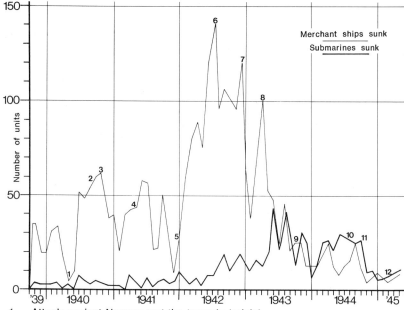

1. Attack against Norway and the torpedo 'crisis'.
2. Beginning of the use of French Atlantic ports by the U-boats.
3. Beginning of surface night attacks against convoys.
4. Beginning of the large-scale use of 'wolf pack' tactics.
5. Entry of the United States into the war and beginning of the operations in the Western Atlantic.
6. Highpoint of the Battle of the Atlantic – greatest successes of the U-boats.
7. Beginning of the intensive use of patrol aircraft armed with depth-charges and fitted with radar and searchlights.
8. Beginning of anti-submarine operations by support groups composed of escort carriers, destroyers and anti-submarine frigates.
9. Beginning of the use of acoustic torpedoes against escort vessels.
10. Beginning of the operational use of the schnorkel in *U-boats*.
11. Withdrawal of submarines from French Atlantic bases.
12. Beginning of operations in the North Sea by *Type XXIII* Elektro-boote.

Ratio between Allied construction of merchant tonnage and tonnage lost to German submarines.

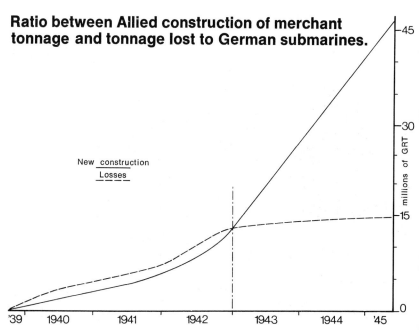

aboard all British and American escorts operating in the Atlantic in 1942.

The principal limitations of asdic/sonar were: its range, usually not greater than 2,000–3,000 yards (1,828–2,743.2m), but which often fell below 1,000 yards (914.4m) under particular conditions of water temperature and salinity; its inability to function when the ship's speed was in excess of 9–11 knots; its inability to determine the precise depth of a target and the fact that the sonar 'beam' could not scan the area immediately beneath it, so that the echo was lost if the ship approached the target close enough for the latter to pass beneath the beam. Furthermore, the exploding charges created an area of underwater turbulence which disturbed the propagation of sound waves, and this often allowed a submarine that had survived the first attack to escape before contact could be re-established.

In 1943, Commander Walker (the leading British escort-group commander) was employing a new tactic which went far to counter the limitations of asdic. This was the 'creeping attack' in which, one escort having located the submarine, monitored its progress and guided a second ship to the attack, by short-range radio link. The attacking ships would creep up on the enemy with asdic switched off, and the submarine would find it very difficult to escape. Walker also developed the technique of concerted attack by three escorts, blanketing the area of the U-boat with depth-charges and rendering a kill very likely. These tactics were rapidly promulgated by the Admiralty and resulted in many U-boat sinkings.

In the meantime, anti-submarine aircraft had greatly increased in numbers and thanks to the introduction of new and improved types (especially the American long-range B–24 Liberator), a large area of the Atlantic could be covered. Fitted with radar, searchlights, rockets and depth-charges, they located U-boats well away from the convoys and severely limited their operational possibilities. Numerous boats fell victim to day and night attacks by anti-submarine aircraft, in the lanes to and from the Atlantic bases.

Despite the fact that by 1942, Allied land-based aircraft could patrol a large area of the Atlantic, there remained a central zone which could not be reached, and this gap was closed by the use of small escort carriers. These were converted merchantment fitted with a flight deck, whose aircraft furnished cover in the immediate area of the convoy. Eventually, escorts were stationed in the central Atlantic and supported convoys in the areas not covered by land-based aircraft.

Early in 1943, the Germans sought to improve their U-boat arm by fitting new weapons and equipment in their existing boats and by designing new types with increased underwater speed and range. The principal improvements consisted of:
1. Increasing the anti-aircraft armament.
2. Adopting special paints for conning towers, capable of absorbing enemy radar impulses (Alberich paints).
3. The fitting of an electronic device (Metox) which intercepted the radar impulses from British aircraft, and allowed time for a crash dive. The Metox was a very effective instrument which operated on a 1.69m wavelength, as did, British radar. When the British adopted a centimetric wavelength, the Metox was rendered ineffective and the Germans were unable to build a new device for the short wavelength.
4. The adoption of acoustic torpedoes, capable of homing on propeller noise, and employed chiefly against escort vessels. Torpedoes programmed for a patterned run (zig-zag, spiral, figure of eight, etc.) were also adopted, and their use against convoys and warship formations considerably increased their chances of hitting a target.
5. The mounting of the schnorkel in operational boats. This device allowed the diesel engines (breathing in air and expelling exhaust gases) to be used at periscope depth, thereby enabling the batteries to be recharged without surfacing. The use of a schnorkel greatly increased the underwater speed and range, and reduced the likelihood of being sighted, or detected by radar.

The Germans were well aware that these improvements were, in themselves, insufficient to restore the U-boats to their previous level of effectiveness, and maximum effort was directed to the design of completely new boats.

As early as 1939, a new type of propulsion gear, the Walter turbine, had been tested in Germany. Named after its inventor, it functioned on a closed cycle and had no need to take air from outside the boat. It was a type of gas turbine, in which the oxygen necessary for the combustion of the fuel was obtained from the spontaneous decomposition of hydrogen peroxide in the presence of permanganate of lime. It developed a high specific power which allowed very high underwater speeds.

U 744 of the 9th Flotilla in a sinking condition, after being attacked by British surface forces in the Atlantic on 6 March 1944. Note the shell holes in the conning tower and the British ship's boat alongside.

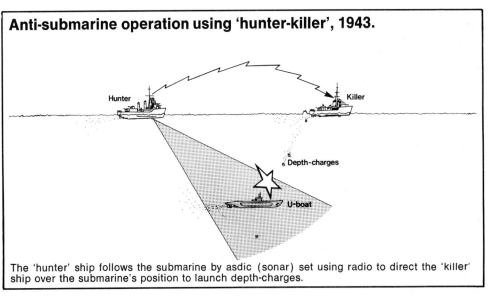

Anti-submarine operation using 'hunter-killer', 1943.

Hunter

Killer

Depth-charges

U-boat

The 'hunter' ship follows the submarine by asdic (sonar) set using radio to direct the 'killer' ship over the submarine's position to launch depth-charges.

Further developed, this turbine could have become the 'dual-purpose motor' that had been the dream of submarine designers from the beginning. But in 1943, despite the building of several experimental boats, the Walter turbine was far from operational, and Submarine Command, unable to wait any longer, sought the solution to their immediate problems in conventional motors, though ordering studies of the Walter to be pursued. Thus, the Elektro-boote or electric submarines were designed. These were boats of high underwater speed, in which the electric component of the propulsion gear was greatly superior to the diesel component, in importance and power. The hull, shape, especially developed for underwater propulsion, and the notable electric power available, allowed the boats to develop underwater bursts of speed almost double that possible in normal submarines.

In a very short space of time, two designs were prepared: Type XXI, ocean-going and Type XXIII, coastal. They were approved in June 1943 and construction was begun on a large scale. To speed up and decentralize production, widespread use was made of prefabrication techniques, and independent hull segments, eight for Type XXI and four for Type XXIII. The first Elektro-boote were ready in the summer of 1944, but the problems inherent in their final preparation and the extensive crew training necessary, did not allow their large-scale employment before the end of the war. The new boats were never fully tested in action, but several single missions carried out experimentally during the final days, demonstrated their exceptional offensive capabilities. Their maximum underwater speed was in the order of 16–17 knots, and their advanced instrumentation enabled them to carry out lightning submerged attacks. Launching their torpedoes from depth, on the basis of hydrophone or echo-ranging data, they were practically immune from attack from escort vessels, whose echo-detection gear was ineffective at speeds of more than 12 knots.

Protection against sighting by aircraft was ensured by the schnorkel and by special air conditioning and regeneration apparatus which enabled the boats to operate almost constantly underwater; range was limited only by the quantity of fuel carried. Hull shape assured good underwater performance and manoeuvrability, but the boats were ill-suited to surface operation. The aircraft had forced the submarine underwater: now the dreams of the early submarine designers—rendered impraticable by the technical limitations of their day—became reality. The underwater vessel had become a true submarine, designed to spend all its time beneath the surface and to perform better there, unlike 'submersible' which is all that previous submarines could be.

While the major attention of Submarine Command was occupied with the implementing of the vast programme of new construction laid down in 1943, and which called for the building, initially, of 200 Type XXI and 100 Type XXIII, the conventional submarines continued the Battle of the Atlantic. Despite increases and improvements to weapons and equipment, their successes continued to decline and at the end of 1943, for the first time, submarine losses were numerically greater than those of merchant ships.

This situation continued until the end of the war. In 1944, losses were so high that Doenitz, who had been promoted to Grand Admiral and had replaced Raeder, thought of withdrawing all submarines from the Atlantic. He refrained from doing so because of the need to maintain pressure on the Allies, and because of the re-development of enormous quantities of Allied ships and equipment to other areas, that would ensue.

During this period, the Allies had perfected a new system for detecting and tracking submarines: sonobuoys. Dropped from aircraft, they registered noise from submerged boats and transmitted it to the aircraft which directed a hunter-killer group to the scene. Many aircraft were also being equipped with M.A.D. (Magnetic Airborne Detector) which, during low-altitude flight, detected the presence of a submerged boat, by measuring variations in the earth's magnetic field caused by the metal bulk of the boat. Furthermore, radar had been perfected to the point that, given favourable weather, even the small 'head' of the schnorkel could be located.

Both M.A.D. and sonobuoys could be used in conjunction with a deadly new weapon dropped from aircraft. This was the homing acoustic torpedo, which was particularly effective when dropped in the swirl of water left by a diving submarine. It was responsible for many of the U-boat losses during the last months of the war.

The Royal Navy had produced an equally effective weapon for surface escorts the ahead-throwing mortar known as the 'squid'. Its triple barrels threw three depth-charges to a point well ahead of the ship. Much larger than Hedgehog bombs they were fitted with hydrostatic fuzes like ordinary depth-charges and did not have to secure a hit in order to cause fatal damage to a U-boat. Another weapon used by the escorts was a huge depth-charge weighing a ton, which had to be fired from the torpedo tubes of destroyers. Because of its rapid sinking and its huge charge of explosives, it was employed against submarines that had gone deep.

When the Allies occupied the ports of Germany in May 1945, they found hundreds of new boats ready for service. Many of them had been scuttled by their crews just before the surrender.

In the Pacific Ocean, immediately after Japan attacked Pearl Harbor, the Americans began unrestricted warfare. The deployment of their submarines became increasingly widespread and audacious, owing much of its inspiration to the German exploits in the Atlantic. About 60 per cent of Japanese merchant shipping was sunk by submarines—equivalent to 4,861,317 GRT, of which, 2 per cent can be credited to British and Dutch boats in the theatre. The percentage of losses was relatively low: 52 of a total of 217 boats, i.e., approximately 15.8 per cent compared to the Atlantic, where the losses were in the order of 80 per cent. These results stemmed largely from the inadequacy of the Japanese defensive measures, and the ineffectiveness of their anti-submarine equipment and weapons which, throughout the war, remained at a much lower level than that reached by the Allies.

The Americans also sank numerous warships including the brand-new Shinano, whose 71,890 tons at full load, made her the largest built during the Second World War. She was torpedoed by the submarine Archerfish off Yokosuka on 29 November 1944.

American boats also played an extremely useful role in the rescuing of aircrew brought down during attacks on Japanese bases: 504 airmen were recovered between August 1943 and August 1945.

The Japanese did not know how to manage their submarine fleet. Designed essentially to operate in support of the surface fleet against warships, there were few occasions when it could be used successfully. Its greatest achievement was the sinking of the aircraft carrier Yorktown, which was torpedoed by I 168 on 5 June 1942 during the battle of Midway. Throughout the war, the Japanese never used their submarine fleet in a concerted operation against American supply lines, although frequently urged by the Germans to do so. Instead, they continued to deploy their boats against warships despite heavy

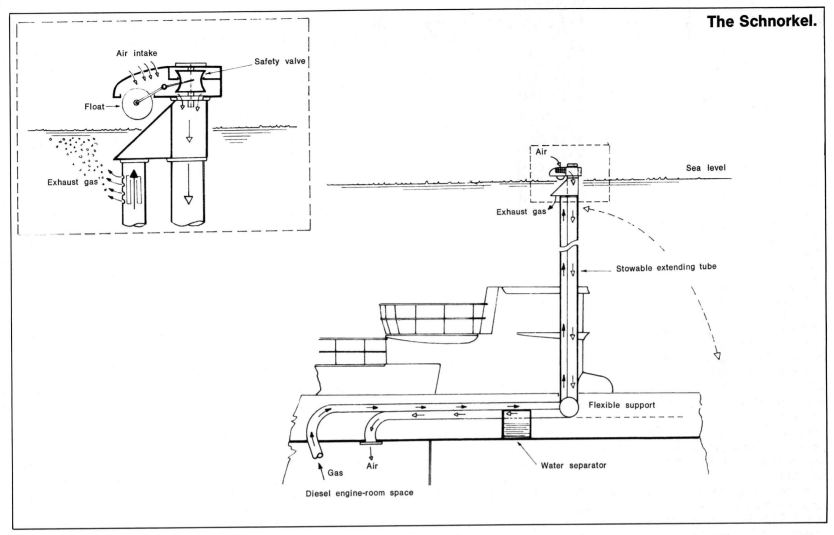

losses (some 130 boats) and modest results. Only during the last phase, when there was a programme of active cooperation with Germany for the building of fast boats in Japan, was the question of attacking merchant shipping re-examined. By then it was too late, and the Japanese submarines were occupied in transporting supplies to their island garrisons, cut off by the American 'leapfrog' strategy, and in transporting kaitens or 'human torpedoes', the naval counterpart of the Kamikaze suicide planes.

During the war, the Japanese developed some interesting types of boats such as the large submarine-aircraft carriers of the *I 400* Class, armed with three floatplanes. They were to have been used to attack the locks in the Panama Canal, but entered service too late to carry out the project.

Excluding the prototypes of fast submarines, built in Japan in 1944, the boats used in the Pacific by the Americans and the Japanese were of the conventional type, without significant innovations. From 1942, all American boats were equipped with radar. The Japanese began equipping only towards the end of the war, and their apparatus was decidedly inferior to the American type. The schnorkel was being fitted in numerous Japanese boats at the end of the war, whereas the Americans were only just beginning to fit the devices.

In the Mediterannean, Axis boats operated mainly against naval vessels while British submarines devoted themselves to attacking Italian warships and the supply lines to North Africa. After the fall of France, French submarines had little opportunity to distinguish themselves, with the exception of several Free French boats which continued to operate with the British.

Submarine warfare in the Mediterranean was strongly influenced by the complete air coverage possible, and losses to air attacks were heavy on both sides. Losses to enemy boats were also high.

German submarines passed through the Straits of Gibraltar in September 1941. Their greatest successes were the sinking of the British aircraft carrier *Ark Royal* by *U 81* and *U 205* in the Western Mediterranean on 13 November 1941; the British battleship *Barham*, torpedoed by *U 331* in the Eastern Mediterranean on 25 November 1941 and the cruiser *Galatea,* sunk by *U 557* on 15 December 1941.

Between 10 June 1940 and 8 September 1943, British boats sank more than 800,000 GRT of Axis merchant shipping, and numerous warships including the Italian cruiser *Trento*, which was torpedoed by *Umbra* on 15 June 1942, after having been damaged by torpedo bombers.

Special use was made of submarines by both the Italian and the British, in the transporting of supplies to North Africa and to the beseiged island of Malta, respectively.

All the submarines deployed in the theatre were of the conventional type and the high level of losses was disproportionate to sinkings, though not to strategic results, at least so far as the British attack against Rommel's supply lines was concerned.

The Black Sea saw limited submarine warfare conducted by a few German coastal boats that had been transferred along the Danube; several Italian 'pocket' submarines which had been transported overland, and numerous Soviet boats. The absence of merchant shipping and of large-scale warship operations precluded any noteworthy results.

In the Baltic, a closed and almost completely mineable sea, Soviet submarine operations were limited to the attacking—with little success—of German coastal traffic during the last phases of the war, and attacks on German boats in training. The lack of enemy targets denied the Germans extensive use of their coastal-boat fleet which was located in the Baltic, but the protected waters were ideal for training.

In the Arctic, German submarine operations, hampered as they were by the extreme severity of the climate, formed a mere appendix to those of the Atlantic and North Sea. Their attacks against convoys to Russia were heavily supported by their air forces, but only sporadically and rarely decisively, by surface units of the Kriegsmarine.

No comprehensive account of submarine activity and evolution during the Second World War can omit mention of the 'pocket' submarines. Although their employment had no noteworthy influence at a strategic level, they represent an interesting type of craft, halfway between the classic submarine and the underwater assault craft. Italy, Germany, Japan and Great Britain built and employed midget submarines during the war.

Italy's *CA* Series (experimental) and *CB,* of about 35 tons, were chiefly employed in the Black Sea, where they achieved several successes. The CA types were later transformed into 'underwater assault team transporters', but the conversions were not ready in time to be employed. The Italian Navy also built and employed with great success, numerous 'human' torpedoes of the *SLC* (siluri a lenta corsa =slow speed torpedoes) type, the famous maiali (pigs) which, transported in special cylinders aboard normal submarines to the proximity of bases, penetrated the defences and attacked anchored ships. On a number of occasions, the Italians used these craft to penetrate the harbours of Gibraltar and Alexandria, in the latter of which, the British battleships *Valiant* and *Queen Elizabeth* were seriously damaged in December 1941.

Germany built numerous midget submarines of various types, intended essentially for defending their coastlines and anchorages, and for use against invasion fleets, but their results were disappointing and failed to justify the building of such large numbers.

Japan also built numerous examples and achieved similar results. Several boats were employed unsuccessfully during the attack on Pearl Harbor. Better results were obtained, however, during the last months of the war, with the kaiten. This was a 'human' torpedo piloted by a volunteer, sworn to sacrifice himself. It was transported by surface vessel or normal submarine to the vicinity of the target where it was released to proceed to the target and explode on impact.

The Royal Navy's most important midgets were the *X-* and later, the *XE*-craft. Their most successful action was against the German battleship *Tirpitz*, which they damaged in Alten Fjord on 22 September 1943. The British also built and employed human torpedoes known as 'chariots'. Copied from Italian craft, their most important success was the sinking of the Italian cruiser *Ulpio Traiano* which was fitting out at Palermo, in January 1943.

The submarine during the post-war period

Emerging from the war in a phase of transformation, the conventional submarines were being replaced by boats with superior underwater characteristics, and increasing emphasis was being given to the concept of the 'pure' submarine. During the immediate post-war period, all navies studied the most recent German types, such as the Elektro-boote and the prototypes fitted with the Walter turbine (though this was never to work satisfactorily), and built experimental examples derived from them. Old conventional submarines were transformed into fast boats, by increasing the battery power and the size of the electric motors, and by modifying the hull and conning tower structures to render them more suitable for high underwater speeds. In 1955, atomic power solved the old problem of dual-purpose propulsion. The American *Nautilus,* launched in 1954, was the first boat equipped with the new propulsion gear. Basically, this is an ordinary closed-cycle steam engine, whose heat source is a nuclear reactor, which provides extremely high specific power and almost unlimited range.

Strategically, the submarine enjoys a more important role today, than at any time in its history. Inter-continental missiles with nuclear warheads can be launched, while submerged, at targets thousands of miles distant, making the submarine the capital ship of modern fleets, and the element upon which, a large part of the strategic deterrence of the major powers is based. Tactically, the fast nuclear-attack submarine, armed with surface-to-surface missiles or torpedoes, capable of underwater speeds in the order of 30 knots, and of diving to depths greater than 1,000ft (300m), is fundamental to the more important navies. It continues to be complemented by types of boats with conventional propulsion gear, many of which are specially designed for an anti-submarine role.

Opposite page.
Top left: the Type XXI boat, *U 3001* during the final phases of fitting out. Top right: *U 2332* during an early trial run. Below left: the Blohm and Voss shipyard in Hamburg, shortly after its capture by the British Army, showing U-boats in various stages of construction. Centre right: installing a diesel engine in the central hull section of a Type XXI boat in 1944. Below right: Type XXIII submarine *U 2361* in dry dock.

The US submarine *Thornback (SS.418)* with post-war conning tower modification.

France

Although the submarine achieved its earliest successes in the United States, it is not inaccurate to say that, as an efficient naval weapon, it was born and developed in France. From the beginning of the century, the French Navy has always paid particular attention to its submarine fleet, regarding it as one of the most important elements of French naval strategy.

During the First World War, French submarines gave a good account of themselves and, if they did not achieve any particular success, this was essentially because of the special kind of war being fought, and the absence of merchant shipping in the Mediterranean and Northern European waters.

In 1919, France emerged from the war with a submarine fleet which was large but outdated. Urgent needs in other areas during the war years had prevented French industry building an adequate number of new boats and the existing boats were worn out. The acquisition of 44 German submarines as reparations, of which only 10 were commissioned, enabled France to make up lost time and to compare her techniques with the more advanced German boats.

The economic and political difficulties of the post-war period, together with the uncertainties that preceded and accompanied the first Naval Disarmament Conference (where France strongly resisted the British proposal to abolish the submarine), prevented the French from immediately resuming construction of underwater craft, and they were confined to modernizing their best boats.

Not until the Washington Naval Treaty of 1922, was a naval programme approved which included the construction of twelve new boats: six ocean-going type (de grande patrouille or first class) and six coastal (de défense côtière or second class). These were the first units of the *Requin* Class and of the Type subsequently designated *600 tonnes*.

The programme for the development of the submarine fleet specified two principal branches: ocean-going for colonial service and for operations against merchant shipping, especially advanced scouting for fleet operations, far from home; and a coastal branch for home waters and the Mediterranean. A third branch was to consist of ocean-going minelaying submarines, whose prototype, *Saphir* was laid down in November 1925 and commissioned in November 1930, followed by five similar boats completed between 1930 and 1937. These boats gave an excellent account of themselves during the war, because of their simple, safe and effective arrangements for laying mines.

The design of the nine boats of the *Requin* Class, whose performance was mediocre, was followed a few years later by that of the *1500 tonnes* Type, which was far superior. A total of 31 examples were built between 1924 and 1939.

The early *600 tonnes* boats (which proved inadequate in many respects) were followed by other series with improved characteristics, known as the *630 tonnes* Type and the *Minerve* Class. Between 1927 and 1939, a total of 34 coastal submarines were commissioned in the French Navy.

Development of French submarines, 1923–1939.

	Ocean-going (1st class)	Coastal (2nd class)	Minelayers
1925	Requin / ---1500 tons / Surcouf	600 tons	P. Chailley (1922) / Saphir
1930		630 tons / Minerve	
1935	Morillot	Aurore / (Phenix)	Emeraude

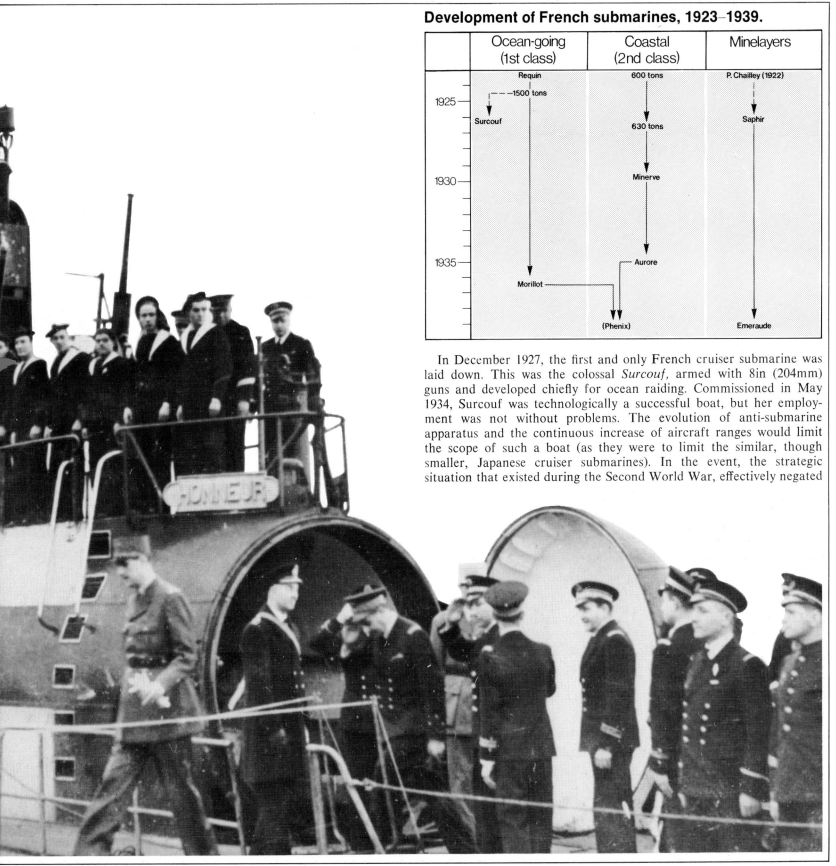

In December 1927, the first and only French cruiser submarine was laid down. This was the colossal *Surcouf,* armed with 8in (204mm) guns and developed chiefly for ocean raiding. Commissioned in May 1934, Surcouf was technologically a successful boat, but her employment was not without problems. The evolution of anti-submarine apparatus and the continuous increase of aircraft ranges would limit the scope of such a boat (as they were to limit the similar, though smaller, Japanese cruiser submarines). In the event, the strategic situation that existed during the Second World War, effectively negated

Rubis in 1931. Note the triple traversing stern mount.

the use of *Surcouf*. One wonders how she might have fared had she reached the Pacific: she was lost en route. However, her building shows that in the twenties, France was already oriented towards the strategic use of submarines against merchant shipping. During the inter-war period, French shipyards built boats for other nations: two for Latvia, six for Greece, three for Poland and two for Yugoslavia.

A characteristic of French boats, all of which were of the double hull type, was the presence of torpedo tubes outside the pressure hull, non-reloadable while submerged. They were either of the single, fixed type, normally located in the cavity between the two hulls, beneath the weather-deck, and capable of firing forward or aft; or they were fitted in traversing mounts. These consisted of two, three or even four tubes, side by side, located athwartships, normally in the casing forward or aft of the conning tower, or else, at the extreme stern of the boat. They were electrically controlled and could be traversed while surfaced or submerged.

In the *1500* tonnes Type boats, one of the two mounts at the stern had torpedo tubes of different calibres: two 21in (533mm) and two 15.7in (400mm).

The use of multiple traversing mounts was questioned by many submariners, who considered that this arrangement led to structural weakening of the boat, and to a further and almost useless complication of the firing apparatus to achieve a fan-shaped torpedo spread, which other navies achieved by pre-setting the gyro mechanism of the torpedoes on divergent courses, using fixed internal torpedo tubes which were much simpler, stronger and, above all, which could be reloaded while submerged.

To understand the insistence with which the French Navy defended the use of traversing mounts, it should be remembered that French torpedoes were very unreliable when launched at an angle, because the gyro mechanism did not work very well. (Another drawback was that, when submerged, they created considerable resistance and made it difficult to maintain a constant heading when traversed).

The 21in (533mm) model V/1924 torpedoes used by the French during the Second World War gave good results, but French sources indicate that the 15.7in (400mm) model V/1926 were a failure. Both types were steam propelled, and had, respectively, warheads of 684lb (310kg) and 318lb (144kg); ranges of 3,282 yards (3,000m) at 44 knots (or 7,658 yards (7,000m) at 35 knots) and 1,970 yards (1,800m) at 44 knots.

The use of the 15.7in (400mm) torpedoes alongside the 21in (533mm) was motivated by the fact that the latter could not be set at depths less than 10ft (3m) and so were useless against small targets, for which, the smaller torpedoes were adequate in any case.

The French Navy equipped its boats with 3.9in (100mm) deck guns, 40- or 45-cal, and 3in (76mm) 34.5-cal. Both types could be used against aircraft. Their projectiles weighed 30lb (13.5kg) and 14lb (6.5kg) respectively. The anti-aircraft weapons were mainly of the 13.2 'Hotchkiss' type in twin mounts, and 8mm weapons in single and twin mounts.

The mines loaded in the *Saphir* Class boats were normally of the automatic anchoring, Breguet HS 4 type (485lb (220kg) charge). After 1940, British-type mines were also used in *Rubis*, which operated with Free French units.

Generally speaking, French submarines built between the wars were good boats: reliable, strong, seaworthy and manoeuvrable. They were well armed and had adequate range and surface speed. The ocean-going boats of the last series reached 20 knots, surpassing the speed of many boats of other navies.

The principal shortcomings were: complexity of torpedo-launching equipment; relatively slow diving time (a concomitant of the good surface characteristics which required a high buoyancy factor), and large conning towers.

Underwater stability, manoeuvrability and speed were quite good: hulls, appendages and superstructure offered minimum resistance. Training and morale was good, and had the opportunity presented itself during the war, French crews would probably have been successful.

On 1 September 1939, the fleet numbered 77 boats commissioned: 36 were under construction or ready to be laid down, so that the total available within a few years would have exceeded one hundred, thereby achieving parity with Italy, whom France considered her direct opponent at sea. Of the commissioned boats, 38 were ocean-going, 32 coastal, six minelayers and *Surcouf* was a cruiser.

Of the submarines building or in the design stage, eleven were of the *Aurore* Class, eight of the *Morillot* Class (developed from the *1500 tonnes* Type), four of the *Emeraude* Class (a new version of the *Saphir* Class with greater mine-carrying capacity), and thirteen of the *Phénix* Class (a new type of medium boat: improved *Aurore* Class).

With the exception of *Aurore*, completed in 1940, none of these boats entered service with the French Navy during the war. Most of those under construction were sabotaged in June 1940, or were abandoned and subsequently scrapped. Only one of the *Aurore* Class was completed by the Germans, who incorporated her in their navy.

Between September 1939 and May 1940, French submarines operated with the British, chiefly in the Atlantic and North Sea. During this period, the boats in the Mediterranean carried out numerous patrols to supervise Italian non-belligerency. *Poncelet*, a *1500 tonnes* type, ocean-going boat, captured a German merchant ship in the Atlantic during the early days of the war. Results during the first eight months were modest, thanks to the absence of merchant shipping. Several boats operated off Norway, but without much luck. The minelayer *Rubis* laid several offensive minefields in the North Sea.

Early in June 1940, many boats were recalled from northern waters to the Mediterranean. Here, the submarines based in Provence and in Tunisia immediately began operations against the Italian Navy, carrying out patrols in the Tyrrhenian, and laying several minefields off the ports of Cagliari, Trapani and Tripoli. The collapse of the French Army marked France's withdrawal from the war, and the long odyssey of the French fleet began, which was to have its tragic epilogue in the scuttling at Toulon, two years later.

With other naval units, several boats sought refuge in Britain when the Germans occupied the Atlantic bases. They were siezed by the British who subsequently returned them to de Gaulle's Free France.

Other boats, unable to move, were scuttled in northern French ports, but most of them reached their African bases in the Mediterranean and the Atlantic. The British attack against Mers-el-Kebir (July 1940) to gain control of, or neutralize or destroy the French fleet, and the attacks of the Anglo-Gaullist forces against Dakar (September 1940), Gabon (November 1940), Syria (June 1941) and Madagascar (May 1942) led to the loss of seven boats. During these operations, however, the French displayed some aggressive spirit and *Beveziers* damaged the British battleship *Resolution* off Dakar.

Meanwhile, the few boats commissioned by the Free French naval forces operating with the British (*Surcouf, Junon, Minerve, Rubis, Narval, Ondine* and *Orion*), were employed in the North Sea, where the minelayer *Rubis* performed hazardous and fruitful missions in

Top: the salvage of *Pascal*, which had been scuttled at Toulon on 27 November 1942. Above: *Rubis* at sea in 1941. Below left: the Italian *Bronzo*, later renamed French *Narval* by the French, in port at Syracuse after her capture in July 1943. Below right: General de Gaulle visiting the submarines *Junon* and *Minerve* (foreground) in 1942.

enemy waters, and in the Mediterranean, where *Narval* was lost.

The Allied landings in North Africa in 1942, resulted in the loss of another nine boats in action, and another three were scuttled in port. Several escaped to Toulon where, a few days later, they were included in the general scuttling ordered by the Commander of the Fleet, when the Germans occupied the base. Of the 21 boats at Toulon on 27 November 1942, 16 were sabotaged by their crews, in the port or in the roadstead, and four escaped. Of these, three, *Casabianca, Marsouin* and *Le Glorieux* reached African ports and *Iris* sought refuge in Spain where she was interned. At the same time, the nine boats at Bizerte (all de-commissioned) were captured by Italo-German forces and were later lost.

In December 1943, the French Navy, once again united under the Algiers government, had a force of about 22 boats available: some had operated with Free France until that time, others were from overseas bases, still others had escaped from Toulon. This strength remained essentially unchanged until the end of the war, despite the cession of four boats from the Royal Navy (three *U* and *V* Class, and one ex-Italian of the *Acciaio* Series) and the loss of two boats in action.

On the whole, the operations conducted alongside the Allies by the survivors of the French submarine fleet from 1943 to 1945, achieved good results. Several of the French boats distinguished themselves; for example, *Casabianca* in the Mediterranean, and *Junon* and *Minerve* in the North Sea and in Norwegian waters.

At the end of the war, only about twenty boats were left of the once proud and numerous French submarine fleet of 1939, and all the survivors had become obsolete. More than fifty boats had been lost between 1939 and 1945—about 70 per cent of the original force.

The second rebuilding of the fleet began practically on the day after the war ended, and today, more than twenty years later, it includes nuclear-powered boats which carry a large part of the French strategic nuclear deterrent.

Above: *L'Espoire*. Right: *Le Glorieux*. Below: the hull of the *Morillot* Class boat *La Praya* under construction in June 1939.

Requin Class

Requin, Souffleur, Morse, Narval, Caïman:
Builder: Cherbourg Dockyard.
Date: 1923–1926/27.
Marsouin, Phoque:
Builder: Brest Dockyard.
Date: 1923–1926/27.
Dauphin, Espadon.
Builder: Toulon Dockyard.
Date: 1923–1926/27.
Normal displacement: 1,150

Requin.

tons surfaced; 1,441 tons submerged.
Dimensions: 256ft 6in x 22ft 4in x 16ft 6in (78.2m x 6.8m x 5.1m)
Machinery: diesel: 2 Sulzer or Schneider; electric: 2.
Maximum power: 2,900 hp surfaced; 1,800hp submerged.
Maximum speed: 15 knots surfaced; 9 knots submerged.

Range: 7,700 miles at 9 knots surfaced; 70 miles at 5 knots submerged.
Torpedo tubes: ten 21.7in (550mm); 4 forward, 2 aft, 4 external in traversing mounts; torpedoes: 16.
Guns: one 3.9in (100mm); two 8mm (2 x 1) machine-guns.
Complement: 54.

Double hull ocean-going submarines (1st class). Maximum operational depth: 256ft (80m); normal fuel load: 115 tons. Built under the 1922 and 1923 Programmes, they were the first long-range boats built by the French Navy

after the First World War. They underwent major rebuilds between 1935 and 1937, mostly of machinery and hull arrangements.

They were only partially successful, mainly because of their poor handling and their surface speed which was adjudged inadequate.

From September 1939 to June 1940, they operated mainly in the Mediterranean, patrolling the French and North African coasts. While so engaged, *Morse* was mined in a French minefield off Sfax. When France was defeated, *Narval* joined the Free French forces and was subsequently lost. *Souffleur* was sunk during the brief Syrian campaign in June 1941; *Marsouin* reached North Africa from Toulon in November 1942. All the others were lost by scuttling, or were captured by Axis forces in November 1942. *Phoque, Dauphin, Espadon* and *Requin* were incorporated in the Italian Navy with the designations *FR.111, FR.115, FR.114* and *FR.113*, but only the first of these actually served under the Italian flag. She was lost in 1943.

Fates

date:	location:	boat:	cause (see page 7):
1940	Mediterranean	*Morse, Narval*	m
1941	Mediterranean	*Souffleur*	s
1942	Mediterranean	*Caïman*	sb
		Requin, Dauphin, Phoque, Espadon	c
1946	—	*Marsouin*	r

600/630 tonnes Types

600 tonnes Type (10 units).
Three *Loire-Simonot* Design
A.
Sirène, Naïade, Galathée:
Builder: A. Chantier de la
Loire, Nantes.
Date: 1925–1927/27.
Three *Normand-Fenaux*
Design *B*
Ariane, Eurydice, Danaé:
Builder: Chantier Normand,
Le Havre.
Date: 1923–1928/29.
Four *Schneider-Laubeuf*
Design *C.*
Circé, Calypso, Thétis, Doris:
Builder: Schneider, Chalon-
sur-Saône.
Date: 1923–1929/30.

630 tonnes Type (16 units).
Five *Schneider-Laubeuf*
Design *D.*
*Argonaute, Aréthuse,
Atalante, La Vestale,
La Sultane*:
Builder: Schneider, Chalon-
sur-Saône.
Date: 1927–1932/35.
Two *Loire-Simonot* Design *E.*
Orion:
Builder: A. Chantier de la
Loire, Nantes.
Date: 1928–1932.
Ondine.
Builder: Chantier Dubigeon,
Nantes.
Date: 1928–1932.
Nine *Normand-Fenaux*
Design *F.*
*Diane, Méduse, Amphitrite,
Orphée, La Psyché.*

Builder: Chantier Normand,
Le Havre.
Date: 1927–1932/33.
*Antiope, Amazone, Oréade,
La Sybille.*
Builder: Chantier de la Seine,
Rouen.
Date: 1928–1932/34.
Normal displacement:
A 609 tons surfaced; 757 tons
submerged.
B 626 tons surfaced; 787 tons
submerged.
C 615 tons surfaced; 776 tons
submerged.
D 630 tons surfaced; 798 tons
submerged.
E 656 tons surfaced; 822 tons
submerged.
F 651 tons surfaced; 807 tons
submerged.
Dimensions:
A 210ft 0in x 17ft 0in x 14ft
0in (64m x 5.2m x 4.3m).
B 216ft 2½in x 16ft 0in x 13ft
6in (65.9m x 4.9m x 4.1m).
C 204ft 9in x 17ft 9in x 12ft
9in (62.4m x 5.4m x 3.9m).
D 208ft 0in x 16ft 9in x 11ft
9in (63.4m x 5.1m x 3.6m).
E, F 211ft 3in x 16ft 9in x
12ft 9in (64.4m x 5.1m x
3.9m).
Machinery: diesel: 2 Schneider,
Sulzer or Vickers; electric: 2.
Maximum power:
A 1,300 hp surfaced; 1,000 hp
submerged.
B 1,200 hp surfaced; 1,000 hp
submerged.
C 1,250 hp surfaced; 1,000 hp
submerged.

D 1,300 hp surfaced; 1,000 hp
submerged.
E 1,420 hp surfaced; 1,000 hp
submerged.
F 1,300 hp surfaced; 1,000 hp
submerged.
Maximum speed:
A 13.5 knots surfaced; 7.5
knots submerged.
B, C 14 knots surfaced; 7.5
knots submerged.
D, E 14 knots surfaced; 9
knots submerged.
F 13.7 knots surfaced; 9
knots submerged.
Range:
A, B, C 3,500 miles at 7.5
knots surfaced; 75 miles at
5 knots submerged.
D, E, F 4,000 miles at 10
knots surfaced; 82 miles at
5 knots submerged.
Torpedo tubes: *A, B, C*: seven
21.7in (550m); 3 forward (2
external), 2 aft (external), 2
amidships (external in twin
traversing mount); torpedoes:
13; *D, E, F*: six 21.7in
(550mm); (2 external), 1 aft
(external in traversing mount),
2 amidships (external in twin
traversing mount); two
15.75in (400mm); aft (external
in traversing mount);
torpedoes: 9.
Guns: *A, B, C*: one 3in
(76mm) 35-cal, *B*: one 3.9in
(100mm) 40-cal plus two 8mm
(2 x 1) machine-guns each;
D, E, F: one 3in (76mm)
35-cal, one 8mm machine-gun.
Complement: 41.

Double hull medium-displacement submarines (2nd class).
Maximum operational depth: 256ft (80m); normal fuel
load: approximately 60–65 tons.

Built between 1925 and 1934, these 26 boats were
divided into two types, designated *600 tonnes* and *630
tonnes*. The latter was an improved version of the former,
and several of the original shortcomings had been eliminated: limited transverse stability while submerged, and
low standard of habitability. The *600 tonnes* boats were
modernized between 1937 and 1938. *Ondine* (1st) of the
Sirène Series sank in 1928 after having been rammed by
a merchant ship and *Nymphe* of the *Ariane* Series was
paid off in 1938.

Among both types were several differences of size and
external appearance, because the boats were built to
several different designs, developed by different shipyards,
based however, on common technical specifications.

On the whole, both types had reasonable characteristics,
were quite manoeuvrable and had a good torpedo armament. Their layout was thought to be too complex (fixed
internal and external tubes, traversing mounts, etc.).

In 1939, they were the largest group of medium-range
submarines in the French Navy and until June 1940, they
operated extensively, despite the limited operational effectiveness of the oldest of the boats. During that period,
Doris was torpedoed by the German *U 9*.

In June 1940, *Orion* and *Ondine* were in Britain and
were seized. The others, under the orders of the Vichy
government, were partially de-commissioned in French
bases at home and overseas. In November 1942, six boats
were lost in action against Anglo-American forces in
North Africa, two were captured by the Italians at Bizerte
but not used, five were scuttled at Toulon and three in
North Africa.

In 1943, *Orion* and *Ondine* which had been used for
spare parts, were discarded in Britain. The remaining seven
boats, having operated with Free French forces until the
end of the war, were paid off in 1946.

Fates			**cause**
date:	location:	boats:	(see page 7):
1940	North Sea	*Doris*	s
1942	Atlantic	*La Psyché, Méduse,*	a
		Amphitrite, Oréade	
		Sybille	uc
	Mediterranean	*Argonaute*	n
		Circé, Calypso	c
		Thétis, Sirène, Naïade,	sb
		Galathée, Eurydice,	
		Ariane, Danaé, Diane	
1943	Britain	*Orion, Ondine*	r
1946	—	*Orphée, Aréthuse, Atalante,*	
		Amazone, Antiope,	
		La Sultane, La Vestale	

The *600 tonnes* type *Calypso*
in 1935.

0   20

Saphir Class

Saphir, Turquoise, Nautilus, Rubis, Diamant, Perle.
Builder: Toulon Dockyard.
Date: 1925–1930/37.
Normal displacement: 761 tons surfaced; 925 tons submerged.
Dimensions: 216ft 3in x 23ft 3in x 14ft 1in (65.9m x 7.1m x 4.3m).
Machinery: diesel: 2 Vickers; electric: 2.
Maximum power: 1,300hp surfaced; 1,100hp submerged.
Maximum speed: 12 knots surfaced; 9 knots submerged.
Range: 7,000 miles at 7.5 knots surfaced, 4,000 miles at 12 knots surfaced; 80 miles at 4 knots submerged.
Guns: one 3in (75mm) 35-cal; one 13.2mm, two 8mm machine-guns.
Mines: 32 in 16 lateral wells, 8 per side.
Complement: 42.

Medium-displacement double hull minelaying submarines. Maximum operational depth: 256ft (80m); maximum fuel load: approximately 95 tons. These were among the best boats built in France between the wars. The Normand-Fenaux minelaying system of 16 vertical tubes, each containing two mines, located in the side tanks, stemmed from methods which had already been tested in *Pierre Chailley*, built between 1917 and 1922, and discarded in 1936. The system was particularly safe and effective and overshadowed all other features, which were not outstanding, especially the speed.

From September 1939 to June 1940, the boats were stationed in the Mediterranean and the North Sea, and carried out several minelaying missions in enemy waters: *Saphir*: Cagliari, 13 June 1940; *Turquoise*: Trapani, 14 June 1940; *Nautilus*: Tripoli, 14 June 1940. When the French surrendered, *Rubis* was in Britain, and joined the Free French. From April 1940 until the end of the war, under the successive commands of the then Lieutenant-Commanders Cabanier and Rousselot, *Rubis* carried out 22 minelaying patrols in the Bay of Biscay and along the Norwegian coast. A total of 683 mines were laid, which caused the sinking of 14 merchant and auxiliary vessels, of approximately 21,000 GRT, and seven patrol boats and a minelayer as well as damaging two other vessels. During one patrol, *Rubis* torpedoed a merchantman of 4,300 GRT. Paid off in 1949, *Rubis* accidentally sank in the South of France while being towed to the breakers. In 1971, her hull, lying vertically on a rocky bottom at no great depth, was discovered by divers who made an interesting documentary film which was shown throughout the world, reviving memories of one of France's most glorious submarines.

The other five boats were all lost during the war. *Diamant* was sabotaged at Toulon in November 1942; *Saphir*, *Turquoise* and *Nautilus* were captured at Bizerte as Italian war booty, but none entered service in the Italian Navy; *Perle* was sunk accidentally by a British aircraft in July 1944.

Fates

date:	location:	boat:	cause (see page 7):
1942	Mediterranean	*Diamant*	sb
		Nautilus, Saphir, Turquoise	c
1944	Atlantic	*Perle*	e
1949	—	*Rubis*	r

Rubis at Toulon before the War.

1500 tonnes Type

Redoubtable, Vengeur:
Builder: Cherbourg Dockyard.
Date: 1924–1931/31.
Pascal, Pasteur, Achille, Ajax, Le Centaure, Le Héros*:
Builder: Brest Dockyard.
Date: 1925–1931/34.
Archimède, Persée:
Builder: Chantiers Navals Français, Caen.
Date: 1927–1932/33.
Monge, Protée, Le Tonnant*:
Builder: F. Chantier de la Méditerranée, La Seyne:
Date: 1927–1932/35.
Fresnel:
Builder: Penhoët Shipyards, St. Nazaire.
Date: 1927–1931.
Henri Poincaré, Poncelet:
Builder: Lorient Dockyard.
Date: 1925–1931/32.
Actéon, Achéron, Pégase, Le Conquérant*, *Sfax, Casabianca*:
Builder: A. Chantier de la Loire, Nantes.
Date: 1927–1931/35.
Argo:
Builder: Dubigeon Shipyards, Nantes.
Date: 1927–1932.
L'Espoir, Le Glorieux, Agosta, Beveziers, Ouessant, Sidi Ferruch.
Normal displacement: 1,570 tons surfaced; 2,084 tons submerged.
Dimensions: 302ft 9in x 26ft 11in x 15ft 6in (92.3m x 8.2m x 4.7m).
Machinery: diesel: 2 Sulzer or Schneider; electric: 2.
Maximum power: 6,000hp surfaced (*Le Héros, Le Tonnant, Le Conquérant, L'Espoir, Le Glorieux*, 7,200hp; *Sfax, Casabianca, Agosta, Beveziers, Ouessant, Sidi Ferruch*, 8,600hp); 1,000hp submerged.

Maximum speed: 17 knots surfaced (*Le Héros, Le Tonnant, Le Conquérant, L'Espoir, Le Glorieux*, 19 knots; *Sfax, Casabianca, Agosta, Beveziers, Ouessant, Sidi Ferruch*, 20 knots); 10 knots submerged.
Range: 10,000 miles at 10 knots surfaced, 4,000 miles at 17 knots surfaced; 100 miles at 5 knots submerged.
Guns: one 3.9in (100mm) 40-cal; two 13.2mm (2 x 1) machine-guns.
Complement: 61.

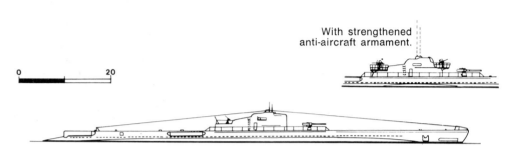

With strengthened anti-aircraft armament.

Double hull ocean-going submarines (1st class). Maximum operational depth: 256ft (80m); normal fuel load: 95 tons; minimum crash-dive time: 45–50 seconds.

The largest standardized group serving in the French Navy during the Second World War and the most successful.

Designed in 1922, the first two boats, *Redoutable* and *Vengeur* were laid down at Cherbourg in 1924: they were launched in 1928 and entered service in 1931. Between 1931 and 1939, a total of 31 boats of this type were built. Two of them were lost before the war. *Prométhée* in a diving accident off Cherbourg in 1932 and *Phénix*, cause unknown, in Indo-Chinese waters in 1939.

Apart from several constructional details which differed in boats built in different yards, the important distinguishing item was the progressive increase in power of the diesel engines. The boats authorized under the 1928–1929 Programmes went from 6,000hp to 7,200hp. The 1930 Programme boats reached 8,600hp. Consequently, maximum speed increased from the 17 knots of the first series to 20 knots in the last.

In 1941, Redoutable was modified. Part of the ballast tanks were adapted for use as fuel tanks, which almost doubled the range of the boat. The modification was subsequently made to other boats.

After 1942, some of the few surviving serviceable *1500 tonnes* boats were modernized in Britain and the United States: the anti-aircraft armament was strength--ened and the two 15.75in (400mm) torpedo tubes were

replaced by a single 21in (533mm) tube, so that the stern traversing mount was now fitted with three 21in (533mm) instead of two 15.75in (400mm) and two 21in (533mm) tubes.

Overall, these were good ocean-going boats, fast, strong, with excellent surface handling and adequate submerged characteristics, though they were rather slow in diving. They were often employed in tropical climates and their habitability was always acceptable.

When France declared war on Germany in 1939, *1500 tonnes* type were stationed in all the operational theatres of the French Navy, from Europe to Indo-China. The largest concentration was in the Atlantic home ports from which they operated against German shipping. Up to June 1940, the most important success was achieved by *Poncelet* which captured the German merchant ship *Chemnitz* (5,900 GRT) in the Atlantic, off the Spanish coast, on 28 September 1939.

When the Germans occupied the French Atlantic ports, *Agosta, Ouessant, Achille* and *Pasteur,* which were refitting at Brest, were scuttled by their crews, as they could not be moved. After the surrender, *Protée* was interned at Alexandria, and *Persée, Poncelet* and *Ajax* were lost during British attacks on French African bases, during the summer of 1940.

During the same period, *Pégase*, stationed in Indo-China, was de-commissioned, and *Sfax* was mistakenly torpedoed by a German submarine. *Beveziers, Héros* and *Monge* were

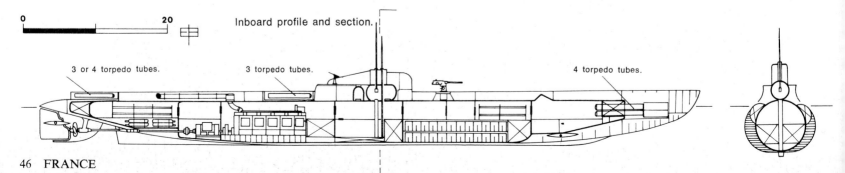

Inboard profile and section.

3 or 4 torpedo tubes.   3 torpedo tubes.   4 torpedo tubes.

lost in May 1942 during the attack on Madagascar. In November 1942, *Actéon*, *Sidi Ferruch* and *Le Conquérant* were lost during the Allied landings in North Africa. *Vengeur*, *Redoutable*, *Pascal*, *Poincaré*, *Achéron*, *L'Espoir* and *Fresnel* were scuttled at Toulon and *Le Tonnant* was scuttled off the coast of Spain. The remaining boats joined the Free French and operated with the Allies; *Protée* was lost while so engaged.

Of the boats scuttled at Toulon, several were salvaged by the Italians and the Germans, but only *Poincaré* was transferred to Genoa for overhaul. As *FR.118*, she was lost in September 1943.

From 1943 to 1945, the five survivors, *Argo*, *Archimède*, *Le Centaure*, *Le Glorieux* and *Casabianca* operated extensively, and *Casabianca* distinguished herself in the Mediterranean, where she obtained several successes against German coastal traffic and played an important part in the French recapture of Corsica. Shortly after the war ended, the five survivors were paid off, together with *Pégase* which had not been re-commissioned after 1940.

Fates

date:	location:	boat:	cause (see page 7):
1940	North Sea	*Achille, Agosta, Ouessant, Pasteur*	sb
	Atlantic	*Persée, Poncelet, Ajax*	n
		Sfax	s
1942	Mediterranean	*Pascal, Redoutable, Le Tonnant, Vengeur, Achéron, L'Espoir, Fresnel, Poincaré*	sb
	Atlantic	*Actéon*	n
		Sidi Ferruch, Le Conquérant	a
	Indian Ocean	*Beveziers, Monge*	n
		Le Héros	a
1943	Mediterranean	*Protée*	n
1946–52	—	*Argo, Pégase, Archimède, Le Centaure, Le Glorieux, Casabianca*	r

Top: submarines moored at a French base before the war. In the foreground is *Achéron* of the 1500 tonnes type. Above: *Archimède*. The anti-aircraft armament has been strengthened by the addition of two 20mm cannon, one forward and one aft of the conning tower. Below: *Casabianca*. Note the stern traversing mount fitted with two 21in (533mm) torpedo tubes (centre) and two 15.7in (400mm) tubes.

Surcouf

Surcouf.
Builder: Cherbourg Dockyard.
Date: 1927–1934.
Normal displacement: 3,250 tons surfaced; 4,304 tons submerged.
Dimensions: 360ft 10in x 29ft 6in x 29ft 9in (110m x 9m x 9.07m).
Machinery: diesel: 2 Sulzer; electric: 2.
Maximum power: 7,600hp surfaced; 3,400hp submerged.
Maximum speed: 18 knots surfaced; 8.5 knots submerged.
Range: 10,000 miles at 10 knots surfaced, 6,800 miles at 13.8 knots surfaced; 70 miles at 4.5 knots submerged.
Torpedo tubes: eight 21.7in (550mm); 4 forward, 4 amidships (external in quadruple traversing mount); torpedoes: 14; four 15.75in (400mm) aft in quadruple traversing mount; torpedoes: 8.
Guns: two 8in (204mm) in twin turret; two single 37mm; four 13.2mm (2 x 2) machine-guns; one reconnaissance floatplane.
Complement: 118.

Double hull cruiser type submarine. Maximum operational depth: 256ft (80m); normal fuel load: approximately 280 tons.

The building of *Surcouf* was authorized under the 1926 naval programme and until the large Japanese aircraft-carrying submarines were commissioned, she was the largest submarine in the world. Intended for raiding far afield, she could carry stores for a cruise of 90 days. The most interesting feature of her armament was the two 8in (204mm) 50-cal guns, of the same type as mounted in French 10,000 ton 'Treaty' cruisers. They were housed in a water-tight turret, forward of the conning tower. Their range at maximum elevation of 30°, was 30,000 yards (27,500m). Ammunition basic load was 600 rounds, each of which weighed 271lb (123.2kg). She was the only example of a submarine armed with the largest guns permitted to undersea craft by the naval treaties.

Her fire-direction centre was equipped with a stereoscopic rangefinder mounted on a 13ft (4m) base, with a range of 13,128 yards (12,000m), corresponding to the effective range of the 8in (204mm) guns, which could open fire some 2.5 minutes after surfacing, at a rate of three rounds per minute. Torpedo armament was also noteworthy, consisting of eight 21in (533mm) tubes with a total load of 14 torpedoes, and four 15.75in (400mm) tubes with 8 torpedoes. Eight of the torpedo tubes (four 21in (533mm) and four 15.75in (400mm)) were arranged in quadruple traversing mounts, situated in the casing aft. *Surcouf* was the only French boat equipped with spare torpedoes for reloading the external tubes.

In the after part of the conning tower was a watertight hangar which housed a partially dismantled Besson MB 411 small reconnaissance floatplane which could be lowered to the water and retrieved by a crane. These operations took about thirty minutes. The original design also specified the carrying of a large motorboat with a speed of 16 knots and a range of 70 miles, to be used for boarding and for spotting targets. After a time, however, it was no longer carried.

With a maximum surface speed of 18 knots, long range and good submerged handling and stability (considering her size), *Surcouf* was undoubtedly a technologically successful boat, but her employment created problems. Briefly, she could not be effectively employed during the Second World War because of the absence of enemy ocean-going shipping. The original programme called for another two similar boats, but their construction was never ordered.

In June 1940, *Surcouf* left Brest where she had been undergoing a major refit, and sought refuge in Britain where, during the same month, she was seized and handed over to the Free French, in whose navy she served from 1940 until 18 February 1942 when she sank after colliding with an American merchant ship in the Gulf of Mexico, en route to the Pacific.

From July 1940 to February 1942, after a refit in England, *Surcouf* had carried out several uneventful Atlantic patrols and had taken part in the seizure of St. Pierre-et-Miquelon by the Gaullist forces.

Fates

date:	location:	boat:	cause (see page 7):
1942	Atlantic	*Surcouf*	v

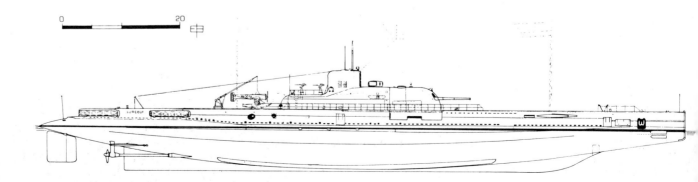

Minerve Class

Minerve:
Builder: Cherbourg Dockyard.
Date: 1931–1936.
Junon, Pallas:
Builder: Chantier Normand, Le Havre.
Date: 1932–1937/39.
Vénus, Cérès:
Builder: Chantier Worms, Le Trait.
Date: 1932–1936/39.
Iris.
Builder: Dubigeon Shipyards, Nantes.
Date: 1932–1936.
Normal displacement: 662 tons surfaced; 856 tons submerged.
Dimensions: 223ft 6in x 18ft 4in x 11ft 9in (68.1m x 5.6m x 3.6m).
Machinery: diesel: 2 Vickers or Schneider; electric: 2.
Maximum power: 1,800hp surfaced; 1,230hp submerged.
Maximum speed: 14 knots surfaced; 9 knots submerged.
Range: 4,000 miles at 10 knots surfaced, 2,500 miles at 13 knots surfaced; 85 miles at 5 knots submerged.
Torpedo tubes: six 21.7in (550mm); 4 forward, 2 aft; torpedoes: 6; three 15.75in (400mm) amidships external in triple traversing mount); torpedoes: 3.
Guns: one 3in (76mm) 35-cal; two 13.2mm (2 x 1) machine-guns.
Complement: 42.

```
0                    20
```

Minerve.

Double hull medium-range submarines (2nd class) developed from the *630 tonnes* type. Maximum operational depth: 256ft (80m); normal fuel load: approximately 60 tons.

Built to an official design, the six boats of this Class represented an improvement on the medium-range boats that had been built hitherto. Torpedo armament was increased and its arrangement was improved, with an increased number of internal tubes (4 forward and 2 aft) and the external 15.75in (400mm) tubes concentrated in a single triple traversing mount, in the casing aft of the conning tower.

In 1939, they were the most modern medium-range boats in service with the French Navy. At the surrender, *Junon* and *Minerve* were in Britain and were seized and handed over to the Free French, with whom they operated until 1945. The other boats remained under the orders of the Vichy government. In November 1942, *Iris* sought refuge in Spain, where she was interned until the end of the war. *Cérès* and *Pallas* were scuttled by their crews at Oran, and *Vénus* was scuttled at Toulon.

Fates			cause
date:	location:	boat:	(see page 7):
1942	Mediterranean	*Cérès, Pallas, Vénus*	sb
1945–54	—	*Minerve, Junon, Iris*	r

L'Aurore Class

L'Aurore:
Builder: Toulon Dockyard.
Date: 1935–1940.
La Créole, La Bayadère, L'Artémis:
Builder: Chantier Normand, Le Havre.
Date: 1937–/–.
La Favorite, L'Africaine, L'Andromaque, L'Armide:
Builder: Chantier Worms, Le Trait.
Date: 1937–/–.
L'Astrée, L'Andromède:
Builder: Dubigeon Shipyards, Nantes.
Date: 1938–/–.
L'Antigone:
Builder: Schneider, Chalon-sur-Saône.
Date: 1938–/–.
L'Hermione, La Gorgone, ordered but not laid down:
Builder: Chantier Normand, Le Havre.
La Clorinde:
Builder: Dubigeon Shipyards, Nantes.
La Cornélie: order cancelled.
Normal displacement: 893 tons surfaced; 1,170 tons submerged.
Dimensions: 241ft 2in x 21ft 4in x 13ft 9in (73.5m x 6.5m x 4.2m).
Machinery: diesel: 2 Sulzer or Schneider; electric: 2.
Maximum power: 3,000hp surfaced; 1,400hp submerged.

Maximum speed: 15 knots surfaced; 9 knots submerged.
Range: 5,600 miles at 10 knots surfaced, 2,250 miles at 15 knots surfaced; 80 miles at 5 knots submerged.
Torpedo tubes: nine 21.7in (550mm); 2 forward, 2 aft, 3 amidships; external in triple traversing mount.
Guns: one 3.9in (100mm); two 13.2mm (2 x 1) machine-guns.
Complement: 44.

Double hull medium-range submarines (2nd class) developed from the *630 tonnes* type, but considerably improved. Maximum operational depth: approximately 328ft (100m); normal fuel load: approximately 85 tons.

The construction of the fifteen boats which were to have constituted the *Aurore* Class, was approved under the 1934, 1937 and 1938 Programmes but, when the French surrendered in June 1940, only eleven boats had been laid down, and none were yet commissioned.

Compared to the preceding medium-range boats, these had greater displacement and range; armament had been further increased by standardizing the torpedo calibre at 21in (533mm) and raising the calibre of the deck gun to 4in (102mm).

Aurore underwent trials in June 1940 and was completed in that year. She was sunk by her crew at Toulon without having been operational.

La Créole was towed incomplete to Britain in 1940. She was seized by the British who returned her to France in 1945. She was commissioned during the post-war period with four other boats, *L'Africaine, L'Andromède, L'Artémis* and *L'Astrée*, whose building was resumed in 1945, to a design which had been modified from the original.

L'Africaine, L'Andromède and *La Favorite*, still under construction, were captured by the Germans and incorporated in their navy with the designations *UF.1, UF.2* and *UF.3*. Only *UF.2* ex-*La Favorite*, was commissioned, and she was used for training; she was lost in 1944. The other two boats were returned to the French after the war.

All the other units under construction in 1940, were sabotaged or abandoned on the ways and subsequently scrapped, with the exception of *L'Artémis* and *L'Astrée*, whose construction was resumed after the war.

Fates

date:	boat:	cause (see page 7):
1940	*L'Africaine, L'Andromède, La Favorite, La Créole*	c
1942	*L'Aurore*	sb

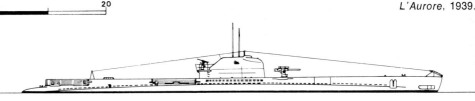

L'Aurore, 1939.

L'Aurore, salvaged at Toulon by the Italians in 1943, but considered beyond repair.

Submarines incomplete in 1940

Table 8: Design characteristics of submarines under construction in 1940 and not completed

Class:	Normal displacement (tons): surfaced/ submerged	Dimensions:	Machinery: type/hp	Maximum speed (knots): surfaced/ submerged	Range (miles at knots): surfaced/ submerged	Armament:
Morillot (*Roland Morillot, La Praya, La Martinique, La Réunion, La Guadeloupe,* plus three units not laid down)	1,817/2,416	336ft 3in x 27ft 3in x 15ft 0in (102.5m x 8.3m x 4.6m)	two diesels/12,000 two electric/2,300	22/9	10,000 at 10 85 at 9	ten 22in (572mm) torpedo tubes 14–18 torpedoes one 3.9in (100mm) gun two 13.2mm (2 x 1)
Emeraude (*Emeraude, L'Agate, Le Corail, L'Escarbouche,* plus three units not laid down)	862/1,119	238ft 6in x 23ft 11in x 13ft 6in (72.7m x 7.3m x 4.1m)	two diesels/2,000 two electric/1,270	15/9	5,600 at 12 90 at 4	four 22in (572mm) torpedo tubes 6 torpedoes, 40 mines one 3.9in (100mm) gun two 13.2mm (2 x 1)
Phénix (*Phénix, Brumaire, Floréal, Frimaire, Fructidor, Germinal, Messidor, Nivôse, Pluviôse, Prairial, Thermidor, Vendémiaire, Ventôse*)	1,056/1,212	246ft 0in x 21ft 0in x 12ft 9in (74.9m x 6.4m x 3.9m)	two diesels/4,200 two-electric/1,400	18/9	8,000 at 10	ten 22in (572mm) torpedo tubes 12 torpedoes one 40mm, one 20mm

In June 1940, several boats were under construction and were sabotaged or abandoned on the ways, and construction was discontinued. They were boats of the *Morillot* Class, an improvement of the *1500 tonnes* Type, and the *Emeraude* Class, a larger version of the *Saphir* Class mine-laying boats.

The *Morillot* Class was to have consisted of eight boats. These had already been ordered, but only five had been laid down between 1937 and 1939.

The three whose building was most advanced, were *Morillot, La Praya* and *La Martinique,* and they were demolished on the ways on 23 June 1940, before the German occupation. The other two, which were in the initial stages of construction, were abandoned.

Of the four boats of the *Emeraude* Class, *Emeraude* had been laid down at Toulon in May 1938 and was sabotaged on 18 June 1940.

The 1939 and 1940 Programmes authorized another 13 boats of the *Phenix* Class, a larger version of the *Aurore* Class, developed for employment in tropical climates. None of these were laid down and their building was cancelled in June 1940.

Foreign submarines in French service

Curie, ex-British *Vox*, at Toulon in 1944.

During the war, the French Navy commissioned four boats which had been ceded by the Royal Navy:

Narval ex *P.714*, ex *Bronzo*. An Italian-built boat (*600 Class, Acciaio* Series) captured off Augusta, Sicily in July 1943, and ceded, after having been incorporated in the Royal Navy as *P.714*, to France on 29 January 1944.

Curie ex *P.67*, ex *Vox*. U Class boat ceded in May 1943; *Doris* ex *Vineyard* and *Morse* ex *Vortex*. V Class boats, built in England and ceded in June and December 1944, respectively. All the boats were returned to Britain on 11 September 1946.

Germany

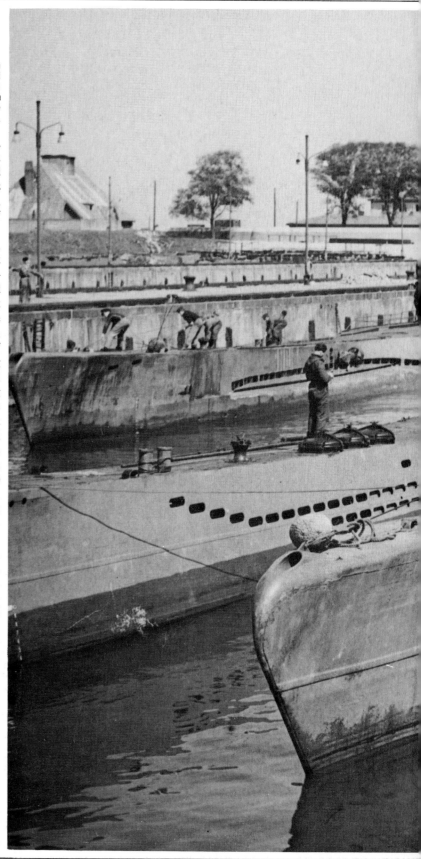

U-boats at Wilhelmshaven in 1945, shortly before their formal surrender. On the far left of the picture is *U 883* (Type IXD2) with three Type VIIC boats in the foreground.

On 16 March, 1935, Germany repudiated the Treaty of Versailles, one clause of which, forbade her to build and employ submarines. In June of that year, the Anglo-German Agreement was signed, and this allowed Germany to build a fleet whose overall displacement was not to exceed 35 per cent of that of the British fleet. For submarines, the proportion was established as 45 per cent, with the possibility of achieving parity (in terms of total tonnage).

On 29 June, eleven days after the effective date of the agreement, the first boat of the new German undersea fleet, *U 1,* was fitted out at Kiel. Apart from the obvious violation of the Treaty, this demonstrated the extent to which the German shipbuilding industry and Navy were able to build modern boats, despite the seventeen years that had passed, during which submarines were prohibited. War experience had been updated by the design and building of several boats in foreign yards: the ocean-going *Birinci Inonu* and *Ikinci Inonu* of 505/620 tons, built in Holland for Turkey in 1927; the sea-going *Vetehinen, Vesihiisi* and *Iko-Turso* of 490/715 tons, and the coastal *Saukko* of 100/136 tons, built in Finland in 1930–31; the ocean-going *Gur* of 750/960 tons, built in Spain for Turkey in 1932; and the coastal *Vesikko* of 250/300 tons, built in Finland in 1933. These eight boats enabled the German General Staff to test its strategic and tactical theories and to plan the development of the future submarine fleet with the following basic types: ocean-going of 500/750 tons; ocean-going-minelaying of about 1,000 tons: 'cruiser' of about 1,500 tons; coastal of about 250 tons; coastal-minelaying of about 500 tons.

From these types, derived all the major conventional submarines employed by the Reich during the Second World War, whose prototypes were built in Germany before 1939.

The ocean-going type of 500/750 tons later became the Type VII, the ocean-going-minelaying of 1,000 tons became the Types I and IX, and the coastal type of 250 tons became the Type II. The 500-ton coastal-minelaying type was not built, and the building of the prototype of the cruiser submarine (Type XI) was not pursued: it would have greatly exceeded the 1,500 tons initially planned.

The building of these large displacement boats was one of the primary causes of contention between the German Naval Staff and the then Commander of Submarines, Captain Karl Doenitz. He was opposed to the construction of large boats, because the new tactics which he was developing and testing, called for the large-scale employment of smaller boats. Furthermore, obliged as he was, to keep within the overall displacement limitations imposed by the Anglo-German Naval Agreement, he preferred to have the greatest possible number of submarines, and this could be achieved only by building boats of limited displacement.

Briefly, Doenitz's theories were based upon the following considerations deriving chiefly from experience of undersea warfare during the First World War: first, enemy merchant shipping was the principal target of submarines and should be attacked without restrictions; second, operations should be carried out on a strategic level, so that

tonnage sunk should exceed new construction, until the enemy's maritime communications were strangled.

These theories clearly presupposed a war with the Western powers, and their successful prosecution called for a numerous fleet of suitable boats and, above all, new tactics deriving from the knowledge that an isolated submarine had small chance of success against escorted convoys.

The limited search capacity of periscope and hydrophones, the low underwater speed and the limited range of batteries rendered a boat almost blind and immobile during patrols of vast ocean spaces. Furthermore, a favourable position, preferably ahead of the convoy, was a prerequisite of successful attack by a submerged boat, and any deviation from course by the convoy, could leave the submarine too far away to launch torpedoes accurately.

In view of these difficulties, it was decided to use submarines primarily on the surface as torpedo-boats submerging only to avoid air attack, or when conditions favoured a submerged attack. The boat's greater surface speed and range greatly increased its search area. Attacking by night, simultaneously from different sides of a convoy, a group of submarines could disorient and scatter the escorts. The concept of groups in coordinated attacks led to the 'wolf pack' tactics which required about twenty boats, stationed along a patrol line perpendicular to the probable course of a convoy, which, when sighted, was shadowed until the pack had gathered. The attack was launched by night, on the surface at high speed, from several angles and from within the area of the convoy itself. At dawn, the boats would retire, and would resume the process the following night, until the convoy was annihilated. The technique called for boats of high speed and surface range, good seakeeping and manoeuvrability, a large supply of torpedoes, and topsides and conning tower of reduced dimensions so as to be as inconspicuous as possible.

The boat that best embodied these requirements was Type VII, an ocean-going submarine of reduced dimensions, in which, at the expense of habitability, a considerable offensive fire power had been concentrated. Type VII formed the backbone of the German flotillas in the Battle of the Atlantic.

The tactics described above were tested extensively by U-Boat Command with the few boats available before the war. They proved practicable, but Admiral Doenitz wanted a minimum of 300 boats ready at the outbreak of hostilities (reckoning that only a third of these could be operative at one time). His strategic requirements were met only in small measure by the German Naval Staff. At that time, the Supreme Commander of the German Navy was Grand Admiral Raeder, whose ideal of naval warfare, based on the direct encounter of battle fleets, was partly inspired by a pointed study of naval operations of the First World War, published by Admiral Wegener in the 1920s.

When war started in 1939, therefore, the German submarine fleet consisted of 55 boats, with another thirty or so building. Little more than half of them were capable of ocean-going operations; the remainder were coastal or prototypes for training or tests, and as several were under repair, Germany began operations in the Atlantic with not more than about twenty submarines.

In addition to the limitations imposed by his small fleet, Doenitz's plans were thwarted by Hitler's decision to adhere scrupulously to international conventions, which excluded the sinking of merchant ships without warning, but on 17 October 1939, these limitations were lifted.

The most interesting tactic, which was to have produced the greatest results, the wolf pack, could not be implemented because of insufficient boats. The operations of the first months of the war, therefore, consisted of the traditional isolated attacks from ambush.

The German boats operating from 1939 to 1940 differed little from those used towards the end of the First World War; only with respect to weapons had there been significant improvements. At first, they were armed with normal 21in (533mm) 'steam' torpedoes of the Type G7a, and with a new type derived from the preceding model, G7e, which was propelled electrically and had a magnetic fuze. The realization of the electric torpedo, whose major advantage was its complete absence of wake, had been made possible by the adoption of super-light lead storage batteries, so that the overall weight was about 3,528lb (1,600kg), almost the same as a normal torpedo. Speed and running distance, however, were significantly inferior to thermal torpedoes: 28 knots for 3,829 yards (3,500m) as opposed to 50 knots for 4,376 yards (4,000m) and 30 knots for 10,940 yards (10,000m).

The magnetic fuze was intended to detonate the warhead under the target's hull, the best position for maximum damage. When first used operationally, G7e proved so erratic that they were withdrawn and replaced by normal G7a torpedoes. During the campaign in Norway, faulty fuzes caused many torpedoes to explode prematurely, and many failed to explode because of defective depth-setting mechanism. It has been estimated that, had the torpedoes functioned properly, hits would have been registered on at least one battleship of the four attacked; seven cruisers out of twelve and seven destroyers out of ten, apart from numerous attacks which failed against transport vessels. Apparently, irregularities in the earth's magnetic field in Northern latitudes, played a part in these failures.

The electric torpedo, its defects remedied, was again operational from the summer of 1941, this time, successfully. Other important innovations were an effective system of firing without bubbles, and a fire-direction centre for calculating torpedo-firing data. The new firing system ingeniously prevented the escape from the tube of the compressed air needed for launching: instead, it was discharged (unfortunately, mixed with the exhaust gas of the thermal torpedo) into the interior of the boat, thereby eliminating the surfacing bubbles which betrayed the presence of the submerged boat. The fire-direction centre was a miniature electro-mechanical calculator which received heading, speed and distance data, observed or estimated, and rapidly furnished the information necessary for launching torpedoes with a fair degree of accuracy.

All German ocean-going submarines could be used as minelayers. They could carry a certain number of mines in lieu of spare torpedoes (two or three, depending on the type, for each torpedo). The mines were of the magnetic type and were normally dropped through the stern torpedo tubes. Carrying capacity varied according to the type of boat and mine.

Table 9: Mine/Torpedo capacity of German ocean-going submarines

Submarine type:	TMA type mine:	TMB type mine:	Alternative torpedo load:
I A	28	42	14
II	12	18	5
VII	22–26	33–39	11–14
IX	44	66	22
XXI	12	—	*
XXIII	—	—	—

* Only 6 of the 23 torpedoes carried could be replaced by mines.

Until June 1940, U-boat successes against Allied merchantmen were modest, 103,544 GRT in 1939 and 525,000 GRT during the first five months of 1940. Their Atlantic and North Sea operations had been inhibited by the small number of boats available at any one time (not more than ten, on average), the troublesome G7e torpedoes and the withdrawal of some boats to support operations in Norway. During this period, several important successes were achieved against warships. Notable, were the sinking of the British aircraft carrier *Courageous* in the Atlantic, and the battleship *Royal Oak* inside the great British base at Scapa Flow in the Orkney Islands.

From June 1940, however, the Germans were able to use the French Atlantic ports as bases and, with the progressive increase of boats in service (reaching approximately 70 in October-November), operations began to be conducted in a more effective manner. Operational Command was set up in Paris, whence operations were directed and coordinated, and the first group of Focke-Wulf Condor long-range reconnaissance aircraft was stationed in France. The construction of numerous new boats had been approved, but production rate was still low and the minimum 300 boats for large-scale operations against merchant shipping was not reached until two years later, by which time, the situation had changed radically, chiefly because of the countermeasures adopted by the Allies.

Wide-scale attacks by large groups of surfaced boats began in mid 1941. Results were excellent and demonstrated the value of the technique, but it had been too long delayed. Already, towards the end of 1941, larger areas of sea were being patrolled by increasing numbers of British offensive reconnaissance aircraft.

In 1941, German submarines sank 445 ships totalling 2,171,890 GRT for the loss of 38 boats. The submarines used were the Type VII (in its different versions) in the North Atlantic, Type IX in the central Atlantic and Type II ('canoes') for coastal operations in the North Sea.

In September 1941, in accordance with Italo-German agreements, several Type VII were stationed in the Mediterranean and continued to operate there, achieving successes, particularly against British warships, until May 1944. The loss of his boats to the Mediterranean, following those removed to Norway, were a new cause of contention between Doenitz and the Staff. The Commander of Submarines insisted that every diversion of boats from their primary objective against merchant shipping be avoided. The sinking of a warship or two in the Mediterranean would in no way compensate the considerable decrease in merchant tonnage sunk in the Atlantic.

In June 1942, the U-boats scored their greatest number of sinkings, 131 ships totalling 616,904 GRT. In November, the record for the war was achieved, with 118 ships totalling 743,321 GRT. The total sinkings for this, the U-boats' best year, was 1,094 ships totalling 5,819,025 GRT. The 259 operational boats in January increased to 397 in December 1942. The majority of these were variants of Type VII and Type IX. U-boat losses for the year totalled 88 boats, about twice the number with which Germany had started the war. In 1942, however, new merchant building exceeded—for the first time—tonnage sunk, signalling the failure of the German Atlantic campaign.

During this period, another special type of U-boat appeared. Type XIV, known as 'Milchkuh' (milch cow), was an ocean-going supply boat carrying approximately 600 tons of diesel fuel. The replenishing of fuel tanks at sea, extended the cruise time of twelve Type VIIs by four weeks or five Type IXs by eight weeks, enabling Type VII to operate as far afield as the Antilles, or off the coast of South

Development of German submarines, 1930–1945.

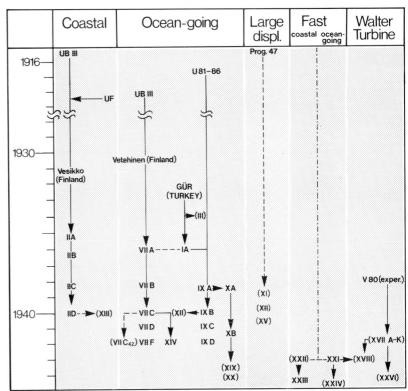

A Type IX boat leaves her bunker in a French base, bound for the Atlantic.

Africa, and allowing Type IX unlimited range in the Atlantic. The use of supply submarines increased the number of U-boats in operational areas by 50 per cent, despite the increasingly long passages from their bases. The Type XIV 'milch cows' were complemented by two Type IX (Variant D1) for replenishing fuel, and four Type VII (Variant F) for reloading torpedoes.

In one respect, the U-boats were their own enemy. A vital factor of the wolf pack and of the system of centralization from U-Boat Command, was that boats frequently had to break radio silence to transmit sightings or position reports to base and to their comrades. Allied shore stations could use these transmissions to fix the positions of U-boats which enabled the Admiralty to divert convoys away from the lurking packs. Even more importan was the use of high-frequency radio direction-finding sets fitted in ships, to detect the presence of submarines near convoys. Known as H/F D/F or 'Huffduff', this British development was fitted in numbers of escorts in 1941, though it remained unknown to the Germans throughout the war. It was at least as important as radar in the defence of convoys and the sinking of U-boats.

The Germans adopted a number of ruses to help a detected boat to evade attack. The most important was a device known as 'pillenwerfer'. This emitted a 'pill' or bubble of gas which gave the same sonar return as the U-boat herself, whose escape could be screened by this before the escorts detected the trick.

At the beginning of 1943, the U-boats operated across half the world: Type VII in the Atlantic, Arctic and Mediterranean; Type II in the North Sea, Baltic and Black Sea (several had been transferred via the Danube since June 1942); Type IX in the Atlantic, Arctic and—from October 1942—Indian Oceans. Following a peak in March 1943, when merchant sinkings reached 105 ships totalling 590,234 GRT, sinkings diminished until they reached the levels of the early days of

Above and right: A German Type VII C boat being launched.

the war: 9 ships totalling 30,726 GRT in November 1943. At the same time, submarine losses were appreciably higher: 245 boats from January to December 1943, with a high point of 42 in May.

One of the chief causes of the decline in U-boat successes was the Allied use of aircraft. The activity of Allied aircraft fitted with radar was particularly intense in the Bay of Biscay, where submarines were in transit. In addition, operations were started by groups of escort carriers (merchantmen converted to carry about twenty aircraft) and escort vessels, and almost complete air coverage of the central Atlantic was assured, when Portugal allowed the Allies to use airfields in the Azores from the autumn of 1943.

The most important result achieved by aircraft, was the forcing of the submarine underwater, depriving it of all the advantages of mobility which, hitherto, Doenitz's torpedo-boat technique had conferred upon it. Again, the submarine became comparatively blind and immobile, and all the measures adopted by the Germans to limit their losses were in vain. These consisted of: the increasing of anti-aircraft armament; the fitting of Metox, which revealed radio-electrical emissions on the wavelength of ship and aircraft radar, but which soon became obsolete because the Allies changed the frequency of their radar sets; and the adoption of a new type of torpedo whose acoustic head (Zaunkönig) guided itself to the target by propeller and engine noise, and was used mainly against escorts.

Clearly, the U-boats' problems could no longer be solved by modifying existing boats or improving their tactics and strategy. A completely new type was needed, able to move underwater at high speed for long periods, and able to evade attack by diving deep. The concept had been under study in Germany since 1939. It was based on a single system for surface and underwater propulsion—the Walter turbine. The oxygen necessary for combustion, was provided by the spontaneous decomposition of hydrogen peroxide in the presence of permanganate of lime. This breakdown into oxygen and water vapour enabled any fuel to be burned. The Germans used a sulphur-free synthetic diesel oil to avoid corrosion of the closed-cycle machinery. In pursuit of their single propulsion gear, the Germans

Relationship between submarines lost and new boats commissioned, 1939–1945.

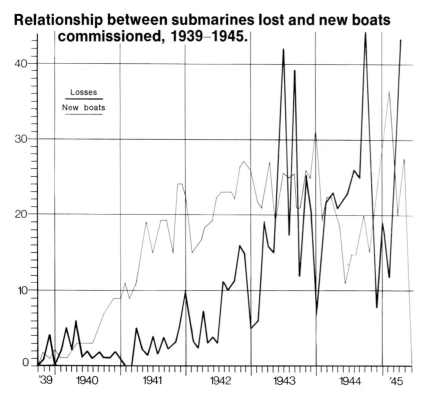

Top right: The Type XVII B boat, *U 1407*, built for experiment with the Walter turbine. Above: The experimental Walter turbine boat, *V 80* of 1940.

also studied a type of closed-cycle diesel engine fuelled by oxygen, highly pressurised in steel containers. It never passed the experimental stage but it was to have been fitted in the Type XVII K which were building in 1945, and in the Types XXXII, XXXIII and XXXVI which were being developed in the same year (see Table 13, pages 88-93).

The first Walter submarine, *V 80* was tested in 1940. Results were encouraging and she was followed by other experimental boats (Type XVII in several variants), but in 1943, the hydrogen peroxide turbine was still far from operational, and the first operational Walter boats (Type XXVI W) were still under construction at the end of the war.

As neither of these single-propulsion system boats could be made available rapidly, the German designers sought another solution. They adopted light-weight high-capacity batteries; hull shapes developed specially for underwater propulsion, and the schnorkel, which allowed diesels to be used at periscope depth (it had been tested successfully in 1943). The results were embodied in the Elektro-boote (electric submarines) which had high underwater speeds. They were designed to operate almost exclusively submerged, and the electric power installed, considerably exceeded that furnished by the diesels for surface propulsion. They could still be defined as 'conventional' because of the two types of propulsion gear, but in their characteristics, they constituted the first step towards the 'pure' submarine which would become practical after the war with the arrival of atomic power.

Designed in 1943, the first Elektro-boote began trials in mid 1944. Built in two types, the ocean-going XXI and the coastal XXIII, they were equipped with good acoustic instruments which, together with their high underwater speed (Type XXI was capable of bursts of 17.5 knots as opposed to the 7–8 knots of conventional boats) allowed precise swift attacks to be made from depth, and escape was easy. Had they been available earlier, they would have imparted a new turn to the Battle of the Atlantic.

Several actions fought by approximately ten Type XXIII boats, fully demonstrated the validity of their design principles, and proved the boats comparatively invulnerable to the Allied anti-submarine weapons of that period. From the beginning of 1944, the construction of electric boats had absolute priority over any other type. Almost all new contracts for Type VII and IX were cancelled and many boats already begun were demolished for their materials. A vast Elektro-boote programme was begun, on which Doenitz placed his last hopes of successfully resuming the war against merchant shipping.

At the end of 1943, the German submarine fleet reached its highest number with 442 operational boats, but losses were enormous and successes continued to decline. The only immediate possibility of restoring the balance rested in the schnorkel, and at the beginning of 1944 it was installed in all boats assigned to the Atlantic. Its use, which did not become widespread until the middle of the year, took the Allies by surprise and, for a time, lowered German losses to an acceptable level and achieved a modest increase in sinkings. In a very short time, however, the Allies produced a type of radar whose wavelength could detect even the small head of the schnorkel, and so its effectiveness was limited.

By late 1943, U-boat Command was well aware that the battle was lost, but Doenitz did not completely suspend operations because the disappearance of U-boats from the seas would have had serious repercussions on the war elsewhere, allowing the Allies to re-deploy the huge forces that had been engaged in the defence of shipping.

In 1944, the number of U-boats lost exceeded that of new boats entering service (264 against 230), and the size of the operational forces (408 in December) began to diminish for the first time since the war began. The first months of 1945 saw a slight decrease in losses which, however, remained high without a corresponding amount of shipping sunk. In April, losses rose again to reach the high point of the war with 64 boats sunk. At the surrender on 8 May 1945, there were still some 360 operational boats. Of these, almost a hundred were of the Types XXI and XXIII which had not yet been employed on a large scale. Many boats, especially the most recent (about 230) were scuttled by their own crews, and more than a hundred surrendered to the Allies.

Three views of *U 995* (Type VIIC). Right: conning tower. Far right: forward torpedo room and crew quarters. Below: after end of control room.

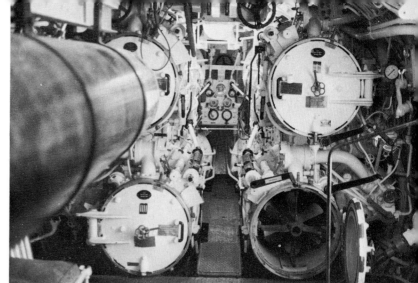

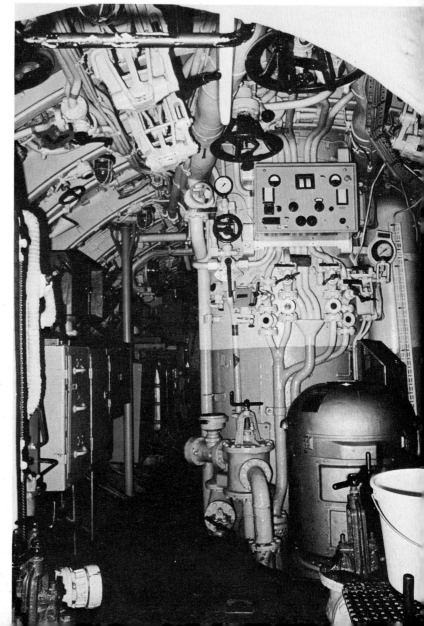

Between June 1935 and May 1945, the German submarine fleet totalled 1,162 boats in operational service, divided into 33 flotillas. Approximately 55,000 men served aboard them. Of this impressive fleet, some 920 boats carried out 3,000 patrols during the war and sank 2,840 merchant ships totalling 14,333,082 GRT, and 150 warships of all types. Losses in action or from scuttling amounted to 1,060 boats with 27,491 dead or missing and some 5,000 prisoners.

Analysis reveals that about 75 per cent of the boats were lost in action during the 69 months of the war; approximately 43 per cent of the losses were to air attack. These figures exclude the so-called 'pocket' submarines, a large number of which, were built and manned from 1943, chiefly for defensive purposes. Their results were disappointing and had little or no effect on the great battle.

The losses of operational boats from the bombing of bases were relatively low compared to those suffered by boats under construction in German yards. This was because of the defensive measures adopted by the German Navy. At the main operational bases in France, Germany and Norway (Brest, St. Nazaire, Bordeaux-La Pallice, Hamburg, Trondheim) bombproof shelters of reinforced concrete protected the boats during refit and resupply.

Submariners, a high percentage of whom were volunteers, were the élite of the German Navy. The young commanders emulated the examples of such 'aces' as Kretschmer, Luth, Schutze, Prien, Rosing, Thiesenhausen and others. Esprit de corps, while never reaching the point of fanaticism, was an ever-present and determining factor, even during the worst periods of 1944 and 1945, when only one boat in three was likely to return to base. New crews underwent an intensive training programme, during which, the veterans passed on their experience to the newcomers. Throughout the war, training was considered of primary importance and was always carried out in a very realistic manner.

Until mid 1943, the traditional system of building submarines was used: boats were laid down on the ways of sixteen yards, where all the necessary materials were gathered. This resulted in a building time of 7–9 months for Type VII and IX boats, and exposed them throughout that period, to Allied bombing which was becoming ever more frequent and effective. Towards the end of 1943, wide-scale prefabrication techniques were introduced. The building ways became assembly points and the time spent by each boat there was reduced to a few days. Production rate accelerated to a monthly average of 30–35 boats, compared to the 20–25 for the period 1942–43.

The Type XXI and XXIII fast submarines were successfully prefabricated in three phases. The major structural components of the various hull sections—frames, pressure plating, outer plating—were processed in thirty-two centres throughout Germany. These sections were transferred, generally by river, to sixteen shipyards where the main engines, piping and electrical cables and other components were installed. The sections were then concentrated in three yards where they were welded and completed.

Type IA

U 25, U 26.
Builder: Deschimag, Bremen.
Date: 1935–1936/36.
Normal displacement: 862 tons surfaced; 983 tons submerged.
Dimensions: 237ft 6in x 20ft 3in x 14ft 0in (72.4m x 6.2m x 4.3m).
Machinery: diesel: 2 MAN; electric: 2 BBC.
Maximum power: 2,800hp surfaced; 1,000hp submerged.
Maximum speed: 17.7 knots surfaced; 8.3 knots submerged.
Range: 7,900 miles at 10 knots surfaced; 78 miles at 4 knots submerged.
Torpedo Tubes: six 21in (533mm), 4 forward, 2 aft; torpedoes: 14.
Guns: one 4.1in (105mm) 45-cal; one 20mm.
Complement: 43.

Single hull ocean-going boats with large side tanks. Maximum operational depth: 472ft (150m); maximum fuel load: 96 tons; minimum crash-dive time: 30 seconds.

This type, directly derived from the Turkish *Gur* (ex-Spanish *E 1*) built in Spain in 1932 to a German design, served as a test bed for the development of the subsequent Type IX. Both boats of this series were lost during the first months of the war.

Fates			cause
date:	location:	boat:	(see page 7):
1939	North Sea	*U 25*	m
		U 26	n–a

1939.

U 25 at the beginning of the war.

Type II

Right: *U 56* and another Type II boat used for training at Gdynia, Poland, in 1944. *U 18* heading for the open sea in 1937. Bottom: *U 2* in heavy seas.

Variant II A (6 units).
U 1–U 6:
Builder: Deutsche Werke, Kiel.
Date: 1934–1935/35.

Variant II B (20 units).
U 7–U 12, U 17–U 24:
Builder: Krupp Germania, Kiel.
Date: 1935–1935/36.
U 13–U 16:
Builder: Deutsche Werke, Kiel.
Date: 1935–1935/36.
U 120 – U 121 (building for China: requisitioned in 1939):
Builder: Flender Werft, Lubeck.
Date: 1939–1940/40.

Variant II C (8 units).
U 56–U 63:
Builder: Deutche Werke, Kiel.
Date: 1937–1938/40.

Variant II D (16 units).
U 137 – U 152.
Builder: Deutsche Werke, Kiel.
Date: 1939–1940/41.

Normal displacement:
Variant II A: 254 tons surfaced; 303 tons submerged.
Variant II B: 279 tons surfaced; 329 tons submerged.
Variant II C: 291 tons surfaced; 341 tons submerged.
Variant II D: 314 tons surfaced; 364 tons submerged.
Dimensions:
Variant II A: 134ft 3in x 13ft 6in x 12ft 6in (40.9m x 4.1m x 3.8m).
Variant II B: 140ft 0in x 13ft 6in x 12ft 6in (42.7m x 4.1m x 3.9m).
Variant II C: 144ft 0in x 13ft 9in x 12ft 6in (43.9m x 4.2m x 3.8m).
Variant II D: 144ft 3in x 16ft 0in x 12ft 9in (44m x 4.9m x 3.9m).
Machinery: diesel: 2 MWM; electric: 2 SSW.
Maximum power:
Variant II A: 700hp surfaced; 360hp submerged.
Variant II B: 700hp surfaced; 360hp submerged.
Variant II C: 700hp surfaced; 410hp submerged.
Variant II D: 700hp surfaced; 410hp submerged.

Maximum speed:
Variant II A: 13 knots surfaced; 6.9 knots submerged.
Variant II B: 13 knots surfaced; 6.9 knots submerged.
Variant II C: 13 knots surfaced; 7.4 knots submerged.
Variants II D: 13 knots surfaced; 7.4 knots submerged.
Range:
Variant II A: 1,600 miles at 8 knots surfaced; 35 miles at 4 knots submerged.
Variant II B: 3,100 miles at 8 knots surfaced; 40 miles at 4 knots submerged.
Variant II C: 3,800 miles at 8 knots surfaced; 40 miles at 4 knots submerged.
Variant II D: 5,650 miles at 8 knots surfaced; 56 miles at 4 knots submerged.
Torpedo tubes: three 21in (533mm) forward; torpedoes: 5.
Guns: one 20mm (from 1942: four 20mm 2 x 2).
Complement: 25.

IIA, 1942.

IIA, 1942.

IIA–B, 1938.   IIC, 1939.   IID, 1942.

Inboard profile and section of Type II.

IID and U120-121, 1942.

Single hull coastal boats with internal main rapid-dive tank. Maximum operational depth: 394ft (120m); maximum fuel load: 12 tons (II A), 21 tons (II B), 23 tons (II C), 38 tons (II D); minimum crash-dive time: 35–25 seconds.

This type was the first to be built in Germany after the First World War. It derived from the *Vesikko,* built in Finland in 1931–33, to a German design, in turn derived from the Type UB II of 1915 and the Type UF of 1918.

These small boats were strong and manoeuvrable. In the subsequent versions (A, B, C, D), several characteristics were improved: range, for example was increased significantly, which enabled the D version to operate in the Atlantic during the first year of the war.

After 1941, Type II was no longer produced: ocean-going boats were built instead. During the war, these boats operated predominantly in German coastal waters and in the English Channel (1939–40), and in the Baltic against the Russians, from the summer of 1941. Many were assigned to training; several were transferred, via the German canals and the Danube, to the Black Sea, where they operated until 1944. *U 57* and *U 58* were fitted with schnorkel apparatus for trials in 1943. Few of these boats were lost in action at sea: most of them were destroyed by bombing or were scuttled at the surrender.

Fates date:	location:	boat:	cause (see page 7):
1939	North Sea	*U 1*	s
		U 12	m
		U 16	n
1940	North Sea	*U 13*	n
		U 15	v
		U 22	m
		U 63	n
1941	Atlantic	*U 138, U 147*	n
	Baltic	*U 144*	s
1943	Baltic	*U 5*	v
1944	Baltic	*U 2*	v
		U 3, U 4, U 6, U 10, U 21	r
		U 7	v
	Black Sea	*U 9*	b
		U 18, U 19, U 20, U 23, U 24	sb
1945	North Sea	*U 8, U 11, U 14, U 17, U 27, U 58,*	
	Baltic	*U 60, U 61, U 62, U 120, U 121,*	
		U 137, U 139, U 140, U 141,	
		U 142, U 146, U 148, U 151, U152	sb
		U 56	
		U 59	r
		U 143, U 145, U 149, U 150	x

60 GERMANY

Type VII

Variant VII A (10 units).
U 27–U 32:
Builder: Deschimag AG Weser, Bremen.
Date: 1935–1936/37.
U 33–U 36:
Builder: Krupp Germania Werft, Kiel.
Date: 1935–1936/36.

Variant VII B (24 units).
U 45–U 55, U 99–U 102 (ex *U 69–U 72*):
Builder: Krupp Germania Werft, Kiel.
Date: 1936–1938/40.
U 73–U 76:
Builder: Veg. Vulcan, Bremen.
Date: 1938–1940/40.
U 83–U 87:
Builder: Flender Werft, Lubeck.
Date: 1939–1941/41.

Variant VII C and VII C–41
(661 units + 27).
U 69–U 72 (ex *U 99–U 102*):
Builder: Krupp Germania Werft, Kiel.
Date: 1938–1940/41.
U 77–U 82, U 132–U 136:
Builder: Veg. Vulcan, Bremen.
Date: 1939–1941/41.
U 88–U 92:
Builder: Flender Werft. Lubeck.
Date: 1939–1941/42.
U 201–U 212, U 221–U 232:
Builder: Krupp Germania Werft, Kiel.
Date: 1939–1941/42.
U 235–U 250:
Builder: Krupp Germania Werft, Kiel.
Date: 1941–1942/44.
U 251–U 300, U 1271–U 1279:
Builder: Veg. Vulcan, Bremen.
Date: 1939–1941/44.
U 301–U 329, U 903–U 904:
Builder: Flender Werft. Lubeck.
Date: 1940–1941/44.
U 331–U 350, U 1101–

U 1110:
Builder: Nordseewerke, Emden.
Date: 1939–1941/44.
U 351–U 370:
Builder: Flensburg Schiffbau.
Date: 1939–1941/44.
U 371–U 400, U 1131–U 1132:
Builder: Howaldtswerke, Kiel.
Date: 1939–1941/44.
U 401–U 430, U 1161–U 1172:
Builder: Danziger Werft, Danzig.
Date: 1939–1941/44.
U 431–U 450, U 731–U 750, U 825–U 828, U 1191–U 1210:
Builder: F. Schichau, Danzig.
Date: 1939–1941/44.
U 451–U 458, U 465–U 486:
Builder: Deutsche Werke, Kiel.
Date: 1939–1941/44.
U 551– U 650:
Builder: Blohm & Voss, Hamburg.
Date: 1939–1940/42.
U 651–U 683:
Builder: Howaldtswerke, Hamburg.
Date: 1939–1941/44.
U 701–U 722:
Builder: Stulcken Sohn, Hamburg.
Date: 1939–1941/43.
U 751– U 779:
Builder: KM Werft, Wilhelmshaven.
Date: 1939–1941/44.
U 821–U 822:
Builder: Stettiner Oderwerke, Stettin.
Date: 1941–1943/44.
U 901:
Builder: Stettiner Vulcan Werke, Stettin.
Date: 1941–1943.
U 905–U 908:
Builder: H. C. Stulcken, Hamburg.
Date: 1942–1944/–.
U 921–U 930:
Builder: Neptun Werft, Rostock.
Date: 1941–1943/44.

U 951–U 1032:
Builder: Blohm & Voss, Hamburg.
Date: 1941–1942/–.
U 1051–U 1058, U 1063–U 1065:
Builder: Germania Werft, Kiel.
Date: 1941–1944/44.
U 1301–U 1308:
Builder: Flensburg Schiffbau.
Date: 1942–1944/45.

Variant VII C and VIII C–41 boats, contracts for which were cancelled in 1943/44 or which were designed only and no contracts placed (shown in brackets).
U 330, U 684–U 686, (U 687–U 698), U 723–730, U 780–U 782, U 823–U 824, U 829–U 840, U 902, U 909–U 912, (U 919–U 920), U 931–U 936, (U 943–U 950), U 1033–U 1050, U 1066–U 1068, U 1111–U 1113, (U 1121–U 1130), U 1133–U 1146, (U 1153–U 1160), U 1173–U 1190, U 1211–U 1214, U 1280–U 1285, (U 1298–U 1300), U 1309–U 1312, (U 1319–U 1330), U 1331–U 1338, (U 1351–U 1400), U 1401–U 1404, U 1417–U 1422, U 1435–U 1439, U 1801–U 1804, U 1823–U 1828, (U 1829–U 1900), (U 1905–U 2000), (U 2005–U 2100).

Variant VII C–42 (168 units) planned but none completed); contracts cancelled in 1944 or (in brackets) no orders placed:
U 699–U 700, U 783–U 790, U 913–U 918, U 937–U 942, U 1069–U 1080, U 1093–U 1100, U 1115–U 1120, U 1147–U 1152, U 1215–U 1220, U 1286–U 1297, U1313–U 1318, U 1339–U 1350, U 1423–U 1434, U 1440–U 1463, (U 1464–U 1500), U 1805–U 1822, U 1901–U 1904, U 2001–U 2004, U 2101–U 2104,

(U2105–U 2110), U 2301–U 2318, (U 2319–U 2320).

Variant VII D (6 units).
U 213–U 218:
Builder: Krupp Germania Werft, Kiel.
Date: 1940–1941/42.

Variant VII F (4 units).
U 1059–U 1062:
Builder: Krupp Germania Werft, Kiel.
Date: 1941–1943/43.

Normal displacement:
Variant VII A: 626 tons surfaced; 745 tons submerged.
Variant VII B: 753 tons surfaced; 857 tons submerged.
Variant VII C: 769 tons surfaced; 871 tons submerged.
Variant VII C–42: 999 tons surfaced; 1,050 tons submerged.
Variant VII D: 965 tons surfaced; 1,080 tons submerged.
Variant VII F: 1,084 tons surfaced; 1,181 tons submerged.
Dimensions:
Variant VII A: 211ft 9in x 19ft 3in x 14ft 6in (64.5m x 5.85m x 4.37m).
Variant VII B: 218ft 3in x 20ft 3in x 15ft 6in (66.5m x 6.20m x 4.74m).
Variant VII C: 218ft 3in x 20ft 3in x 15ft 6in (66.5m x 6.20m x 4.74m).
Variant VII C–42: 225ft 6in x 22ft 3in x 16ft 3in (67.3m x 6.80m x 5.0m).
Variant VII D: 252ft 3in x 21ft 0in x 16ft 6in (76.9m x 6.38m x 5.01m).
Variant VII F: 254ft 3in x 24ft 0in x 16ft 0in (77.6m x 7.30m x 4.91m).
Machinery: diesel: 2; electric: 2 of various types.
Maximum power:
Variant VII A: 2,310hp surfaced; 750hp submerged.
Variant VII B: 3,200hp surfaced; 750hp submerged.

Variant VII C: 3,200hp surfaced; 750hp submerged.
Variant VII C–42: 2,700hp surfaced; 750hp submerged.
Variant VII D: 3,200hp surfaced; 750hp submerged.
Variant VII F: 3,200hp surfaced; 750hp submerged.
Maximum speed:
Variant VII A: 17 knots surfaced; 8 knots submerged.
Variant VII B: 17.9 knots surfaced; 8 knots submerged.
Variant VII C: 17.6 knots surfaced; 7.6 knots submerged.
Variant VII C–42: 16.7 knots surfaced; 7.6 knots submerged.
Variant VII D: 16.7 knots surfaced; 7.3 knots submerged.
Variant VII F: 17.6 knots surfaced; 7.9 knots submerged.
Range:
Variant VII A: 6,200 miles at 10 knots surfaced; 94 miles at 4 knots submerged.
Variant VII B: 8,700 miles at 10 knots surfaced; 3,850 miles at 17.2 knots submerged; 90 miles at 4 knots submerged.
Variant VII C: 8,500 miles at 10 knots surfaced; 130 miles at 2 knots submerged; 3,250 miles at 17 knots surfaced; 80 miles at 4 knots submerged.
Variant VII C–42: 10,000 miles at 12 knots surfaced; 80 miles at 4 knots submergd.
Variant VII D: 11,200 miles at 10 knots surfaced; 127 miles at 2 knots submerged; 5,050 miles at 16 knots surfaced; 69 miles at 4 knots submerged.
Variant VII F: 14,700 miles at 10 knots surfaced; 130 miles at 2 knots submerged.
Torpedo tubes: five 21in (533mm) 4 forward, 1 aft; torpedoes: 11 (VII A), 12 (VII B), 14 (VII C, VII D, VII F).
Guns: one 3.4in (88mm) 45-cal; one 20mm (VII A, VII B, VII C see notes); one 37mm; two 20mm.
Mines: 15 in 5 tubes (VII D).
Complement: 44 (46 VII F).

U 32, Type VIIIA at the time of the Spanish Civil War.

Single hull ocean-going boats of medium displacement, with external ballast tanks and main negative tanks inside the pressure hull. The latter was of carbon steel approximately 22mm thick (Variant VII C) entirely welded except for the area above the main engines, which was riveted to facilitate replacement. The storage batteries were located in separate compartments. There were two parallel rudders; the forward bow planes could not be folded. Type VII, built in successive variants (VII A, VII B, VII C, VII C–41, VII C–42, VII D, VII F) with a total of more than 700 boats between 1935 and 1945, formed the backbone of the German submarine fleet, and represents the most numerous and uniform group of submarines ever to have been built.

The variants, though stemming from a single basic type and retaining several common structural characteristics, differed from each other in performance and function: attack submarines (Variants VII A, VII B, VII C, VII C–41, VII C–42), minelayers (VII D) and torpedo re-supply boats (VII F).

Variant VII A

The first VII, *U 27*, was launched on 24 June 1936. The design was inspired by the boats of the *Vetehinen* Class, built in Finland between 1926 and 1931, deriving from the Type UB III of 1918. In these boats, it was sought to

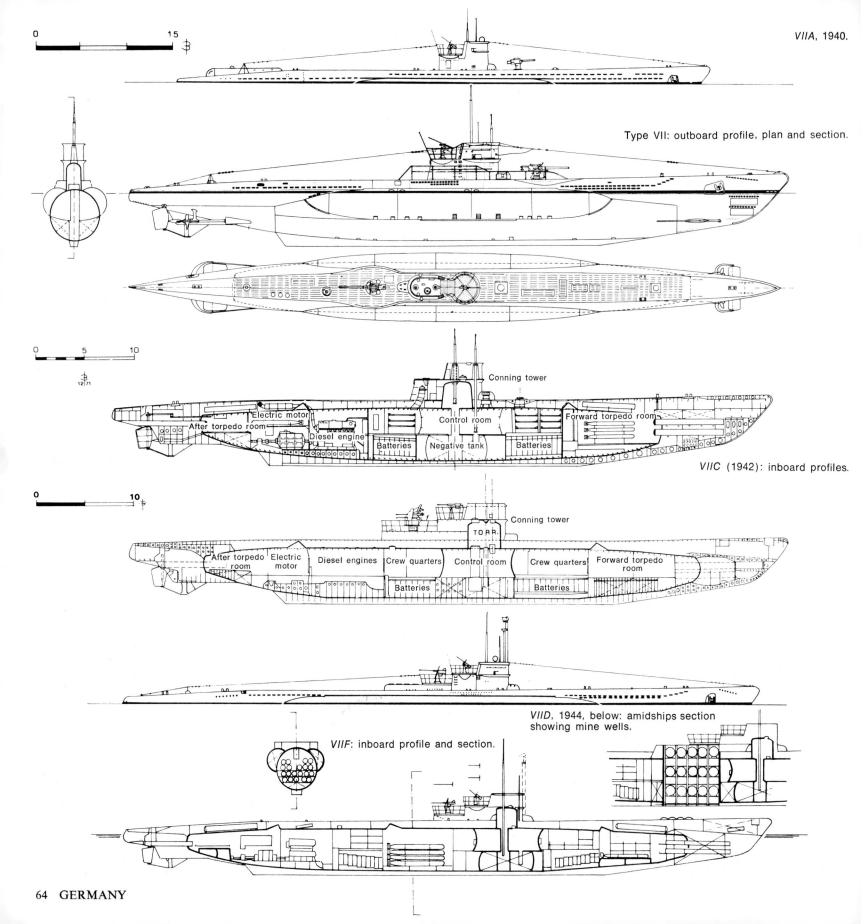

VIIA, 1940.

Type VII: outboard profile, plan and section.

0   5   10

12|71

Conning tower

Electric motor

After torpedo room

Diesel engine

Control room

Batteries   Negative tank   Batteries

Forward torpedo room

VIIC (1942): inboard profiles.

0   10

Conning tower

TORR.

After torpedo room   Electric motor

Diesel engines   Crew quarters

Control room

Crew quarters

Forward torpedo room

Batteries   Batteries

VIID, 1944, below: amidships section showing mine wells.

VIIF: inboard profile and section.

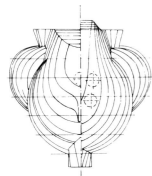

VIIC (1942): section.

The conning tower of the captured Type VIIC boat *U 826*.

maximize strength, sea-keeping, surface and underwater handling, surface speed, diving speed, range, torpedo load, speed of construction and ease of maintenance. All this was to be achieved while limiting size and displacement as much as possible and sacrificing habitability to offensive and structural qualities.

The result was a boat of a mere 915 tons displacement submerged, and only 218ft 3in (64.5m) in length, but which incorporated a noteworthy degree of offensive power, and was suitable for ocean-going operations. Type VII's qualities were not exceptional, per se, but their well-balanced characteristics and the high average level of performance made them a formidable weapon, and one of the most successful types ever built. The urge to limit dimensions and displacement was prompted by the desire to have a manoeuvrable ocean-going boat, with a restricted silhouette. By limiting the displacement of individual boats, Germany would be able to build a greater number.

The first version of the Type VII was distinguished by the single stern torpedo tube mounted outside the pressure hull, in the casing, which was open to the flow of water. This arrangement precluded reloading while submerged

and was eliminated from the subsequent variants. Two reserve torpedoes and the fuel tanks were located under the casing—also open to the free circulation of water. Maximum operational depth: 472ft (150m); maximum fuel load: 67 tons; minimum crash-dive time: 30 seconds.

Variant VII B
Appearing two years after Variant VII A with the launching of *U 45* on 27 April 1938, Variant VII B derived directly from its predecessor and had slightly increased dimensions and displacement because of its more powerful diesel engines and greater fuel load. The stern torpedo tubes were located in a torpedo room inside the pressure hull, and the reserve torpedoes were increased by one. Maximum operational depth: 472ft (150m); maximum fuel load: 108.3 tons; minimum crash-dive time: 30 seconds.

Variants VII C and VII C–41
These two, between which there were only minor differences, were produced in the greatest number of examples. *U 69* (ex-*U 99*), the first of the Variant VII C, entered service on 18 April 1940. *U 292* was the first boat of Variant VII C–41, and was delivered to the navy on 25 August 1943. The construction of numerous boats was cancelled in 1943–44, in favour of a more modern type. Variant VII C had a slightly greater displacement than VII B, as a result of increased storage space, and (in VII C–41) a reinforced hull, giving greater depth. Maximum operational depth: 472–590ft (150–180m); maximum fuel load: 113.5 tons; minimum crash-dive time: 25–30 seconds.

Variant VII C–42
No boats of this variant ever entered service because construction was cancelled or suspended in 1944—the Series having become obsolete. It represented a significant improvement to the preceding VII C–41 version, with increased size, displacement, range and, thanks to structural reinforcement, maximum operational depth, which was to have exceeded 984ft (300m). The design also called for armour plating for the conning tower, and a strong anti-aircraft armament of numerous 37mm and/or 20mm weapons and the installation, during construction, of a schnorkel. Maximum fuel load: 180 tons.

Variant VII D
This minelaying version of the Type VII was a modification of Variant VII C, with an additional centre section of approximately 32ft (10m), bringing the overall length to 252ft (76.9m). In this section, located immediately behind the conning tower, were five vertical tubes, each capable of holding three moored mines, similar to those laid by surface ships. Increased fuel load extended the range. The increase of dimensions and displacement with installed power unchanged, led to a slight loss of surface and submerged speed.

U 213, the first Variant VII D, was launched on 24 July 1941: the last to enter service was *U 127* on 31 January 1942. Only six boats were built. The German Navy's need of specialized minelaying boats was limited: all German submarines could lay moored and magnetic mines, which had been specially developed for them. They were released from the 21in (533mm) torpedo tubes. Normally, 2 to 3 mines could be carried (depending on type) in place of each reserve torpedo. Consequently, a

normal VII C boat could carry 26 to 39 mines in lieu of torpedoes. Maximum operational depth: 492ft (150m); maximum fuel load: 169.4 tons; minimum crash-dive time: 30 seconds.

Variant VII E

This variant remained in the design stage only. It was to have represented an improvement to Variant VII C, by the adoption of a new, considerably lighter propulsion gear which would have increased storage space and range for the same displacement. Delays in perfecting the new engine, and the building of new boats with more advanced characteristics, led to the abandoning of the project, probably in 1944.

Variant VII F

The four boats of this variant entered service between May and August 1943. In essence, they were of the VII D minelayer design, modified for supplying torpedoes to boats in operational areas. The centre section, which in the VII D contained the mine wells, was used to stow 25 torpedoes. Another 14 torpedoes comprised the normal torpedo armament of the boats, which were to be employed as normal operational submarines, in addition to their supply role. Maximum fuel load: 198.8 tons; minimum crash-dive time; approximately 35 seconds. As the transfer of torpedoes at sea would leave the boats concerned stranded on the surface, Variant VII F were used mainly for the transfer of torpedoes between bases.

The conventional gun armament of the Type VII boats, like that of all German submarines, underwent considerable changes during the war. In particular, from 1942, the various types and calibres of anti-aircraft cannon were considerably strengthened and, with the elimination of the deck gun, became the only form of surface armament in this type of boat. With the increasing threat from enemy aircraft, the calibre of cannon passed from the original 20mm in single and twin mounts, to 37mm in single mounts and, in some cases, to 20mm in highly effective quadruple mounts.

The number of weapons also increased significantly: in May 1943, U 441 and the other VII C boats (U 256, U 271, U 621, U 953, etc.) were armed with a 37mm gun (1,160 rounds) and eight 20mm cannon in two quadruple mounts (6,000 rounds per mount). The Variant C boats underwent the greatest changes and the last of them were commissioned minus the deck gun. In 1943, the deck gun was removed from most of the surviving boats of the earlier variants operating in the Atlantic, to make room for anti-aircraft weapons.

In the Mediterranean, where enemy air activity was less intense than in the Atlantic, the deck gun was retained until the end of the war, but the number of anti-aircraft weapons was increased.

The first boats of Variant VII D were armed with an 88mm 45-cal deck gun with a normal supply of 220 rounds, and with a single 20mm anti-aircraft gun. In 1942, the deck gun was removed and the armament was changed to one 37mm and two 20mm cannon in single mounts, as in the boats of the VII F variant. The following illustrations show several examples of the armament of the Type VII boats, and the evolution of the conning tower profile from 1939 to 1945.

From 1943, the Type VII boats began to receive the first folding-type schnorkel devices, generally mounted alongside the conning tower, towards the bow. By the end of that year, all operational boats were so equipped, and the schnorkel was included in the construction of all boats that had not yet entered service.

The schnorkel considerably increased the operational capabilities of the Type VII boats. Batteries could be recharged while submerged, and this permitted long distances to be covered underwater, using the main engines to develop a speed of 6 knots. The chance of survival was increased, even in areas where there was a high degree of aerial opposition. Nevertheless, the Type VII had concluded its brief but extensive operational cycle by 1943–44. Like other conventional boats, it had been decisively beaten by the anti-submarine weapons and tactics of the times.

On 1 September 1939, there were 19 Type VII boats in service. Ten were of the Variant A that had been present at the Spanish Civil War without seeing any action, and nine were Variant B boats. Another 15 Variant B were under construction together with numerous boats of the new Variant C.

Between 1939 and 1945, 705 Type VII boats entered service, operating primarily in the Atlantic, the North Sea and the Arctic. Several boats were stationed in the Baltic and 64 operated in the Mediterranean.

A Type VII boat, U 30 commanded by Lieutenant Commander Lemp, torpedoed the British passenger liner *Athenia* (13,581 GRT). She sank the next day, the first victim to a submarine in the Second World War. The first and last German boats lost during the war were also Type VIIs: U 27, sunk with depth-charges by the British destroyers *Forester* and *Fortune,* south of the Hebrides on 22 September 1939, and U 320, sunk by aircraft off Bergen on 7 May 1945, only a few hours before the end of hostilities in Europe.

The first boat to be captured during the war was a Type VII: U 570 surrendered after having been damaged by British aircraft on 27 August 1941, and became HMS *Graph.* The first boat handed over to the British at the surrender was the Type VII U 249: she reached the English coast off the Lizard on 8 May 1945, and proceeded to Weymouth.

Of the almost 3,000 merchant ships sunk by German boats during the Second World War, more than 50 per cent were sunk by Type VII boats. Two Type VIIs achieved the highest scores of the war: U 48 with 53 ships sunk totalling 318,111 GRT, and U 99 with 37 ships totalling 242,658 GRT. To these results can be added the damaging of several major warships and the sinking of numerous vessels of lesser displacement.

Particularly important, were the sinking of the British aircraft carrier *Courageous* by U 29, the first major warship lost during the war; *Ark Royal,* torpedoed in the Western Mediterranean by U 81 and U 205, which deprived Gibraltar's Force H of its aircraft carrier; and the battleship *Royal Oak,* in her supposedly secure base at Scapa Flow.

Of the 705 Type VII boats which entered service before May 1945, 437 were lost in action. The remainder were lost to other causes, chiefly the bombing of ports and shipyards. A total of 165 boats were scuttled by their crews

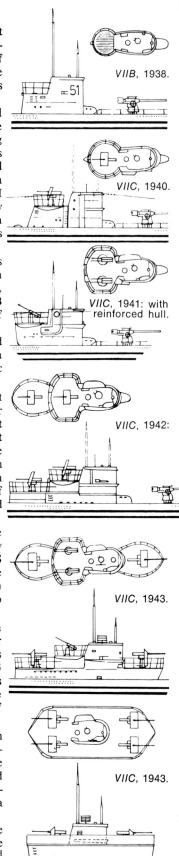

VIIB, 1938.

VIIC, 1940.

VIIC, 1941: with reinforced hull.

VIIC, 1942:

VIIC, 1943.

VIIC, 1943.

Table 10: Major successes of Type VII U-boats during the Second World War

Boat:	Commander:	Date:	Result:	Type:	Ship:	Location:
U 29	Schuhart	17 Sept 1939	sank	carrier	Courageous	Atlantic
U 47	Prien	14 Oct 1939	sank	battleship	Royal Oak	Scapa Flow
U 81	Guggenberger	14 Nov 1941	sank	carrier	Ark Royal	Mediterranean
U 331	von Tiesenhausen	25 Nov 1941	sank	battleship	Barham	Mediterranean
U 557	Paulssen	14 Dec 1941	sank	cruiser	Galatea	Mediterranean
with Italian Dagabur						
U 751	Bigalk	21 Dec 1941	sank	escort carrier	Audacity	Atlantic
U 565	Jebsen	11 Mar 1942	sank	cruiser	Naiad	Mediterranean
U 73	Rosenbaum	11 Aug 1942	sank	carrier	Eagle	Mediterranean
U 617	Brandi	1 Feb 1943	sank	cruiser	Welshman	Mediterranean
U 410	Fenski	18 Feb 1944	sank	cruiser	Penelope	Mediterranean

VIIC, armoured conning tower, 1943.

VIIC, 1944.

VIIC, 1944.

20mm x 1. Twin 20mm. 37mm x 1.

Quadruple 20mm.   88mm.

or handed over to the Allies at the surrender. *U 977* left Norway and after a continuously submerged passage of 66 days, reached Argentina on 17 August 1945: her crew were interned.

Fates

date:	location:	boat:	cause (see page 7):
1939	Atlantic	U 45	n
	North Sea	U 27, U 35	n
		U 36	s
1940	Atlantic	U 31, U 32	n
		U 51	s
	North Sea	U 33, U 49, U 50, U 53, U55	n
		U 54	s
		U 102	cs
1941	Atlantic	U 41, U 47, U 76, U 99, U 100, U. 207, U 208, U 401, U 434, U 551, U 556, U 567, U 574, U 651	n
		U 206	a
		U 570	c
	North Sea	U 452	n
	Mediterranean	U 75, U 79, U 204, U 433	n
		U 95	s
		U 451	a
		U 557	v
	Baltic	U 580, U 583	v
1942	Atlantic	U 82, U 85, U 90, U 93, U 94, U 136, U 210, U 213, U 215, U 252, U 352, U 353, U 356, U 357, U 379, U 581, U 587, U 588, U 619, U 626	n
		U 98, U 132, U 216, U 253, U 254, U 408, U 578, U 582, U 597, U 599, U 611, U 627, U 654, U 658, U 661, U 701, U 751, U 754, U 756	a
		U 705	b
	North Sea	U 261, U 412	a
		U 88	n
		U 335	s
		U 702	cs
	Mediterranean	U 74, U 372, U 411, U 559, U 568, U 605, U 652, U 670	n
		U 259, U 331, U 577, U 595	a
		U 133	m
		U 374	s
		U 573	r
	Arctic	U 457, U 585, U 589, U 655	n
	Baltic	U 222, U 272	v
1943	Atlantic	U 69, U 87, U 135, U 201, U 202, U 209, U 225, U 226, U 229, U 274, U 282, U 306, U 334, U 340, U 381, U 405, U 432, U 436, U 438, U 444, U 449, U 576, U 600, U 606, U 607, U 609, U 613, U 631, U 634, U 635, U 638, U 640, U 645, U 648, U 710, U 732	n
		U 84, U 86, U 89, U 134, U 211, U 217, U 221, U 232, U 258, U 265, U 266, U 268, U 273, U 279, U 280, U 284, U 304, U 332, U 336, U 337, U 338, U 341, U 359, U 376, U 383, U 384, U 388, U 391, U 402, U 403, U 404, U 417, U 418, U 419, U 420, U 422, U 435, U 440, U 442, U 447, U 454, U 456, U 465, U 467, U 468, U 469, U 470, U 558, U 563, U 564, U 566, U 569, U 572, U 584, U 590, U 591, U 594, U 598, U 604, U 610, U 614, U 615, U 620, U 623, U 624, U 628, U 630, U 632, U 633, U 643, U 646, U 657, U 662, U 663, U 664, U 665, U 669, U 706, U 707, U 752, U 759, U 951, U 954, U 964, U 966	a
		U 553, U 753	cs
		U 439, U 659	v
	North Sea	U 227, U 389	a
		U 308, U 644	s
		U 769, U 770	b
		U 647	m
	Mediterranean	U 73, U 83, U 205, U 224, U 375, U 409, U 414, U 443, U 458, U 561, U 562, U 593	n
		U 77, U 297, U 617, U 755	a
		U 301, U 303, U 431	s
		U 602	cs
	Baltic	U 34, U 346, U 649, U 670, U 718, U 768, U 983	v
		U 395	b
		U 345	b–r
		U 639	s
		U 101	r
1944	Atlantic	U 91, U 238, U 257, U 264, U 302, U 305, U 322, U 333, U 358, U 386, U 392, U 400, U 406, U 424, U 445, U 448, U 473, U 575, U 603, U 608, U 618, U 621, U 641, U 709, U 719, U 731, U 734, U 736, U 743, U 744, U 757, U 761, U 762, U 962, U 984, U 986, U 1200	n
		U 231, U 243, U 270, U 271, U283, U 311, U 342, U 364, U 373, U 378, U 385, U 426, U 441, U 571, U 592, U 625, U 629, U 653, U 666, U 741, U 765, U 821, U 955, U 970,	

		Boats	Code
		U 976, U 981	a
		U 263, U 415, U 667, U 703	m
		U 377, U 925, U 972	cs
	North Sea	U 212, U 214, U 247, U 269, U 297, U 390, U 413, U 671, U 672, U 678, U 713, U 767, U 961, U 971, U 988, U 1006	n
		U 240, U 241, U 292, U 317, U 319, U 394, U 423, U 476, U 477, U 478, U 484, U 674, U 675, U 715, U 735, U 740, U 742, U 772, U 777, U 906, U 908, U 959, U 973, U 980, U 982, U 990, U 993, U 966	a
		U 771, U 974, U 987	s
		U 673, U 737, U 1209	v
		U 92	b
		U 228, U 437, U 998	b–r
	Mediterranean	U 223, U 343, U 371, U 407, U 450, U 453, U 616, U 960	n
		U 81, U 596	a
		U 380, U 410, U 421, U 486, U 642, U 952, U 967, U 969	b
		U 230, U 466, U 471, U 565	sb
		U 455	m
	Arctic	U 289, U 314, U 344, U 360, U 362, U 387, U 472, U 601	n
		U 277, U 288, U 347, U 354, U 355, U 361, U 365, U 366, U 921	a
	Baltic	U 28, U 80, U 416, U 738, U 1013, U 1015	v
		U 239	b–r
		U 250	n
		U 479	m
		U 474	b
1945	Atlantic Ocean	U 248, U 285, U 300, U 636, U 722, U 774, U 1001, U 1051, U 1172	n
		U 321, U 396, U 1055, U 1107	a
		U 260, U 1169	m
		U 650	cs
		U 963	sb
		U 485, U 977, U 1277	x
	North Sea	U 246, U 309, U 325, U 327, U 399, U 480, U 482, U 683, U 711, U 714, U 965, U 989, U 1003, U 1014, U 1018, U 1021, U 1024, U 1063, U 1191, U 1195, U 1199, U 1208, U 1274, U 1278, U 1279, U 1302	n
		U 242, U 296, U 320, U 393, U 579, U 681, U 905, U 927, U 1106, U 1276	a
		U 72, U 96, U 329, U 339, U 348, U 350, U 382, U 429, U 430, U 682, U 747, U 1011, U 1012, U 1017, U 1167	b
		U 275, U 287, U 326, U 1020	m
		U 398	cs
		U 486	s
		U 1053, U 1206	v
		U 71, U 370, U 446, U 475,	
		U 552, U 554, U 704, U 708, U 822, U 828, U 922, U 979, U 1032, U 1131	sb
		U 218, U 244, U 245, U 249, U 255, U 256, U 262, U 276, U 278, U 281, U 291, U 293, U 294, U 295, U 298, U 299, U 310, U 312, U 313, U 315, U 318, U 324, U 328, U 363, U 368, U 369, U 427, U 481, U 483, U 622, U 637, U 668, U 712, U 716, U 720, U 739, U 760, U 764, U 773, U 775, U 776, U 778, U 779, U 825, U 826, U 901, U 907, U 926, U 928, U 930, U 953, U 956, U 957, U 968, U 975, U 978, U 991, U 992, U 994, U 995, U 997, U 1002, U 1004, U 1005, U 1009, U 1010, U 1019, U 1022, U 1023, U 1052, U 1057, U 1058, U 1064, U 1102, U 1103, U 1104, U 1105, U 1108, U 1109, U 1110, U 1163, U 1165, U 1171, U 1194, U 1197, U 1198, U 1201, U 1202, U 1203, U 1271, U 1272, U 1275, U 1301, U 1305, U 1307	x
	Arctic Baltic	U 286, U 307, U 425	n
		U 78, U 679	n
		U 251, U 1007, U 1008, U 1065, U 1210	a
		U 676, U 745, U 923, U 1273	m
		U 1000	m–r
		U 367, U 1054	v
		U 1166	v–r
		U 1196	v–r–sb
		U 555	r
		U 235	e
		U 237, U 677, U 749, U 758, U 763, U 904	b
		U 1164	b–r
		U 29, U 30, U 46, U 48, U 52, U 236, U 267, U 290, U 316, U 323, U 349, U 351, U 397, U 428, U 560, U 612, U 717, U 721, U 733, U 746, U 748, U 750, U 827, U 903, U 924, U 929, U 958, U 999, U 1016, U 1025, U 1026, U 1027, U 1028, U 1029, U 1030, U 1031, U 1056, U 1101, U 1132, U 1161, U 1162, U 1168, U 1170, U 1192, U 1193, U 1204, U 1205, U 1207, U 1303, U 1304, U 1306, U 1308	sb

Top left:
Conning tower of the Type VII C boat, U 581.

Top right:
A Type VII boat comes alongside a sister boat in a British port after the surrender.

Centre left:
U 249 heading for Portland after the surrender on 8 May 1945. Note the deck housing for the stowable schnorkel tube.

Centre right:
A Type VIIC boat in 1941.

Bottom, opposite page:
Type VIIC U-boats at Loch Ryan awaiting scuttling in 'Operation Deadlight', 3 December 1945.

U 1305, one of the last Type VII C–41 boats to enter service, bound for Britain escorted by a British ship, after having surrendered in May 1945.

Below:
The ex-U 570 (Type VII C), sailing under the British flag as Graph, after her capture in August 1941.

Type IX

Variant IX A (8 units).
U 37–U 44:
Builder: Deschimag AG
Weser, Bremen.
Date: 1936–1938/39.

Variant IX B (14 units).
*U 64–U 65, U 103–U 111,
U 122–U 124* (ex *U 66–U 68*):
Builder: Deschimag AG
Weser, Bremen.
Date: 1937–1939/41.

Variant IX C (54 units).
U 66–U 68 (ex *U 122–U 124*),
*U 125–U 131, U 153–U 160,
U 171–U 176*:
Builder: Deschimag AG
Weser, Bremen.
Date: 1939–1940/41.
U 161–U 166:
Builder: Deschimag Seebeck,
Wesermunde.
Date: 1939–1941/42.
U 501–U 524:
Builder: Deutsche Werft,
Hamburg.
Date: 1939–1941/42.

Variant IX C–40 (87 units +
8).
U 167–U 170, U 801–U 806:
Builder: Deschimag Seebeck,
Wesermunde.
Date: 1940–1942/44.
*U 183–U 194, U 841–U 846,
U 853–U 858, U 865–U 870,
U 877–U 881, U 889–U 894*:
Builder: Deschimag AG
Weser, Bremen.
Date: 1940–1942/44.
U 525–U 550:
Builder: Deutsche Werft,
Hamburg.
Date: 1940–1942/43.
U 1221–U 1238:
Builder: Deutsche Werft,
Hamburg.
Date: 1941–1943/–.
Contracts cancelled in 1944 or
(shown in brackets) not
ordered:
*U 807–U 816, (U 817–U 820),
U 882, U 892–U 894, U 1501–
U 1530, U 1239–U 1262*:

Variant IX D1 (2 units).
U 180, U 195:
Builder: Deschimag AG
Weser, Bremen.
Date: 1940–1942/42.

Variant IX D2 and IX D–42
(29 units + 2).
*U 177–U 179, U 181, U 182,
U 196–U 200, U 847–U 852,*

*U 859–U 864, U 871–U 876,
U 883, U 885, U 886*:
Builder: Deschimag AG
Weser, Bremen.
Date: 1940–1942/–.
Contracts cancelled in 1944 or
(shown in brackets) not
ordered:
*U 884, U 887, U 888, U 895–
U 900, U 1531–U 1542,
(U 1543–U 1600)*.
Normal displacement:
Variant IX A: 1,032 tons
surfaced; 1,153 tons
submerged.
Variant IX B: 1,051 tons
surfaced; 1,178 tons
submerged.
Variant IX C: 1,120 tons
surfaced; 1,232 tons
submerged.
Variant IX C–40: 1,144 tons
surfaced; 1,247 tons
submerged.
Variant IX D1: 1,610 tons
surfaced; 1,799 tons
submerged.
Variant IX D2 and IX D–42:
1,616 tons surfaced;
1,804 tons submerged.
Dimensions:
Variant IX A: 251ft 0in x 21ft
3in x 15ft 6in (76.5m x
6.51m x 4.70m).
Variant IX B: 251ft 0in x
22ft 3in x 15ft 6in (76.5m x
6.76m x 4.70m).
Variant IX C: 252ft 0in x
22ft 9in x 15ft 6in (76.7m x
6.76m x 4.70m).
Variant IX C–40: 287ft 6in x
24ft 6in x 17ft 9in (76.7m x
6.86m x 4.67m).
Variant IX D1, IX D2,
IX D–42: 287ft 6in x 24ft 6in
x 17ft 9in (87.5m x 7.50m
x 5.35m).
Machinery:
Variant IX A, IX B, IX C,
IXC–40; IX D1: diesels: 2;
electric: 2, of various types.
Variant IX D2, IX D–42:
diesels: 2; diesel generators: 2;
electric: 2.
Maximum Power:
Variant IX A, I XB, IX C,
IX C–40: 4,400hp surfaced;
1,000hp submerged.
Variant IX D1: 2,800hp
surfaced; 1,100hp submerged.
Variant IX D2, D–42: 5,400hp
surfaced, 1,100hp submerged.
Maximum speed:
Variant IX A, IX B, IX C,
IX C–40: 18.2 knots surfaced;
7.7 knots submerged.

Variant IX D1: 15.8 knots
surfaced; 6.9 knots submerged.
Variant IX D2, IX D–42:
19.2 knots surfaced; 6.9 knots
submerged.
Range:
Variant IX A: 10,500 miles at
10 knots surfaced; 78 miles
at 4 knots submerged.
Variant IX B: 12,000 miles at
10 knots surfaced; 3,800 miles
at 18.2 knots surfaced; 63
miles at 4 knots submerged.
Variant IX C: 13,450 miles
at 10 knots surfaced; 128
miles at 2 knots submerged.
Variant IX C–40: 13,850
miles at 10 knots surfaced;
63 miles at 4 knots
submerged.
Variant IX D1: 12,750 miles
at 10 knots surfaced; 245
miles at 2 knots submerged.
Variant IX D2, IX D–42:
31,500 miles at 10 knots
surfaced; 8,500 miles at 19.2
knots surfaced; 121 miles at 2
knots submerged; 57 miles at 4
knots submerged.
Torpedo tubes: six 21in
(533mm) 4 forward, 2 aft;
torpedoes: 22 all variants
except IX D1.
Guns: one 4.1in (105mm) 45-
cal; one 37mm; one 20mm (all
variants except IX D1) one
37mm; four 20mm (2 x 2)
IX D1.
Complement: 48 (IX A, IX B,
IX C); 49 (IX C–40); 57 (IX
D1, IX D2, IX D–42).

Conning tower of a Type IX
boat.

Double hull ocean-going boats whose design derived from
the U–81–86 Series of 1916 and was similar in many respects
to the Type I A of 1936.

With more than 200 boats built in seven successive
variants (IX A, IX B, IX C, IX C–40, IX D2, and IX
D–42), Type IX was second only to Type VII in numbers
built and results achieved.

Possessing good seakeeping qualities and long range,
which even in the early models reached 10,500 miles and
rose to 31,500 miles at 10 knots in the last variants, Type
IX were the ocean-going boats par excellence of the
German Navy. They operated chiefly along the coasts of
the United States, in the South Atlantic and in the Indian
Ocean. Their characteristically wide and flat deck, with
bulwarks almost perpendicular to the surface, gave them
excellent seaworthiness on the surface but increased their
crash-dive time, which, in all versions, was approximately
35 seconds compared to 25–30 seconds for the Type VII.
This was acceptable, however, and compared favourably
to equal displacement boats of other navies: but not the
British, whose boats were superior in this respect.
Maximum operational depth for all variants was approximately 492ft (150mm). As with Type VII, the different
variants represented successive improvements to the
original version, even when they differed little from it:
only Variant D 1, designed for refuelling other boats, had
markedly different characteristics.

Variant IX A
The first Type IX boat, *U 37* was commissioned on 4
August 1938, less than three months after having been
launched at Bremen on 4 May. Compared to Type VII,
which was almost a contemporary, Type IX had greater
displacement, was more habitable and, above all, had
greater range, having been developed for operating in
distant waters. The layout was totally different. A double

A Type IX boat with the original armament of one 4.1in (105mm) deck gun, one 37mm anti-aircraft cannon on deck and one 20mm in the conning tower.

hull had been adopted instead of the single hull with saddle tanks of the Type VII. This had been done, primarily to achieve better surface seaworthiness and to allow the stowing of part of the fuel load in the space between the hulls. All the ballast tanks were located in the double hull. The original surface armament consisted of a 4.1in (105mm) 45-cal deck gun and a 20mm anti-aircraft gun, mounted on the platform behind the conning tower, which, as in all German boats from 1942 on, was of very limited dimensions so as to be as inconspicuous as possible during surface operations at night. Maximum fuel load: 154 tons.

Variant IX B
Designed only a few months after the prototype of the Type IX, Variant B was practically identical with it save for a slight increase in fuel load from 154 to 165 tons, which increased maximum surface range to 12,000 miles at 10 knots. U 64, the first of a total of 14, entered service on 16 December 1939: U 124 was the last to be commissioned on 11 February 1941.

Externally, the Variant B boats differed from the earlier model in that the deck gun was mounted closer to the conning tower.

Variant IX C and Variant IX C–40
A total of 151 boats were built in these two variants. All 54 of the C variant entered service between March 1949 and July 1942. Of the C–40 Variant which was practically identical, only 87 of the 95 boats begun, entered service between July 1942 and May 1944. The contracts for the other 76 were cancelled in 1944, in favour of the new Type XXI electric submarines to whose construction, all the resources of the German shipbuilding industry were to be dedicated.

The fuel load was even further increased, reaching 208 and 214 tons, respectively: greater use was made of fuel tanks in the space between the hulls. Maximum surface range increased by about 1,500–1,800 miles.

Variants IX D1, IX D2 and IX D–42
In 1940, a new variant of Type IX was designed, the D, which was larger and had considerably increased range and speed. The two boats which constituted Variant D1, were modified during construction for use as refuelling boats. They lacked torpedo tubes, but carried 252 tons of fuel in addition to their own load of 203 tons. Daimler-Benz

MB 501 fast diesel engines, of the type used in torpedo-boats, were installed in place of the lower rpm engines normally used in submarines. These engines (three on each shaft, for a total power rating of 9,000hp), though giving a maximum surface speed of about 20.8 knots, gave poor results in reliability and range. About a year after commissioning, they were replaced by normal submarine engines of lower power; with notable lowering of top speed. The boats of Variants D2 and D–42 were equipped with conventional engines of higher power which could develop a speed of 19.2 knots. High speed was indispensable to operations in the South Atlantic and Indian Ocean, for which the boats had been designed.

The range of these boats reached record levels, largely because of the installation, alongside the two normal 2,200hp diesel engines, of two diesel dynamos of 5,500hp each, to be used as generators for the electric motors. They gave a maximum surface range of 31,500 miles at 10 knots, with a maximum fuel load of 441 tons.

The first boat of Variant D1 to enter service was U 178 in February 1942: the first and only D–42, was U 883, completed on 27 March 1945. The contracts for 78 boats of the D–42 variant, which differed only in minor details from the preceding type, were cancelled in favour of the Type XXI Elektro-boote.

Numerous boats of the D variant assigned to the Indian Ocean, were equipped with a small Focke-Achgelis FA–330 single-seat helicopter for reconnaissance. More precisely, the machine was an autogyro which, with the help of the submarine's high speed, and the considerable force of the winds during the monsoon period, took off, and (tethered to the deck by a cable) rose approximately 300ft (100m). This 'kite' increased the boat's horizon appreciably.

The conventional gun armament of the Type IX underwent considerable development during the war. Originally (all versions except D1), it consisted of a 4.1in (105mm) gun forward of the conning tower; a 37mm automatic on the after-deck, and a single 20mm on a platform to the rear of the conning tower. It was subsequently modified by eliminating the deck gun and increasing the number and calibre of the automatics, and by changing their disposition. The practice of mounting cannon on the weather-deck was abandoned because it was usually awash in rough seas; preference was given to installation on the conning tower.

From 1942–43, armament normally consisted of a single 37mm gun on an after extension of the conning tower (two spare torpedoes could be stowed in this extension), and two 20mm twin mountings, also on the conning tower, aft of the periscopes. From 1943, schnorkel apparatus consisting of a foldable tube alongside the conning tower, was installed in Type IX boats, as shown in the photographs and drawings.

The increased armament, and the installation of the schnorkel and other equipment, such as radar detection devices, increased the volume of the conning tower, and this led to an increase in the minimum crash-dive time, which, originally, had been approximately 35 seconds. A partial compensation was achieved by reducing the weather-deck in several boats: a section of the forward casing was eliminated at the expense of several spare torpedoes. All variants except D1 were fitted with three periscopes.

On 1 September 1939, there were only 9 Type IX boats in service: 8 of Variant IX A and one, U 64, of Variant

IX B. On that date, another 13 boats of Variant IX B, and 54 of the new Variant IX C were under construction. By the end of the war, 194 Type IX boats had entered operational service, another 10 had been bombed while fitting out, or scrapped while incomplete.

The Type IX, because of their excellent seaworthiness and range, were chiefly employed at great distances from base, usually alone against unescorted ocean shipping. They operated chiefly in the north and south Atlantic in 1940-41, along the coasts of Africa and South America and, after December 1941, along the North American coast as far as the Caribbean Sea. Between October 1942 and February 1945, 25 Type IX boats operated singly in the Indian Ocean where, from October to November 1942, *U 159* sank eight ships, the record for that sector. A number of boats, replenished at pre-arranged rendezvous, reached the Pacific Ocean to maintain contact with the Japanese. In 1943-44, *U 511* and *U 1224* were ceded to the Japanese Navy as part of a programme of cooperation.

The most notable sinking by a Type IX was that of the British transatlantic liner *Laconia* (19,695 GRT) on 12 September 1942 in the Central Atlantic, by *U 156* commanded by Lieutenant-Commander Hartenstein. In addition to her 930 passengers and crew, the British ship was carrying 1,800 Italian prisoners of war. The German boat immediately began rescue operations together with other German and Italian boats and French warships. The rescue lasted several days, during which the Allies made several air attacks against boats loaded with survivors, which resulted in Admiral Doenitz prohibiting further rescue operations of this kind.

The principal successes achieved by Type IX boats against warships were: British escort carrier *Avenger* sunk on 15 November 1942 by *U 155* (Commander Piening); American escort carrier *Block Island* sunk on 29 May 1944 by *U 549* (Commander Krankenhagen); British cruiser *Dunedin* sunk on 24 November 1941 by *U 124* (Commander Mohr), all in the Atlantic.

Of the 194 Type IX boats which operated during the war, 150 were sunk in action; the remainder were lost to a variety of causes. *U 505* was captured at sea by the American escort carrier *Guadalcanal* and the escort vessel *Pillsbury*. Renamed *Nemo*, the ex-*U 505* has been displayed since 1945 at the Chicago Museum. *U 181*, *U 195* and *U 862* were in the Far East in May 1945, and were captured and incorporated in their navy by the Japanese, as *I.501*, *I.506* and *I.502*.

Fates

date:	location:	boat:	cause (see page 7):
1939	Atlantic	*U 39, U 42*	n
	North Sea	*U 40*	m
1940	Atlantic	*U 41, U 104*	n
	North Sea	*U 44*	n
		U 64	a
		U 122	cs
1941	Atlantic	*U 65, U 110, U 111, U 127, U 131, U 501*	n
1942	Atlantic	*U 153, U 157, U 162, U 173, U 184*	n
		U 158, U 166, U 502, U 503, U 512, U 517, U 520	a
		U 165, U 171	m
	Indian Ocean	*U 179*	a
1943	Atlantic	*U 124, U 125, U 128, U 130,*	
		U 175, U 182, U 186, U 187, U 191, U 192, U 504, U 521, U 522, U 523, U 528, U 531, U 536, U 538, U 841, U 842	n
		U 43, U 67, U 105, U 106, U 109, U 126, U 156, U 159, U 160, U 161, U 164, U 167, U 169, U 172, U 174, U 176, U 185, U 189, U 194, U 199, U 200, U 506, U 507, U 508, U 509, U 513, U 514, U 519, U 524, U 525, U 527, U 529, U 535, U 540, U 542, U 844, U 847, U 848, U 849, U 850	a
		U 163	s
		U 526	m
	Indian Ocean	*U 197, U 533*	a
	Pacific	*U 511*	r
1944	Atlantic	*U 154, U 549, U 550, U 845, U 856, U 877*	n
		U 66, U 68, U 107, U 177, U 193, U 515, U 543, U 544, U 545, U 801, U 846, U 860, U 863, U 871, U 1222, U 1226, U 1229	a
		U 123	r
		U 129	r-sb
		U 178	sb
		U 180	m
		U 505	c
		U 851	cs
	North Sea	*U 855, U 865, U 867, U 1225*	a
		U 890, U 891, U 872	b
	Indian Ocean	*U 198*	n
		U 852	a
		U 859	s
	Pacific	*U 168, U 537*	s
		U 196	cs
		U 1224	r
	Baltic	*U 547*	r
		U 803	m-r
		U 854	m
		U 1234	v-sb
1945	Atlantic	*U 518, U 546, U 548, U 853, U 857, U 866, U 869, U 878, U 879, U 880, U 881, U 1235, U 170, U 190, U 510, U 530, U 541, U 805*	n
	Pacific	*U 183*	s
		U 181, U 195, U 862	c
	North Sea	*U 534, U 843*	a
		U 864	s
		U 870	b
		U 876	b-sb
		U 885	sb
		U 886	b
		U 155, U 516, U 532, U 539, U 802, U 806, U 858, U 861, U 868, U 873, U 874, U 875, U 883, U 889, U 1228, U 1230, U 1231, U 1232, U 1233	x
	Baltic	*U 1221, U 1223*	a
		U 1227	b-sb
		U 103	b
		U 37, U 38, U 108	sb

Above:
U 505, captured in action off Dakar on 4 June 1944, is taken in tow by an American vessel which towed her 2,500 miles to Bermuda.

Centre
U 861 (right) alongside a Type VII boat, moored outside the bunkers in Trondheim in 1945. Note the hatches at the base of the conning tower for loading two spare torpedoes.

Right:
U 185 sinking in the central Atlantic after having been attacked by aircraft from the American escort carrier *Core* on 24 August 1943.

IXA/B, 1940.

IXC, 1943.

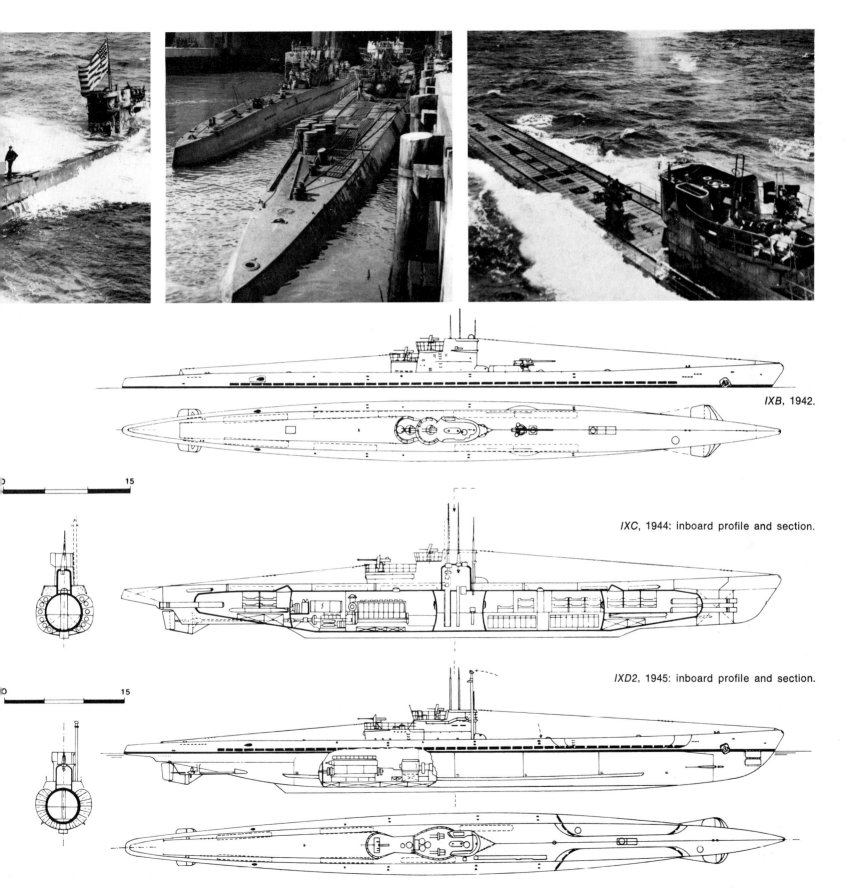

IXB, 1942.

IXC, 1944: inboard profile and section.

IXD2, 1945: inboard profile and section.

0   15

0   15

Type XB

U 116–U 119, U 219, U 220, U 233, U 234:
Builder: Krupp Germania Werft, Kiel.
Date: 1939–1941/44.
Normal displacement: 1,763 tons surfaced; 2,177 tons submerged.
Dimensions: 294ft 9in x 30ft 3in x 13ft 6in (89.8m x 9.20m x 4.71m).
Machinery: diesel: 2 F46; electric: 2 AEG.
Maximum power: 4,200hp surfaced; 1,100hp submerged.
Maximum speed: 16.4 knots surfaced; 7 knots submerged.
Range: 18,450 miles at 10 knots surfaced, 6,750 miles at 16.9 knots surfaced; 188 miles at 2 knots submerged, 93 miles at 4 knots submerged.
Torpedo tubes: two 21in (533mm); torpedoes: 15.
Guns: one 4.1in (105mm) 45-cal (until 1943); one 37mm; two 20mm single (4 after 1943).
Mines: 66 in 30 tubes.
Complement: 52.

Below:
A Type XB minelaying submarine in a floating dock.

Below right:
U 118, surprised on the surface and attacked by aircraft from the escort carrier *Bogue*, off the Canary Islands on 12 June 1943.

Full double hull ocean-going minelaying boats, derived from the Type XA, which was not built, but which was inspired by Type IA and Type IX A. Maximum operational depth: 492ft (150m); maximum fuel load: 368 tons; minimum crash-dive time: 35 seconds. Equipped with schnorkel from 1943. The installations for mines consisted of 30 vertical tubes forward, and 12 on each side, amidships. Most of the reserve torpedoes were stowed in the space between the deck and the pressure hull. In 1943, the deck gun was eliminated and the anti-aircraft armament was increased by another two 20mm cannon. These boats were more often used as supply vessels. They were all lost except *U 219* which was captured by the Japanese and designated *I.505,* and *U 234* which was handed over to the Allies at the surrender.

Fates

date:	location:	boat:	cause (see page 7):
1942	Atlantic	U 116	cs
1943	Atlantic	U 117, U 118, U 220	a
		U 119, U 233	n
1945	North Sea	U 234	x
	Pacific	U 219	c

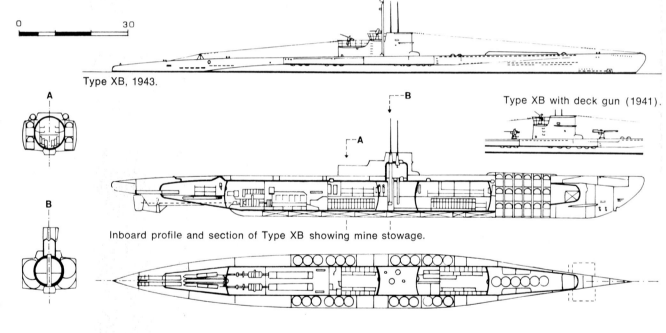

Type XB, 1943.

A

B

Type XB with deck gun (1941).

Inboard profile and section of Type XB showing mine stowage.

Type XIV

U 459–U 464, U 487–U 490:
Builder: Deutsche Werke, Kiel.
Contracts cancelled in 1944: U 494–U 500, U 2201–U 2204.
Date: 1940–1941/43.
Normal displacement: 1,688 tons surfaced; 1,932 tons submerged.
Dimensions: 220ft 3in x 30ft 9in x 21ft 3in (67.10m x 9.35m x 6.51m).
Machinery: diesel: 2; electric 2 SSW.
Maximum power: 2,800hp surfaced; 750hp submerged.
Maximum speed: 14.4 knots surfaced; 6.2 knots submerged.
Range: 12,350 miles at 10 knots surfaced, 5,500 miles at 14.4 knots surfaced; 120 miles at 2 knots submerged, 55 miles at 4 knots submerged.
Guns: two 37mm single (from 1943: one 37mm; four 20mm twin); one 20mm.
Cargo: 423 tons diesel fuel; four torpedoes.
Complement: 53.

Ocean-going tanker boats derived from Type VII C, and used for supplying other boats. Maximum fuel load (in addition to own fuel): 203 tons. In 1943, they were equipped with schnorkel apparatus, and anti-aircraft armament was modified. They were widely employed, mostly in the Atlantic, and all were lost, mainly to air attack.

Fates

date:	location:	boat:	cause (see page 7):
1942	Atlantic	U 464	a
1943	Atlantic	U 459, U 460, U 461, U 462, U 463, U 487, U 489	a
1944	Atlantic	U 488	n
		U 490	n–a

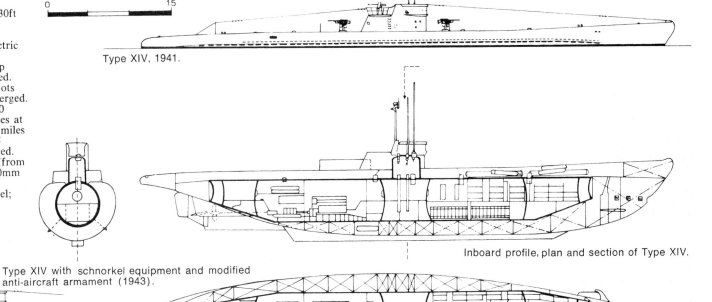

Type XIV, 1941.

Type XIV with schnorkel equipment and modified anti-aircraft armament (1943).

1943

Inboard profile, plan and section of Type XIV.

A Type XIV re-supply submarine in 1941.

Type XXI

U 2501–U 2551:
Builder: Blohm & Voss, Hamburg.
Date: 1943–1944/45.
U 2552–U 2564:
Builder: Blohm & Voss, Hamburg.
Date: 1943–   /–.
U 3001– U3051:
Builder: Deschimag AG, Bremen.
Date: 1943–1944/45.
U 3052–U 3063:
Builder: Deschimag AG, Bremen.
Date: 1943–   /–.
U 3501–U 3537:
Builder: F. Schichau, Danzig.
Date: 1943–1944/45.
U 3538–U 3695:
Builder: F. Schichau, Danzig.
Date: 1943–   /–.
Series ordered or (shown in brackets) designed, but construction or assembly not begun:
U 2565–U 2643, (U 2644–U 3000), (U 3696–U 4000).
Normal displacement: 1,621 tons surfaced; 1,819 tons submerged.
Dimensions: 251ft 9in x 21ft 9in x 20ft 9in (76.7m x 8m x 6.20m).
Machinery: diesel: 2 MAN; electric: 2 SSW + 1 (for silent running).
Maximum power: 4.000hp surfaced; 4,200–4,800 + 226hp submerged.
Maximum speed: 15.5 knots surfaced; 17.5 knots submerged, 3.5 knots silent running.
Range: 15,500 miles at 10 knots surfaced, 5,100 miles at 15.6 knots surfaced; 365 miles at 5 knots submerged, 110 miles at 10 knots submerged.
Torpedo tubes: six 21in (533mm) forward; topedoes: 23, or 17 + 12 mines.
Guns: four 30mm (2 x 2) or, in some units, 20mm (2 x 2).
Complement: 57.

Double hull ocean-going boats with high submerged speed. The design was approved by Admiral Doenitz on 13 June 1943, and a programme of 200 boats was ordered: it was later to exceed 1,300 boats.

The first of the Type XXI boats, *U 2501,* entered service on 17 June 1944. Speed of construction was achieved by prefabricating entire sections. Her most interesting characteristic was her underwater speed, which was considerably higher than that of any conventional boat then in service. It was achieved by streamlining the hull and increasing the power of the electric propulsion gear.

A double hull configuration was adopted, formed of two superimposed cylinders, connected by light outer plating to afford streamlining. The pressure hulls were formed from carbon steel plates, 28mm thick, increasing to 37mm around the hatches To simplify prefabrication, the frames were on the outside of the pressure hull, and were particularly numerous and strong. The upper hull was the larger in diameter of the two, and contained the living quarters, engines and torpedo rooms. The storage batteries and some fuel and trim tanks were in the lower hull. The ballast tanks were sited in the space between the external hull and the two pressure hulls. The conning tower was of the 'closed' type (to minimize drag) and had two 30mm twin 'disappearing' mounts. Large tail surfaces were specially designed to give manoeuvrability and stability, and to cut down drag. The bow planes, unlike those on preceding German boats, were located directly beaneath the main-deck and could be withdrawn by rotation on a vertical axis.

This particular hull shape, together with the stern arrangement, gave the boat a thrust output close to the value of 0.65, compared to 0.45 in conventional twin-screw boats. Maximum operational depth was approximately 492–656ft (150–200m), and crush depth was in the order of 1,082ft (330m). Minimum crash-dive time reached an exceptional 18 seconds.

The hull was subdivided longitudinally into eight sections: each, complete with all equipment and electrical cables, was built in a different production centre. The sections were then transported overland or by river, to assembly yards where they were rapidly joined and completed.

As the Walter turbine and the closed-cycle diesel were not yet operational in 1943, the Germans used a combination of normal diesels and electric motors for the Type XXI, in which, for the first time, the maximum power of the electric motors (4,200hp surfaced, 800hp submerged) exceeded that of the diesel engines (4,000hp).

The number and power of the new super-light high-capacity batteries, was particularly high. In addition to the main electric motors, a 225hp electric motor was installed for silent running. The underwater propulsion gear gave a top speed of 16 knots for one hour, or enabled the boat to run at 4 knots for more than three days without having to recharge the batteries or ventilate the boat, which was fitted with air-regenerating and conditioning equipment. A few hours of schnorkel running enabled the boat to re-submerge for a further prolonged period. Maximum surface range was in excess of 15,000 miles at economical speed, with a fuel load of 250 tons. Internal layout provided as much comfort as possible: the boats were designed for cruises of more than five months duration almost exclusively underwater. For the first time, a compartment was set aside exclusively for launching torpedoes.

The electronic and acoustic equipment were notable. Type XXI was fitted with radar, whose 'disappearing' antenna was located in the conning tower, together with two periscopes, echo-ranging antenna and telescoping schnorkel. An ultra-short wave radar-emission warning device was fitted on the head of the schnorkel, which was sheathed in synthetic rubber (buna) to absorb the radiations of search devices. Sonar and an improved type of highly sensitive hydrophone consisting of forty-eight microphones, were located in a circular pattern on the bow, beneath the torpedo tubes. An effervescent substance (pillenwerfer) could be expelled through two ejection devices into the sea, to produce false echoes in enemy sonar.

Underwater armament consisted of six bow tubes, three on each side, with twenty-three torpedoes, all located in the spacious torpedo room within the pressure hull. A varying number of mines (launched through the torpedo tubes) could be carried as an alternative. Surface armament was reduced to four 30mm cannon: these were of a new type, and insufficient numbers caused many boats to carry 20mm guns instead.

Two variants of Type XXI were designed in 1944. Variants XXI B and XXI C differed from the basic type mainly in the quantity and location of the underwater armament. Type XXI B was to have had six more tubes, three per side, located in the bow but firing astern at an angle of 10° from the centre-line of the boat. In the XXI C variant, whose maximum length was to have been 263ft (83m), there were to have been 18 torpedo tubes: six for forward firing, and twelve, in two groups of three on each side, angled towards the stern. Designs of other variants (XXI D, XXI E and XXI T) were studied, but none was ever built.

Attack by Type XXI boats was carried out in a very different manner from that in conventional boats. Once the target had been sighted or revealed by radar or hydrophones, the manoeuvre consisted of running at high speed on a collision course at depth, until the target area was reached. Without recourse to the periscope, target distance and bearing could be determined with a high degree of accuracy by sonar and hydrophone, and computed in a

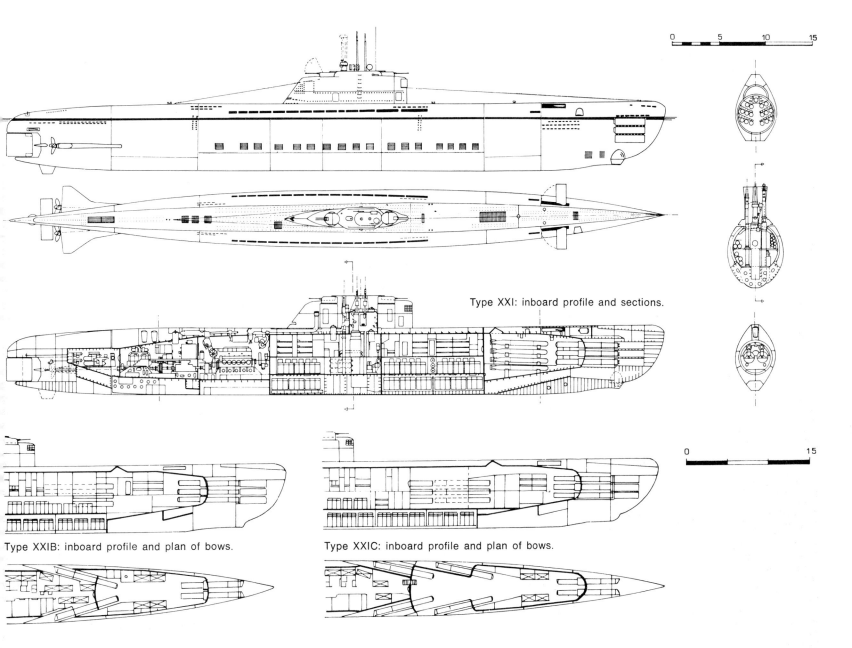

Type XXI: inboard profile and sections.

Type XXIB: inboard profile and plan of bows.

Type XXIC: inboard profile and plan of bows.

fire-control centre. Escape could be achieved at high speed at depth: the enemy's sonar became ineffective at speeds in excess of 12–13 knots.

These exceptional boats were not entirely free from faults. When they were designed, minimum underwater drag had been achieved at the expense of surface seakeeping. They were, nevertheless, the best type of operational boat built during the Second World War.

Between 27 June 1944 and the end of the war in Europe, 118 Type XXI boats entered service. Others were in advanced stages of completion in May 1945, and many more had been destroyed in air raids during the assembly stage. The vast programme, which would have produced more than 1,300 boats at the rate of one every 2–3 days, was begun to the detriment of other types, which were cancelled in 1944. Although built rapidly and in large numbers, they were unable to take an active part in the

war. The necessarily long training, slowed their entry into service. In May 1945, only 13 boats surrendered to the Allies: 88 were sabotaged by their own crews. Six boats were lost to air attack on the surface, three were mined and 25 were destroyed during air raids on ports.

The captured boats were incorporated in Allied navies and used for tests after the war. *U 2518* served in the French Navy as *Roland Morillot* until 1958. *U 2540* was salvaged in 1957 and served as *Wilhelm Bauer* in the navy of the Federal Republic of Germany from 1960 until 1971.

Fates   cause

date:	location:	boat:	(see page 7):
1945	North Sea	*U 2509, U 2514, U 2515, U 2523,*	
		U 2530, U 2532, U 2537, U 2547,	
		U 2549, U 2550, U 3007, U 3036,	
		U 3042, U 3043, U 3045, U 3046,	
		U 3502, U 3508	b

	U 2521, U 2524, U 2534	a
Baltic	U 2538	m
	U 2501, U 2504, U 2505, U 3004,	
	U 3005, U 3006, U 3503, U 3506,	
	U 3509, U 3518	sb
	U 2502, U 2506, U 2511, U 2513,	
	U 2518, U 3017, U 3035, U 3041,	
	U 3514, U 3515	x
	U 2503, U 2510, U 2516, U 2542,	
	U 3003, U 3505, U 3512	b
	U 3028, U 3030, U 3523	a
	U 3519, U 3520	m
	U 2507, U 2508, U 2512, U 2517,	
	U 2519, U 2520, U 2022, U 2525,	
	U 2526, U 2527, U 2528, U 2531,	
	U 2533, U 2535, U 2536, U 2539,	
	U 2540, U 2541, U 2543, U 2544,	
	U 2545, U 2546, U 2548, U 2551,	
	U 2552, U 3001, U 3002, U 3009,	
	U 3010, U 3011, U 3012, U 3013,	
	U 3014, U 3015, U 3016, U 3018,	
	U 3019, U 3020, U 3021, U 3022,	
	U 3023, U 3024, U 3025, U 3026,	
	U 3027, U 3029, U 3030, U 3031,	

U 3033, U 3034, U 3038, U 3039,
U 3040, U 3044, U 3047, U 3048,
U 3049, U 3050, U 3051, U 3501,
U 3504, U 3507, U 3510, U 3511,
U 3513, U 3516, U 3517, U 3521,
U 3522, U 3524, U 3525, U 3526,
U 3527, U 3528, U 3529, U 3530,
U 3536   sb
U 2529, U 3008, U 3032   x

Right:
U 3503, being scuttled by her own crew, like many other Type XXI boats at the surrender.

Left:
U 2534 being sunk by a British B–24 Liberator bomber, having been surprised on the surface off Göteborg on 6 May 1945.

Below, left and right:
Three Type XXI and a Type VII boats, moored at a base in Norway in 1945. U 2511 is in the foreground.

Type XXIII

U 2321–U 2331, U 2334–
U 2371:
Builder: Deutsche Werft,
Hamburg.
Date: 1943–1944/45.
U 2332, U 2333:
Builder: Germania Werft, Kiel.
Date: 1943–1944/44.
U 2372–U 2377:
Builder: Naval shipyard,
Toulon.
Date: 1944–   /–.
U 4001–U 4120:
Builder: Deutsche Werft,
Hamburg.
Date: 1944–   /–.
U 4701–U 4712:
Builder: Krupp Germania
Werft, Kiel.
Date: 1944–1944/45.
U 4713–U 4718:
Builder: Krupp Germania
Werft, Kiel.
Date: 1944–   /–.
Series ordered or (shown in
brackets) designed, but
construction or assembly not
begun:
U 2378–U 2400 (Toulon),
U 2401–U 2430 (Ansaldo,
Genoa), U 2431–U 2445
(C.R.D.A., Monfalcone),
U 2446–U 2460 (Nikolaev
and Linz naval shipyards)
(U 2461–U 2500), U 4719–
U 4891, (U 4892–U 5000).

Normal displacement: 232
tons surfaced; 258 tons
submerged.
Dimensions: 113ft 9in x 9ft
9in x 12ft 3in (34.6m x 4m x
3.66m).
Machinery: diesel: 1 MWM;
electric: 1 AEG + 1 (for
silent running).
Maximum power: 575–630hp
surfaced; 550 + 35hp
submerged.
Maximum speed: 9.7 knots
surfaced; 12.5 knots
submerged, 3.5 knots silent
running.
Range: 4,300 miles at 6 knots
surfaced, 1,350 miles at
9.7 knots surfaced; 175 miles
at 4 knots submerged, 43
miles at 10 knots submerged.
Torpedo tubes: two 21in
(533mm) forward; torpedoes: 2.

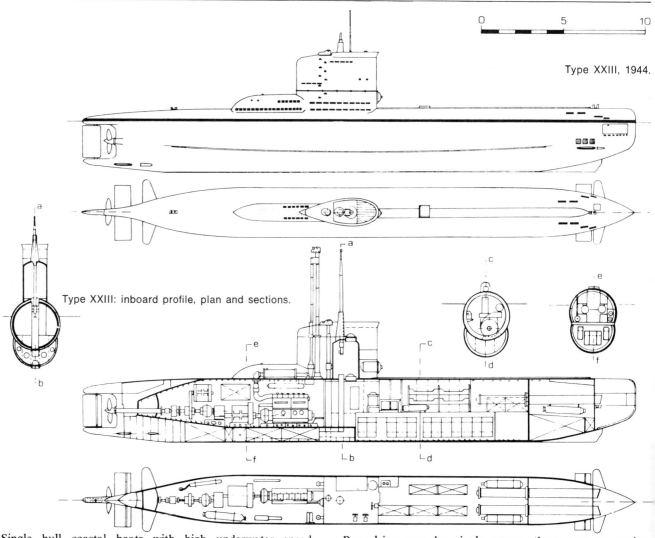

Type XXIII, 1944

Type XXIII: inboard profile, plan and sections.

Single hull coastal boats with high underwater speed, designed to meet the same needs as Type XXI. The first, designated Type XXII (see Table:13 Types of experimental or design-stage boats) called for similar performance to Type XXI, but with coastal characteristics. It was never built, being quickly outdated by a slightly larger boat with better performance, designated Type XXIII.

As in Type XXI, the hull consisted of two superimposed pressure hulls, but lacked the external sheathing except in the stern section. The upper hull, the larger in diameter of the two, contained crew's quarters, engines and torpedo tubes: the lower hull contained the storage batteries and some of the fuel and dive tanks. The hull was streamlined and was built in four separate sections.

Propulsion was by single screw; there was no casing and the conning tower was small and streamlined. The control surfaces, forward and aft, were complemented by stabilizing fins, and the tail and directional rudders together with the 5.9ft (1.78m) diameter propeller, had been specially developed to give a high overall propulsion output while submerged. Maximum operational depth was approximately 492ft (150m) and minimum crash-dive time reached a record of approximately 9 seconds.

The batteries had a particularly high capacity which, through a 550hp electric motor, enabled the boat to maintain a maximum submerged speed of 12.5 knots for more than an hour, and an economical speed of 4 knots for almost two days. An additional electric motor for silent

Type XXIII submarine *U 2361* in dry dock.

U 2332 during an early trial run.

running was installed. With a maximum fuel load of 18 tons, range at 6 knots reached 4,300 miles.

Type XXIII was equipped with a telescoping schnorkel, but only one periscope. Maximum schnorkel speed was 8 knots. Although equipped with less acoustic gear than the Type XXI, a fire-control centre was installed, which could compute torpedo-launching data from hydrophone readings.

Armament consisted of only two bow torpedo tubes and, because of limited space, no spare torpedoes were carried. Seakeeping qualities on the surface, were modest but, overall, Type XXIII was considered to have been very successful.

The first Type XXIII boat, *U 2321*, was launched at Hamburg on 17 April 1944 and entered service on 12 June. The assembly of 83 boats had begun, and 62 of them had entered service when the war ended. Another six boats (*U 4713–U 4718*) were ready for assembly, and another six (*U 2372–U 2377*) were to have been assembled at Toulon, but the sections were lost during the retreat from southern France in the previous year. Of the 280 boats

programmed, only 95 had been begun. Several series were to have been assembled in Italian yards and employed in the Tyrhennian Sea and the Adriatic, and in yards on the Danube for employment in the Black Sea. Unlike the Type XXI, Type XXIII boats saw action during the final months of the war. In ten missions during March–May 1945, six merchant ships were sunk without loss. The last sinking of the war, by a German submarine, occurred off the coast of Scotland at 23.00 hours on 7 May 1945, when *U 2336* (Lieutenant-Commander Klusmeier) sank the British merchantmen *Avondale Park* (2,878 GRT) and *Snealand* (1,791 GRT) with a single torpedo each. She returned to base unscathed and later surrendered to the British.

Two Type XXIII boats were sunk by air attack at sea: many more were destroyed by bombing, mines and various accidents. The majority were scuttled or surrendered to the Allies, who incorporated several into their own navies for experimental use. *U 2365* and *U 2367* were salvaged in 1956, and served for some years in the navy of the Federal Republic of Germany.

Fates

date:	location:	boat:	cause (see page 7):
1944	Baltic	U 2331	v
1945	North Sea	U 2359	a
		U 2340	b
		U 2327, U 2332, U 2365, U 2370, U 2371	sb
		U 2322, U 2326, U 2328, U 2329, U 2334, U 2335, U 2336, U 2337, U 2341, U 2345, U 2348, U 2350, U 2351, U 2353, U 2354, U 2356, U 2361, U 2363, U 4706	x
	Baltic	U 2338	a
		U 4708, U 4709, U 4711, U 4712	b
		U 2323, U 2342	m
		U 2344, U 2367	v
		U 2330, U 2333, U 2339, U 2343, U 2346, U 2349, U 2352, U 2355, U 2357, U 2358, U 2360, U 2362, U 2363, U 2364, U 2366, U 2368, U 2369, U 4701, U 4702, U 4703, U 4704, U 4705, U 4707, U 4710	sb
		U 2321, U 2324, U 2325	x

Midget submarines

During the war, mainly after 1943, the German Navy devoted considerable energy to the design and construction of midget submarines and 'human' torpedoes.

Unlike the British, Italian and Japanese, the Germans intended their small boats for defence rather than offensive operations. By the time of their appearance early in 1944, the German role in the war had been reduced to one of pure defence, and the midgets were designed to oppose Allied ships during large-scale operations such as the invasion of Normandy.

The first to be built were the *Neger* and *Marder* types. They took the form of two superimposed torpedoes, the lower of which, was the weapon itself. The upper one was fitted with a control-station or cockpit towards the forward end. The operator was protected by a watertight plexiglas canopy.

The *Biber* type, which followed, was larger and more seaworthy and was armed with two torpedoes which were fastened side by side under the hull. Unlike its predecessors, *Biber* had an internal combustion engine for surface propulsion. The prototype, *Adam*, was built in the Flender yard at Lubeck between 9 February and 15 March 1944.

Another type built in substantial numbers was the *Molch*, armed with two torpedoes and equipped, like the *Neger* and *Marder* types, with an electric torpedo motor for surface and submerged propulsion. The foregoing types can best be clasified as 'human' torpedoes; but 1944 saw the first true 'pocket' submarines enter service with the *Hecht* (Type XXVII) and the *Seehund* (Type XXVII B). These, unlike the other 'pocket' types, were included in the normal numbering system of German submarines.

Of the 186 originally proposed, only three examples of the *Hecht* were built, but the construction of more than 1,300 *Seehund* was ordered. These were undoubtedly the best of the German midgets, but only 67 of them were completed before the war ended.

Although smaller, the general characteristics of the *Seehund* can be compared to the Italian CB types. Other types such as the *Hai* and *Delphin* remained in the proto-type or design stage: *Grosser Delphin,* an enlarged and

Table 11: Details of German midget submarines

Type:	U-boat series numbers:	Number units entered service/(not completed):	Year first unit ready:	Displace-ment (tons):	Dimensions: Max. length	Dimensions: Max. breadth	Propulsion gear: surfaced/submerged
Neger (Negro)	—	approx. 200	1944	2.7	26ft 3in (8m)	1ft 9in (.53m)	E torpedo motor
Marder (Sable)	—	approx. 300	1944	3	26ft 3in (8m)	1ft 9in (.53m)	E torpedo motor
Biber (Beaver)	—	324	1944	6.3	29ft 6in (9.04m)	5ft 3in (1.6m)	Internal combustion motor. 1 E torpedo motor
Molch (Salamander)	—	390	1944	11	35ft 6in (10.8m)	6ft (1.82m)	E torpedo motor
Hechet (Pike)	XXVII A U 2111–U 2200 U 2205–U 2300	3(87)	1944	12.5–11.8	34ft 0in (10.5m)	5ft 6in (1.7m)	E torpedo motor
Seehund (Seal)	XXVII B U 2251–U 2300 U 5001–U 6351	67 (1,284)	1944	14.9	39ft 0in (12m)	5ft 6in (1.7m)	I D / I E
Hai (Shark)	—	1	1944	3.5	26ft 3in (11m)	1ft 9in (.53m)	E torpedo motor
Delphin (Dolphin)	—	3	1944	2.8	16ft 9in (5.1m)	3ft 4in (1.01m)	1 E
Grosser Delphin (Large Dolphin)	U 5790 (?)	—	1945	approx. 8	28ft 6in (8.68m)	—	1 D + 1 E or 1 Walter turbine

Speed (knots): surfaced/ submerged	hp: surfaced/ submerged	Range (miles at knots): surfaced/ submerged	Number of torpedoes/ (mines):	Comple- ment:	Notes:
4.2/3.2	12	30–3	1	1	Capable of reaching a maximum speed of 20 knots.
4.2/3.2	12	30–3	1	1	Improved version of *Neger*.
6.5/5.3	32/13	130–6/8.6–5	2	1	Petrol load: 0.11 tons. Builder: AG. Weser, Bremen.
4.3/5	13.9	50–4/50–5	2	1	Builder: Flender, Lubeck.
5.6/6	13	78–3/40–6	1 (1)	2	Builder: Krupp Germania Werft, Kiel. Units commissioned: *U 2111, U 2112* and *U 2113*.
7.7/6	60/12	300–7/63–3	2	2	Fuel load: 0.5 tons. Builder: various. Units commissioned: *U 2251–U 2295, U 5034–5037, U 5251–U 5269.*
4.2/3.2	12	63–3	1	1	Experimental model developed from *Neger* type.
19/15	13	3–10	1 (1)	1	Experimental model. The torpedo was carried underneath the hull; the mine was towed.
17/30	60/25	100/30	2 (2)	2	Development of the preceding model; remained in design stage.

developed version of the *Delphin*; *Schwertal*, a 36ft
(10.24m) boat with a Walter turbine and armed with two
torpedoes; *Elefant*, a 30 ton boat with tracks for land
travel and a crew of two—the prototype, begun in 1944,
was destroyed while building in May 1945; Type K, an
improved *Seehund* with a displacement of 18 tons and a
crew of two.

Despite the large number built (more than 1,200),
operational results were limited and disappointing. The
Neger, Marder and *Biber* types saw the most action.
Neger and *Marder* were employed against the Allied landings at Anzio on 20/21 April 1944, and in Normandy early
in July 1944. The *Biber* types operated mainly in Belgian
and Dutch coastal waters. In January 1945, several were
stationed at Harstadt in Norway. Transported there by
Type VII C submarines, they were to have attacked the
battleship *Arkhangelsk* (ex-*Royal Sovereign*) at Murmansk,
but the action was never carried out.

At the surrender, several hundreds of midgets of all
types, were captured by the Allies in German ports and
yards. Most of them were destroyed, but several of the
Seehunds were commissioned by the French Navy and
remained in service as experimental and training boats
until the mid fifties.

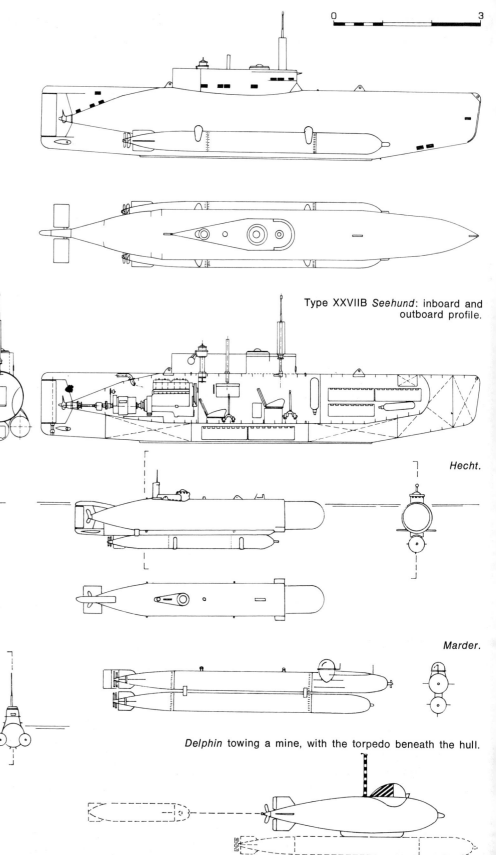

Type XXVIIB *Seehund*: inboard and outboard profile.

Molch.

Hecht.

Biber.

Marder.

Delphin towing a mine, with the torpedo beneath the hull.

Submarines captured or requisitioned

The conning tower of *U–A*
ex-Turkish *Batiray*.

During the war, The German Navy gained possession of numerous boats belonging to other nations, after the occupation of Holland and France, and of northern Italy after the surrender on 8 September 1943. Exceptions, were the ex-Turkish *Batiray* which was building in Germany in 1939 and was requisitioned, and the ex-British *Seal,* captured in May 1940.

Only the best of these boats were manned by the German Navy. Non-standard equipment made their maintenance difficult and costly and their general effectiveness was always low; they were operational only for brief periods. *U–A* (ex-*Batiray*), of German construction and similar to the Type IX, was the first boat to operate in the South Atlantic in the summer of 1940. The Italian ocean-going boats captured at Bordeaux were used as Transports to and from the Far East. The remaining foreign boats were used for training in the Baltic or in Norwegian waters, and were scuttled in 1945. The only modifications to these boats were the rebuilding of conning towers, and the replacement of anti-aircraft armament by weapons of German manufacture.

Table 12: Submarines requisitioned or captured by the German Navy

Boat:	Details:	Career and fate:
U –A, ex-Turkish *Batiray*	Normal displacement: 1,044 tons surfaced; 1,357 tons submerged Dimensions: 282ft 3in x 22ft 3in x 14ft (86m x 6.8m x 4.1m) Machinery: 1 diesel; 1 electric Maximum power: 4,600hp surfaced; 1,300hp submerged Maximum speed: 18 knots surfaced; 8.4 knots submerged Range: 13,100 miles at 10 knots surfaced; 146 miles at 2 knots submerged Armament: Six 21in(533mm) torpedo tubes; 4 forward 2 aft One 4.1in(105mm) 45-cal gun; two 20mm Maximum mine load: 36 (launched through torpedo tubes)	Minelaying boat building in 1939 at Germania Werft, Kiel. Requisitioned and designated *U A* in 1940. Fate: Date — Location — Cause (see page 7): 1945 — North Sea — sb
U –B, ex-British *Seal*	See Great Britain, *Porpoise* Class	Minelaying boat captured in the Kattegat on 2 May 1940. Recommissioned in November 1940 and used for training. Disarmed in 1943. Fate: Date — Location — Cause (see page 7): 1945 — North Sea — sb
UC 1, UC 2, ex-Norwegian *B 5*, *B 6*	See Norway, *B* Class	'Holland' type coastal boats captured in 1940. Fates: Date — Boat — Cause (see page 7): 1942 — *UC 1* — r 1944 — *UC 2* — r
UC 3, ex-Norwegian *A 3*	See Norway, *CA* Class	Built in Germany in 1914 and captured in 1940: not recommissioned.
UD 1, ex-Dutch *O.8*	See Holland, *O.8* Class	'Holland' type coastal boats captured in 1940. Fate: Date — Location — Cause (see page 7): 1945 — North Sea — sb
UD 2, ex-Dutch *O.12*	See Holland, *O.12* Class. (From 1941, armed with one 20mm in place of original two 40mm guns)	Captured at Den Helder in 1940. Fate: Date — Location — Cause (see page 7): 1945 — North Sea — sb
UD 3, UD 4, UD 5, ex-Dutch *O.25*, *O.26*, *O.27*	See Holland, *O.21* Class	Modern type boats captured in 1940 while still building. Fitted with Dutch type schnorkel. *UD 5* survived the war and returned to Dutch Navy in 1945. Fates: Date — Location — Boat — Cause (see page 7): 1945 — North Sea — *UD 3, UD 4* — sb
UF 1, UF 2, UF 3, ex-French *L'Africaine*, *La Favorite*, *L'Astrée*	See France, *Aurore* Class	Captured on ways (*UF 1*, *UF 3*) or fitting out in 1940. Building of *UF 1* and *UF 3* was not completed and was resumed by the French in 1945. Fate: Date — Location — Boat — Cause (see page 7): 1945 — North Sea — *UF 2* — sb
UIT 1, UIT 2, UIT 3, ex-Italian *R 10*, *R 11*, *R 12*, UIT 4, UIT 5, UIT 6, ex-*R 7*, *R 8*, *R 9*	See Italy, *R* Class	Transport boats captured building or fitting out in 1943. None completed. Fates: Date — Location — Boat — Cause (see page 7): 1944 — Mediterranean — *UIT 1, UIT 4, UIT 5, UIT 6* — b 1945 — Mediterranean — *UIT 2, UIT 3* — sb

Boat:	Details:	Career and fate:
UIT 7, ex-Italian *Bario*; UIT 8, ex-*Litio*; UIT 9, ex-*Sodio*; UIT 10, ex-*Potassio*; UIT 11, ex-*Rame*; UIT 12, ex-*Ferro*; UIT 13, ex-*Piombo*; UIT 14, ex-*Zinco*; UIT 15, ex-*Sparide*; UIT 16, ex-*Murena*; UIT 19, ex-*Nautilo*; UIT 20, ex-*Grongo*	See Italy, *Flutto* Class	Coastal boats captured building or fitting out. None completed.

Fates:

Date	Location	Boat	Cause (see page 7):
1944	Mediterranean	UIT 15, UIT 16, UIT 19, UIT 20	b
1945	Mediterranean	UIT 7, UIT 8, UIT 9	b
		UIT 10, UIT 11, UIT 12, UIT 13, UIT 14	sb

Boat:	Details:	Career and fate:
UIT 17, ex-Italian *CM 1*; UIT 18, ex-*CM 2*	See Italy, *CM* Class	Midgets captured incomplete.

Fates:

Date	Location	Boat	Cause (see page 7):
1945	Mediterranean	UIT 17	c
		UIT 18	sb

Boat:	Details:	Career and fate:
UIT 21, ex-Italian *Finzi*	See Italy, *Calvi* Class	Captured at Bordeaux in September 1943 and sunk there in 1945 without having been put back into service.
UIT 22, ex-Italian *Bagnolini*; UIT 23, ex-*Giuliani*; UIT 24, ex-*Cappellini*; UIT 25, ex-*Torelli*	See Italy, *Liuzzi*, *Marcello* and *Marconi* Classes	Ocean-going boats adapted for transporting materials to Far East. UIT 22 captured at Bordeaux, UIT 23 and UIT 25 at Singapore and UIT 24 at Sabang.

Fates:

Date	Location	Boat	Cause (see page 7):
1944	Atlantic	UIT 22	
	Indian Ocean	UIT 23	s
1945	Pacific Ocean	UIT 24, UIT 25	c

Left:
The ex-Dutch *UD 4* (left) and *UD 3*.

Below:
UB, ex-H.M.S. Seal, at Kiel in 1940 after her capture.

Experimental/design projects

The following table illustrates the principal technical characteristics of experimental submarines built in Germany between 1939 and 1945, and the more important types which were designed but never built.

These experimental types were important to the technical evolution of German submarines. Their building led to the development of propulsion gear with revolutionary characteristics such as the Walter turbine, and the fast diesel closed-cycle engine which never progressed beyond the experimental stage: they also led to the development of new hull shapes for high underwater speeds. These designs, which had no practical outcome, complete the picture of the technical evolution of German boats during the Second World War. The first of these, from Type III to Type XVI, were abandoned because they were already superseded by other boats in service or because they were no longer fitted to operational needs of the moment (Types III, XI, XII, XV and XVI).

Table 13: German experimental/design projects

Type:	Series numbers:	Number of boats built:	Years ordered/ completed:	Displacement (tons): surfaced/ submerged	Dimensions:	Machinery: surfaced/ submerged	hp: surfaced/ submerged
III	—	—	—	—	254ft 3in x 26ft 3in x 17ft 0in (77.4m x 7.96m x 5.2m)	2 D/2 E	2,800/1,000
IV, V, VI	—	—	—	—	—	—	—
VIII	—	—	—	—	—	—	—
X A	—	—	—	approx. 2,500/—	—	—	—
XI	U 112–U 115	4	1939–—	3,140/3,630	377ft 3in x 31ft 3in x 20ft 3in (114.9m x 9.5m x 6.1m)	8 D/2 E on 2 shafts	17,600/2,200
XII	—	—	—	1,600/—	—	2 D/2 E	7,000/1,680
XIII	—	—	—	400/—	—	—	—
XV	—	—	—	2,500/—	—	2 D/2 E	2,800/750
XVI	—	—	—	5,000/—	—	2 D/2 E	2,800/750
V 80	—	1	1939–40	approx. 73¼/76	72ft 3in x 7ft 0in x 10ft 6in (26m x 2.6m x 2.2m)	1 Walter turbine 1 E	2,000 + 15
XVII V 300	U 791	1	1942–—	610/655	171ft 0in x 13ft 3in x 18ft 0in (52m x 4.03m x 5.4m)	2 Walter turbines 2 D/2 E	4,360 330/150
Wa 201	U 792, U 793	2	1942–1943–44	313/343	111ft 3in x 11ft 3in x 15ft 0in (34m x 3.43m x 4.5m)	2 Walter turbines 1 D/1 E	5,000 230/77.5
Wa 202	U 794, U 795	2	1942–1943–45	236/259			

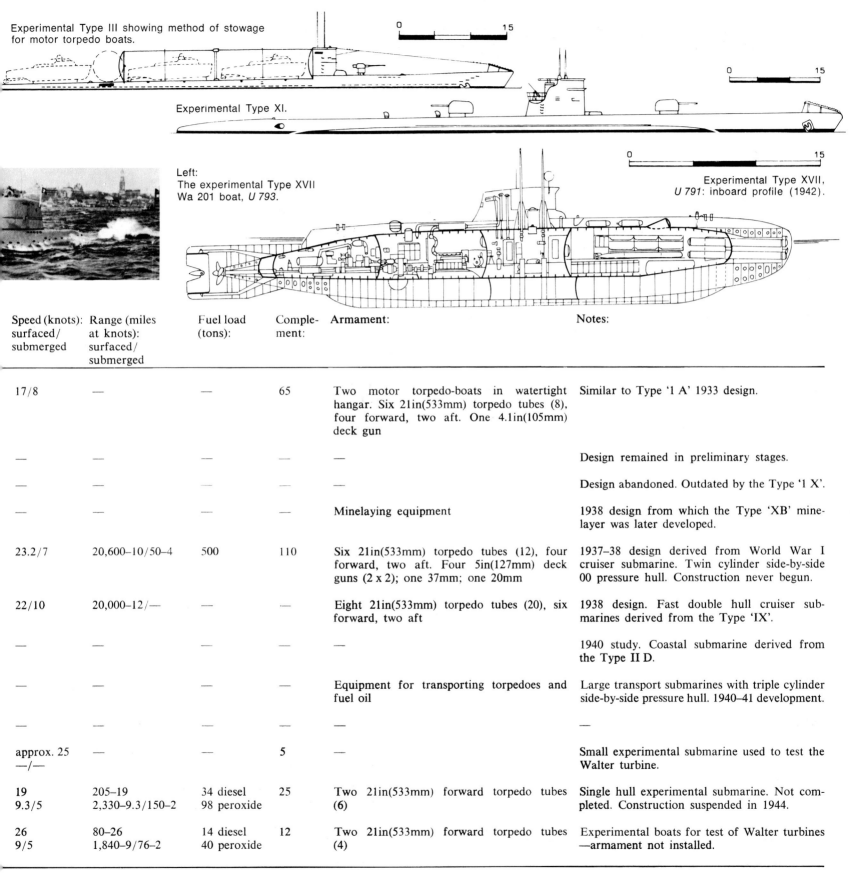

Experimental Type III showing method of stowage for motor torpedo boats.

Experimental Type XI.

Left:
The experimental Type XVII
Wa 201 boat, U 793.

Experimental Type XVII,
U 791: inboard profile (1942).

Speed (knots): surfaced/ submerged	Range (miles at knots): surfaced/ submerged	Fuel load (tons):	Comple- ment:	Armament:	Notes:
17/8	—	—	65	Two motor torpedo-boats in watertight hangar. Six 21in(533mm) torpedo tubes (8), four forward, two aft. One 4.1in(105mm) deck gun	Similar to Type '1 A' 1933 design.
—	—	—	—		Design remained in preliminary stages.
—	—	—	—		Design abandoned. Outdated by the Type '1 X'.
—	—	—	—	Minelaying equipment	1938 design from which the Type 'XB' mine-layer was later developed.
23.2/7	20,600–10/50–4	500	110	Six 21in(533mm) torpedo tubes (12), four forward, two aft. Four 5in(127mm) deck guns (2 x 2); one 37mm; one 20mm	1937–38 design derived from World War I cruiser submarine. Twin cylinder side-by-side 00 pressure hull. Construction never begun.
22/10	20,000–12/—	—	—	Eight 21in(533mm) torpedo tubes (20), six forward, two aft	1938 design. Fast double hull cruiser sub-marines derived from the Type 'IX'.
—	—	—	—	—	1940 study. Coastal submarine derived from the Type II D.
—	—	—	—	Equipment for transporting torpedoes and fuel oil	Large transport submarines with triple cylinder side-by-side pressure hull. 1940–41 development.
—	—	—	—	—	—
approx. 25 —/—	—	—	5	—	Small experimental submarine used to test the Walter turbine.
19 9.3/5	205–19 2,330–9.3/150–2	34 diesel 98 peroxide	25	Two 21in(533mm) forward torpedo tubes (6)	Single hull experimental submarine. Not com-pleted. Construction suspended in 1944.
26 9/5	80–26 1,840–9/76–2	14 diesel 40 peroxide	12	Two 21in(533mm) forward torpedo tubes (4)	Experimental boats for test of Walter turbines —armament not installed.

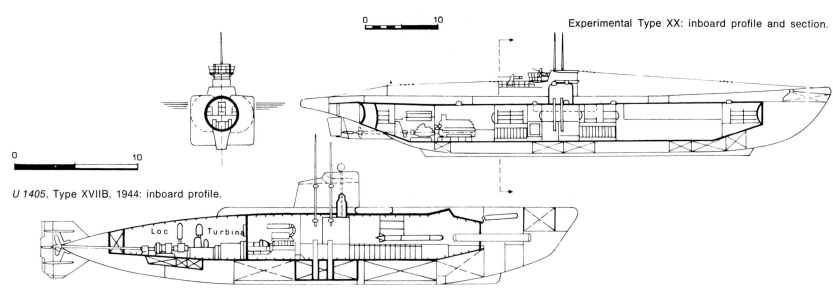

Experimental Type XX: inboard profile and section.

U 1405, Type XVIIB, 1944: inboard profile.

Type:	Series numbers:	Number of boats built:	Years ordered/ completed:	Displacement (tons): surfaced/ submerged	Dimensions:	Machinery: surfaced/ submerged	hp: surfaced/ submerged
XVII B	U 1405–U 1409 U 1410–U 1416	5 7	1943–1944– 1943–	312/337	136ft 3in x 10ft 9in x 14ft 9in (41.5m x 3.4m x 4.3m)	1 Walter Turbine 1 D/1 E	2,500 230/77.5
XVII G	U 1081–U 1092	12	1943–	314/345	129ft 9in x 11ft 3in x 15ft 6in (39.5m x 3.4m x 4.3m)	1 Walter Turbine 1 D/1 E	2,500 230/77.5
XVII K	U 798 (U 799, U 800)	1	1944–	368/425	133ft 6in x 11ft 3in x 16ft 0in (40.7m x 4.5m x 4.9m)	1 D/1 E closed cycle	1,500/ 12 + 1,500
XVIII	U 796, U 797	2	1943–	1,485/1,652	235ft 3in x 20ft 3in x 21ft 0in (71.5m x 8.0m x 6.36m)	2 Walter turbines 1 D/1 E	15,000 2,000/77
XIX	—	—	—	2,000/—	—	—	2,800/750
XX	U 1601–U 1615 (U 1616–U 1700) U 1701–U 1715 (U 1716–U 1800)	200	1943–	2,708/2,962	255ft 0in x 30ft 3in x 21ft 9in (77.1m x 9.1m x 6.6m)	2 D/2 E	3,200/750
XXII	—	—	—	155/200	89ft 0in x 9ft 9in x 12ft 9in (32m x 2.9m x 3.9m)	1 Walter Turbine 1 D/1 E	2,500 210/77
XXIV (XXV)	—	—	—	1,800/—	234ft 6in x 20ft 3in x 21ft 9in (71.5m x 6.2m x 6.6m)	2 Walter turbines 2 D/2 E	15,000 4,000/550
XXVI A & B	—	—	—	950/— (A) 1,150/— (B)	190ft 3in x 21ft 0in x 21ft 3in (A) (58m x 6.4m x 6.5m) 203ft 6in x 21ft 0in x 21ft 3in (B) (62m x 6.4m x 6.5m)	1 Walter Turbine 1 D/1 E	7,500
XXVI W	U 4501–U 4700	200	1944–	842/926	184ft 6in x 18ft 0in x 19ft 6in (56.2m x 5.5m x 5.9m)	1 Walter Turbine 1 D/1 E	7,500 580/70

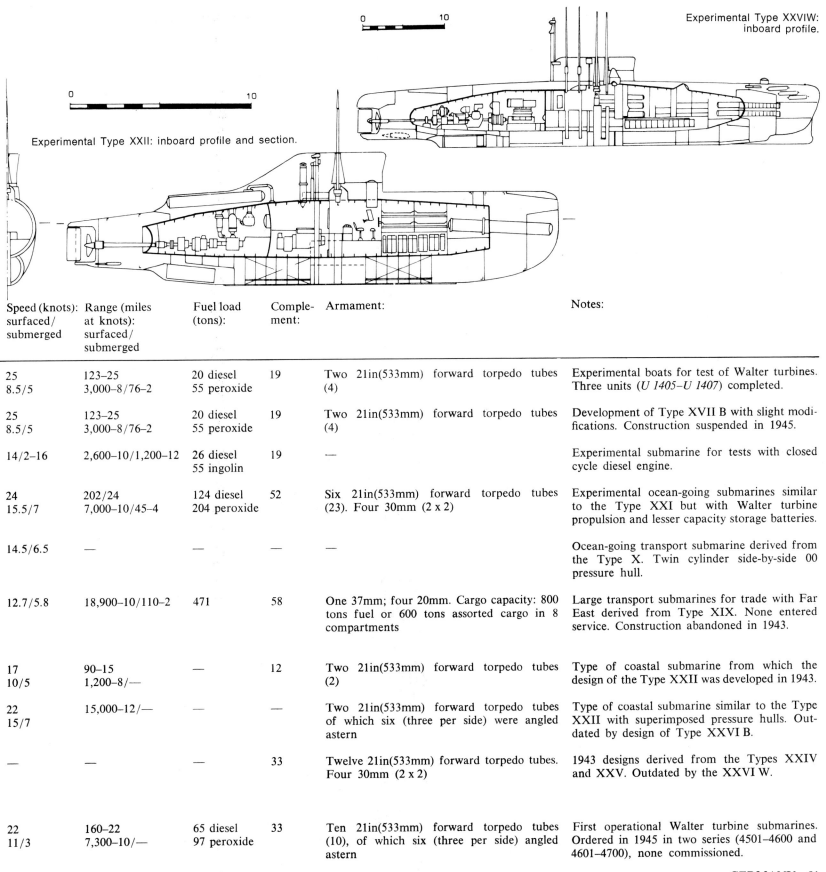

Experimental Type XXVIW: inboard profile.

Experimental Type XXII: inboard profile and section.

Speed (knots): surfaced/ submerged	Range (miles at knots): surfaced/ submerged	Fuel load (tons):	Comple-ment:	Armament:	Notes:
25 8.5/5	123–25 3,000–8/76–2	20 diesel 55 peroxide	19	Two 21in(533mm) forward torpedo tubes (4)	Experimental boats for test of Walter turbines. Three units (U 1405–U 1407) completed.
25 8.5/5	123–25 3,000–8/76–2	20 diesel 55 peroxide	19	Two 21in(533mm) forward torpedo tubes (4)	Development of Type XVII B with slight modifications. Construction suspended in 1945.
14/2–16	2,600–10/1,200–12	26 diesel 55 ingolin	19	—	Experimental submarine for tests with closed cycle diesel engine.
24 15.5/7	202/24 7,000–10/45–4	124 diesel 204 peroxide	52	Six 21in(533mm) forward torpedo tubes (23). Four 30mm (2 x 2)	Experimental ocean-going submarines similar to the Type XXI but with Walter turbine propulsion and lesser capacity storage batteries.
14.5/6.5	—	—	—	—	Ocean-going transport submarine derived from the Type X. Twin cylinder side-by-side 00 pressure hull.
12.7/5.8	18,900–10/110–2	471	58	One 37mm; four 20mm. Cargo capacity: 800 tons fuel or 600 tons assorted cargo in 8 compartments	Large transport submarines for trade with Far East derived from Type XIX. None entered service. Construction abandoned in 1943.
17 10/5	90–15 1,200–8/—	—	12	Two 21in(533mm) forward torpedo tubes (2)	Type of coastal submarine from which the design of the Type XXII was developed in 1943.
22 15/7	15,000–12/—	—	—	Two 21in(533mm) forward torpedo tubes of which six (three per side) were angled astern	Type of coastal submarine similar to the Type XXII with superimposed pressure hulls. Outdated by design of Type XXVI B.
—	—	—	33	Twelve 21in(533mm) forward torpedo tubes. Four 30mm (2 x 2)	1943 designs derived from the Types XXIV and XXV. Outdated by the XXVI W.
22 11/3	160–22 7,300–10/—	65 diesel 97 peroxide	33	Ten 21in(533mm) forward torpedo tubes (10), of which six (three per side) angled astern	First operational Walter turbine submarines. Ordered in 1945 in two series (4501–4600 and 4601–4700), none commissioned.

Type:	Series numbers:	Number of boats built:	Years ordered/ completed:	Displacement (tons): surfaced/ submerged	Dimensions:	Machinery: surfaced/ submerged	hp: surfaced/ submerged
XXVI E$_2$	—	—	—	830/approx. 1,150	186ft 6in x 18ft 0in x 21ft 0in (52m x 5.5m x 6.4m)	1 D/1 E	2,000/2,500
XXVIII	—	—	—	approx. 200/—	105ft 0in x — x — (32m x —m x —m)	—	—/2,000
XXIX A	—	—	—	681/—	176ft 3in x 15ft 9in x 16ft 9in (53.7m x 4.8m x 5.1m)	1 D/1 E	1,035/1,400
B, B$_2$, C, D, F, G, K$_{1-4}$	—	—	—	753 to 825 (D) 1,035/—	188ft 9in x 15ft 9in x 16ft 9in (A) (57.5m x 4.8m x 5,1m) 218ft 9in x 17ft 9in x 17ft 6in (D) (66.7m x 5.4m x 5.3m)	1 D/1 E (D, K$_4$) 2 D/1 E	1,035 to 2,000/— (C) 2,100/2,800
XXX A	—	—	—	1,180/—	226ft 0in x 17ft 9in x 20ft 3in (68.9m x 5.4m x 6.2m)	1 D/1 E	2,000/2,100
XXXI	—	—	—	1,200/—	177ft 3in x 20ft 3in x 23ft 0in (53.5m x 7m x 6.9m)	1 D/1 E	2,000/2,100
XXXII	—	—	—	approx. 90/—	—	1 D closed cycle	1,500
XXXIII	—	—	—	approx. 360/—	131ft 3in x 20ft 3in x 23ft 0in (40m x 6.5m x 6.9m)	1 D closed cycle	—
XXXIV	—	—	—	90/—	78ft 0in x 8ft 3in x 8ft 6in (23.7m x 2.5m x 2.6m)	1 D closed cycle	—
XXXV	—	—	—	approx. 850/—	164ft 0in x — x — (50m x —m x —m)	1 Walter turbine	7,500
XXXVI	—						
		—		approx. 930/—	—	4 D closed cycle	6,000/—

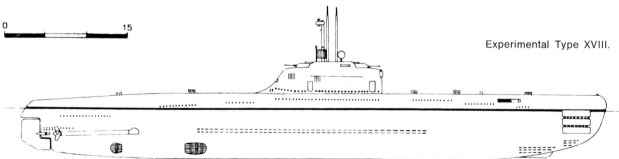

0   15

Experimental Type XVIII.

Experimental Type XXIXB: inboard profile.

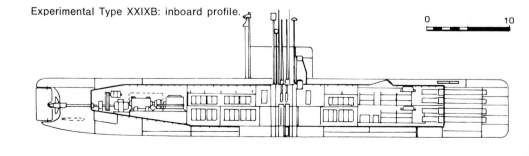

0   10

Speed (knots): surfaced/ submerged	Range (miles at knots): surfaced/ submerged	Fuel load (tons):	Comple- ment:	Armament:	Notes:
14.5/16	8,500–10/—	—	—	Eight 21in(533mm) torpedo tubes (8), four forward, four aft around propeller	Similar to Type XXVI W with conventional propulsion gear and high-capacity batteries.
—	—	—	—	Four 21in(533mm) forward torpedo tubes	'Pure' submarine for coastal use, with single propeller.
12.5/14	7,500–12/—	—	—	Eight 21in(533mm) forward torpedo tubes	Fast coastal submarine with single propeller.
12 to 13/ 14 to 16 (C) 11.5/16.5	—	—	—	Eight 21in(533mm) torpedo tubes (8) in various configurations. (D) twelve 21in (533mm) torpedo tubes (12)	Fast coastal submarine with single propeller.
14.6/15.6	15,000–10/—	—	—	Twelve 21in(533mm) forward torpedo tubes (12), of which four (two per side) angled astern	Fast ocean-going submarine with single screw; performance similar to Type XXI.
12/14.6	15,000–10/—	—	—	Twelve 21in(533mm) torpedo tubes (24), eight forward, four aft	Fast ocean-going submarine with single screw developed from preceding model.
—/22	200–12/80–21	6 oxygen	—	Two torpedoes in external tubes	Experimental coastal submarine for tests with closed cycle diesel.
—	1,500–6	—	—	Four 21in(533mm) forward torpedo tubes (6)	Experimental coastal submarine.
approx. 14/—	—	—	—	—	Experimental coastal submarine.
approx. 22/—	—	—	—	Eight 21in(533mm) forward torpedo tubes (8) of which two (one per side) angled astern	Single-screw ocean-going submarine.
approx. 16	—	—	—	—	Ocean-going submarine with closed cycle diesel propulsion and twin screws.

Experimental Type XXXA: inboard profile.

Experimental Type XXXI: inboard profile.

Great Britain

Right: HMS *Severn*.

"Of all branches of men in the Forces, there is none which shows more devotion and faces grimmer perils than the submarine . . . Great deeds are done in the air and on the land; nevertheless, nothing surpasses your exploits." With these words, Winston Churchill emphasized the difficulties and dangers faced by the submarine branch of the Royal Navy during the Second World War. The task which confronted them was different in kind from that faced by the Americans or the Germans. Not for the Royal Navy, the juicy and, at first, ill-protected targets that the German submarines found in the Atlantic, nor the wholesale destruction of an enemy's merchant marine, as accomplished by the Americans. There was little opportunity to wage a strategic and semi-independent war against merchant ships on the high seas. As in the First World War, British naval power was such that the commerce of her European enemies disappeared from the trade routes as soon as war was declared.

Instead, the British submariners were faced with the interminable boredom of long patrols off enemy bases, and the hazardous attacking of heavily guarded trade routes, close to enemy shores. Inevitably, targets would be few, and casualties high.

The single opportunity of conducting a really decisive submarine campaign, lay in the Mediterranean. Here, the Axis needed a steady supply line to North Africa. The Mediterranean, comparatively shallow, enclosed and with clear water, is not ideal for submarine warfare, but it was here that British submarines achieved their greatest successes against merchant shipping. At the expense of many casualties, their actions, together with those of aircraft and surface units operating from Malta, had a decisive effect on the Desert campaign. Despite the heroism of Italian merchant seamen, victory in the battle of the Mediterranean supply lines went to the Allies. British submarines also achieved good results against warships in the Mediterranean.

During the Norwegian campaign, British successes against warships formed one of the few bright patches in that tale of disaster. Later, other successes were achieved in Northern European waters, and British submarines did much to curtail the freedom of action of enemy warships including submarines. On 9 February 1945, HMS *Venturer* (relying entirely on asdic and hydrophone bearings) sank *U 864* and became the first submarine to sink another, while both boats were submerged.

British boats played little part in the war against Japan until the end of 1943 when they began to obtain some successes in the Indian Ocean. Although by the end of the war, quite a number of British boats had been employed in this theatre, their score was not large and forms a mere footnote to the great American campaign in the Pacific. This resulted partly from the fact that the British boats were too small to have adequate range for the immense distances involved, but mostly, because of insufficient targets.

As we have seen, Britain has had a record of public opposition to the submarine from the time of Lord St. Vincent. The Admiralty

realised that it posed one of the greatest threats to the supremacy of the Royal Navy. At The Hague in 1899, Washington in 1921 and London in 1930, British diplomats strove to secure the abolition of this hated weapon. During both World wars, there was great popular hatred of the U-boats, and it is significant that the British took the lead in prosecuting Admiral Doenitz at Nuremburg, as much, it would seem, because of his position, as for what he had done.

However, nothing prevented Britain building submarines as soon as practicable designs appeared, or in having her own highly efficient submarine service. It has usually been equipped with excellent boats, fully equal to foreign contemporaries, and her submarine commanders have been as skilful and inventive as any in the world.

On 1 September 1939, the Royal Navy had 58 boats available, 47 of which were of modern type. The remaining boats belonged to old classes (H and L) built during the First World War. During the inter-war period, the Royal Navy concentrated on the quality rather than quantity of her underwater fleet. Good results had been obtained and the latest types of boats were suited to the planned operational needs. This was fully demonstrated during five years of war, when the prototypes created during the thirties were reproduced in large numbers, without any important modifications.

At the end of the First World War, the greatest part of the British submarine fleet had been placed in reserve, and during the following years, the older boats had been scrapped. The survivors of many famous classes such as the A, B and E, thus disappeared.

At the beginning of the twenties, the fleet had consisted of about 60 boats belonging to the H (coastal), L (ocean-going, attack and minelaying), K (Fleet submarines with steam propulsion), M (monitor, experimental) and R (submarine killer, soon to be scrapped) Classes. The first boat designed after the war was X 1, an experimental submarine, the largest in the world at that time, inspired by the German cruiser submarines. With her, the Royal Navy proved that a hull, 363ft 6in (110m) long and of about 3,600 tons displacement, could be manoeuvred quite easily underwater. Her diving performance, in fact, was surprisingly good. Operationally, however, X 1 could be seen as a complete failure. The premises which had prompted the development of cruiser submarines during the First World War were no longer valid in the twenties, and it would have been difficult for the Royal Navy to employ units of that type profitably. It is difficult to see why she was ordered at all. Because of this and because of constant trouble with her very unreliable diesels, X 1 was paid off and scrapped in 1936 and, in accordance with the terms of the Treaty of London, her displacement was utilized to build an equivalent displacement of smaller boats.

By the late twenties, the Royal Navy had to begin to think in terms of replacing the obsolescent boats in service, by new units which were technically more advanced, but whose roles were the same as those of the existing types. Over a period of years, the following types were decided upon: coastal boats replacing the H Class; ocean-going boats replacing the L Class; minelaying boats with ocean-going characteristics replacing—in that specific role— the L Class; diesel-propelled Fleet boats, with high surface speed for use with battle squadrons replacing the K Class steam-driven boats.

The first new type built was the O Class, derived from the L Class and scheduled to replace them. The first unit, Oberon (ex O.1) was launched in 1929 and commissioned the following year. Because of the increasing estrangement of Japan, Oberon was designed for greater range, with a view to her possible employment in the Pacific.

The more than 200 tons of fuel required for 6,500 miles at 10 knots, the increased underwater and surface armament, and the strengthened pressure hull, considerably increased the displacement and size of the O Class. The result was a larger degree of manoeuvrability, and of safety in terms of reserve speed. The first three boats were followed two years later by another six, in which several of the defects, especially with regard to safety, were eliminated by an increase in size. On the whole, the O Class boats were not particularly successful.

From the modified O Class (2nd group) derived the P and R Classes, ten examples of which, entered service between 1931 and 1932. Like their predecessors, they were not very manoeuvrable.

At the same time (1930), the design of the new Fleet submarines scheduled to replace the K Class was completed. Given the names of rivers, only three were built: Thames, Severn and Clyde. They were commissioned between 1932 and 1935. Technically, they were successful but their operational doctrine had already been eclipsed before it could be put into practice. The insistence of the 'budget conscious' Royal Navy, on a method of submarine employment which had never given any positive results, is puzzling. Originally, the lack of success of Fleet submarines in combined operations with surface forces was attributed to the difficulties of inter-communication. Despite developments in telecommunications, the employment of submarines with battle squadrons continued to be a difficult operation, and the incidence of confusion and accidents was high. Furthermore, the continuous increase in the speed of major warships (at that time, 30 knot battleships were being designed) made it difficult if not impossible to design boats capable of operating with them. Almost contemporaneously with the building of the three 'River' boats, the concept of the Fleet submarine was abandoned by the Royal Navy. There were other tasks, however, where the great speed and range of the River Class (they were faster than all except some Japanese boats) would prove useful.

During this period, the Royal Navy revised its modernization programme for submarines. It was decided to standardize construction on the basis of two main types: medium-range boats for the North Sea, and ocean-going boats to replace those units of the O, P and R Classes that had not given good results. At the same time, a minelaying type—already building—was confirmed, and it was decided that all new boats would have the fuel tanks inside the pressure hull and not between the double hulls nor in the bulges as hitherto. This was to obviate the fuel leaks which had plagued the preceding classes.

Swordfish, the prototype of the new S Class, was launched in November 1931. She was a medium-displacement boat whose construction and internal layout had been inspired by criteria of the utmost simplicity. Swordfish, and the twelve boats which followed between 1932 and 1938, proved excellent from all viewpoints. Their design was revived at the beginning of the war, and was used without many changes for another 51 boats commissioned between 1942 and 1945.

Almost simultaneously with the S Class, were launched the first minelaying boats of the Porpoise Class. These also were particularly well-designed, and their intensive wartime employment, both as minelayers and as transport submarines during the siege of Malta, confirmed their good qualities.

At Barrow on 5 October 1937, Vickers-Armstrong launched the prototype of the new ocean-going submarines which were intended to replace the O, P and R Classes. Entering service in December 1938,

Triton was the first of the 22 boats of the *T* Class, laid down between 1936 and 1938 and commissioned between 1938 and 1942. Classified as 'patrol submarines', the *T* Class were eminently successful, possibly the best boats built by the Royal Navy between the wars.

The design, of the utmost simplicity and rationality, resulted in boats easy to build, manoeuvre and maintain. The war service of the *T* Class which, like the *S* Class, was reproduced in some thirty examples without major changes, clearly demonstrated their high level of effectiveness and confirmed the wisdom of the formula adopted. Strong, safe and very manoeuvrable, they were fitted with a heavy armament of 10–11 internal and external torpedo tubes. This had been demanded because of forseeable rapid improvement of anti-submarine techniques and equipment. (In 1936, the British had asdic which already was very effective, and it was thought that other navies would have it soon). Boats would be forced to fire their torpedoes from continually increasing ranges, and a spread of ten torpedoes could make up for the inevitable lack of accuracy. In addition, the continuing increase in effectiveness of underwater protection systems would require even more torpedoes to achieve a sinking.

Three years before the war, the Royal Navy decided to build some small unarmed boats for the training of surface vessels in anti-submarine operations. These were the *U* Class, single hull coastal boats derived from the *H* Class. Because of the deteriorating international situation, they were modified during construction, by the addition of six torpedo tubes; four internal and two external. The first three boats, ordered in 1936 and commissioned late in 1938, proved very successful and it was immediately decided to build another twelve identical boats which were laid down in 1939. They were small, built simply and rapidly at low cost, and all frills had been eliminated. Propulsion was of the diesel-electric type, and the hull was completely welded. Because of their limited range, they were intended for the North Sea and other restricted waters. Their chief virtues of manoeuvrability and ease of handling were to prove very important during the war. Like the *S* and *T* Classes, the *U* Class was reproduced in some thirty units without many changes. The 22 boats of the *V* Class, built between 1943 and 1945, were little more than an improved and further simplified version of the *U* Class.

At the outbreak of war, the Royal Navy did not possess a numerically impressive submarine fleet, but qualitative development between 1932 and 1939 had been excellent. To achieve the necessary buildup, the Royal Navy made the simplest and surest decision and, as it turned out, the wisest: to immediately and rapidly reproduce the prototypes which had already been tested, making only small necessary changes from time to time. This resulted in a good number of boats

Development of British submarines, 1926–1944.

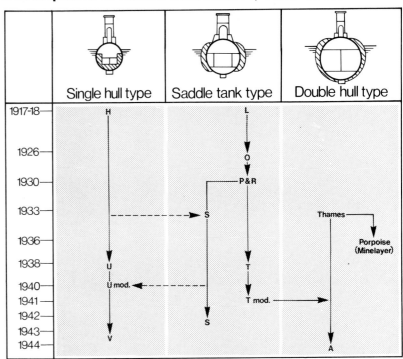

of proven effectiveness, available in a relatively short time, almost entirely eliminating the delays inherent to the drawing of new designs.

The only exception to this principle was the design, late in the war, of a type of long-range boat for use in the Pacific: the *A* Class, ordered in 1944, only two units of which were able to enter service before the war ended. They were large ocean-going boats, whose speed, range and armament had been developed to the limit, even to the detriment of simplicity and manoeuvrability, to suit them to operations against Japanese merchant shipping, whose anti-submarine measures were ineffective.

All British (and most other) warships have recognition numbers (known as pendant numbers) and the submarine is no exception. During the inter-war years, all numbered submarines simply reversed their designation: *H 20* wore 20–H as her pendant number, and so on. Named submarines of the *P* Class were allocated numbers ending in –P, as were the *O* Class. The *R, S* and *T* Classes used their own letter, while the three 'River' boats were –F for Fleet; the *U* Class –C for coastal, and the minelayers, naturally, –M.

In 1939, all submarines were allocated numbers ending with the letter N. On the outbreak of war, instructions were given for submarines to have their number painted in large figures on the sides of the conning tower. Further confusion arose from the Admiralty's decision in 1940, to place the letter N *before* instead of after the number, and the giving of numbers beginning with the letter P to all wartime-built submarines. None of these latter boats were to have names, but their crews frequently gave them unofficial names, beginning with the appropriate Class letter. These were soon in general use, and early in 1943 the Admiralty finally decided to recognize them officially. Thereafter, all submarines were again named. The changes between numbers and names can be followed in subsequent pages of this work.

Table 14: Location of operational submarines of the Royal Navy in September 1939

1st Flotilla (Mediterranean)	Three *O* Class, four *S* Class, two *Porpoise* Class
2nd Flotilla (Dundee, North Sea)	One *O* Class, eight *S* Class, one *T* Class
4th Flotilla (China)	Thirteen *O, P* and *R* Classes, one *Porpoise* Class plus two *en route*
5th Flotilla (Portsmouth, Channel)	Eight *H* Class, one *L* Class, one *O* Class, one *Thames* Class
6th Flotilla (Blyth, North Sea)	One *H* Class, two *L* Class, three *U* Class
7th Flotilla (being organized at Freetown)	Two *Thames* Class (being transferred)

The sinking of the *S* Class *Shark* in the North Sea on 6 July 1940. Damaged by depth-charges from the German auxiliary mine-sweepers *M. 1803, M. 1806* and *M. 1807*, she was forced to surface but sank while the German ships were trying to capture her.

The *U* Class *Unruffled*, returning to Malta from a patrol.

Ultimatum, one of the first boats of the second group.

Rorqual. Note that the periscopes are offset to allow free passage of mines in the casing above the pressure hull.

A group of British boats alongside their tender. From the left: one *S* Class (second group), one *U* Class, one *S* Class (ex-Turkish) and two *U* Class.

Unrivalled returning to Malta from a patrol.

During the early days of the war, several boats were transferred from the Far East to the Mediterranean and thence, when Italy had declared her status of non-belligerency, to home waters.

British submarines at sea, received the order to commence hostilities against Germany at 11.00 hrs on 3 September. Four minutes later, torpedoes from a German U-boat missed *Spearfish* by a few yards. During the first few months, several boats patrolled as far as the Baltic but were unable to find targets. The first success was achieved by *Sturgeon* which sank a small anti-submarine vessel in the Skaggerak, but the first worthwhile results were not achieved until the Norwegian campaign in April–May 1940. Then, the North Sea submarines played an important role in opposing the German naval invasion forces:

Table 15: Location of British submarines and boats controlled by the Royal Navy in January 1942

1st Flotilla (Alexandria, Mediterranean)	Four *O* and *P* Classes, eight *T* Class
2nd Flotilla (Malta, Mediterranean)	Thirteen *U* Class, five Greek boats, one Polish, one Yugoslav
3rd Flotilla (Clyde, Atlantic)	Three *T* Class, two ex American, two ex Turkish (requisitioned)
5th Flotilla (Portsmouth, Channel)	One *U* Class, one *T* Class, three *S* Class, one *Porpoise* Class, one *R* Class, one *P* Class, one ex Turkish (requisitioned), one Norwegian, four Free French, one ex German (*Graph*)
6th Flotilla (Blyth, North Sea)	One *T* Class, one *L* Class
7th Flotilla (west coast of Britain)	Two *O* Class, two *L* Class, seven *H* Class, three Dutch, one Norwegian, one Polish
8th Flotilla (Gibraltar)	Two *Thames* Class, one *O* Class, one Dutch
9th Flotilla (Dundee, North Sea)	One *U* Class, three Dutch, two Free French
Indian Ocean	*X 2* (ex Italian *Galilei*)
Pacific Ocean	Two *T* Class, one *R* Class
Atlantic Ocean (Central America)	One Dutch, one Free French
Undergoing complete refit in USA	One *P* Class

Table 16: Location of British submarines in May 1944

1st Flotilla (Malta, Mediterranean)	Eight *U* Class, two *S* Class, four Greek boats, one Dutch, one Yugoslav
3rd Flotilla (Holy Loch, North Sea)	Five *U* Class, seven *T* Class, nine *S* Class, three Dutch, two Free French
4th Flotilla (Trincomalee, Indian Ocean)	Ten *T* Class, one *S* Class, one *Porpoise* Class, one *Thames* Class
5th Flotilla (Portsmouth, Channel)	Four *U* Class, one *T* Class, three *S* Class, one *Porpoise* Class, one Free French, three Polish, one ex American
6th Flotilla (Blyth, North Sea)	Four *U* Class, two *T* Class, one *O* Class
7th Flotilla (Rothesay, Atlantic)	Four *U* Class, two *T* Class, one *S* Class, one *P* Class, one *O* Class, four Dutch, one Norwegian, one ex American
8th Flotilla (Trincomalee, Indian Ocean)	Nine *S* Class
9th Flotilla (Dundee, North Sea)	Five *U* Class, one *T* Class, three *S* Class, one ex Turkish (requisitioned), two Dutch
10th Flotilla (La Maddalena, Mediterranean)	Three *U* Class, one *T* Class

21 ships, merchantmen and warships totalling 75,869 GRT were sunk and another 12 were damaged by mines laid by submarines. The most important warship sunk was the light cruiser *Karlsruhe*, torpedoed by *Truant* off Christiansand on 9 April 1940. Six submarines were lost, of which, *Seal* was captured by the Germans during a minelaying operation in the Kattegat.

Italy's entry into the war in June 1940, led to the recall of numerous British boats to the Mediterranean. Their operations were marked by a high degree of aggression and daring and, from the outset, were in accordance with the best traditions of British 'seadogs'. Results, though not exceptional, were good, partly as a result of the ineffective anti-submarine measures of the Italian escorts which did not have asdic.

From the summer of 1940 until mid 1943, the Mediterranean was the main operational area of British submarines. Here they achieved their most important successes against warships (sinking of the cruisers *Bande Nere* and *Trento* on 23 March and 15 June 1942 by *Umbra* and *Urge;* serious damage to the battleship *Littorio* and the cruisers *Bolzano, Gorizia* and *Attilio Regolo*) and merchant ships (transatlantic liners *Conte Rosso, Esperia, Neptunia* and *Oceania*).

Most of the boats operating in the Mediterranean during this period were of the *T* and *U* Classes. The latter, in particular, because of their ease of handling, manoeuvrability and small size, proved eminently suitable for the Mediterranean where long range was not needed and where opposition continually increased as Italian anti-submarine units gained experience and suitable equipment. It was in the Mediterranean that the British suffered their greatest underwater losses: approximately 60 per cent of all British submarines lost during the war.

An interesting detail clearly illustrates the difficulties under which the British boats operated. During the period in which the Italo-German air offensive against Malta reached its maximum intensity (spring of 1942), the boats of the 2nd Flotilla were forced to pass the daylight hours resting on the harbour bottom, during their brief periods between operations. Because of this and other precautions, the submarine base at Malta remained operational, if at a reduced level, throughout the siege and only *P 36, P 39* and *Pandora* were sunk.

With the extension of the war in the Pacific, and Italy's exit from the war, the situation began to change appreciably. The number of units stationed in the Mediterranean remained virtually static, while new units, as they were commissioned, were assigned on a preferential basis to the Pacific Ocean and Indian Ocean, in relation to the considerable increase of activities in those areas.

In May 1944, the disposition of the submarine forces in the various areas had changed to those shown in Table 16. There were no important changes until the end of the war, except for a slight increase in the number of units operating in the Indian Ocean and the Pacific Ocean.

British submarines did not undergo any great technical changes throughout the war. The single innovation was the mounting of the early types of radar in an increasing number of boats from 1942. Although of short range, these were effective sets, with air as well as surface scan capabilities.

The standard weapon was the 21in (533mm) 'steam' torpedo, 20ft (6.7m) long, with a warhead of approximately 661,500lb (300kg), capable of a speed of 30–35 knots on an average run of 8,750 yards (8,000m)–10,950 yards (10,000m). The fuzes were of impact and magnetic type. Overall, British torpedoes were excellent and the Royal

Navy experienced none of the problems of malfunction which so plagued the German and American Navies. Torpedo tubes were either internal, reloaded from within the pressure hull and located forward and/or aft; or external, located in the casings, either on the sides or forward and/or aft, and which could not be reloaded while submerged. The number of internal tubes was fixed for each class: the number of external tubes varied from boat to boat, even within the same class.

British mines could be laid through the torpedo tubes and were carried in lieu of spare torpedoes. *T* Class boats could carry up to 12 mines.

The calibre of British deck guns was 4in (102mm) for ocean-going or medium range boats and 3in (76mm) or virtually identical 12-pounder for coastal boats. Machine-guns were usually .303in or 20mm (*T*, *S* and *A* Classes).

The majority of British submarines were painted grey or sometimes, black, but some had more unusual colour schemes, For example, *U* Class boats operating out of Malta were painted a deep 'Mediterranean' blue, and at least one three-ton camouflage scheme was prepared for submarines, though few seem to have used it.

An obvious, and very important, feature of British submarines was their narrow casing. This contributed to the rapid diving in which, the British boats excelled, and is a further indication that the Admiralty were very conscious of these boats having to operate in difficult conditions near enemy bases. It was not until very late in the war that the Germans began to modify some of their boats, with similar narrow casings, in order to speed up their dives.

Particular attention was paid to training and safety. Following the loss of numerous boats and personnel to various types of accidents during the inter-war years, the crews of British boats were provided with adequate equipment, and were intensively trained in escape techniques at the main British submarine base, Fort Blockhouse

Table 17: Submarines of occupied powers operating under the control of the Royal Navy

Poland: *Orzel, Wilk, Sokol, Dzik, Jastrzab.*

Norway: *B. 1, Uredd, Ula, Utsira.*

Holland: *K. 9, K. 11, K.12, K. 14, K. 15, O. 9, O. 10, O. 14, O. 15, O. 19, O. 21, O. 22, O.23, O. 24, Zeehond, Zwaardvish, Dolfijn.*

Free France: *Casabianca, Capes, Junon, Le Glorieux, Marsouin, Minerve, Narval* (I), *Ondine, Orion, Pallas, Perle, Protée, Rubis, Surcouf, Curie, Doris, Morse, Narval* (II).

Greece: *Glafkos, Katsonis, Nereus, Papanicolis, Triton, Pipinos, Delfin, Matrozos.*

Yugoslavia: *Nebojsca.*

Italy (co-belligerent units after 8 September 1943): *Alagi, Atropo, Bragadin, Brin, Cagni, Galatea, Giada, Mameli, Jalea, Menotti, Platino, Zoea.*

Table 18: Merchant vessels sunk or damaged by British submarines during the Second World War

Sector:	Ships sunk:		Ships damaged:		Sunk by mines:
	no.	GRT	no.	GRT	
North Sea and Atlantic Ocean	84	270,000	16	69,000	23
Mediterranean	361	1,157,000	86	435,000	12
Indian Ocean and Pacific Ocean	48	97,000	7	14,000	

(HMS *Dolphin*) at the entrance to Portsmouth harbour.

During the war, many boats belonging to Axis-occupied countries or to countries whose governments were in exile in Great Britain, operated under the control of the Royal Navy. These are listed in Table 17.

During the war, British submarines sank 493 merchant ships totalling 1,524,000 GRT and seriously damaged 109 ships (518,000 GRT)

Umbra, which sank the Italian cruiser *Trento*—the most successful exploit by a British submarine against the Italian Navy in the Mediterranean.

The *1500 tonnes* type *Casabianca* leaving a French North African port in 1943.

Unbroken returning home in 1944 from the Mediterranean, where she had particularly distinguished herself.

to which should be added 35 ships destroyed by mines laid by submarines. The division of these results between the three main operational theatres is shown in Table 18.

Results against naval vessels were: 169 ships sunk (6 cruisers, 16 destroyers, 35 submarines and 112 minor units) and 55 seriously damaged (2 battleships, 10 cruisers, 2 destroyers, 6 submarines and 35 minor units) plus 6 vessels (1 destroyer, 3 escorts and 1 submarine) destroyed by mines laid from submarines.[1]

British losses were quite high, totalling 75 boats, of which 68 were lost in action and 7 to various types of accidents, divided between the theatres as follows:

North Sea, Atlantic, Baltic	27 boats (36%)
Mediterranean	45 boats (60%)
Indian Ocean, Pacific Ocean	3 boats (4%)

British submarine losses were high: approximately 35 per cent of the 215 boats that served during the Second World War. In the 75 boats sunk, 3,142 submariners lost their lives and 359 were taken prisoner out of a total of approximately 25,000 men in the underwater fleet which, in 1945, represented about 3 per cent of the entire personnel of the Royal Navy.

Comparing the total number of warships and merchantmen sunk by British submarines to total losses, records show that 9.3 enemy ships were sunk for every boat lost, which represents the highest ratio of any navy during the war, except the US Navy, which reached the exceptional value of 24.6.

During the immediate post-war period, the majority of British boats were placed in reserve, scrapped or ceded to other countries. Only a few T Class and S Class boats remained in service, while construction continued at the end of the war, on those A Class boats in an advanced stage of construction or completion. All were fitted with a schnorkel and many were not fitted with surface armament.

During subsequent years, several T Class and A Class boats were radically modernized along the lines of the American 'Guppy' Programme. Higher capacity batteries were installed, and the streamlining of hulls and conning towers was improved, to obtain higher underwater speeds.

H Class

H.28, H.31, H.32:
Builder: Vickers, Barrow.
Date: 1917–1918/19.
H.33, H.34:
Builder: Cammell Laird, Birkenhead.
Date: 1917–1919.
H.43, H.44:
Builder: Armstrong, Walker.
Date: 1917–1919/20.
H.49, H.50:
Builder: Beardmore, Dalmuir.
Date: 1918–1920.
Normal displacement: 440 tons surfaced; 500 tons submerged.
Dimensions: 171ft 0in x 15ft 9in x 12ft 6in (52.1m x 4.8m x 3.8m).
Machinery: diesel: 2 New London Ship & Engine Co.; electric: 2.
Maximum power: 480hp surfaced; 320hp submerged.
Maximum speed: 13 knots surfaced; 10.5 knots submerged.
Range: 1,900 miles at 8 knots surfaced; 23 miles at 4 knots submerged.
Torpedo tubes: four 21in (533mm) forward; torpedoes: 6.
Guns: two .303in Lewis machine-guns.
Complement: 22.

Single hull, internal ballast tank submarines of Electric Boat (Holland) design. Fuel capacity: 16 tons; maximum operational depth: 100ft (30m). During the First World War, not all Royal Naval submarines were British built. The Admiralty ordered ten boats from the Electric Boat Co. at Groton, built to roughly the same design as the American H Class. At the same time, another ten were ordered from Canadian Vickers at Montreal. The Canadian boats (H.1–H.10) were soon delivered, but the ten American vessels (H.11–H.20) were held up by the US government until that nation declared war on Germany. Two boats (H.11, H.12), then served, as had been intended, with the Royal Navy, but H.14 and H.15 were transferred to the Royal Canadian Navy, and the remaining six were given to Chile as a compensatory gesture for the Chilean warships building in Britain, but taken over at the outbreak of war.

In service, the design proved very successful, and the Italians ordered eight (see Italy) and the Russians, six. Meanwhile, the Royal Navy had been so impressed by them, that another 33 were ordered from British yards. The opportunity was taken to slightly enlarge the design. The 18in (457mm) torpedo tubes were replaced by 21in (533mm), and a more powerful radio set was installed.

By the outbreak of war, only the nine boats listed above were left in service. They had spent most of the inter-war years training submarine crews and anti-submarine ships, and for most of the war, this was still their task. During the first year of the war, however, there were not yet enough modern submarines, and so the small and old H boats were pressed into operational service. One (H.49) was lost to the enemy; H.31 was lost through unknown causes. Four of the remainder were sold for scrapping late in 1944, the other three were scrapped in 1945. The class could carry a 3in (76mm) gun, but these had been removed, early in the inter-war period.

H. 44.

L Class

L.23, L.26, L.27.
Builder: Vickers, Barrow (completed at Chatham, Devonport and Sheerness Dockyards respectively).
Date: 1917–1924/26.
Normal displacement: 890 tons surfaced; 1,080 tons submerged.
Dimensions: 238ft 6in x 23ft 6in x 11ft 2in (72.7m x 7.2m x 3.4m).
Machinery: diesel: 2 Vickers; electric: 2.
Maximum power: 2,400hp surfaced; 1,600hp submerged.
Maximum speed: 17.5 knots surfaced; 10.5 knots submerged.
Range: 3,800 miles at 10 knots surfaced; 75 miles at 4 knots submerged.
Torpedo tubes: four 21in (533mm) forward; torpedoes: 8.
Guns: one 4in (102mm); two .303in Lewis machine-guns.
Complement: 35.

Single hull, saddle tank submarines, they were basically improved developments of the excellent and famous *E* Class, direct descendants of the earliest overseas patrol submarines of the *D* Class. Fuel capacity: 76 tons.

The first group of these submarines (*L.1–L.8*) were armed with six 18in (457mm) torpedo tubes, two of which were on the beam. The next series (*L.9–L–12, L.14–L.36*), to which all three surviving boats belonged, were slightly lengthened, and were fitted with 21in (533mm) torpedo tubes. Some of this Class had six tubes: others had four, and were minelayers with vertical tubes on the German pattern. The 4in (102mm) gun was carried in an unusual position, high in the conning tower. The final boats of the Class (*L.50–L.74*) had two guns instead of one.

The *L* Class was a very successful and admired design, but by 1939 it had become obsolete and most of its boats had been scrapped. The three survivors spent about a year on operational patrols and were then taken over for training. L.26 was scrapped in 1945, and *L.27* was sunk as a target during the same year. In 1946, the remaining boat foundered on her way to the shipbreakers.

L.26 minus her 4in (102mm) deck gun which was used for training.

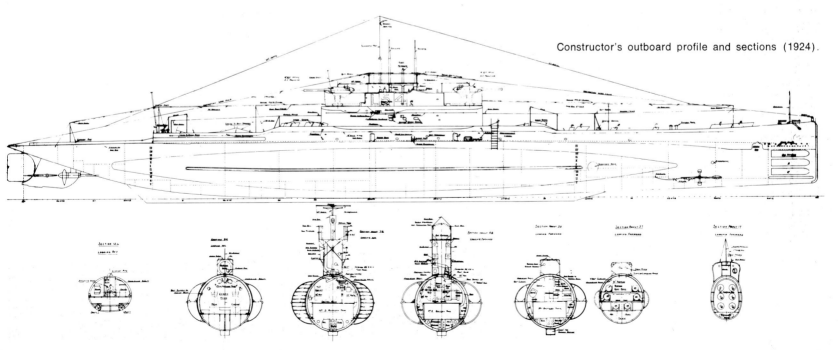

Constructor's outboard profile and sections (1924).

O Class

Group 1.
Oberon ex-*O.1*:
Builder: Chatham Dockyard.
Date: 1924–1927.
Otway ex-*OA.2*, *Oxley* ex-*OA.1*:
Builder: Vickers Armstrong, Barrow.
Date: 1925–1927/27.

Group 2.
Odin:
Builder: Chatham Dockyard.
Date: 1927–1929.
Olympus, Orpheus:
Builder: Beardmore, Glasgow.
Date: 1927–1930.
Osiris, Oswald, Otus.
Builder: Vickers Armstrong, Barrow.
Date: 1927–1929/29.

Normal displacement:
Oberon: 1,490 tons surfaced; 1,892 tons submerged.
Group 1: 1,636 tons surfaced; 1,870 tons submerged.
Group 2: 1,784 tons surfaced; 2,038 tons submerged.

Dimensions:
Oberon: 269ft 8in x 28ft 0in x 13ft 2in (83.4m x 8.5m x 4.6m).
Group 1: 275ft 0in x 27ft 7in x 13ft 3in (84.5m x 8.3m x 4.6m).
Group 2: 283ft 6in x 29ft 10in x 13ft 8in (86m x 9.1m x 4.8m).
Machinery:
Group 1: diesel: 2 Vickers; electric: 2.
Group 2: diesel: 2 Admiralty; electric: 2.
Maximum power:
Oberon: 2,950hp surfaced; 1,350hp submerged.
Group 1: 3,000hp surfaced; 1,350hp submerged.
Group 2: 4,400hp surfaced; 1,320hp submerged.
Maximum speed:
Group 1: 15 knots surfaced; 9 knots submerged.
Group 2: 17.5 knots surfaced; 9 knots submerged.

Range:
Oberon: 5,000 miles at 9.5 knots surfaced; 60 miles at 4 knots submerged.
Group 1: 4,560 miles at 10.3 knots surfaced; 60 miles at 4 knots submerged.
Group 2: 5,180 miles at 11.4 knots surfaced; 50 miles at 4 knots submerged.
Torpedo tubes: eight 21in (533mm); 6 forward, 2 aft; torpedoes: 16; Group 2, 14.
Guns: one 4in (102mm); two 0.303in Lewis machine-guns.
Mines: Group 2 could carry 18 mines instead of torpedoes.
Complement: 56.

Ocean-going saddle tank type submarines, derived from the *L* Class, which was designed during the First World War. Normal fuel load: 160 tons (*Oberon*), 166 tons (Group 1), 170 tons (Group 2); maximum operational depth: 230ft (70m): designed maximum was 500ft (155m).

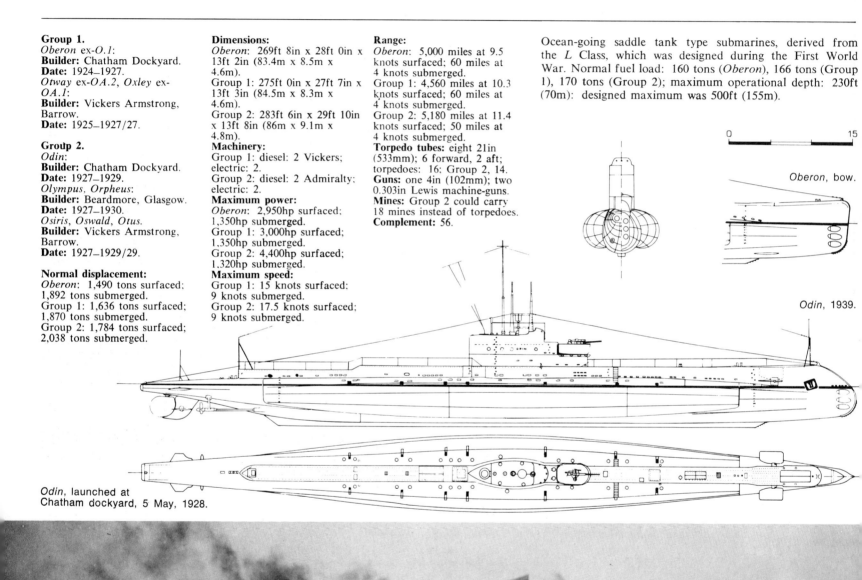

0   15

Oberon, bow.

Odin, 1939.

Odin, launched at Chatham dockyard, 5 May, 1928.

The ending of the Anglo-Japanese Treaty of Alliance in 1922, led the Royal Navy to order a new type of submarine, of a more advanced design, for long-range operations and possible employment in the Far East. The prototype, *Oberon* (originally *O.1*) was included in the 1923 Programme, and was launched at Chatham Dockyard on 24 September 1926.

Compared to the *L* Class the new submarines were longer by approximately 32ft (10m) and broader by 3ft (1m). Top speed was lowered by two knots, but the range was considerably greater, and the number of torpedo tubes and torpedoes was doubled.

Vickers Armstrong built two similar boats at the same time as *Oberon* for the Australian Navy (*AO.1* and *AO.2*, later, *Oxley* and *Otway*). After about three years service, they were transferred to the Royal Navy, following budget cuts. The two Australian boats were slightly larger, but had no significant differences from the prototype, other than a different bow shape, which can be seen in the drawings and photographs.

Oberon was the first Royal Naval submarine to have asdic fitted while building.

In the 1926 Programme, it was decided to build another six boats of the *O* Class and these were laid down during the following year. The second group did not differ greatly from the first: they were an improvement of the Australian boats, with a slight increase in displacement, dimensions and speed, thanks to the installation of more powerful diesel engines. Surface range was also increased.

The design changes to the second group of boats did not eliminate the shortcomings of this type of vessel; lack of submerged manoeuvrability and poor buoyancy factor. These stemmed from the considerable increase in displacement without a corresponding increase in size. The structural strengthening, and the stowage of almost 200 tons of fuel had so weighed down the boats, that diving became dangerously rapid and difficult to control.

For these reasons, and because of difficulties caused by the fuel tanks being located outside the pressure hull, the boats of the Class were considered mediocre performers and, already before the war, their replacement had been scheduled within a short time. Three units, very similar to the *O* Class, were built for Chile by the Vickers Armstrong yard at Barrow, between 1927 and 1929.

At the outbreak of war, the nine *O* Class boats in service, were stationed in the Mediterranean (3 units), North Sea (1 unit), Atlantic (1 unit) and Far East (4 units). Initially, they were employed in combat operations and their stations underwent several changes. Later, they were used for training purposes. Between 1941 and 1942, *Otus* was used to carry supplies to Malta. Five boats were lost in action. *Oxley* was sunk by mistake by the British submarine *Triton* on 10 September 1939; the first boat lost by the Royal Navy during the Second World War. The remaining four boats were scrapped between 1945 and 1946.

Fates

date:	location:	boat:	cause (see page 7):
1939	North Sea	*Oxley*	e
1940	Mediterranean	*Odin, Orpheus, Oswald*	n
1942	Mediterranean	*Olympus*	m
1945	—	*Oberon, Otway, Osiris, Otus*	r

Below:
Oberon, O Class prototype.
Centre:
Otway (*O* Class, first group).
Bottom,
Oswald (*O* Class, second group). Note the position of the forward rudder planes compared to the boats of the first group.

P/R Classes

Parthian:
Builder: Chatham Dockyard.
Date: 1928–1931.

Perseus, Poseidon, Proteus, Pandora ex-*Python*:
Builder: Vickers-Armstrong, Barrow.
Date: 1928–1930/30.

Phoenix:
Builder: Cammell Laird, Birkenhead.
Date: 1928–1931.

Rainbow:
Builder: Chatham Dockyard.
Date: 1929–1932.

Regent, Regulus, Rover.
Builder: Vickers-Armstrong, Barrow.
Date: 1929–1930/31.

Normal displacement:
P Class: 1,775 tons surfaced; 2,040 tons submerged.
R Class 1,772 tons surfaced; 2,030 tons submerged.
Dimensions:
P Class: 289ft 2in x 29ft 10in x 13ft 8in (88.8m x 9.1m x 4.2m).
R Class: 287ft 2in x 29ft 10in x 13ft 10in (87.5m x 9.1m x 4.2m).
Machinery: diesel: 2; electric: 2.
Maximum power: 4,400hp surfaced; 1,320hp submerged.
Maximum speed: 17.5 knots surfaced; 9 knots submerged.
P Class: 7,050 miles at 9.2 knots surfaced; 62 miles at 4 knots submerged.
Range:
P Class: 7,050 miles at 9.2 knots surfaced; 62 miles at 4 knots submerged.
R Class: 7,050 miles at 9.2 knots surfaced; 70 miles at 4 knots submerged.
Torpedo tubes: eight 21in (533mm); 6 forward, 2 aft; topedoes: 14.
Guns: one 4in (102mm) 40-cal; two 0.303in Lewis machine-guns.
Mines: 18 (alternative load).
Complement: 56.

PLAN Nº 427.

R Class inboard profile (as taken from constructor's plans).

H. M. S. "REGENT," "REGULUS" & "ROVER."

GENERAL ARRANGEMENT.

PORT ELEVATION.

SCALE ⅛ INCH = ONE FOOT.

MODIFIED IN RED AT CHATHAM 27-6-31 FOR "REGULUS" ONLY, VIN A.L.D. 6632/31. 2.6.31.

Parthian.

Regent on patrol. Note the position of the deck gun compared to the P Class.

P Class conning tower.

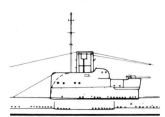

Saddle tank ocean-going submarines, derived from the *O* Class. Normal fuel load: 160 tons (*P*), 156 tons (*R*); maximum operational depth: 300ft (95m): designed maximum was 500ft (155m).

While the second group of the *O* Class were still under construction, the building of another six similar units (*P* Class) was decided upon for the 1927 Programme. Their original design suffered from the same defects that appeared in *Oberon* and several changes were introduced. Six boats (*P* Class) were laid down in 1928, and as part of that year's Programme, it was decided

The appearance of the *P* and *R* Classes differed from the *O* Class boats in the shape of the bow, which was similar to that of *Oberon*. The *R* Class differed from the *P* Class in that the 4in (102mm) 40-cal deck gun was lower, and lacked the shield which had been introduced in the *P* Class.

Between 1941 and 1942, two units, *Pandora* and *Parthian* were modified for employment as transport submarines for Malta. To make room for cargo, spare torpedoes were not carried, and one of the two battery banks was eliminated: numerous ballast tanks were adapted to carry petrol, as were some of the fuel and fresh water tanks. Without undergoing any alterations, *Regent* was also used to supply Malta during the same period. Wartime employment of the boats of this Class followed almost the same path as those of the *O* Class, and the survivors ended the war as training boats.

Poseidon was lost in a collision with a merchant ship on 9 June 1931. During the war, seven boats were lost, all

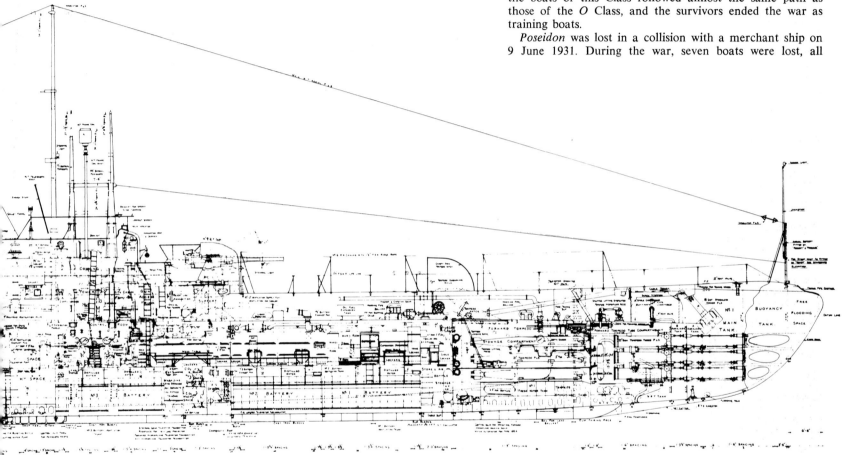

R Class conning tower.

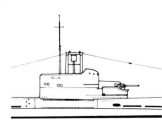

to build a further series of six (*R* Class) of which, only four units were laid down in 1929. The orders for *Royalist* and *Rupert* which had already been given to Beardmore at Dalmuir and Cammell Laird of Birkenhead, were cancelled. This cancellation was brought about largely through economic and political reasons, though the mediocre results displayed by the second group of the *O* Class must have contributed to the decision. The same observations made about the O Class are valid for the P and R Classes: despite the modifications they also turned out to be difficult to manoeuvre while submerged, and were somewhat unsafe.

in the Mediterranean. The only two survivors were broken up in 1946.

Fates

date:	location:	boat:	cause (see page 7):
1940	Mediterranean	*Phoenix*	n
		Rainbow	s
		Regulus	uc
1941	Mediterranean	*Perseus*	s
1942	Mediterranean	*Pandora*	b
1943	Mediterranean	*Parthian, Regent*	m
1946	—	*Proteus, Rover*	r

River (Thames) Class

Thames, Severn, Clyde.
Builder: Vickers-Armstrong, Barrow.
Date: 1931–1932/35.
Normal displacement: 2,165 tons surfaced; 2,680 tons submerged.
Dimensions: 344ft 10in x 28ft 2in x 15ft 9in (105.1m x 8.6m x 4.8m); *Thames* 15ft (4.6m).
Machinery: diesel: 2 Admiralty; electric: 2.
Maximum power: 10,000hp surfaced; 2,500hp submerged.
Maximum speed: 22.25 knots surfaced; 10 knots submerged; *Thames:* 21.5 knots surfaced; 10 knots submerged.
Range: 6,260 miles at 12.4 knots surfaced, 19,900 miles at 5 knots surfaced; 115 miles at 4 knots submerged.
Torpedo tubes: six 21in (533m) forward; torpedoes: 14.
Guns: one 4in (102mm) 40-cal; two 0.303in Lewis machine-guns.
Mines: 12 (alternative load).
Complement: 61.

Double hull ocean-going boats, designed for employment as Fleet submarines. Normal fuel load: 202 tons; maximum operational depth: 200ft (60m): designed maximum was 300ft (95m).

With the 1929 Programme, the Royal Navy decided to build a new class of squadron submarines which were to have replaced the, by now, obsolete *K* Class. In order to operate in direct conjunction with battleships, a high surface speed of at least 20 knots was required. For many reasons (including speed of diving, and the series of disasters to the *K* Class) the Royal Navy did not wish to use steam propulsion machinery, which would have furnished the necessary power, but opted instead for a large type of boat, with a high-powered diesel engine, specially developed for the purpose. This plant consisted of two 10 cylinder, 5,000hp diesels, and was very large: the stern torpedo tubes had to be eliminated from the design, to make room for it.

The first unit of this, the *River* Class, was launched on 26 January 1932 and was commissioned at the end of the year. On trial, the prototype *Thames,* reached a maximum speed of 21.5 knots which for the period, represented an absolute record for diesel-powered boats, broken only by a few Japanese boats.

This outstanding speed, however, did not guarantee that the boats would be able to operate with large surface warships, because the speed of the latter had also continued to increase: in the early thirties, battleships were being built with a designed speed of thirty knots. This outclassed the submarines of the day, and the Royal Navy abandoned the concept of Fleet submarines.

Nevertheless, *Thames* was followed by two more boats, *Clyde* and *Severn.* Authorized in the 1931 and 1932 Estimates, they were laid down in 1934 and entered service in the following year. They differed slightly from the prototype and were about one knot faster.

The *River* Class boats were quite successful despite the operational limitations imposed by their large size (which reduced manoeuvrability) and the low ratio of armament to displacement. Everything had been sacrificed for the high surface speed essential for Fleet submarines, and the location of the large fuel load in tanks outside the pressure hull gave rise to several problems, including the relatively frequent loss of diesel fuel.

At the outbreak of war, *Thames* was stationed in home waters, and *Clyde* and *Severn* were en route to Freetown where the 7th Submarine Flotilla was being organized. Shortly afterwards, however, they returned to England and operated from British bases until 1941. During this period, *Clyde* seriously damaged the German battlecruiser *Gneisenau* off the Norwegian coast on 20 July 1940. *Thames* was mined off Norway in June 1940. In 1941, the other two boats were transferred to the Mediterranean where, despite their large size which proved fatal to many boats of the *O, P* and *R* Classes, they operated from Gibraltar with a certain degree of success.

In 1944, *Severn* and *Clyde* were transferred to the Far East where their excellent range and surface speed could be better utilized. Only *Severn* could be used for operations, however, as *Clyde* was precluded by her bad state of repair.

At the end of the war, after *Severn* had been partially dismantled for spares at Trincomalee, she was broken up in Ceylon. *Clyde* was broken up in South Africa.

Fates			cause
date:	location:	boat:	(see page 7):
1940	North Sea	*Thames*	m
1946	—	*Severn, Clyde*	r

Thames under way.

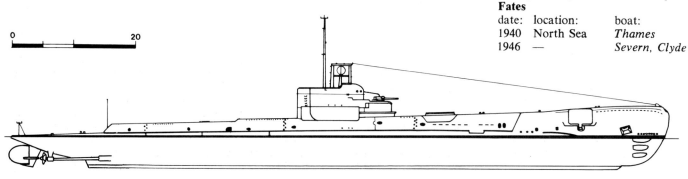

0   20

Porpoise Class

Porpoise, Narwhal, Rorqual:
Builder: Vickers-Armstrong, Barrow.
Date: 1931–1933/37.
Grampus, Seal:
Builder: Chatham Dockyard.
Date: 1934–1937/39.
Cachalot.
Builder: Scotts, Greenock.
Date: 1936–1938.
Normal displacement: 1,810 tons surfaced; 2,157 tons submerged;
Porpoise; 1,782 tons surfaced; 2,053 tons submerged.
Dimensions: 288ft 0in x 29ft 10in x 13ft 9in (89.1m x 7.7m x 5.1m).
Machinery: diesel: 2; electric 2.
Maximum power: 3,300hp surfaced; 1,630hp submerged.
Maximum speed: 15.75 knots surfaced; 8.75 knots submerged;
Porpoise 15 knots surfaced; 8.75 knots submerged.
Range: 5.880 miles at 9.3 knots surfaced; 64 miles at 4 knots submerged;
Porpoise 6,300 miles at 10.6 knots surfaced; 64 miles at 4 knots submerged.
Torpedo tubes: six 21in (533mm) forward; torpedoes: 12.
Guns: one 4in (102mm) 40-cal; two 0.303in Lewis machine-guns.
Mines: 50.
Complement: 59.

Porpoise.

Porpoise Class excluding Porpoise.

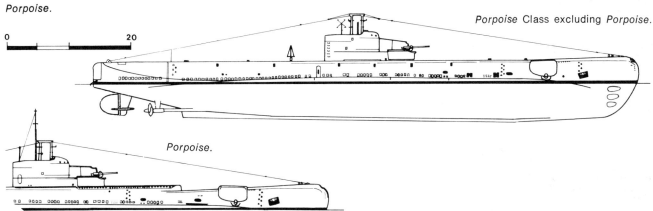

Porpoise.

Double hull minelaying submarines. Normal fuel load: 150 tons; maximum operational depth: 220ft (66m): designed maximum was 300ft (95m).

This class of excellent minelaying boats stemmed from the experience gained by the Royal Navy in the twenties, when one of the large submarine-monitors of the *M* Class, *M.3*, was transformed into an experimental minelayer. The system adopted for laying mines was very similar to that used by surface vessels. The mines were not contained in more or less vertical tubes, as in most minelaying boats of the period, but in a long, high casing above the pressure hull. The casing was fitted on a rail which rested on the pressure hull, and the mines were winched along the rail to the stern by a chain mechanism. The mines were of the standard British Mk XVI self-mooring type, and left the boat through a hatch in the stern. The system was very simple, and minelaying operations were quite safe and easy, though carrying the mines outside the pressure hull could be hazardous in certain circumstances.

Porpoise, the first of the Class, was authorized under the 1930 Estimates and was launched on 30 August 1932.

Her design was influenced by the contemporaneous *Thames* Class boats with which, she had many technical aspects in common. Between 1933 and 1939, *Porpoise* was followed by another five boats, differing from the prototype in that their dimensions and mine capacity were increased. In *Porpoise*, the casing for the mines ended about 60ft (19m) from the bow: on the other units, it ran clear from stem to stern. With a full load of 50 mines, the displacement of these boats reached 1,810 tons surfaced; 2,155 tons submerged.

The 1940 Emergency Programme called for the construction of another three vessels of the same type, at Scotts shipyard at Greenock, but the contract was cancelled in September 1941, because a special type of mine—which could be launched through the 21in (533mm) torpedo tubes—had been developed. This enabled all normal attack submarines to be used as minelayers, as in the German and American Navies. During the war, however, attack submarines were rarely used for minelaying, which remained almost exclusively the task of the *Porpoise* Class boats. They laid a total of 2,599 mines, divided among

The minelayer *Rorqual* at Malta; a *T Class* boat is moored in the foreground.

the various boats as follows: *Grampus* 50; *Seal* 50; *Cachalot* 300; *Narwhal* 450; *Porpoise* 465; *Rorqual* 1,284.

At the beginning of the war, *Cachalot* and *Narwhal* were stationed in the Mediterranean; *Rorqual* was in China and *Seal* and *Grampus* were en route to join her: only *Porpoise* was operating in home waters.

Seal and *Narwhal* were ordered to return immediately for employment in the North Sea, and *Rorqual* and *Grampus* were subsequently sent to the Mediterranean. The first casualty was *Seal*. Seriously damaged by a mine while laying an offensive barrier in the Kattegat, she was captured and after repair, was commissioned in the *Kriegsmarine* as *UB*. Between 1940 and 1943, the various boats were employed, primarily in the North Sea and Mediterranean, where they also contributed to the relief of Malta between 1941 and 1942. In 1944, the two boats still in service, *Rorqual* and *Porpoise* were sent to the Far East: *Porpoise* was lost and *Rorqual* remained there until the end of the war.

Fates

date:	location:	boat:	cause (see page 7):
1940	North Sea	*Seal*	c
		Narwhal	uc
	Mediterranean	*Grampus*	n
1941	Mediterranean	*Cachalot*	n
1945	Pacific	*Porpoise*	a
1946	—	*Rorqual*	r

S Class

Group 1 (4 units).
Sturgeon, Swordfish, Seahorse, Starfish:
Builder: Chatham Dockyard.
Date: 1930–1932/33.

Group 2 (8 units).
Sealion, Salmon, Spearfish:
Builder: Cammell Laird, Birkenhead.
Date: 1933–1934/36.

Shark, Snapper, Sunfish, Sterlet:
Builder: Chatham Dockyard.
Date: 1933–1934/38.

Seawolf:
Builder: Scotts, Greenock.
Date: 1934–1936.

Group 3 (51 units).
Safari ex-*P.211*, ex-*P.61*, *Sahib* ex-*P.212*, ex-*P.62*, *Saracen* ex-*P.213*, ex-*P.63*:
Builder: Cammell Laird, Birkenhead.
Date: 1940–1942/42.

Satyr ex-*P.214*, ex-*P.64*, *Sceptre* ex-*P.215*, ex-*P.65*:
Builder: Scotts, Greenock.
Date: 1941–1942/43.

Sea Dog ex-*P.216*, ex-*P.66*, *Sibyl* ex-*P.217*, ex-*P.67*, *Sea Nymph* ex-*P.225*:
Builder: Cammell Laird, Birkenhead.
Date: 1941–1942/43.

Sea Rover ex-*P.218*, ex-*P.68*, *Sirdar* ex-*P.226*, *Spiteful* ex-*P.227*:
Builder: Scotts, Greenock.
Date: 1941–1943/43.

Seraph ex-*P.219*, ex-*P.69*, *Shakespeare* ex-*P.221*, ex-*P.71*, *P.222* ex-*P.72*:
Builder: Vickers-Armstrong, Barrow.
Date: 1940–1942/42.

Splendid ex-*P.228*, *Sportsman* ex-*P.229*:
Builder: Chatham Dockyard.
Date: 1941–1942/42.

Stoic ex-*P.231*, *Stonehenge* ex-*P.232*, *Storm* ex-*P.233*, *Stratagem* ex-*P.234*, *Stubborn* ex-*P.238*, *Surf* ex-*P.239*, *Syrtis, Shalimar, Spirit, Statesman*:
Builder: Cammell Laird, Birkenhead.
Date: 1942–1943/44.

Strongbow ex-*P.235*, *Spark* ex-*P.236*, *Scythian* ex-*P.237*, *Scotsman**, *Sea Devil**:
Builder: Scotts, Greenock.
Date: 1943–1944/45.

Shalimar:
Builder: Chatham Dockyard.
Date: 1942–1943.
Sturdy, Stygian, Subtle*, *Supreme**, *Seascout**, *Selene**, *Saga**, *Scorcher**, *Sidon**, *Sleuth**, *Solent**, *Spearhead**, *Springer**, *Spur**, *Sanguine**:
Builder: Cammell Laird, Birkenhead.
Date: 1943–1943/45.

Senescal*, *Sentinel**:
Builder: Scotts, Greenock.
Date: 1943–1945/45.

Units cancelled in 1945:
Sea Robin, Sprightly, Surface, Surge.
Builder: Cammell Laird, Birkenhead.

Normal displacement:
Group 1: 737 tons surfaced; 927 tons submerged.
Group 2: 768 tons surfaced; 960 tons submerged.
Group 3: 814–872 tons surfaced; 990 tons submerged.
Dimensions:
Group 1: 202ft 6in x 24ft 0in x 10ft 6in (61.7m x 7.3m x 3.2m).
Group 2: 208ft 8in x 24ft 0in x 10ft 6in (63.6m x 7.3m x 3.2m).
Group 3: 217ft 0in x 23ft 6in x 11ft 0in (66.1m x 7.2m x 3.4m).
Machinery:
Group 1: diesel: 2 Admiralty; electric: 2.
Group 2: diesel: 2 Admiralty; electric: 2.
Group 3: diesel: 2 Admiralty or Scott; electric: 2 General Electric or Metrovick.

Maximum power:
Group 1: 1,550hp surfaced; 1,300hp submerged.
Group 2: 1,550hp surfaced; 1,300hp submerged.
Sunfish: 1,900hp surfaced; 1,300hp submerged.
Group 3: 1,900hp surfaced; 1,300hp submerged.
Maximum speed:
Group 1: 13.75 knots surfaced; 10 knots submerged.
Group 2: 13.75 knots surfaced; 10 knots submerged.
Sunfish: 15 knots surfaced; 10 knots submerged.
Group 3: 15 knots surfaced; 10 knots submerged.
Range:
Group 1: 3,800 miles at 10 knots surfaced;
Group 2: 6,000 miles at 10 knots surfaced;
Group 3:
Torpedo tubes: six 21in (533mm) forward; torpedoes: 12.
Guns: one 3in (76mm) 50-cal.
Complement: Group 1, 36; Group 2, 39; Group 3, 48.

Medium range saddle tank submarines. Normal fuel load: 38 tons (Group 1), 38–40 tons (Group 2), 48, later 72, then 91–98 tons (Group 3); maximum operational depth: 300ft (95m) (Groups 1 & 2), 350ft (110m) (Group 3); minimum crash-dive time: approximately 25–30 seconds.

In 1930, the Royal Navy, in accordance with the plan to modernize the submarine force, decided to build a new type of boat, suitable for employment in the North Sea and restricted waters such as the Mediterranean. They were to replace the, by now, obsolete *H Class*. Staff requirements called for a boat of medium size, simple to build and operate, and with surface speed, range and armament, superior to those of the *H* Class, but retaining the latter's excellent handling, diving time and underwater manoeuvrability. The resulting *S* Class was among the most successful, and certainly was the largest class, ever built for the Royal Navy. Sixty-three boats were built and the Class remained in service for more than fifteen years. The first two boats were authorized under the 1929

Programme, and these were followed between 1930 and 1935 by another ten. The last eight boats were slightly larger than the first four (*Swordfish, Sturgeon, Seahorse* and *Starfish*) and differed from them in appearance, because of an extension forward of the conning tower. The 3in (76mm) deck gun, on a 'disappearing' mount, withdrew into the extension, which also contained a small boat. This method of mounting the deck gun was eliminated soon after entry into service, and was replaced by a

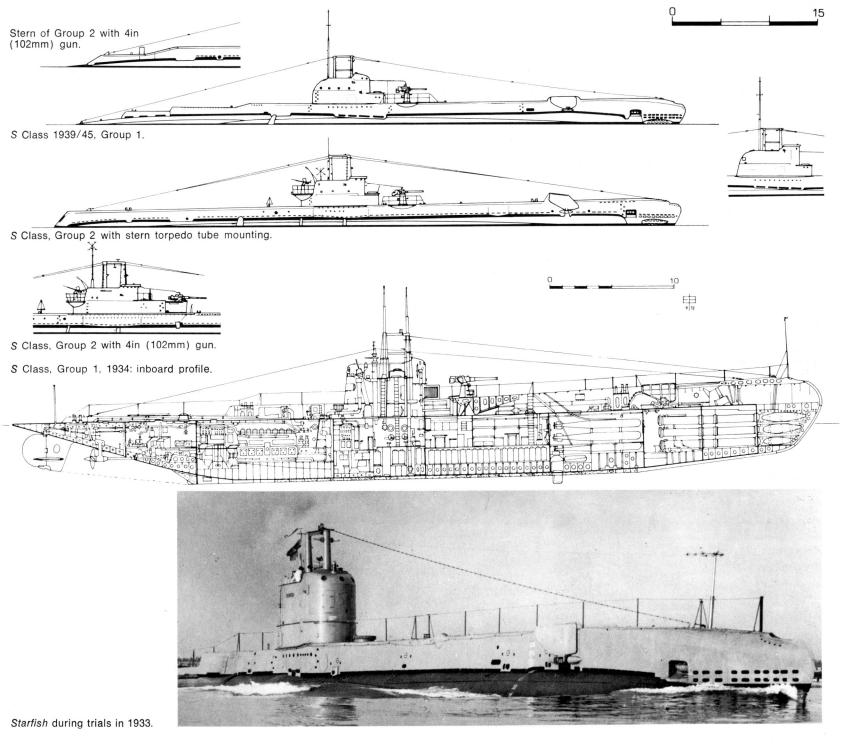

Stern of Group 2 with 4in (102mm) gun.

S Class 1939/45, Group 1.

S Class, Group 2 with stern torpedo tube mounting.

S Class, Group 2 with 4in (102mm) gun.

S Class, Group 1, 1934: inboard profile.

Starfish during trials in 1933.

normal fixed deck mount, as was fitted from the start in the rest of the Class. At the same time, the extension was reduced in length and became the small ammunition store which had been fitted, from the start, in all other boats.

On the outbreak of war, construction was ordered of a first group of another five boats of the S Class, followed by another thirteen in 1940, fifteen in 1941, twelve in 1942 and nine in 1943. Four of the latter were subsequently cancelled.

This second group did not differ markedly from the first group, but they were larger and had increased power and speed. At first, only minor modifications were made (suggested by experience gained from the first group of boats); subsequently, in the light of war experience, more substantial changes were introduced in armament and internal arrangements. Hull construction changed from partial to totally welded, and the assembly of pre-fabricated units was speeded up. Structural strength was increased.

After the first five units of the War Programme had been commissioned (*Safari, Sahib, Saracen, Satyr* and *Sceptre*), it was decided to install an external stern torpedo tube. This brought the number of tubes up to seven, and the number of available torpedoes to thirteen. In many boats, in place of or in addition to the .303 machine-guns, which could be removed at the time of diving, a 20mm Oerlikon cannon was mounted on a platform aft of the periscopes. In eighteen boats, all built during the final years of the war and intended to operate mainly in the Far East, the 3in (76mm) 50-cal deck gun was replaced by a 4in (102mm) 40-cal gun, mounted inside a low breastwork, forward of the conning tower.

In the boats armed with the 4in (102mm) gun, the external stern torpedo tube was eliminated, from weight considerations. The stern tube was mounted in several boats of the second group which had not originally been fitted with it.

To achieve a greater range for the boats bound for the Far East, several sections of the ballast tanks were adapted for use as fuel tanks (in the S Class, the fuel tanks were inside the hull), and the fuel load was increased to a maximum of 91–98 tons. Stores, especially food and ammunition were increased and were stowed in any available space; a small ammunition locker was placed under the table in the officers' quarters.

By these measures, the small S Class boats managed to achieve long patrol times in operational areas; the record of 48 days was set by *Sirdar*. Fitted with asdic from 1932, between 1941 and 1942, the S Class boats began to mount the first radar sets for surface as well as air search. The Class were among the most successful conventional submarines of the Second World War. The combination of their qualities—none of which, in itself was above average—together with the reliability of their equipment and the great ease of operation and maintenance, made them very effective and safe.

Left, top to bottom: *Sturgeon* surfacing; *Saracen* flying the 'Jolly Roger'; *Storm*; and *Satyr*.
Opposite page. Top left: *Sportsman*. Top right: *Seawolf*. Centre left: *Sahib* in May 1942, after mounting of external stern torpedo tubes. Centre right: *Solent*, armed with a 4in (102mm) deck gun and minus the stern torpedo tubes. Bottom: *Seahorse* and *Starfish* alongside the old destroyer Mackay, which was acting as tender to the 2nd Submarine Flotilla at Portland in May 1939.

At the beginning of the war, four of the *S* Class were serving in the Mediterranean and eight, in home waters. Later, most of the first and second groups were concentrated in the North Sea, but were again divided between the Mediterranean and home waters when Italy entered the war in June 1940. During this period, the boats were very active, and major successes were achieved by *Salmon* which seriously damaged the light cruisers *Leipzig* and *Nürnberg* in one attack off Jutland on 13 September 1939; and by *Spearfish* which damaged the heavy cruiser *Lützow* (ex pocket battleship *Deutschland*) in the Kattegat on 11 April 1940. Losses were rather heavy: in the North Sea alone, six of the Class were lost in 1940.

The boats of the third group, built under the War Programmes, began to enter service in 1942 and were stationed mainly in home waters and the Far East. The *S* Class were particularly successful against submarines. From 1939 to 1945, six submarines (*Salmon, Saracen, Sahib, Sickle, Shakespeare* and *Satyr*) sank seven German and Italian boats (*U 36, U 335, Granito, U 301, U 303, Velella, U 987*).

Seventeen boats were lost during the war: nine in the North Sea and the Atlantic, six in the Mediterranean and two in the Pacific and Indian Oceans. One boat was ceded to the Dutch Navy in 1943 and one to the Soviet Navy in 1944. The construction of four boats was suspended at the end of the war, and the majority of those in service were placed in reserve. Many were subsequently scrapped, a number were sold or given to other navies, and others, stripped of armament and with a modified conning tower, were used for a time in anti-submarine training.

Fates

date:	location:	boat:	cause (see page 7):
1940	North Sea	*Swordfish*	uc
		Salmon	m
		Spearfish	s
		Seahorse, Starfish, Shark, Sterlet	n
1941	Atlantic	*Snapper*	uc
1942	Mediterranean	*P.222*	n
1943	Mediterranean	*Sahib, Saracen, Splendid*	n
		Simoon	uc
	—	*Sturgeon* (Dutch *Zeehond*)	r
1944	Mediterranean	*Sickle*	m
	Indian Ocean	*Stonehenge*	uc
	Pacific	*Stratagem*	n
	North Sea	*Syrtis*	m
	—	*Sunfish* (Soviet *V.1*)	r
1945	—	*Sealion, Seawolf*	r
1946–1952		*Safari, Satyr, Sceptre, Seadog, Searover, Sea Nymph, Shakespeare, Sybil, Spiteful, Sportsman, Stoic, Storm, Strongbow, Spark, Scythian, Stubborn, Surf, Shalimar, Spirit, Statesman, Stygian, Supreme, Saga, Spearhead, Spur*	r

Left: two views of *Syrtis* in April 1943. (Note that the censor has seen fit to obliterate the tug in the lower photograph, but has omitted to paint out its funnel.)

T Class

Group 1 (22 units).
Triton, Triumph, Thistle, Triad, Truant, Tetrarch, Trusty, Turbulent:
Builder: Vickers-Armstrong, Barrow.
Date: 1936–1938/41.

Thunderbolt ex-*Thetis*, *Trident, Taku, Talisman, Tempest, Thorn, Thrasher*:
Builder: Cammell Laird, Birkenhead.
Date: 1936–1939/41.

Tribune, Tarpon, Tuna, Traveller, Trooper:
Builder: Scotts, Greenock.
Date: 1937–1939/42.

Tigris, Torbay:
Builder: Chatham Dockyard.
Date: 1938–1940/40.

Group 2 (31 units + 2).
P.311 ex-*Tutankhamen*, ex-*P.91, Tactician* ex-*P.314*, ex-*P.94, Taurus* ex-*P.313*, ex-*P.93, Templar* ex-*P.316* ex-*P.96, Trespasser* ex-*P.312*, ex-*P.92, Truculent* ex-*P.315*, ex-*P.95*:
Builder: Vickers-Armstrong, Barrow.
Date: 1940–1942/42.

Thule ex-*P.325, Tudor* ex-*P.326*:
Builder: Devonport Dockyard.
Date: 1941–1944/44.

Tireless ex-*P.327, Token* ex-*P.328*:
Builder: Portsmouth Dockyard
Date: 1941–1945/45.

Talent (I) ex-*P.322, Tally-Ho* ex-*P.317*, ex-*P.97, Tantalus* ex-*P.318*, ex-*P.98, Tantivy* ex-*P.319*, ex-*P.99, Telemachus* ex-*P.321, Terrapin* ex-*P.323, Thorough* ex-*P.324, Tiptoe*:
Builder: Vickers-Armstrong, various yards.
Date: 1942–1943/44.

Totem, Truncheon:
Builder: Devonport Dockyard.
Date: 1942–1943/44.

Tradewind ex-*P.329, Trenchant, Turpin, Thermopylae*:
Builder: Chatham Dockyard.
Date: 1942–1944/45.

Trump, Taciturn, Tapir, Tarn, Tasman (from 1945), *Talent* (III), *Teredo*:
Builder: Vickers-Armstrong, various yards.
Date: 1942–1944/46.

Tabard:
Builder: Scotts, Greenock.
Date: 1944–1946.

Thor, Tiara.
Builder: Portsmouth Dockyard.
Date: 1944–

Units cancelled in 1945: *Talent* (II), *Theban, Threat* (Vickers-Armstrong), *Typhoon* and three boats, names for which had not been assigned.

Normal displacement:
Triton: 1,330 tons surfaced; 1,585 tons submerged.
Group 1: 1,326–7 tons surfaced; 1,523–1,575 tons submerged.
Group 2: 1,321–1,422 tons surfaced; 1,571 tons submerged.
Dimensions:
Group 1: 275ft 0in x 26ft 7in x 12ft 0in (83.6m x 8.1m x 3.6m).
Triton: 277ft 3in x 26ft 7in x 12ft 0in (84.2m x 8.1m x 3.6m).
Group 2: 273ft 6in x 26ft 6in x 12ft 0in–15ft 3in (83.1m x 8.1m x 4.5m–4.8m).
Machinery: diesel: 2 Admiralty, Vickers, Sulzer or MAN; electric: 2 L. Scotts.
Maximum power: 2,500hp surfaced; 1,450hp submerged.
Maximum speed: 15.25 knots surfaced; 9 knots submerged.
Range:
Group 1: 8,000 miles at 10 knots surfaced.
Group 2: 8,000–11,000 miles at 10 knots surfaced.
Torpedo tubes:
Group 1: ten 21in (533mm); 8 forward (2 external); 2 midships (external); torpedoes: 16.
Group 2: eleven 21in (533mm); 8 forward (2 external), 2 midships (external), 1 aft (external); torpedoes: 17.
Guns:
Group 1: one 4in (102mm) 40-cal; three 0.303in machine-guns (later replaced or supplemented by one 20mm).
Group 2: one 4in (102mm) 40-cal; one 20mm; three 0.303in machine-guns.
Mines:
Group 1: 18 mines (alternative load).
Complement: Group 1, 56; Group 2, 61.

Ocean-going saddle tank type submarines. Normal fuel load: 132 tons (Group 1), 132–230 tons (Group 2); maximum operational depth: 300ft (95m).

In the early thirties, the Royal Navy decided to build a new ocean-going type to replace the *O, P* and *R* Classes which had not proved satisfactory. Features required for the new boats (defined as patrol submarines) included a patrol duration of at least 42 days, and a strong armament. The limitations imposed by the London Naval Treaty, allowed the Royal Navy at that time, only 16,500 tons for the construction of new submarines, and because of this, displacement was established at about 1,000 tons, so that a sufficient number of boats could be built.

The prototype of the new class was approved in the 1935 Programme, and construction began at Vickers Armstrong, Barrow in August 1936.

Launched on 5 October 1937, *Triton* entered service in December 1938. She was followed—with slight modifications, mainly in dimensions—by another 21 boats all of whose names began with the letter *T*. Ordered between 1936 and 1939, the last entered service in 1941.

Although they displaced almost 400 tons less than the *O, P* and *R* Classes, the *T* Class were superior in many respects (more torpedo tubes, thicker-skinned pressure hull, greater speed and safety in diving, better surface and underwater handling, etc), with the sole exception of maximum surface speed, which was lower as a consequence of the lesser installed power necessitated by the displacement limitations.

The design was based on rigid criteria of simpliciy of construction, ease of operation and maintenance of all equipment. Noteworthy success was achieved in this, and few types can claim the high level of technical efficiency displayed by the *T* Class during five years of war.

One of the most notable characteristics was the high number of torpedo tubes installed: eight bow tubes, six of which were reloadable from inside the pressure hull and two (external) contained in a large bulge in the upper part of the bow. Another two external tubes were situated in the casing at the base of the conning tower, so arranged as to fire ahead. This gave a salvo of ten torpedoes which, the Royal Navy reckoned, would compensate the inevitable errors attendant on long-range attacks.

Under the 1940 War Programme, it was decided to build another nine boats of a slightly modified design without departing from its basic characteristics. Essentially, the design was a copy of the first group, modified in the light of several years of service. The entire construction was electrically welded. The main changes were in the number and disposition of the torpedo tubes, and the outer hull shape.

An additional external tube was fitted at the extreme stern, and the two tubes amidships were shifted aft of the conning tower, angled to fire astern. The shape and silhouette of the casing amidships were modified as a consequence of the re-location of the tubes. The large bulge containing the two external bow tubes was eliminated, as its presence had created a notable bow wave which, when running at periscope depth, hampered visibility and the correct trim of the boat. Consequently, the bow shape of the second group of boats was more streamlined, and the openings for the two external tubes were much more visible.

The boats of the second group were fitted with a 20mm Oerlikon cannon on a platform aft of the periscopes, in addition to the three 0.303in machine-guns on removable mountings, common to almost all British submarines.

Subsequently, the external stern torpedo tube and the 20mm gun were retrospectively fitted in several boats of the first group. In other boats of the first group, the two midships external torpedo tubes were re-positioned in a manner similar to that of the second group.

The order for the first nine modified boats of the *T* Class were followed by orders for another 31 units (17 in 1941 and 14 in 1942); a total of 40 boats of which, however, only 31 entered service between 1942 and 1946.

The construction of nine units was cancelled in 1944 and replaced by a like number of boats of the more modern A Class. Two of them, Thor and Tiara, already in an advanced stage of construction, were not completed and were scrapped between 1946 and 1947.

Many boats of the second group were modified for employment in the Far East, by transforming several ballast tanks into fuel tanks, thereby increasing fuel load from 132 to 230 tons, and surface range from 8,000 to 11,000 miles at 10 knots. This increase in range, essential in a theatre where it took a week to get from base to operational area, together with increased stores capacity, enabled long patrols to be carried out: the record was achieved by Tantalus with 56 days, 40 of which were spent in the patrol area. Like other British boats, from 1941 to 1942, the T Classs began to be fitted with surface and air search radar sets.

During the Second World War, the T Class boats operated successfully in all the theatres in which the Royal Navy was committed. While obtaining satisfactory results, they were subjected to the highest loss rate: 13 boats were sunk in the Mediterranean, where they were employed in substantial numbers, despite the fact that large boats were very vulnerable in that sea. The most important successes are listed in Table 19.

The T Class were particularly successful against submarines: 13 boats (Thunderbolt, Triumph, Torbay, Thorn, Tigris, Tuna, Truculent, Trooper, Taurus, Tally-Ho, Trenchant, Telemachus and Tapir) sank 13 enemy submarines, six Italian, four German and three Japanese. In January 1943, Thunderbolt transported 'chariot' type assault craft which penetrated the harbour of Palermo and sank the hull of the Italian light cruiser Ulpio Traiano, which was being fitted out.

At the end of the war, many T Class boats were placed in reserve or stricken, and several were ceded to other navies: the first had already been ceded to Holland in 1944. Many boats remained in service in the Royal Navy. Several of these were modernized in a manner similar to the American 'Guppy' Programme, and continued in service until 1970. At present (1972), T Class submarines which have been refitted many times, are still active in the Israeli Navy.

Left, top to bottom: Triumph, one of the first of the T Class to enter service, armed with ten torpedo tubes; Thule returning from a patrol in the North Sea; Tantivy leaving a British base during the war. (note the rather rare camouflage.); and two T Class (first group) boats at a mooring. In Turbulent (left) the two midships external torpedo tubes have been modified to fire astern; in Taku (right) they are still in the original configuration. Both boats have the external stern tube that was added in 1942.

Taku returning from a patrol.

Thunderbolt after fitting of the external stern torpedo tube and the 20mm anti-aircraft gun.

Thistle at high speed. The bulge, containing the two external bow tubes, and the opening for the port midships torpedo tube are clearly visible.

Traveller, one of the first group of the *T* Class, in which the two external midships torpedo tubes were moved and aligned towards the stern.

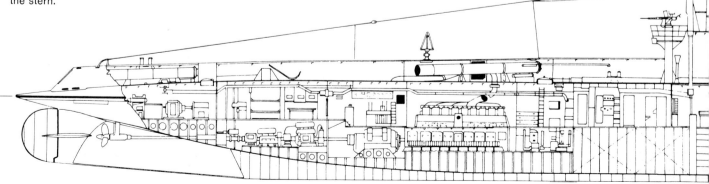

derbolt (ex-*Thetis*).
s sank, as the result of
lfunction of the forward
do tubes, during trials
erpool Bay in June
most of the crew
hed together with the
ard personnel aboard.
was raised and re-
nissioned in April 1940 as
derbolt.

-*Ho* leaving a base in
ndian Ocean.

T Class, Group 1.

T Class, Group 2.

Table 19: Major successes of T Class submarines during the Second World War

Boat:	Commander:	Date:	Result:	Type:	Ship:	GRT:
Truant	Hutchinson	9 April 1940	sank	cruiser	*Karlsruhe*	8,350
Triumph	Woods	24 August 1941	damaged	cruiser	*Bolzano*	12,000
Trident	Sladen	23 February 1942	damaged	cruiser	*Prinz Eugen*	14,800
Tally-Ho	Bennington	11 January 1944	sank	cruiser	*Kuma*	5,700
Templar	Beckley	27 January 1944	damaged	cruiser	*Kitakami*	5,700
Trenchant	Hezlet	8 June 1945	sank	cruiser	*Ashigara*	13,000

Fates

date:	location:	boat:	cause (see page 7):
1940	Mediterranean	*Triton*	n
		Triad	uc
	North Sea	*Tarpon*	n
		Thistle	s
1941	Mediterranean	*Tetrarch*	uc
1942	Mediterranean	*Tempest, Thorn*	n
		Triumph, Talisman, Traveller	uc
1943	Mediterranean	*Thunderbolt, Turbulent*	n
		Trooper, P.311	m
		Tigris	uc
1944	—	*Talent* (Dutch *Zwardvisch*)	r
1945–46	—	*Trident, Taku, Truant, Tuna, Torbay, Thrasher, Terrapin, Tarn* (Dutch *Tijgerhaae*)	r
1948–1950	—	*Taurus* (Dutch *Dolfijn*), *Truculent, Tantalus, Tantivy, Tapir* (Dutch *Zeehond*), *Trusty, Templar*	r

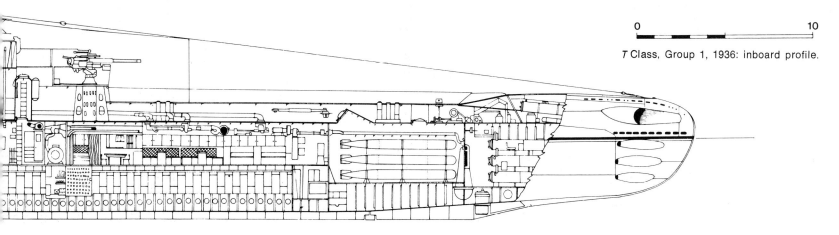

T Class, Group 1, 1936: inboard profile.

U Class

Group 1 (15 units).
Undine*, Unity*, Ursula*:
Builder: Vickers-Armstrong, Barrow.
Date: 1937–1938/38.

Umpire ex-*P.31*, ex-*Umpire*, *Una* ex-*P.32*, ex-*Una*:
Builder: Chatham Dockyard.
Date: 1939–1941/41.

Unbeaten ex-*P.33*, ex-*Unbeaten*, *Undaunted* ex-*P.34*, ex-*Undaunted*, *Union* ex-*P.35*, ex-*Union*, *Unique** ex-*P.36*, ex-*Unique*, *Upholder** ex-*P.37*, ex-*Upholder*, *Upright** ex-*P.38*, ex-*Upright*, *Urchin* ex-*P.39*, ex-*Urchin*, *Urge* ex-*P.40*, ex-*Urge*, *Usk* ex-*P.41*, ex-*Usk*, *Utmost** ex-*P.42*, ex-*Utmost*:
Builder: Vickers-Armstrong, Barrow.
Date: 1939–1941/41.

Group 2 (34 units).
Uproar ex-*Ullswater*, ex-*P.31*, *P.32*, *P.33*, *Ultimatum* ex-*P.34*, *Umbra* ex-*P.35*, *P.36*, *Unbending* ex-*P.37*, *P.38*, *P.39*, *P.41*, *Unbroken* ex-*P.42*, *Unison* ex-*P.43*:
Builder: Vickers-Armstrong, Barrow.
Date: 1940–1941/42.
United ex-*P.44*, *Unrivalled* ex-*P.45*, *Unruffled* ex-*P.46*, *P.47*, *P.48*, *Unruly* ex-*P.49*, *Unseen* ex-*P.51*, *P.52*, *Ultor* ex-*P.53*, *Unshaken* ex-*P.54*:
Builder: Vickers-Armstrong, Barrow.
Date: 1941–1942/43.

Unsparing ex-*P.55*, *Usurper* ex-*P.56*, *Universal* ex-*P.57*, *Vitality* ex-*Untamed*, ex-*P.58*, *Untiring* ex-*P.59*, *Varangian* ex-*P.61*, *Uther* ex-*P.62*, *Unswerving* ex-*P.63*:
Builder: Vickers-Armstrong, Tyne.
Date: 1941–1943/44.

Vandal ex-*P.64*, *Upstart* ex-*P.65*, *Varne* ex-*P.66*, *Vox* (I) ex-*P.67*:
Builder: Vickers-Armstrong, Barrow.
Date: 1941–1943/43.

Normal displacement:
Group 1: 630 tons surfaced; 730 tons submerged.
Group 2: 648 tons surfaced; 735 tons submerged.
Dimensions:
Group 1: 190ft 7in x 15ft 9in x 15ft 9in (58.1m x 4.8m x 4.8m).
Group 2: 195ft 6in x 15ft 9in x 15ft 10in (59.6m x 4.8m x 4.9m).
Machinery: diesel: 2 Admiralty or Davey Paxman; Electric: 2 General Electric.
Maximum power: 615hp surfaced; 825hp submerged.
Maximum speed: 11.5 knots surfaced; 9 knots submerged.
Range: 4,050 miles at 10 knots surfaced.
Torpedo tubes: four 21in (533mm) forward, or six 21in (533mm) forward (2 external); torpedoes: 8 or 10.
Guns: one 3in (76mm) 50-cal (not in *Undine* and *Unity*); three 0.303in machine-guns.
Complement: 33 (*Undine* and *Unity*: 27).

Single hull coastal submarines derived from the *H* Class of the First World War. Normal fuel load: 38–59 tons; maximum operational depth: 200ft (60m). In 1936, it was decided to build three unarmed boats as training craft for anti-submarine vessels, in lieu of the old *H* Class. *Undine, Unity* and *Ursula* were laid down in February 1937, but soon afterwards, their design was modified and they were armed so that they could undertake short offensive missions. The bow was modified to allow installation of six torpedo tubes: two on each side in the hull, and two external tubes, which could not be reloaded while submerged, in a large bulge above the bow, similar to that of the *T* Class. The hull was reinforced forward of the conning tower, to allow installation of a small deck gun.

Launched between October 1937 and February 1938, the first three boats were commissioned during 1938. From their first sea trials, they demonstrated their excellent handling and manoeuvrability. The design was particularly successful, easy to produce and inexpensive. They were small boats, with a single hull, tapered at its extremities, and a short narrow casing above. All the ballast and fuel tanks were inside the pressure hull. Surface propulsion was diesel-electric; the engines were connected directly to two generators which furnished the power for two electric motors, connected to the propellers.

For submerged propulsion, the electric motors were powered by two series of storage batteries, which, in turn, were recharged on the surface.

The diesel-electric propulsion system greatly simplified the layout of the propulsion gear and offered greater flexibility and ease of operation.

When war seemed inevitable, the Royal Navy immediately decided to build more of this type of boat, and twelve identical units were ordered under the 1939 Supplementary Programme. They began to enter service in 1941.

Only four boats carried six torpedo tubes (*Unique, Upholder, Upright* and *Utmost*). The two external bow tubes and their bulge, were eliminated from the others, because of the notable bow wave caused by the bulge when running at periscope depth, and because of the difficulty of keeping the boat trimmed longitudinally, as a result of the reduced length of the periscopes fitted in this Class.

Under the 1940 and 1941 War Programmes, a further 41 boats were ordered, but only 34 were completed. The contracts for seven (*P.81–P.87*) were cancelled and replaced by seven boats of the *V* Class, very similar to the *U* Class and developed directly from them.

The second group of *U* Class boats did not differ substantially from the first. They were approximately 5ft 9in (1.78m) longer in the stern, to give a more streamlined shape aft and improve the flow of water over the propellers; this increased the displacement slightly. Fuel load was increased by several tons, which increased the range considerably.

Individual characteristics, speed, range armament, etc., were inferior to those of contemporaneous boats of other navies. Layout was inadequate in several respects, based as it was, on the original design of the *U* Class as unarmed training craft. There was no ammunition hatch for the deck gun which had to be supplied through the conning tower hatch. This prevented rapid crash-diving if the gun crew were in action.

Nevertheless, the *U* Class boats had undeniable qualities: their very small dimensions gave excellent surface and submerged manoeuvrability; their equipment and design were admirably simple, rational and safe, giving a high level of operational reliability. They were easy to build, handle and repair.

The limited offensive potential of the boats, individually, was compensated by the considerable number of boats that could be, and were, commissioned in a short time. Their limited range confined them exclusively to the Mediterranean and the North Sea. After 1944, their activity in the Mediterranean declined appreciably and many of them returned to their original training role.

In September 1939, the only three *U* Class boats in service were stationed in home waters and began their wartime activity in the North Sea. When the first War Programme boats entered service in 1941, they began to be stationed in the Mediterranean where they operated mainly as part of the Second Flotilla based at Malta. They achieved notable successes against warships and merchantmen. In the Central Mediterranean, the British developed techniques for attacking merchant vessels, using aircraft, submarines and surface vessels in concert. In the Sicilian Channel, two *U* Class boats sank several major Italian merchant ships which were transporting troops and supplies to Africa.

Like other British boats, several of the *U* Class were particularly successful against submarines. Five boats (*Upholder, Unbeaten, Ultimatum, Unruly* and *United*) sank a total of eight, six Italian and two German, all in the Mediterranean.

During the war, 19 boats of the Class were lost, six in the Atlantic and North Sea, and 13 in the Mediterranean. Another boat, *Untamed,* sank in May 1943, but was salvaged two months later and returned to service as *Vitality.* From 1941, numerous boats were ceded to: Poland, USSR, Holland, Norway and Free France. Several of these boats were lost, but the others were returned to the Royal Navy at the end of the war. During the post-war period, most of the survivors were put into reserve and several were lent or sold to other countries: later, the remainder were scrapped. The last of the Royal Naval boats of the Class were broken up in 1950: some boats were later returned by other navies and then broken up.

One of the first group, *Utmost,* alongside an *S* Class boat moored to a tender.

Unity, one of the first three boats of the *U* Class, armed with six bow tubes, two of which were external.

Below: *Unbending* at her moorings in Malta; and *Unison* in 1944.

Fates			cause
date:	location:	boat:	(see page 7):
1940	North Sea	*Undine*	n
		Unity	v
1941	North Sea	*Umpire*	e
	Mediterranean	*Undaunted*	uc
		Union	n
		Usk, P.32, P.33	m
		P.41, Urchin	r
1942	Atlantic	*Unique*	uc
		Unbeaten	e
	Mediterranean	*Upholder, Urge, Utmost, P.38,*	
		P.48	n
		P.36, P.39	b
		P.47, P.52	r
1943	Mediterranean	*Usurper*	n
	North Sea	*Vandal*	v
	—	*Varne, Vox*	r
1944	—	*Ursula, Unbroken, Unison*	r
1945–46	—	*Upright, Uproar, Umbra, United,*	
		Unrivalled, Unruffled, Unruly,	
		Ultor, Unshaken, Unsparing,	
		Universal, Vitality, Untiring,	
		Upstart	r
1949–1950	—	*Una, Ultimatum, Unbending,*	
		Unseen, Varangian, Uther,	
		Unswerving	r

PLAN Nº 650.

H.M.S. UNTIRING, "VARANGIAN", "UTHER", "UNSWERVING".

GENERAL ARRANGEMENT. (AS FITTED)

PORT ELEVATION AND PLAN VIEWS.

SCALE:- $\frac{1}{4}$ INCH = ONE FOOT.

DESIGNED PARTICULARS

LENGTH OVERALL	196'- 10½"
LENGTH BETWEEN PERPENDICULARS	180'- 0"
BREADTH MOULDED	16'- 0"
DEPTH MOULDED KEEL TO TOP OF P.H. FRAME	16'- 0"

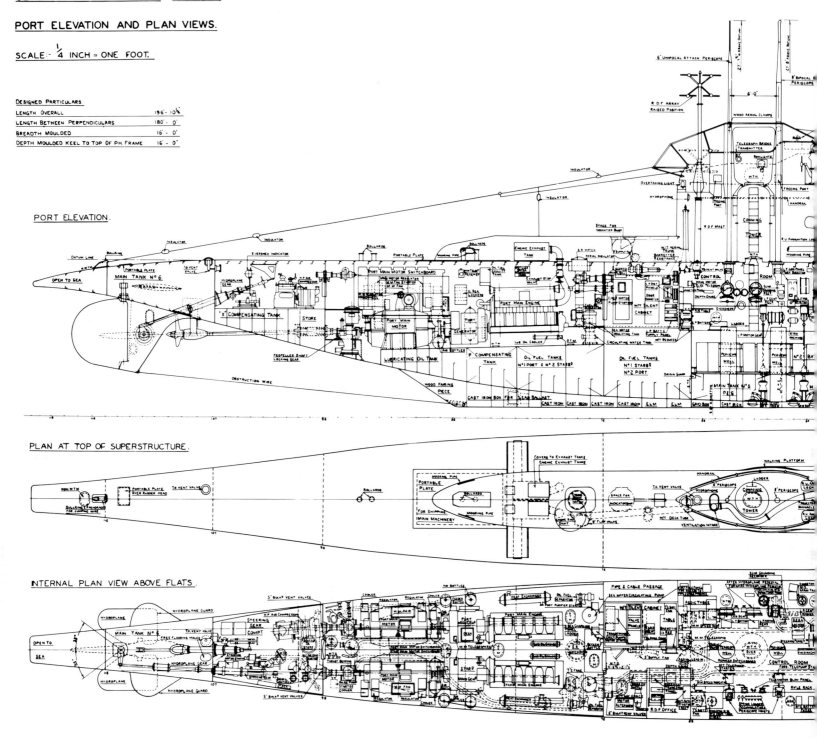

PORT ELEVATION.

PLAN AT TOP OF SUPERSTRUCTURE.

INTERNAL PLAN VIEW ABOVE FLATS.

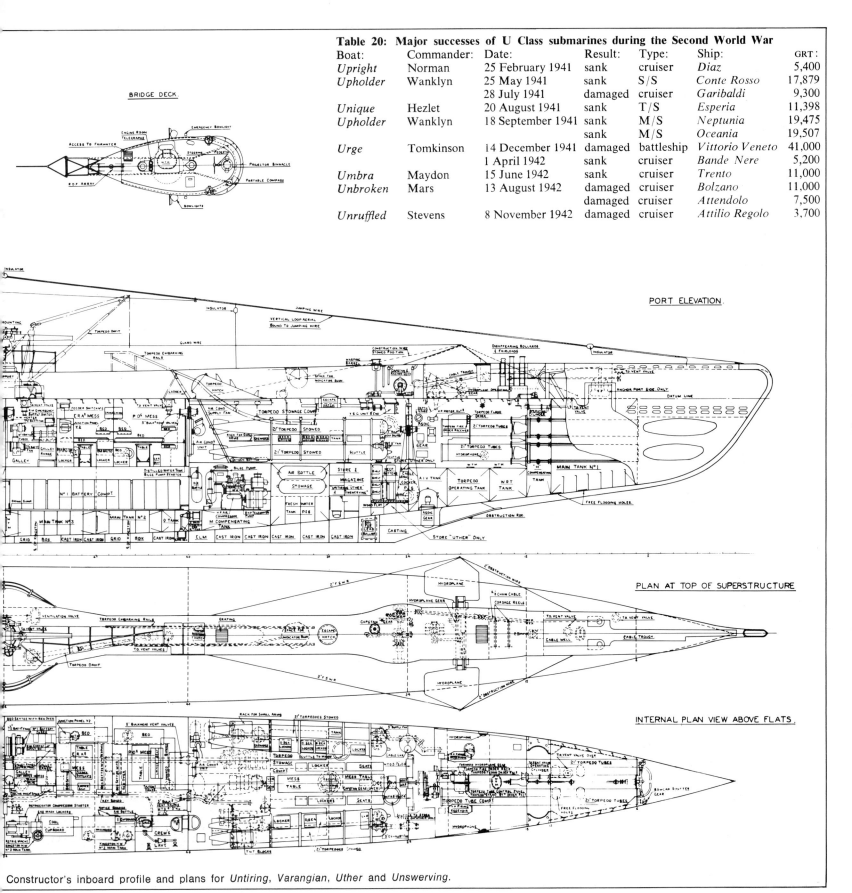

Table 20: Major successes of U Class submarines during the Second World War

Boat:	Commander:	Date:	Result:	Type:	Ship:	GRT:
Upright	Norman	25 February 1941	sank	cruiser	*Diaz*	5,400
Upholder	Wanklyn	25 May 1941	sank	S/S	*Conte Rosso*	17,879
		28 July 1941	damaged	cruiser	*Garibaldi*	9,300
Unique	Hezlet	20 August 1941	sank	T/S	*Esperia*	11,398
Upholder	Wanklyn	18 September 1941	sank	M/S	*Neptunia*	19,475
			sank	M/S	*Oceania*	19,507
Urge	Tomkinson	14 December 1941	damaged	battleship	*Vittorio Veneto*	41,000
		1 April 1942	sank	cruiser	*Bande Nere*	5,200
Umbra	Maydon	15 June 1942	sank	cruiser	*Trento*	11,000
Unbroken	Mars	13 August 1942	damaged	cruiser	*Bolzano*	11,000
			damaged	cruiser	*Attendolo*	7,500
Unruffled	Stevens	8 November 1942	damaged	cruiser	*Attilio Regolo*	3,700

PORT ELEVATION.

PLAN AT TOP OF SUPERSTRUCTURE

INTERNAL PLAN VIEW ABOVE FLATS.

Constructor's inboard profile and plans for *Untiring*, *Varangian*, *Uther* and *Unswerving*.

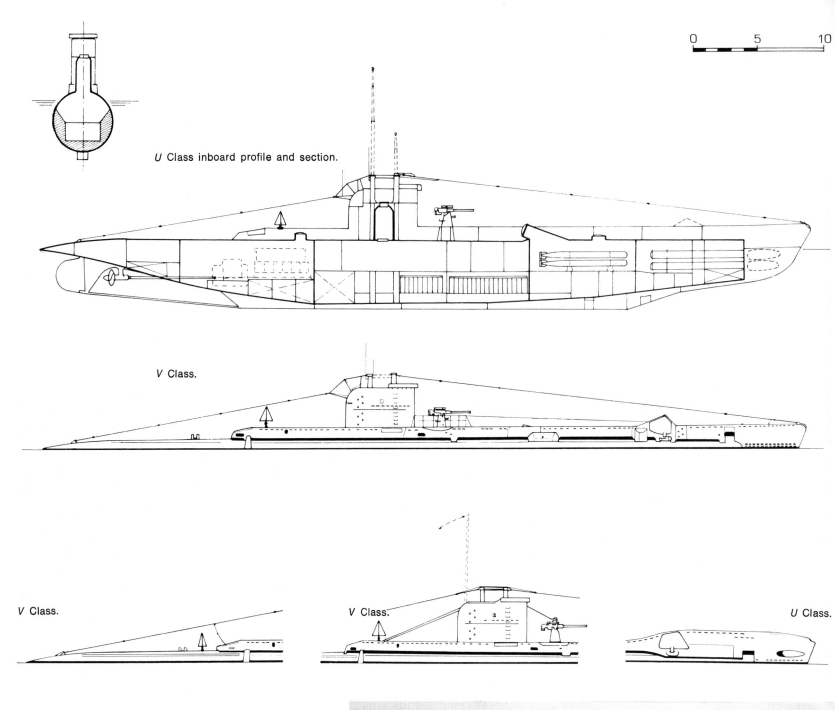

U Class inboard profile and section.

V Class.

V Class.

V Class.

U Class.

Vulpine, with an experimental schnorkel in place of the second periscope. (The photograph was taken at some time before April 1945.)

V Class

Upshot, Urtica, Vampire, Variance, Veldt, Vengeful, Venturer, Vigorous, Viking, Vineyard, Virtue, Visigoth, Vortex, Vox (II):
Builder: Vickers-Armstrong, Barrow.
Date: 1943–1944/44.

Vagabond, Varne (II), *Virulent, Vivid, Volatile, Voracious, Votary, Vulpine.*
Builder: Vickers-Armstrong, Tyne.
Date: 1943–1944/45.

Units cancelled between 1944 and 1945:
Ulex, Unbridled, Upas, Upward, Utopia, Vantage, Vehement, Venom, Verve, Veto, Virile, Visitant and eight unnamed units ordered from Vickers-Armstrong, Tyne shipyards.

Normal displacement: 670 tons surfaced; 740 tons submerged.
Dimensions: 203ft 5in x 15ft 9in x 15ft 9in (62m x 4.8m x 4.8m).
Machinery: diesel: 2 Davey Paxman; Electric: 2 General Electric.
Maximum power: 800hp surfaced; 760hp submerged.
Maximum speed: 12.5 knots surfaced; 9 knots submerged.
Range: 4,700 miles at 10 knots surfaced; 30 miles at 9 knots submerged.
Torpedo tubes: four 21in (533mm) forward; torpedoes: 8.
Guns: one 3in (76mm) 50-cal; three 0.303in machine-guns.
Complement: 37.

Venturer manoeuvring in a British port. Note the shape of the outer hull and bow compared to the *U* Class boats.

Below:
Vineyard in April 1944, before being ceded to the Free French Navy.

Single hull coastal submarines derived from the *U* Class. Normal fuel load: 59 tons; maximum operational depth: 300ft (95m).

In 1941, while the *U* Class building programme was in full swing, the Royal Navy decided to modify the design slightly in order to quickly obtain a type of boat which, while retaining the same characteristics, would be stronger but simpler and less expensive. The *V* Class were slightly longer and faster than the *U* Class and could reach a greater operational depth because of the strengthened pressure hull. Electric welding of all hull assemblies gave a quicker building time.

The first eight units were ordered under the 1941 Programme and were followed by another 19 boats in the 1942 Programme, and 15 in the 1943 Programme. When Italy surrendered in 1943, the need of coastal boats in the Mediterranean decreased and twenty of the boats were suspended and, with the imminent end to hostilities in Europe, cancelled: only 22 boats were completed between 1944 and 1945. As these boats differed but little from the *U* Class, all the remarks made about the earlier submarines apply also to their successors.

Venturer, the first boat completed, distinguished herself by sinking two German submarines, one in November 1944, the other in February 1945.

No *V* Class boats were lost during the war. In 1944, several boats were ceded to allies: two to Greece, one to Norway and three to Free France. Another three were ceded during the immediate post-war period. The last of the Class in service with the Royal Navy, was scrapped in 1958.

Fates		cause
date:	boat:	(see page 7):
1944	*Variance, Vengeful, Vineyard, Vortex, Veldt, Vox* (II)	r
1946–47	*Venturer, Viking, Virtue, Virulent, Volatile, Vulpine*	r
1949–1950	*Upshot, Urtica, Vagabond, Vampire, Vigorous, Visigoth, Vivid, Voracious, Varne*	r

A Class

Opposite page:
Left: *Alderney* at the time of
her commissioning in
December 1945. Note the two
stern torpedo tubes. Right: the
launching of *Auriga* on 29
March 1945.

Ace, Achates:
Builder: Devonport Dockyard.
Date: 1944–
Acheron:
Builder: Chatham Dockyard.
Date: 1944–1948.
Aeneas, Affray, Alaric:
Builder: Cammell Laird,
Birkenhead.
Date: 1944–1946/46.
*Alcide, Alderney, Alliance,
Ambush, Anchorite, Amphion ex-
Amphion, Amphion ex-
Anchorite, Andrew, Astute,
Auriga, Aurochs:*
Builder: Vickers-Armstrong.
Date: 1944–1945/48.
Artemis, Artful:
Builder: Scotts, Greenock.
Date: 1944–1947/48.
Units cancelled in 1945:
*Abelard, Acasta, Adept,
Admirable, Adversary, Agate,
Aggressor, Agile, Aladdin,
Alcestis, Andromache,
Answer, Antaeus, Antagonist,
Anzac, Aphrodite, Approach,
Arcadian, Ardent, Argosy,
Asgard, Asperity, Assurance,
Astarte, Atlantis, Austere,
Awake, Aztec.*
Normal displacement: 1,385
tons surfaced; 1,620 tons
submerged.
Dimensions: 280ft 6in x 22ft
4in x 16ft 9in (85.5m x 6.8m x
5.1m).
Machinery: diesel: 2
Admiralty; electric: 2 English
Electric.
Maximum power: 4,300hp
surfaced; 1,250hp submerged.
Maximum speed: 18.5 knots
surfaced; 8 knots submerged.
Range: 10,500 miles at 11
knots surfaced; 16 miles at
8 knots submerged, 90 miles
at 3 knots submerged.
Torpedo tubes: ten 21in
(533mm); 6 forward (2
external), 4 aft (2 external);
torpedoes: 20.
Guns: one 4in (102mm) 40-
cal; one 20mm; three 0.303in
machine-guns.
Complement: 61.

Double hull ocean-going submarines derived from the *Thames* and *T* Classes. Normal fuel load: 159 tons; maximum operational depth: in excess of 350ft (110m).

This Class represents the only new submarine design produced by the Royal Navy during the Second World War. It was prepared in 1943 and basically, was an enlargement of the *T* Class, but with a different hull form, more like that of the *River* Class.

The design stemmed from the need of a type of boat suited to operations in the Pacific Ocean: optimum speed and surface range, and very heavy armament. Their construction was to be simple, fast and so organized as to utilize many of the materials set aside for the *T* Class boats. The completely welded hull, and the armament was similar to the *T* Class, but the dimensions were slightly larger. The new boats were faster and had greater range, were fitted with an effective air-conditioning system and were equipped with air warning radar which could function at periscope depth.

Forty-six boats were ordered under the 1943 Programme: several contracts replaced contracts already signed for *T*

Class boats, but subsequently cancelled. *Anchorite*, the first of the Class (her name was exchanged with *Amphion* during construction), was laid down on 14 November 1943 and launched on 31 August 1944. Only *Amphion* (ex-*Anchorite*) and *Astute* were completed before the war ended. They entered service on 27 March and 31 June 1945, respectively, but neither had time to see any action. With the end of the war imminent, construction was cancelled for 30 of the 46 boats ordered. Sixteen *A* Class boats were completed: the last of them were commissioned in 1948. *Ace* and *Achates,* already in an advanced state of construction when their contracts were cancelled, were delivered incomplete and were subsequently scrapped. After having been modernized in accordance with the 'Guppy' Programme, between 1955 and 1960, the *A* Class boats began to be scrapped in 1968. *Aurochs*, the only boat not to have been converted, was broken up in 1965. By 1972, only three boats of the Class were still in service with the Royal Navy, and all have now been scrapped.

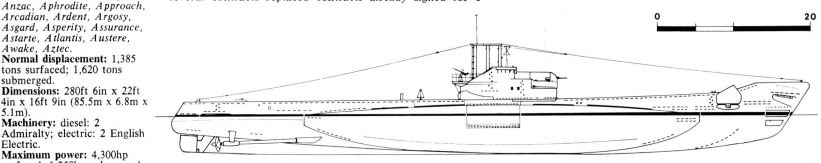

Alderney at speed.

Midget submarines

PROTOTYPES (2 boats).
X.3, X.4.
Builder: Varley Marine
(*X.4.* was completed at
Portsmouth Dockyard).
Date: 1940–43.
Normal displacement:
With charges: 30 tons
surfaced; 32¾ tons
submerged.
Without charges: 22 tons
surfaced; 24 tons submerged.
Dimensions:
X.3: 43ft 6in x 8ft 0in with
side charges, 5ft 6in without
(13.3m x 2.4m/1.7m).
X.4: 45ft 0in x 8ft 0in with
side charges, 5ft 6in without
(13.7m x 2.4m/1.7m).
Displacement:
With charges: 30 tons
surfaced; 32¼ tons submerged.
Without charges: 22 tons
surfaced; 24 tons submerged.
Machinery: diesel: 1 Gardner;
electric: 1.
Power: 32hp surfaced; 32hp
submerged.
Speed: 5.5 knots with charges,
6 knots without, surfaced.
Range:
With charges: 1,100 miles at
4.5 knots surfaced; 85 miles at
2 knots submerged.
Without charges: 1,400 miles
at 4.5 knots surfaced; 85
miles at 2 knots submerged.
Armament: 2 side charges.
Complement: 3.

X.5 CLASS (12 boats).
*X.5, X.6, X.7, X.8, X.9,
X.10:*
Builder: Vickers-Armstrong,
Barrow.
Date: 1942–43.

X.20, X.21:
Builder: Broadbent,
Huddersfield.

Date: 1943.

X.22, X.23:
Builder: Markham,
Chesterfield.
Date: 1943.

X.24, X.25.
Builder: Marshall,
Gainsborough.
Date: 1943.

Displacement without charges:
27 tons surfaced; 29½ tons
submerged.
Dimensions: 51ft 7in x 5ft
9½in, 8ft 6in with charges, x
7ft 5in (15.7m x 1.8m/2.6m x
2.3m).
Machinery: diesel: 1 Gardner;
electric: 1.
Power: 42hp surfaced; 30hp
submerged.
Speed with charges: 6.5 knots
surfaced; 5 knots submerged.
Range:
With cargo: 1,320 miles at
4 knots surfaced; 80 miles at
2 knots submerged.
Without cargo: 1,860 miles at
4 knots surfaced.
Human endurance: 7–10
days.
Armament: 2 side charges,
each of 2 tons of explosive;
weight of each: 4 tons in air,
neutral buoyancy underwater.

XT CRAFT (6 units + 12).
*XT.1, XT.2, XT.3, XT.4,
XT.5, XT.6:*
Builder: Vickers-Armstrong,
Barrow.
Date: 1943–44.
The following units were
cancelled before completion
in 1944:
*XT.7, XT.8, XT.9, XT.10,
XT.11, XT.12, XT.14, XT.15,
XT.16, XT.17, XT.18, XT.19:*
Builder: Broadbent,
Huddersfield.

XE CRAFT (11 units + 1).
*XE.1, XE.2, XE.3, XE.4,
XE.5, XE.6:*
Builder: Vickers-Armstrong,
Barrow.
Date: 1943–1945.
XE.7, XE.8:
Builder: Broadbent,
Huddersfield.
Date: 1943–1945.
XE.9:
Builder: Marshall,
Gainsborough.
Date: 1943–1945.
XE.11, XE.12:
Builder: Markham,
Chesterfield.
Date: 1943–1945 .
XE.10 (Marshall) cancelled
before completion.

During the war, the Royal Navy developed and employed with a degree of success, a type of 'midget' submarine, designed to attack large ships at moorings. Armament consisted of two large charges, each of two tons of *Amatol* explosive, located on the sides of the boat. These could be laid (from inside the boat), on the bottom beneath the target, or attached to the target's keel by magnetic clamps, fitted by divers who left and rejoined the boat via a floodable chamber.

In 1942, two prototypes were built, and, from these, operational types were quickly developed. The first series were employed in European waters (*X* Craft), but a later type was destined for the Far East (*XE* Craft). A series of six boats of a simplified type (*XT* Craft) were also built for training purposes.

The most important operations carried out by British 'midget' submarines were the damaging of the German battleship *Tirpitz* on 22 September 1943, and the sinking of the Japanese heavy cruiser *Takao* on 31 July 1945.

The first of these operations was carried out by *X.5, X.6, X.7, X.8, X.9* and *X.10*. They were towed by submarines to a point off Alten Fjord, Norway, where *Tirpitz* was moored. All the 'midgets' were lost, but *X.6* and *X.7* seriously damaged the hull of *Tirpitz* without, however, sinking her.

In the second operation, *XE.3* sank *Takao* at her moorings in the Straits of Johore, off Singapore. *XE.3* returned to her base unscathed after the attack. *X* Craft also played an important part as navigational beacons during the invasion of Normandy.

The Royal Navy also built a 'midget' submarine (Welman type) which had a one-man crew. The prototype was built at Welwyn Garden City; it was never particularly successful, and never saw action.

Originally designed as a private venture, it was not until *X.3* was already building that she was ordered officially. Fuel capacity: 1,570lb (712kg); maximum depth: 200ft (60m). Extremely manoeuvrable, their low freeboard when surfaced, made an air induction mast necessary. Used for training and scrapped in 1945.

Improved versions of the prototypes, with a different internal layout. The Vickers-built boats were ordered first. Maximum operational depth: 300ft (95m). Maximum towing speed behind a submarine was 10.5 knots, though up to 12 knots was reached when towing submerged. An *S* Class submarine towing an *X* Craft had its endurance reduced by thirty per cent: the comparable figure for a *T* Class boat was 5½ per cent. The first six boats were lost during the attack on *Tirpitz*.

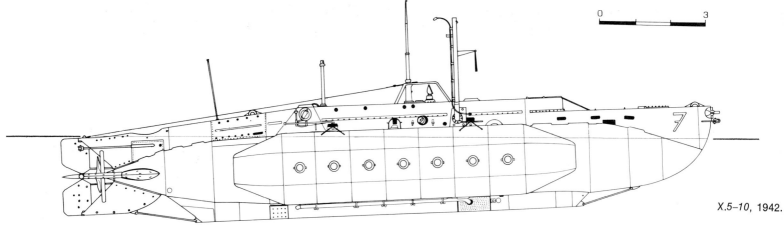

X.5–10, 1942.

Fates

XT Craft

Details as for *X.5* type. They differ from the *X.5* Class only in so far as they were simplified for training purposes. There was no side cargo-release gear, night periscope or automatic helmsman. The day periscope, projector compass and air-induction trunk were fixed in the 'up' position. Bunkerage was sufficient for only 500 miles at 4 knots. All were scrapped after 1945.

XE Craft

As *X.5* Class except: displacement with charges: $30\frac{1}{4}$ tons surfaced; $33\frac{1}{2}$ tons submerged, length: 53ft 3in (16m), complement: 4 or 5; greater range. These were developments of the first *X* Craft production design, for use in the Far East. For this purpose, they were fitted with air-conditioning. Their casing ran the length of the hull instead of ending before reaching the bow, thereby adding to surface seaworthiness. *XE.11* sank in a collision, but was raised in 1945. All survived the war and were scrapped in 1952.

Welman type

Displacement: 4,600lb (2,086.5kg) without warhead (warhead: 1,910lb (540kg); dimensions: 20ft 2in (6.1m) (16ft 10in (4.3m) without charge) x 3ft 6in (1.1m) x 5ft 9in (1.7m); machinery and power: one electric motor; $2\frac{1}{2}$hp; speed: 3 knots; 12 hour human endurance; complement: 1; armament: 560lb (250kg) charge. Test depth 300ft (95m); normal operating depth: 75ft (23m). The earlier examples controlled their trim by a 300lb (136kg) moveable weight. Later craft had compensating tanks for this purpose. There was no periscope. Vision was through armoured glass segments in the 'conning tower'. The charge could be attached to the target by magnets. Transportation was by submarine (in recesses in the casing) or in the davits of a destroyer. MTBs could also be fitted with suitable davits, and high-speed towing was also planned. However, the Welman could never be made to work properly and was finally abandoned. It is not known how many were built. During the war, the Royal Navy built a type of underwater assault craft very similar to the Italian S.L.C. (*Siluro a Lento Corso* = slow-running torpedo) or *pigs*, several examples of which, had been captured during an unsuccessful attack on the harbour at Gibraltar in 1941.

Like the S.L.C., the British 'chariots' were piloted by two men equipped with breathing tanks. The torpedo had a detachable warhead and could carry small limpet mines.

The chief successes achieved by the chariots were the sinking of the Italian light cruiser *Ulpio Traiano*, which was fitting out at Palermo on 3 January 1943, and the hull of the heavy cruiser *Bolzano* on 21 June 1944 to prevent the Germans using it to block the harbour of La Spezia, where the hull was moored.

Other underwater assault craft were tested towards the end of the war, including submersible canoes and supply craft for clandestine operations. An *X* Craft with a conning tower was designed but not built.

P. 553, ex-S. 21, in the process of diving. She was ceded by the United States.

Foreign submarines in British service

P.611 ex-*Oruc Reis*, *P.612* ex-*Murat Reis*, *P.614* ex-*Burak Reis*, *P.615* ex-*Uluc Ali Reis*.
Builder: Vickers-Armstrong, Barrow.
Date: 1939–1942.
Normal displacement: 687 tons surfaced; 861 tons submerged.
Dimensions: 201ft 6in x 22ft 3in x 11ft 9in (61.1m x 6.8m x 3.1m).
Machinery: diesel: 2 Vickers; electric: 2.
Maximum power: 1,550hp surfaced; 1,300hp submerged.
Maximum speed: 13.75 knots surfaced; 10 knots submerged.
Range: 2,500 miles at 10 knots surfaced; — miles at — knots submerged.
Torpedo tubes: five 21in (533mm); 4 forward, 1 aft, external; torpedoes: 9.
Guns: one 3in (76mm); one 0.303in machine-gun.
Complement: 40.

Ex-Turkish Submarines

These four submarines, generally similar to the British *S* Class except for their lesser number of torpedo tubes, were building for Turkey at the outbreak of war. They were acquired by the Royal Navy, but it was decided to deliver the first two to Turkey on completion, in order to strengthen that country's defensive power. For the voyage out, however, they were temporarily commissioned in the Royal Navy as *P.611* and *P.612*.

Fuel capacity: 38 tons; maximum operational depth: 320ft (100m). With their similarity to the *S* Class, and British build and equipment, these were a sensible addition to the Royal Navy. *P.615* was torpedoed by a U-boat, but the other sister retained by the Royal Navy survived and was returned to Turkey after the war. All three survivors were discarded by the Turkish Navy in 1957.

Fates

date:	location:	boat:	cause (see page 7):
1943	Atlantic	*P.615*	s
1957		*Oruc Reis, Murat Reis, Burak Reis*	r

P.615, one of the boats (similar to the *S* Class) building for Turkey in Britain, and requisitioned by the Royal Navy in 1939.

Captured submarines

German Type VIIC *Graph* ex-*U 570* (see Germany)
Another U-boat, the Type IX, *U 110*, was captured by the Royal Navy, but foundered before she could be towed to port. *U 570*, which surrendered to a Lockheed Hudson of R.A.F. Coastal Command, was the only German boat to serve her captors, before the mass surrender at the end of the war. She was employed on patrols against her former masters but was wrecked in 1944. Later, she was salvaged and scrapped.

Italian submarines

X.2 (*P.711* from 1942) ex-*Galileo Galilei* of the *Archimede* Class, *P.712* ex-*Perla* of the *600* Class, *P.714* ex-*Bronzo* of the *Acciaio Class* (see Italy)
X.2 was captured in the Red Sea in 1940, used initially in the Indian Ocean and then went to the Mediterranean in 1944 for training. She was broken up in 1946.

In 1942, *Perla* was captured by a British trawler. She was handed over to the Royal Hellenic Navy (Greece) in 1943, and served as *Matrozos* until scrapped in 1954.

Bronzo was captured off Syracuse in 1943, and after brief service was passed to the French in 1944. Renamed *Narval*, she was broken up in 1948.

American transfers

American *R* Class: *P.511* ex-*R.3*, *P.512* ex-*R.17*, *P.514* ex-*R.19* (see U.S.A.) These old American submarines were transferred to the Royal Navy between 1941 and 1942, and were returned in 1944 with the exception of *P.514*. They were used for training.

Fate

date:	location:	boat:	cause (see page 7):
1941	Atlantic	*P.514*	e

American *S* Class: *P.551* ex-*S.25*, *P.552* ex-*S.1*, *P.553* ex-*S.21*, *P.554* ex-*S.22*, *P.555* ex-*S.24*, *P.556* ex-*S.29* (see U.S.A.)
Old American submarines 'Lease-lent' between 1941 and 1942. They were used mainly for training and were returned to the U.S. Navy in 1944 with the exception of *P.551*, which was handed over to the Polish Navy as *Jastrzab* in 1941, and lost in 1942.

Allied submarines

Many submarines of the Allied nations served under British operational control, but were manned by their own nationals and flew their own flags. (See the Dutch, French, Polish, Greek and Yugoslav sections of this book). Indeed, some American submarines served briefly under British control, though on one occasion, a British submarine, *Seraph*, flew the Stars and Stripes, with an American in nominal command, as part of the clandestine preparations for the invasion of French North Africa in 1942.

Italy

On 10 June 1940, Italy entered the war on Germany's side against Britain and against a France already reeling under the attacks of the *Panzers* and *Stukas*. For the first time in her brief history as a unified country, Italy was in direct confrontation with the major European naval powers—or more accurately, power—because Italy delayed entry until it was obvious that the French were about to be removed from the conflict, and indeed, that Britain seemed likely to capitulate as well.

The relatively young Italian Navy was about to be faced with the most severe test in its history: 39 months of warfare in the Mediterranean against the most expert, famous and, as yet, largest navy in the world. At first, the Italians had the advantage in numbers, but too often, were handicapped by limited and inadequate equipment. A far more severe handicap was the weakness of the Italian high command, and the deplorable lack of collaboration between different branches of the services. Generally, however, Italian units fought as well as their equipment and orders allowed, often with great gallantry and skill, despite the legends of wartime propaganda. It was not the crews and captains that were lacking in these qualities, but their admirals and admiralty. So although Italy was defeated, the Italian Navy emerged from the war with some honour.

The war in the Mediterranean was chiefly a war of supply lines: defence of one's own and attack on those of the enemy being the chief causes of battle. The opposing capital ships met only in short-lived encounters, partly because of the timidity of the Italian high command and partly because of the increasing dominance of air power, which imposed caution on both sides. In this situation, the activity of light surface units in the defence and attack of convoys was of particular importance, and the role of the submarine was vital.

Unfortunately for the Italians, the results obtained by their submarines rarely met expectations, and failed to justify the resources put into the building up of Italy's underwater fleet during the years before the war. This failure stemmed from a combination of technical and strategic reasons. Few Allied merchantmen appeared in the Mediterranean during the early years of the war, except in the intermittent and heavily defended convoys which broke through the Sicilian Channel en route to Malta or Alexandria. There were large numbers of Allied warships in the Mediterranean, and the Italian boats could show few successes against these, which caused the Germans to send a number of U-boats to the Mediterranean, where they obtained some notable successes.

The real reasons for the poor performance of Italian submarines appear to be technical. In their basic qualities as underwater craft, they compared very unfavourably to their British and German contemporaries. Their diving times were comparatively slow and they were not particularly handy under water. Their large conning towers were very visible on the surface and slowed the dive still more. Diving speed was particularly important in the enclosed and aircraft-dominated waters of the Mediterranean, and the Italian boats' defi-

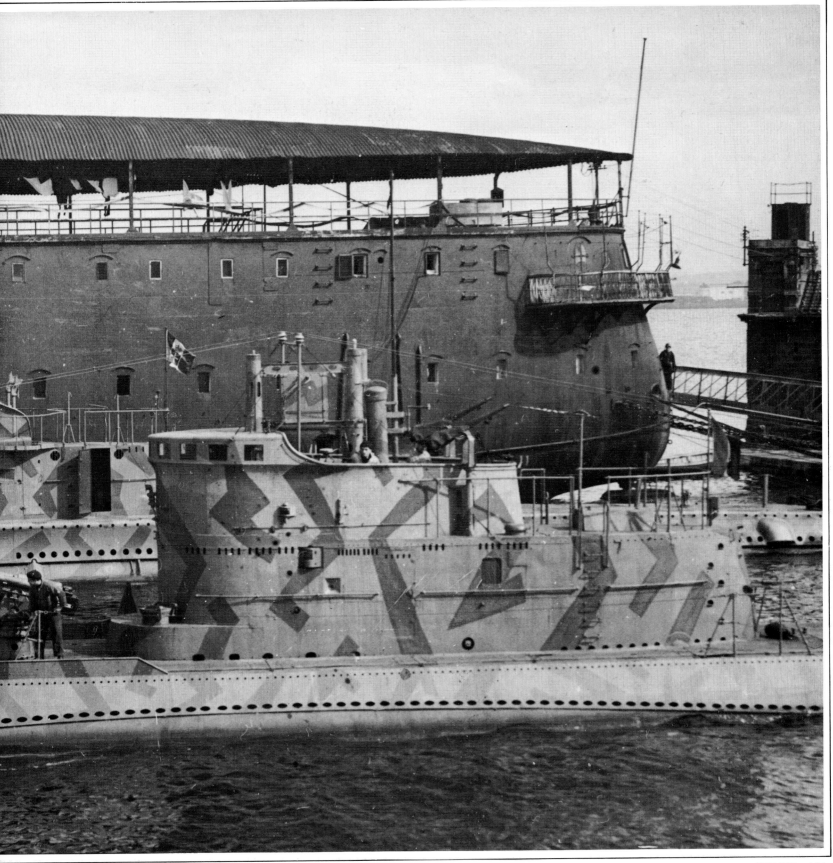

ciency in this respect led to a high proportion of losses. Their situation worsened by the lack of effective fire-control computers, asdic or radar. Against the strong opposition of British anti-submarine forces, these deficiences often proved fatal.

Many of the materials used in the boats built after 1935 (from which time, the Italians had to rely to a great extent on home production) were of poor quality, and the strains of operational employment caused a high degree of unserviceability, and kept a large proportion of the submarine fleet immobilized by frequent refits and repairs. Other deficiencies were remedied by modifying existing boats, and designing new classes, but others, including the poor quality of materials and the lack of radar remained until the Italian government signed an armistice with the Allies in 1943. With such disadvantages, it is not surprising that Italian boats achieved few successes and lost heavily. The only bright spots were the moderate degree of success achieved in the Atlantic under German control, and, more especially, the brilliant and gallant achievements of the 'human torpedoes' and assault swimmers.

When war was declared, the Italian Navy possessed one of the largest submarine fleets in the world: with 115 boats in service, it was surpassed numerically, only by the Soviet Navy which had approximately 160. The Italian boats were concentrated in the Mediterranean with the exception of eight boats in the Red Sea.

Of the 115 units commissioned (of which, on 10 June 1940, 84 were operational, two were completing trials and 29 were undergoing repairs), seven were small boats of old construction, 39 were ocean-going types with surface displacement ranging between 950 and 1,570 tons; and 69 were short- and medium-range 'Mediterranean' boats displacing between 650 and 950 tons.

During the First World War, the Italian Navy's submarine operations were limited to the restricted waters of the Adriatic, against the scanty targets to be found on the coastal routes and among the Dalmatian islands. The lack of experience in ocean warfare was reflected in the training of crews and in the technical character of the boats designed between the wars.

Italy had 56 boats at the end of the First World War. Many of these were scrapped, and at the beginning of the twenties, approximately 40 boats were in service. No new construction was undertaken until 1925 when the upgrading and strengthening of the underwater fleet was begun. The programme was divided into six successive phases between 1925 and 1943:

First phase 1925–1926: development of prototypes, generally in series of four boats for each type.
Second phase 1927–1930: reproduction of the prototypes with improvements, in limited series.
Third phase 1931–1934: increase of the underwater fleet with the ordering of larger series of boats.
Fourth phase 1935–1937: speed-up of construction because of international situation and demands of overseas adventures (German re-armament, Abyssinian War, Spanish Civil War).
Fifth phase 1938–1940: outbreak of war more imminent.
Sixth phase 1940–1943: wartime construction to replace losses and improve quality of boats.

During the first phase, prototypes of different classes were laid down almost simultaneously. Between 1925 and 1929, the four medium-displacement Mameli Class boats were built. These had a circular cross-section, partial double hull, with saddle-type ballast tanks over the pressure hull. The dive and negative tanks were incorporated in the pressure hull, whose extremities were sealed off by hemispherical caps. Designed by the engineer Cavallini, the Mameli Class were particularly successful boats; safe, strong, manoeuvrable and with a good degree of habitability.

Of similar charectistics, but of different design, were the four boats of the Pisani Class, built at the same time as the Mameli Class. Designed by the engineer Bernardis, they were of the single hull type with midships ballast tanks: dimensions and armament were essentially the same as the Mameli Class.

From the designs of Cavallini and Bernardis were later developed almost all the subsequent classes of Italian boats until 1943.

On trials, the Pisani Class displayed limited stability and had to be fitted with blisters; these were always fitted to subsequent boats of the Bernardis type.

Italy also began to build large-displacement long-range ocean-going boats. In 1925, the four Balilla Class boats were laid down. They were based on an Ansaldo-San Giorgio design, of the complete double hull type, with a surface range of more than 7,000 miles, which was rather good for that time.

During the first phase, it was also decided to build another type of large-displacement boat with hull characteristics different from those of the Balilla Class. Based on a Bernardis design, Fieramosca was laid down in 1926. She was a large-displacement single hull boat with midships ballast tanks and external blisters. The original design, especially for the armament (initially, medium-calibre deck guns, an aircraft, and minelaying equipment) was revised several times and the building of the boat took five years. The result was mediocre, however, and Fieramosca was not a successful boat though several characteristics were interesting, for the period; eight torpedo tubes, fourteen torpedoes.

In 1926, the Italians tackled the problem of building minelaying submarines. Their only experience had been the building of two small boats (X Class), derived directly from the German UC type. During the First World War, the Italian Navy had salvaged a specimen of this latter type and had rebuilt and commissioned her as X.1.

The first two minelaying boats of Italian design, Bragadin and Corridoni, were laid down in 1927 and entered service in 1931. They were of the Bernardis type with blisters. They were medium-displacement torpedo and minelaying boats, whose general characteristics were mediocre, and they were decidedly ineffective as mine-layers: even the subsequent changes made to improve their performance could not remedy their serious shortcomings.

The first phase of prototype development closed with the Corridoni design. Despite the fact that Cavallini's boats gave superior results to those of Bernardis, the Italians showed a preference for the latter type, and during the second phase, between 1927 and 1930, a total of fifteen boats, divided among the Bandiera, Squalo and Argonauta Classes, were ordered. At the same time, however, two boats (Settembrini Class) of the Cavallini type were also ordered.

In 1928, the four boats of the Bandiera Class and the four of the Squalo Class were laid down. Slightly larger than the Pisani Class, and again, of the single hull Bernardis type, they were immediately fitted with blisters to achieve greater stability. In general, they gave good results and were decidedly superior to the Pisani Class.

During this period, and also under the guidance of Bernardis, the design of a short-range boat with a surface displacement of about 600 tons was developed. It derived from the earlier Bernardis single hull types with midships ballast tanks, and with external bulges already incorporated in the design. This new Class (*600* Class, *Argonauta* Series), of which, seven examples were ordered, laid down between 1929 and 1930 and completed between 1932 and 1933, gave good results and was later repeated in four successive series with minor changes (*Sirena*, *Perla*, *Adua* and *Acciaio* Series) until the beginning of the war. Several *600* Class were also built for foreign navies (Argentine and Brazil), appreciative of their good qualities, and influenced by Italian government-backed sales techniques and price-cutting.

With 59 boats commissioned between 1932 and 1942, the *600* Class constituted the largest group of boats of the same type, commissioned by the Italian Navy, and provided her major contribution to underwater operations in the Mediterranean during the Second World War.

The Cavallini type was repeated with the two boats of the *Settembrini* Class. Compared to the excellent *Mameli* Class from which they were developed, they had more torpedo tubes, greater range and a more streamlined hull shape which, with an equal power rating, allowed a greater speed. Overall, however, their performance was inferior to the earlier boats, with poor seakeeping, and insufficient stability.

At the beginning of the thirties, the Italian Navy decided to increase its underwater force, and numerous boats were laid down from 1931 to 1934.

This third phase of modernization and development witnessed the building of twelve units of the *600* Class (*Sirena* series) and the design and building of three classes of ocean-going boats (*Archimede*, *Glauco* and *Calvi* Classes) and the prototype of an ocean-going minelayer (*Micca*).

In 1931, the four units of the *Archimede* Class were laid down: with greater dimensions than the *Settembrini* Class (Cavallini type) they gave good results. Two of them (*Archimede* and *Torricelli*) were later ceded to the Spanish Nationalist Navy and their names were transferred to two boats of the *Brin* Class, built 'secretly' between 1937 and 1939.

In 1932, construction of two boats of the *Glauco* Class was begun. This Class was a development of the *Squalo* Class (Bernardis type) which, thanks to a greater displacement and several radical modifications, were quite successful and represented the departure point for the development of the designs of other series of excellent ocean-going submarines.

The three *Calvi* Class boats, with complete double hulls, deriving from the *Balilla* Class, were also laid down. Overall, they were successful: their good seakeeping, long range, high degree of habitability and greater number of torpedoes, accentuated their characteristics as long-range boats.

Their performance with regard to minimum crash-dive time and underwater manoeuvrability, and the considerable bulk of the conning tower, strongly curtailed their chances of success against escorted shipping, and during the war, they were employed chiefly against independent ships in remote areas, where thanks also to their good deck armament, they achieved a reasonable degree of success. They were finally transformed into transport submarines for the Far East.

In 1931, the prototype of a long-range torpedo and minelaying boat was laid down: *Micca* was of the Cavallini type, modified to render her suitable for minelaying. Results were considered good, but the *Micca* type was not repeated because of the high cost and because, at the time of her commissioning studies were already under way for the design of similar boats to carry a greater number of mines on a

Development of Italian submarines, 1925–1943.

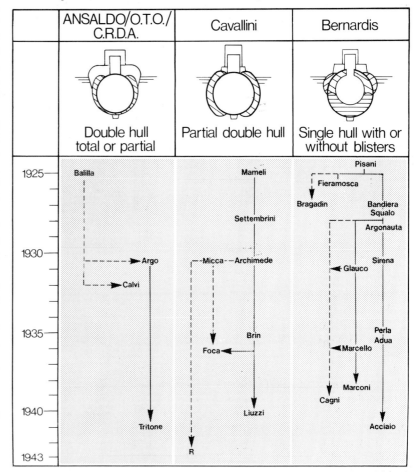

ANSALDO/O.T.O./C.R.D.A.	Cavallini	Bernardis
Double hull total or partial	Partial double hull	Single hull with or without blisters

lesser displacement (*Foca* Class).

The minelaying system was based on a central chamber containing 20 mines laid through a stern aperture. Although it gave rise to certain problems, the system was also adopted for subsequent minelaying boats, in combination with two special stern minelaying tubes.

In 1935, the international complications which arose from the Italian occupation of Abyssinia, pushed the Italian Navy into a renewed programme for strengthening its underwater fleet. German re-armament and the war in Spain later contributed to further intensification.

Between 1935 and 1940, the Italian Navy laid down as many as eight new classes or series of submarines: six ocean-going, of which, one was minelaying (*Brin*, *Marcello*, *Marconi*, *Liuzzi*, *Cagni* and *Foca*), and two were 'Mediterranean' (*Perla* and *Adua* Series of the *600* Class). To these was added the *Argo* Class in 1935, composed of two medium-displacement boats with ocean-going characteristics: their construction had begun in 1931 for the Portuguese Navy.

The total number of ocean-going boats ordered or acquired during this period was almost double (44 against 27) that of the short-range submarines intended for employment in the Mediterranean. This clearly reflected the change in Italian foreign policy which was aiming at an extension of Italy's interests outside the Mediterranean. In support of such a policy, the Italian Navy had to begin to think in terms of ocean-going submarines.

Between 1936 and 1937, the three boats of the *Foca* Class, the five of the *Brin* Class and the nine of the *Marcello* Class, with an additional two in 1938, were laid down. They were developed respectively from the *Micca, Archimede* and *Glauco* Classes. Undoubtedly, the best of these were the *Marcello* Class. They were repeated with several improvements as the *Marconi* Class, of six units, laid down between 1938 to 1939. Of the Bernardis type, they proved excellent boats and operated with success in the Atlantic, within the limits imposed by the general deficiencies of Italian boats, already described.

The minelaying boats of the *Foca* and *Brin* Classes were less successful. The mounting of the deck gun on a revolving platform in the after part of the conning tower proved very ineffective and the arrangement was eliminated during the war.

In 1935, the building of the 10 boats of the *Perla* Series, and the 17 boats of the *Adua* Series was begun: both series belonged to the *600* Class and were developed from the *Sirena* Series.

The four boats of the *Liuzzi* Series were laid down between 1938 and 1939. Developed from the *Brin* Series, they retained many of their shortcomings: poor seakeeping, limited stability and frequent breakdowns.

The only truly new design developed during this period was that of the four *Cagni* Class ocean-going boats, named after admirals. Designed by Cantieri Riuniti dell'Adriatico, they were of the single hull type with bulges, and were inspired by the earlier ocean-going types developed from the Bernardis design which had been built by the same yard. Their most interesting feature was the large torpedo armament: 14 tubes; 36 torpedoes.

These boats had been developed specifically for use against ocean shipping and their torpedo size had been reduced to 18in (457mm). It was thought that the smaller size would cause sufficient serious damage, and of course, more torpedoes could be carried. The French were inclined to this theory and had equipped some of their boats with a mixed armament of small and large torpedoes.

Although only one of the four boats was employed in the Atlantic during the war, the results achieved demonstrated the effectiveness of this type of boat against individual shipping.

In accordance with high command directives which in June 1940, decreed a defensive role for surface forces, and offensive use of the underwater fleet, the Italian Navy, when war began, stationed 55 boats in various areas of the Mediterranean, in individual ambush positions, or in patrol lines of several boats. Two long-range boats, *Finzi* and *Cappellini* were sent to the central Atlantic. The passage through the Straits of Gibraltar, heavily patrolled by British aircraft and ships,

entailed great risks, but thanks to the skill and luck of the Italian commanders, none of the numerous boats which made the passage was lost.

Three days after the beginning of hostilities, half the number of boats at sea had to return to base, and from then until the end of the war, there were never more than 25 to 30 boats at sea.

During the first phase of activity, losses were appreciable (10 boats sunk in twenty days of June 1940) and the serious technological and operational defects of the Italian submarines were soon made apparent.

After the heavy losses of June 1940—partly offset by the sinking, during the first 48 hours of hostilities, of the British cruiser *Calypso* by *Bagnolini* and the tanker *Orkanger* by *Nereide*—submarine losses declined sharply and stabilized in subsequent months at an average of approximately 10 boats every six months, until the end of the war. This rapid decline in losses was brought about by the reduced number of boats at sea, experience gained by boats' crews, and technical improvements to the boats.

A refit was immediately programmed for all boats and it was decided to progressively eliminate all obsolete boats (*X* Class, *Fieramosca*, *Pisani*, *Balilla* Classes, etc.) and to build new medium-range submarines with a diving time of 30 seconds, equipped from the design stage, with all the technological advances, already in service.

For the War Programme, the Italian Navy opted for a medium-displacement type which had proved to be best suited to the requirements of the Mediterranean. To hasten progress, it was decided to update the designs of the two best types then in service: the *600* and *Argo* Classes.

From the *600* Class were developed the 13 submarines of the *Acciaio* Class, laid down in 1940 and completed in 1942. From the *Acciaio* Class was derived the *Flutto* Class, known also as the improved *Argo,* ordered in three successive series (12–24–12 units) between 1941 and 1944. Only eight of the *Flutto* Class entered service before 8 September 1943: the remaining units were destroyed after the surrender, or were never laid down.

The *Flutto* Class were by far the best medium-displacement submarines built by the Italian Navy. Their range of approximately 13,000 miles at economical speed with additional fuel load, should have enabled them to carry out ocean-going operations, but at the time of their entry into service, every available boat was required in the Mediterranean. Operations in the Atlantic had changed, requiring boats of even more advanced characteristics, so the *Flutto* Class were never sent to operate there.

The naval review, honouring Hitler, in the Gulf of Naples on 5 May 1938. During this display, eighty submarines surfaced simultaneously and fired salutes. In the foreground is a *Calvi* Class ocean-going boat.

The War Programmes did not call for ocean-going boats: the number of long-range boats in service was thought to be sufficient, and as they were being modernized, their performance was thought to be acceptable for the types of operations assigned to Italian boats in the Atlantic. The exception, was the building of a type of large transport submarine, designed to carry high-grade materials to and from the Far East, and for the possible transport of fuel to North Africa. Ordered in 1941, the twelve *R* Class boats were all laid down between 1942 and 1943, but only two, *Romolo* and *Remo* entered service before 8 September 1943 and both were lost before they could be used for transport operations.

The War Programmes included numerous short-range boats of the so-called 'midget' or 'pocket' type. The Italian Navy had built several prototypes (*CA* Class) before the war. In 1940, the design was modified and gave rise to the *CB* Class: 24 small boats, only 12 of which entered service before 8 September 1943. They operated principally, and with good results, against the Russians in the Black Sea, where they had been transported by rail, early in 1942.

The *CB* boats were designed essentially for defending bases, especially against submarines. The subsequent *CM* and *CC* Classes were small boats, developed for offensive employment in special 'hot' areas of the Mediterranean, not far from their bases. They were to have been built in large numbers, to replace the medium-displacement boats which were far more expensive and vulnerable in areas such as the Sicilian Channel, and were to have been used en masse during the large-scale enemy re-supply of Malta. Laid down as prototypes in 1943, the first three *CM* and *CC* boats were unable to be completed before the surrender.

On the whole, the boats built during the war were of good quality and design, compared to earlier boats, but they could not rival British and German boats in operational performance. Their number was insufficient and this stemmed from their long construction time (the *Flutto* Class boats built at Monfalcone were delivered, on the average, 25 months after ordering: 17 months after laying down) caused by the shortage of raw materials and skilled labour.

Armament and equipment were fairly well standardized, and generally gave satisfactory results. Like the British, the Italians never had a serious torpedo 'crisis'. Their 21in (533mm) and 18in (457mm) 'steam' torpedoes were always quite accurate and reliable: their performance was adequate for the period.

Initially, the warhead detonators were all of the impact type, but from 1941, the boats began to be equipped with torpedoes which had magnetic fuzes (S.I.C. type), and during this period, the German

Table 21: Performance of Italian torpedoes

Calibre: in(mm)	Type:	Warhead weight: lb(kg)	Length: ft in(mm)	Run: ft(m)	Speed: knots
21(533)	W	595(270)	23 7½(7.2)	13,100(4,000)	48
21(533)	W	550(250)	24 7¼(7.5)	13,100(4,000)	50
				39,350(12,000)	30
21(533)	S.I.	550(250)	24 7¼(7.5)	9,850(3,000)	40
				39,350(12,000)	26
21(533)	W	550(250)	21 4(6.5)	9,850(3,000)	43
				32,800(10,000)	28
21(533)	W	573(260)	22 6(6.86)	13,100(4,000)	43
				39,350(12,000)	30
18(457)	W	440(200)	18 10½(5.75)	9,850(3,000)	44
18(450)	W	242½(110)	17 4(5.28)	6,550(2,000)	38
				22,850(6,000)	26

W = Whitehead Torpedo Works, Fiume; S.I. = Italian Torpedo Works, Naples.

Navy ceded a number of Type G7e torpedoes, with electric propulsion and magnetic detonators, and these were included in the torpedo load of many boats. Subsequently, torpedoes having pre-patterned runs and an acoustic homing-type head were also supplied by the Germans.

Two calibres of deck gun were used: 4.7in (120mm) 45-cal 'O.T.O. 1931' and 4in (102mm) 47-cal 'O.T.O. 1931, 35 and 38' with maximum ranges respectively of 15,863 yards (14,500m) and 13,784 yards (12,600m). Weight of AP shell, 48lb (22kg) and 30lb (13.8kg), muzzle velocity 730 and 840 m/sec. and rate of fire of eight rounds per minute. Anti-aircraft weapons were generally Breda Model 31 13.2mm weapons, with a rate of 400 rounds per minute, fed by 30-round clips and with an effective range of approximately 2,188 yards (2,000m). They were installed on individual or twin mounts, or tripod, or disappearing mounts. Only the captured boats were exempt from this standardization.

There were three main types of mines used by submarines: T 200 with a 441lb (200kg) charge, and P 150 and P 150–1935 with a 330lb (150kg) charge. Of the moored type, with impact detonators, they were not particularly effective, nor safe while being laid, and this was the principal reason for the limited use of Italian minelaying boats during the war.

After the beginning of the war, electronic and acoustic equipment was significantly improved. By the end of the war, Italian boats were fitted with good radio equipment, good hydrophones and an adequate asdic. Numerous boats were fitted with Metox-type apparatus, but

Sinking of the *600* Class *Adua* Series boat, *Gondar*. She was scuttled by her crew after having been seriously damaged by the British destroyer *Diamond* and the Australian destroyer *Stuart*, off the Egyptian coast on 30 November 1940. *Gondar* was carrying 'human' torpedoes to attack the harbour of Alexandria.

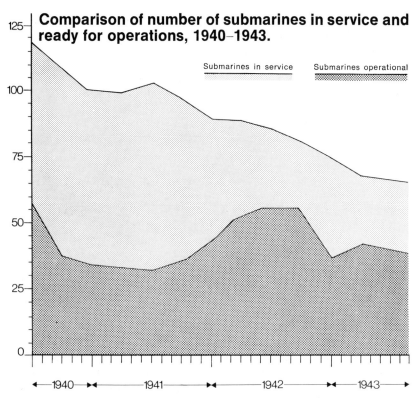

Comparison of number of submarines in service and ready for operations, 1940–1943.

Submarines in service   Submarines operational

◄—1940—►◄—————1941—————►◄—————1942—————►◄————1943————►

no boats were equipped with air- or sea-search radar, because Italian industry during the war, was unable to develop a small device of sufficiently light weight. Similarly, the schnorkel was never fitted in Italian boats, though a device designed for the same purpose and functioning on the same principle had been tested with modest success in the submarine *H.3*, as early as 1926, but was subsequently abandoned without explanation.

Until the beginning of the war, Italian boats often had a recognition sign painted on the sides of the conning tower, consisting of two letters, the first being the initial of the boat's name and the second, generally, a letter of the name (e.g. *Neghelli*, NG; *Ametista*, AA; *Tazzoli*, TZ, etc.) By the outbreak of war, this practice—already curtailed—disappeared, and the identification letters reappeared only in 1945.

From June 1940 to September 1943, Italian boats completed 1,553 patrols, made 173 attacks; fired 427 torpedoes; fought 33 gun actions; sank 23,960 GRT of warships (four light cruisers, two destroyers, one submarine, three minor units and one auxiliary vessel) and sank 69,690 GRT of merchant shipping. Losses were high: 68 boats, 59 of which were sunk in action, two (*Perla* and *Bronzo*) were captured, and seven were lost in various accidents at sea or bombed in port. A total of 10,641 tons of cargo (5,592 tons fuel, 4,193 tons munitions) was carried by 29 boats in 158 missions to North Africa. Six boats were lost while so engaged.

Seven boats, four of which were lost, transported underwater assault craft (S.L.C., 'pigs') and frogmen (gamma) in fifteen missions, contributing to the sinking or damaging of eight merchant or auxiliary ships (59,309 GRT) and seriously damaging the battleships *Queen Elizabeth* and *Valiant*, and one other warship. On the night of 7 February 1943, *Malachite* disembarked a patrol of sappers near Algiers.

The activities of the eight boats which had been stationed in the Red Sea and the Indian Ocean since the beginning of the war was now appreciably reduced, as was the case with the surface units stationed at Massawa. This was mainly because of lack of fuel, but also because defects in air-conditioning led to the poisoning of the crews of several boats (*Perla*, *Archimede*, *Galileo*, etc.) one of which (*Galileo*), was captured by the British. When the defects had been remedied, activity resumed, though on a reduced scale, and lasted until March 1941 when, the fall of Italian East Africa imminent, the four surviving boats (*Ferraris*, *Archimede*, *Guglielmotti* and *Perla*) left Massawa for Bordeaux which they reached in 60 days (12,000 miles approx), having been supplied en route by German submarines and support ships.

Between June 1940 and March 1941, Italian boats based in Italian East Africa sank one destroyer (*Khartoum*, hit by shells from *Torricelli*'s deck gun during an epic fight, in which the Italian boat was also lost) and two tankers, sunk by *Galileo* and *Guglielmotti*, respectively.

From September 1940, Italian boats began to use Bordeaux, where a base was established, with equipment suitable for the supply, maintenance and repair of ocean-going submarines.

Malaspina was the first to arrive at Bordeaux, on 4 September 1940, followed a few days later by *Barbarigo* and *Dandolo*. Between September and December 1940, 27 boats were transferred from Italian bases to Bordeaux. In May 1941, four boats arrived from the Red Sea, and in February 1943, the last boat (*Cagni*) arrived, bringing the total to 32. The greatest number of boats stationed there at one time was 27, in June 1941. This number dropped to eleven from December of the same year until December 1943. At the surrender, there were six Italian boats at Bordeaux.

Of the 32 boats which operated in the Atlantic from Bordeaux, 16 were lost. In 189 patrols, 101 merchant ships and several warships (568,573 GRT) were sunk, and 200,000 GRT of merchant shipping was damaged. For every boat lost, 6.5 ships were sunk.

The employment of Italian ocean-going boats was progressively extended from the Central Atlantic to the Northeast Atlantic, from the Atlantic seaboard of the U.S.A. and Central America to the west coast of Africa and finally, to southern African waters and the Indian Ocean. In the latter area, only four patrols were conducted but they achieved 95,000 GRT of merchant shipping sunk or damaged. After necessary modifications, largely effected at Bordeaux, several boats were employed in combined operations with German boats. In April 1941, *Giuliani* was transferred to the German tactical school for underwater warfare at Gotenhaven (Gdynia in Poland) for training.

A particularly successful period for Italian ocean-going boats was at the time of the entry of the United States to the war, when they operated along the Atlantic seaboard of America and obtained considerable success against heavy shipping which was not yet adequately organized and defended.

At the beginning of 1943, seven ocea-going boats (*Cappellini*, *Tazzoli*, *Giuliani*, *Barbarigo*, *Torelli*, *Bagnolini* and *Finzi*) were transformed at Bordeaux to carriers of high-grade materials, to and from the Far East. To replace them the Germans ceded nine Type VII boats (S Class) to Italy, but they were still training in Germany at the surrender, and were re-commissioned in the German Navy.

On 8 September 1943, the Italian Navy had 53 submarines of ocean-going and 'Mediterranean' type, plus the 'midgets'. Thirty-four were ready to sail, or were at sea, and these sailed to Allied bases in accordance with the terms of the surrender. Several boats, under repair or unable to move, together with boats fitting out or under construction, were sabotaged or scuttled, or were captured by the Germans. This resulted in the loss of approximately 50 boats (23 operational), excluding midgets.

Most of the boats captured by the Germans were not used by them, and were destroyed by Allied air attacks on Italian ports: several were subsequently scrapped or sunk by the Germans themselves. At the end of 1943, there were 33 boats in service (one, *Topazio* had been sunk by mistake by British aircraft), and these began operations alongside the Allies. During the period of co-belligerency, another two boats (*Settembrin* and *Axum*) were lost. From 1940 to 1943, of a total of 145 operational boats, 88 (approximately 53.1 per cent) were lost in action.

Surface vessels accounted for 46.5 per cent of the losses; submarines, 20.4 per cent; aircraft, 17 per cent; miscellaneous causes, 16.1 per cent. Twenty boats were lost in 1940; eighteen in 1941; twenty-two in 1942 and twenty-eight in 1943.

The lack of success of Italian submarines was not the fault of the Italian submariners, whose valour and high spirit of sacrifice was displayed throughout the war: many of them died in the performance of their duty.

Training, however, was not all that could have been desired. Before the war, Italian submarine commanders had not practised any methods of torpedo attack other than waiting submerged for targets to come within range. The inadequate doctrine of submarine employment led to the neglect of such vital technical considerations as rapid diving, fire-control computers, and low silhouettes. In addition, the inadequacy of much of Italian industry, incapable of completely meeting the demands of an ambitious armaments programme and turning out materials of insufficient quality, did not help matters. Despite many brilliant designs and achievements, the Italian shipbuilding industry could not yet match the consistent quality and resources of the shipyards of the major industrial powers, Britain, Germany and the United States. Although continuous efforts to overcome technical and doctrinal handicaps were made throughout the war, it was never possible to remedy the former, except partially, mainly in the few submarines built during the war, and although operational methods were improved, the technical defects were too great to allow them to be put into full effect.

Of the 115 boats with which Italy had entered the war in June 1940 (to which must be added another 30 completed or commissioned before September 1943), only 31 remained at the end, and the majority of these were of limited effectiveness as a result of the intensive activity to which they had been subjected and the poor quality of the materials used in their construction, during the period of 'sanctions' or during the war.

The peace treaty imposed on Italy contained a clause forbidding the Italian Navy to build and commission submarines of any type: the surviving boats, therefore, would have to be discarded. Several were to be scrapped immediately: others were to be delivered to the victorious Allies as war reparation, according to the following schedule: *Dandolo* and *Platino* to the United States; *Giada* and *Vortice* to France; *Atropo* and *Alagi* to Great Britain; *Marea* and *Nichelio* to U.S.S.R.

N.B. No boats were allocated to Yugoslavia, but she salvaged *Nautilo* from the bottom at Pola (Pula), reconditioned and re-commissioned her in 1954 with the name *Sava*.

Only the boats destined for the U.S.S.R. were delivered, in February 1949. The other powers refused those assigned to them, and called for their immediate demolition. All were discarded and only two were saved from being scrapped. These were *Giada* and *Vortice* which, in 1948, were 'secretly' re-commissioned with the provisional designations *P.V.1* and *P.V.2*. They were used for training submariners and anti-submarine units.

In 1952, when the clauses of the peace treaty relating to submarines had expired, the two boats assumed their original names and officially became part of the Italian naval forces. Modernized several times, they served until 1966 and 1967, respectively, complemented by units ceded by the United States, by several small boats newly built in Italy and by *Pietro Calvi* (ex-*Bario*), a *Flutto* Class boat salvaged from the bottom in 1945, and completely rebuilt between 1955 and 1960. With her discarding in January 1972, the last of the large Italian submarine fleet of the Second World War finally left service.

X Class

X.2, X.3.
Builder: Ansaldo, Sestri Ponenti.
Date: 1916–1918/18.
Normal displacement: 403 tons surfaced; 468 tons submerged.
Dimensions: 139ft 9in x 18ft 1in x 10ft 4in (42.6m x 5.52m x 3.15m).
Machinery: diesel: 2 Sulzer; electric: 2 Ansaldo.
Maximum power: 650bhp surfaced; 325bhp submerged.
Maximum speed: 8.2 knots

surfaced; 6.23 knots submerged.
Range: 1,200 miles at 8 knots surfaced; 70 miles at 3 knots submerged.
Torpedo tubes: two 17.7in

(450mm) forward (external); torpedoes: 2.
Guns: one 3in (76mm) 30-cal.
Mines: nine tubes for 18 mines.
Complement: 25.

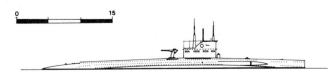

Single hull minelaying submarines with saddle tanks. The design was modified by Bernardis from that of the Austrian *U.24* (ex German *UC. 12*) which accidentally sank herself on one of her own mines off Taranto. She was raised by the Italians, who repaired her and commissioned her as their *X.1*. The two Italian-built boats were neither fast nor handy, and after 1936, were used only for training. Maximum operational depth: 128ft (40m).

Fates		cause
date:	boat:	(see page 7):
1940	*X.2, X.3*	r (laid up in September and not used again)

H Class

H.1, H.2, H.4, H.6, H.8.
Builder: Canadian Vickers, Montreal.
Date: 1916–1916/18.
Normal displacement: 365 tons surfaced; 474 tons submerged.
Dimensions: 150ft 3in x 15.5in x 12ft 5in (45.8m x 4.69m x 3.78m).
Machinery: diesel: 2 New London Ship & Engine Co.; electric: 2 Dynamic Electric Co.
Maximum power: 480hp surfaced: 628hp submerged.
Maximum speed: 12.5 knots surfaced; 8.5 knots submerged.
Range: 3,300 miles at 7 knots surfaced; 120 miles at 3.5 knots submerged.
Torpedo tubes: four 17.7in (450mm) forward; torpedoes: 6.
Guns: one 3in (76mm) 30-cal; (from 1941: one 13.2mm Breda machine-gun).
Complement: 27.

Single hull, internal ballast tank submarines of the Holland (Elco) design. Exact sisters of the first boats of the British *H* Class (see above). Maximum operational depth: 160ft (50m).

Originally, the Italians had eight of these excellent submarines. *H.5* was torpedoed by mistake in 1918, ironically, by her sister ship *H.1. H.7* and *H.3* were discarded in 1930 and 1937, respectively. The remaining members of the Class were still considered fairly seaworthy in 1940,

and were used on operational patrols off the French coast, and in the northern part of the Tyrrhenian Sea. Later, they continued to serve the Italian Navy well, as training submarines—'clockwork mice' for the anti-submarine forces. *H.8* was sunk by bombing at La Spezia in June 1943. Her hull was later raised and used as a battery-charging hulk. Three months later, *H.6* was captured and scuttled by the Germans at Bonifaccio. The others all survived the war.

Fates

date:	location:	boat:	cause (see page 7):
1943	Mediterranean	*H.8*	b
		H.6	c, sb
1947		*H.1, H.2, H.4*	r

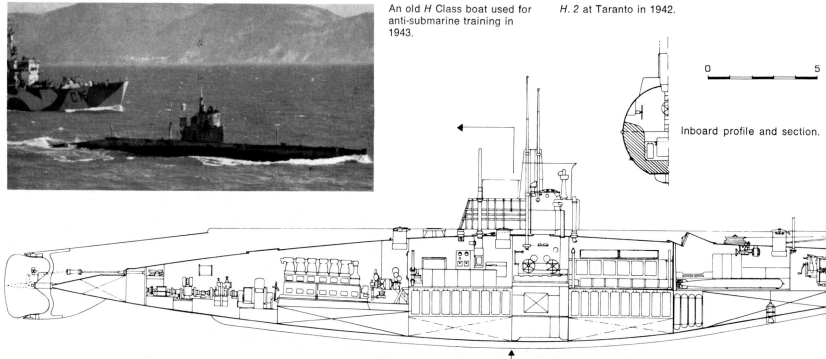

An old *H* Class boat used for anti-submarine training in 1943.

H. 2 at Taranto in 1942.

Inboard profile and section.

Balilla Class

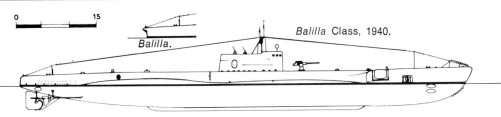

Balilla.

Balilla Class, 1940.

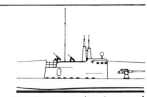

Modified conning tower of
Toti and Sciesa, 1942.

Balilla, Domenico Millelire, Antonio Sciesa, Enrico Toti.
Builder: Odero Terni, La Spezia.
Date: 1925–1928/29.
Normal displacement: 1,450 tons surfaced; 1,904 tons submerged.
Dimensions: 282ft 0in x 24ft 6in x 14ft 0in (86.75m x 7.8m x 4.70m).
Machinery: diesel: 2 Fiat + 1 Fiat auxiliary; electric: 2 Savigliano.
Maximum power: 4,900 + 425hp surfaced; 2,200hp submerged.
Maximum speed: 17.5 knots surfaced, auxiliary 7 knots surfaced; 8.9 knots submerged.
Range: 12,000 miles at 7 knots surfaced, 3,000 miles at 17 knots surfaced; 110 miles at 3 knots submerged, 8 miles at 8.9 knots submerged.
Torpedo tubes: six 21in (533mm); 4 forward, 2 aft; torpedoes: 12.
Guns: one 4.7in (120mm) 45-cal; four 13.2mm (2 x 2).
Mines: one tube; 4 mines (only in *Antonio Sciesa*).
Complement: 77.

The *Balilla* Class *Toti*, used for training, at Pola (Pula in Yugoslavia) in 1942.

Long-range boats with complete double hull. Maximum operational depth: 288ft (90m); maximum fuel load: 140 tons. The *Balilla* Class were the first large-displacement submarines built by the Italian Navy. Between 1929 and 1936, they made numerous ocean cruises and from 1936 to 1937, they participated in the Spanish Civil War. In 1934 they were modernized: the conning tower was modified and the original 4.7in (120mm) 27-cal shielded deck gun was replaced. In 1940, their effectiveness was rather limited: in April 1941, after several operations, *Balilla* and *Millelire* were de-commissioned and used as fuel storage tanks. On 15 October 1940, *Toti* sank the British boat *Rainbow* during a surface engagement in the Gulf of Taranto, and on 1 December 1941, sank the British boat *Perseus* off Zante.

Toti was subsequently posted to training duties and from January 1942, with *Sciesa,* was used to ferry supplies to North Africa. *Sciesa,* damaged by bombs, was destroyed by her crew at Tobruk on 12 September.

Fates			cause
date:	location:	boat:	(see page 7):
1940	—	*Balilla, Millelire*	r
1942	Mediterranean	*Sciesa*	b, sb
1943	—	*Toti*	r

Mameli Class

Millelire in 1938 with
Fieramosca in the background.

Pier Capponi, Giovanni da Procida, Goffredo Mameli ex-Masaniello, Tito Speri.
Builder: Tosi, Taranto.
Date: 1925–1929/29.
Normal displacement: 830 tons surfaced; 1,010 tons submerged.
Dimensions: 213ft 3in x 21ft 3in x 13ft 0in (64.6m x 6.5m x 4.3m).
Machinery: diesel: 2 Tosi; electric: 2 CGE.
Maximum power: 3,100hp surfaced; 1,100hp submerged; from 1942: 4,000hp surfaced; 1,100hp submerged.
Maximum speed: 15 knots surfaced; 7.2 knots submerged; from 1942: 17 knots surfaced; 7.2 knots submerged.
Range: 4,360 miles at 8 knots

surfaced, 2,380 miles at 12 knots surfaced; 110 miles at 3 knots submerged, 8 miles at 7.2 knots submerged.
Torpedo tubes: six 21in (533mm); 4 forward, 2 aft;
torpedoes: 10.
Guns: one 4in (102mm) 45-cal; two single 13.2mm.
Complement: 49.

Da Procida at La Spezia in 1942, after replacement of her propulsion gear.

Short-range boats with partial double hull. Maximum operational depth: 288ft (90m); fuel load: 29 tons. Particularly succcessful boats, fast strong and manoeuvrable. In 1942, higher powered diesels were installed and operational speed was increased to 17 knots.

Before the war, they made several ocean cruises and participated in the Spanish Civil War. From 1940 to 1943, they were employed in the Mediterranean on war patrols and training. From 1944 to 1945, the three boats still in service, were stationed in the Atlantic to train American air-sea forces.

Fates

date:	location:	boat:	cause (see page 7):
1941	Mediterranean	*Pier Capponi*	s
1948		*Da Procida, Mameli, Speri*	r

Pisani Class

Giovanni Bausan,
Marcantonio Colonna,
De Geneys, Vittor Pisani.
Builder: Cantiere Navale
Triestino, Monfalcone.
Date: 1925–1929/29.
Normal displacement: 880
tons surfaced; 1,058 tons
submerged.
Dimensions: 223ft 0in x 19ft
0in x 14ft 0in (68.2m x 6.09m
x 4.93m).
Machinery: diesel: 2 Tosi;
electric: 2 CGE.
Maximum power: 3,000hp
surfaced; 1,100hp submerged.
Maximum speed: 15 knots
surfaced; 8.2 knots submerged.
Range: 4,230 miles at 9.3
knots surfaced, 1,500 miles at
15 knots surfaced; 70 miles
at 4 knots submerged, 7 miles
at 8.2 knots submerged.
Torpedo tubes: six 21in
(533mm); 4 forward, 2 aft;
torpedoes: 9.
Guns: one 4in (102mm) 35-cal;
two single 13.2mm.
Complement: 49.

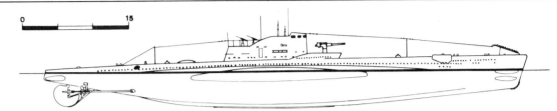

Single hull short-range boats, with internal double hulls and with external bulges. Maximum operational depth: 288ft (90m); fuel load: 38 tons.

Because of their limited stability, after entering service they were fitted with external bulges which decreased their speed by about 2 knots on the surface, and by one knot submerged. They were boats of mediocre performance whose combat effectiveness was rather limited in 1940.

After only a few patrols, they were posted to training duties. Three units were stricken during the war and converted to battery-charging units and fuel-storage vessels. *Vittor Pisani* was discarded in 1947.

Fates

date:	boat:	cause (see page 7):
1942	*Bausan, Colonna, De Geneys*	r
1947	*Vittor Pisani*	r

Conning tower details of *Pisani*, 1942.

Fieramosca Class

Ettore Fieramosca.
Builder: Tosi, Taranto.
Date: 1926–1931.
Normal displacement: 1,556 tons surfaced; 1,965 tons submerged.
Dimensions: 270ft 3in x 27ft 6in x 14ft 9in (84m x 8.3m x 5.3m).
Machinery: diesel: 2 Tosi; electric: 2 Marelli.
Maximum power: 5,200hp surfaced; 2,000hp submerged.
Maximum speed: 15 knots surfaced; 8 knots submerged; on trials: 19 knots surfaced; 10 knots submerged.
Range: 5,300 miles at 8 knots surfaced, 1,600 miles at 15 knots surfaced; 90 miles at 3 knots submerged, 7 miles at 8 knots submerged.
Torpedo tubes: eight 21in (533mm); 4 forward, 4 aft; torpedoes: 14.
Guns: one 4.7in (120mm) 45-cal; four 13.2mm (2 x 2).
Complement: 78.

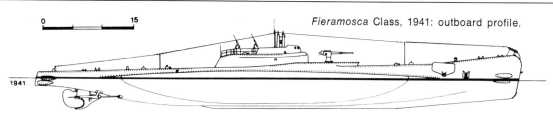

Fieramosca Class, 1941: outboard profile.

Single hull long-range boat with external bulges, developed from the *Pisani* Class. Maximum operational depth: 288ft (90m); fuel load: 145 tons. The original design which, in addition to the heavy deck gun, specified a reconnaissance floatplane and nine launching tubes, was radically modified during construction.

She was not very successful; slow to dive and not very manoeuvrable. In 1940, she carried out only two patrols in the Tyrrhenian Sea. Later, she was posted to training duties and in March 1941, she was de-commissioned.

Fate		cause
date:	boat:	(see page 7):
1941	*Ettore Fieramosca*	r

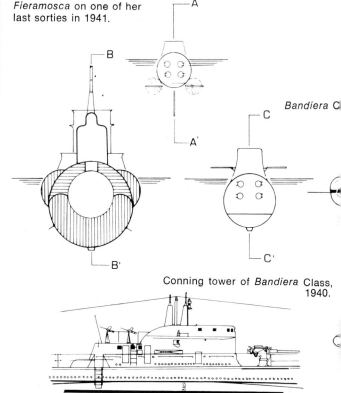

Fieramosca on one of her last sorties in 1941.

Bandiera C

Conning tower of *Bandiera* Class, 1940.

Bandiera Class

Fratelli Bandiera, Luciano Manara:
Builder: Cantiere Navale Triestino, Monfalcone.
Date: 1928–1930/30.
Ciro Menotti, Santorre Santarosa.
Builder: Odero Terni, La Spezia.
Date: 1928–1930/30.
Normal displacement: 993–941 tons surfaced; 1,096–1,153 tons submerged.
Dimensions: 229ft 0in x 24ft 0in/23ft 8in x 13ft 0in/13ft 4in (69.8m x 7.3m/7.2m x 5.18m/5.26m).
Machinery: diesel: 2 Fiat; electric: 2 Savigliano.
Maximum power: 3,000hp surfaced; 1,300hp submerged.
Maximum speed: 15 knots surfaced; 8.2 knots submerged.
Range: 4,750 miles at 8.5 knots surfaced, 1,500 miles at 15 knots surfaced; 60 miles at 4 knots submerged, 6 miles at 8 knots submerged.
Torpedo tubes: eight 21in (533mm): 4 forward, 4 aft; **torpedoes:** 12.
Guns: one 4in (102mm) 35-cal (from 1942: in *Ciro Menotti*, one 3in (76mm) 47-cal); two single 13.2mm.
Complement: 52.

Improvement of the *Pisani* Class. Maximum operational depth: 288ft (90m). Blisters were fitted to these boats to improve stability, with a consequent loss in speed. After entering service, the bow was raised to improve performance in bow-on seas. In 1940, these boats were of limited usefulness. At first, they were employed on normal patrols, but in 1942 they passed to a training role. Later, they were used to transport supplies to North Africa.

After the surrender, the three boats still in service were again used for training, and were de-commissioned at the end of the war.

Fates

date:	location:	boat:	cause (see page 7):
1943	Mediterranean	*Santorre Santarosa*	v sb n
1948		*Fratelli Bandiera, Luciano Manara, Ciro Menotti*	r

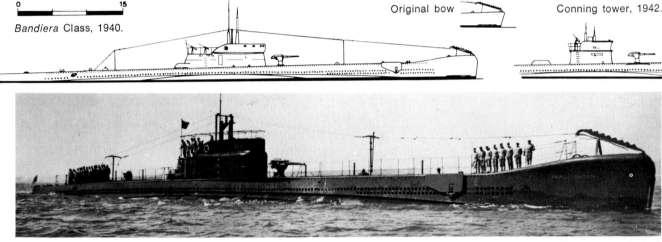

Bandiera Class, 1940.

Original bow

Conning tower, 1942.

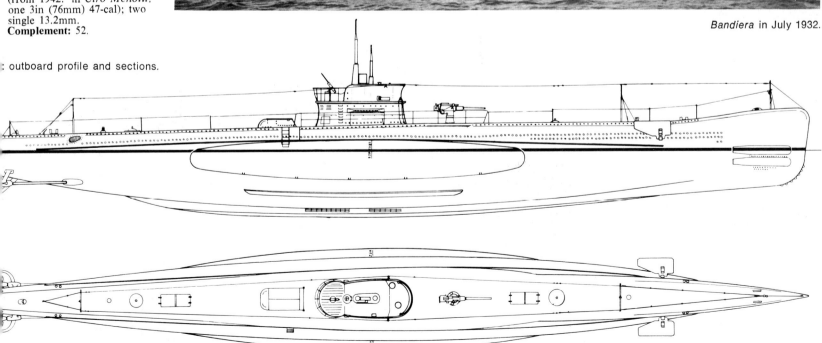

Bandiera in July 1932.

: outboard profile and sections.

Squalo Class

Squalo, Narvalo, Delfino, Tricheco.
Builder: C.R.D.A., Monfalcone.
Date: 1928–1930/31.
Normal displacement: 933 tons surfaced; 1,142 tons submerged.
Dimensions: 229ft 0in x 18ft 9in x 16ft 3in (69.8m x 7.21m x 5.2m).
Machinery: diesel: 2 Fiat; electric: 2 C.R.D.A.
Maximum power: 3,000hp surfaced; 1,300hp submerged.
Maximum speed: 15.1 knots surfaced; 8 knots submerged.
Range: 5,650 miles at 8 knots surfaced, 1,820 miles at 15 knots surfaced; 100 miles at 3 knots submerged, 7 miles at 8 knots submerged.
Torpedo tubes: eight 21in (533mm); 4 forward, 4 aft; **torpedoes:** 12.
Guns: one 4in (102mm) 35-cal; 2 single 13.2mm.
Complement: 53.

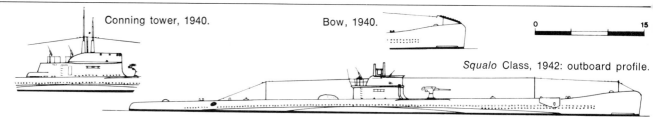

Conning tower, 1940.   Bow, 1940.

Squalo Class, 1942: outboard profile.

Repeat of the *Bandiera* Class with slight modifications. Maximum operational depth: 288ft (90m). Blisters were added and the bow was raised. In 1940, these boats, which still had a modest combat capability, were stationed in the Dodecanese, and operated from there until the beginning of 1941 when they returned to Italian bases. In December 1940, *Tricheco* mistakenly sank *Gemma* of the *Ambra* Series. From 1942, they were used alternately for training and for transporting supplies to North Africa. *Squalo*, the only survivor, was de-commissioned in 1948.

Fates

date:	location:	boat:	cause (see page 7):
1942	Mediterranean	*Tricheco*	s
1943	Mediterranean	*Delfino*	v
		Narvalo	sb, n, a
1948		*Squalo*	r

A *Squalo* Class boat in 1942, after changes to the conning tower.

Bragadin Class

Marcantonio Bragadin,
Filippo Corridoni.
Builder: Tosi, Taranto.
Date: 1927–1931/31.
Normal displacement: 981
tons surfaced; 1,167 tons
submerged.
Dimensions: 234ft 6in x 20ft
2in x 15ft 9in (71.5 x 6.15m
x 4.8m); after modification:
223ft 0in x 23ft 3in x 14ft
1½in (68m x 7.1m x 4.3m).
Machinery: diesel: 2 Tosi;
electric: 2 Marelli.
Maximum power: 1,500hp
surfaced; 1,000hp submerged.
Maximum speed: 11.5 knots
surfaced; 7 knots submerged.
Range: 4,180 miles at 6.5
knots surfaced, 2,290 miles at
11 knots surfaced; 86 miles
at 2.2 knots submerged, 10
miles at 7 knots submerged.
Torpedo tubes: four 21in
(533mm) forward; torpedoes:
6.
Guns: one 4in (102mm) 35-cal;
two single 13.2mm.
Mines: 2 tubes aft; 16 or 24
mines.
Complement: 56.

A *Bragadin* Class minelaying
boat leaving a Mediterranean
base.

Short-range minelaying and torpedo boats, with single hull
and blisters, developed from the *Pisani* Class. Maximum
operational depth: 288ft (90m). In 1935, the extreme stern
was reduced in length by approximately 12ft (4m) and,
as in the *Bandiera* and *Squalo* Classes, the bow section was
raised and blisters were added. These boats were not very
successful and were not repeated. During the war they
were used mainly to transport supplies to North Africa,
and the Aegean, or for training.

Fates   cause
date: boat: (see page 7):
1948   *Bragadin, Corridoni*   r

Corridoni in 1940. Note the
shape of the stern, characteristic of these minelaying
boats.

0 |—————|—————| 15

Outboard profile, 1940.

Conning tower, 1942.

Argonauta Class

Argonauta, Fisalia, Medusa:
Builder: C.R.D.A.,
Monfalcone.
Date: 1929–1932/32.
Serpente ex-*Nautilus, Salpa*:
Builder: Tosi, Taranto.
Date: 1930–1932/32.
Jantina, Jalea.
Builder: Odero Terni,
La Spezia.
Date: 1930–1933/33.
Normal displacement: 650–
665 tons surfaced; 810 tons
submerged.
Dimensions: 218ft 0in x 18ft
6in x 14ft 6in (61.50m x
5.65m x 4.64m).
Machinery: diesel: 2 Fiat-Tosi;
electric: 2 C.R.D.A. or
Marelli.
Maximum power: 1,500hp
surfaced; 800hp submerged.
Maximum speed: 14 knots
surfaced; 8 knots submerged.
Range: 4,900 miles at 9.5
knots surfaced, 2,300 miles at
14 knots surfaced; 110 miles
at 3 knots submerged, 7 miles
at 8 knots submerged.
Torpedo tubes: six 21in
(533mm); 4 forward, 2 aft;
torpedoes: 12.
Guns: one 4in (102mm) 35-cal;
two single 13.2mm.
Complement: 44.

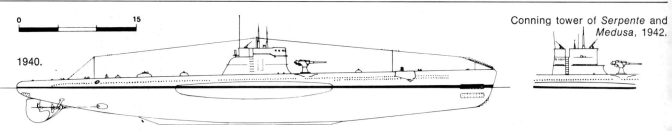

0   15

1940.

Conning tower of *Serpente* and
Medusa, 1942.

Short-range single hull boats with blisters, developed from the *Squalo* Class. Maximum operational depth: 256ft (80m); maximum fuel load: 28 tons. They were strong and manoeuvrable, if not very fast. Prototype of the *600* Class of which, in four successive series, 49 boats were built for the Italian Navy (others were built for several foreign navies).

During the war, they were used extensively in the Mediterranean, in action and for training. All were lost except *Jalea* which was stricken in 1948. In December 1940, *Serpente* sank the British destroyer *Hyperion* off Pantelleria.

Fates

date:	location:	boat:	cause (see page 7):
1940	Mediterranean	*Argonauta*	a
1941	Mediterranean	*Salpa, Jantina*	s
		Fisalia	n
1942	Mediterranean	*Medusa*	s
1943	Mediterranean	*Serpente*	sb
1948		*Jalea*	r

Jalea in 1942.

Settembrini Class

Luigi Settembrini,
Ruggero Settimo.
Builder: Tosi, Taranto.
Date: 1928–1932/1932.
Normal displacement: 953 tons surfaced; 1,153 tons submerged.
Dimensions: 226ft 9in x 25ft 6in x 11ft 2½in (69.1m x 6.6m x 4.4m).
Machinery: diesel: 2 Tosi; electric: 2 Ansaldo.
Maximum power: 3,000hp surfaced; 1,300hp submerged.
Maximum speed: 17 knots surfaced; 17.5 knots submerged.
Range: 3,700 miles at 12.5 knots surfaced, 6,200 miles at 7.3 knots surfaced; 100 miles at 3 knots submerged, 6 miles at 7 knots submerged.
Torpedo tubes: eight 21in (533mm); 4 forward, 4 aft; torpedoes: 12.
Guns: one 4in (102mm) 35-cal; four 13.2mm.
Complement: 56.

Short-range, partial double hull boats, developed from the *Mameli* Class, with considerably increased displacement and dimensions. Maximum operational depth: 288ft (90m); fuel load: 52 tons. On the whole, they were successful boats; fast, manoeuvrable and with good range.

Before 1940, they were stationed in the Red Sea for a long period. From 1940 to 1943, they alternated combat patrols and transport of supplies to North Africa with periods at the Submarine School. After the surrender, they were used for training, and *Settembrini* was lost in the Atlantic after being accidentally rammed by the American destroyer *Framet* in 1944.

Fates			cause
date:	location:	boat:	(see page 7):
1944	Atlantic	*Luigi Settembrini*	v
1948	—	*Ruggero Settimo*	r

Ruggero Settimo at Fiume (now Rijeka, Yugoslavia) in the summer of 1943.

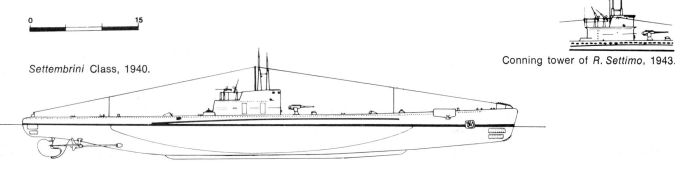

0   15

Settembrini Class, 1940.

Conning tower of *R. Settimo*, 1943.

Sirena Series, 600 Class

Sirena, Naiade, Nereide, Anfitrite, Galatea, Ondina:
Builder: C.R.D.A., Monfalcone.
Date: 1931–1933/34.
Diamante, Smeraldo:
Builder: Tosi, Taranto.
Date: 1931–1933/33.
Rubino, Topazio:
Builder: Cantieri Quarnaro, Fiume.
Date: 1931–1934/34.
Ametista, Zaffiro.
Builder: O.T.O., La Spezia.
Date: 1931–1934/34.
Normal displacement: 679–701 tons surfaced; 842–860 tons submerged.
Dimensions: 197½ft 0in x 21ft 0in x 15ft 0in/15ft 5in (60.18m x 6.45m x 4.6/4.7m).
Machinery: diesel: 2 Fiat or Tosi; electric: 2 C.R.D.A. or Marelli.
Maximum power: 1,350hp surfaced; 800hp submerged.
Maximum speed: 14 knots surfaced; 7.5 knots submerged.
Range: 2,280 miles at 12 knots surfaced, 488 miles at 8.5 knots surfaced; 7 miles at 7.5 knots submerged, 72 miles at 4 knots submerged.
Torpedo tubes: six 21in (533mm); 4 forward, 2 aft; torpedoes: 12.
Guns: one 3.9in (100mm) 47-cal; two-four single-twin 13.2mm.
Complement: 44–45.

Conning tower of *Sirena* and *Galatea*, 1943.

Conning tower of *Topazio*, 1941.

Conning tower of *Topazio*, 1943.

Sirena Series, *600* Class, 1940.

Right:
Topazio with modified conning tower in 1942. She was lost off Sardinia on 12 September 1943 (four days after the surrender) as the result of an error in identification by a British aircraft.

Below:
Smeraldo in 1939.

Short-range boats of the *600* Class. Compared to the earlier *Argonauta* Series, several improvements were introduced and the hull shape at the bow was modified to the *Squalo* type bow.

During the Spanish Civil War, the boats of this Series carried out a total of 18 patrols. From 1940 to 1943, they saw extensive service in the Mediterranean, operating from bases in Italy and the Aegean, and at the surrender, all except *Galatea* had been lost.

Fates

date:	location:	boat:	cause (see page 7):
1940	Mediterranean	*Diamante*	s
		Rubino	a
		Naiade	n
1941	Mediterranean	*Anfitrite*	n
		Smeraldo	uc
1942	Mediterranean	*Zaffiro*	a
		Ondina	n–a

1943	Mediterranean	*Nereide*	
		Sirena, Ametista	sl
		Topazio	e–a
1948		*Galatea*	

Conning tower of a *Sirena* Class boat in 1941. Note the changes to the after section: two 13.2mm Breda Model 31 anti-aircraft weapons in individual mounts (as normally carried), plus two 6.5mm Breda Model 30 automatic rifles (light machine-guns).

Archimede Class

Ferrarris, Galileo.
Builder: Tosi, Taranto.
Date: 1931–1934/35.
Normal displacement: 985 tons surfaced; 1,259 tons submerged.
Dimensions: 231ft 6in x 22ft 6in x 13ft 0in (70.5m x 6.8m x 4.1m).
Machinery: diesel: 2 Tosi; electric: 2 Marelli.
Maximum power: 3,000hp surfaced; 1,100hp submerged.
Maximum speed: 17 knots surfaced; 7.7 knots submerged.
Range: 3,300 miles at 16 knots surfaced, 10,300 miles at 8 knots surfaced; 105 miles at 3 knots submerged, 7 miles at 7.7 knots submerged.
Torpedo tubes: eight 21in (533mm); 4 forward, 4 aft; torpedoes: 16.
Guns: two 3.9in (100mm) 43-cal; two single 13.2mm.
Complement: 55.

Galileo leaving Taranto in 1935.

Galileo, 1940.

Long-range boats with partial double hulls, developed from the *Settembrini* Class whose hull shape they retained, although dimensions were increased and armament strengthened. They were successful boats with good performance. Maximum operational depth: 288ft (90m); fuel load: 60 tons.

Having participated in the Spanish Civil War, they were stationed in the Red Sea in June 1940. *Galileo* was lost on her first patrol: malfunction of her air-conditioning unit forced her to the surface where she engaged British warships until she was captured. She was employed by the Royal Navy as *X 2* until she was scrapped in 1946. *Ferraris* operated in the Red Sea and in the Indian Ocean until 1941 when she transferred to the Atlantic and was subsequently lost.

Fates			cause
date:	location:	boat:	(see page 7):
1940	Red Sea	*Galileo*	c
1941	Atlantic	*Ferraris*	a–n

Glauco Class

Glauco, Otaria.
Builder: C.R.D.A., Monfalcone.
Date: 1932–1935/35.
Normal displacement: 1,055 tons surfaced; 1,325 tons submerged.
Dimensions: 239ft 6in x 23ft 6in x 14ft 6in (73m x 7.2m x 5.12m).
Machinery: diesel: 2 Fiat; electric: 2 C.R.D.A.
Maximum power: 3,000hp surfaced; 1,100hp submerged.
Maximum speed: 17 knots surfaced; 8 knots submerged.
Range: 2,825 miles at 17 knots surfaced, 9,760 miles at 8 knots surfaced; 110 miles at 3 knots submerged, 8 miles at 8 knots submerged.
Torpedo tubes: eight 21in (533mm); 4 forward, 4 aft; torpedoes: 14.
Guns: two 3.9in (100mm) 47-cal; two single 13.2mm.
Complement: 57.

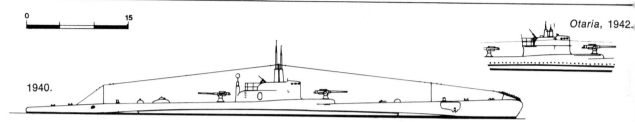

0   15

Otaria, 1942.

1940.

Long-range single hull boats with blisters; developed from the *Squalo* Class. Maximum operational depth: 288ft (90m); fuel load: 59 tons. The two boats of this Class had been ordered by Portugal, as *Delfim* and *Espadarte,* in 1931: the contract was cancelled in the same year, and construction continued on behalf of the Italian Navy. They were very successful boats: strong, fast and manoeuvrable when submerged and on the surface, and they had good internal arrangements.

They took part in the Spanish Civil War and subsequently, were sent to the Red Sea and the Indian Ocean. In 1940, they made several patrols in the Mediterranean and were then transferred to the Atlantic. In 1941, *Glauco* was lost, and *Otaria* returned to the Mediterranean where she was employed on offensive patrols and transport to North Africa, and for training.

Fates

date:	location:	boat:	cause (see page 7):
1941	Atlantic	*Glauco*	n
1948		*Otaria*	r

0   5   10   15

Glauco Class: inboard profile, plan and section.

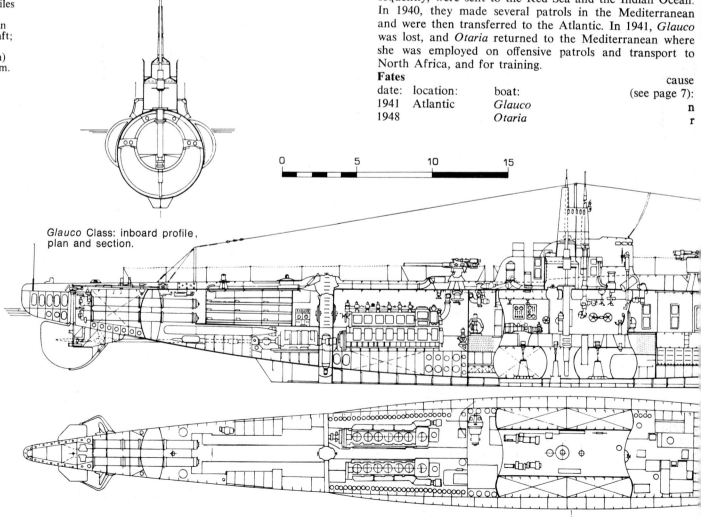

Otaria at the time of her commissioning in 1935.

Pietro Micca

Pietro Micca.
Builder: Tosi, Taranto.
Date: 1931–1935.
Normal displacement: 1,570 tons surfaced; 1,970 tons submerged.
Dimensions: 296ft 6in x 25ft 3in x 17ft 6in (90.3m x 7.7m x 5.3m).
Machinery: diesel: 2 Tosi; electric: 2 Marelli.
Maximum power: 3,000hp surfaced; 1,500hp submerged.
Maximum speed: 14.2 knots surfaced; 7.3 knots submerged.
Range: 2,600 miles at 14.5 knots surfaced, 6,400 miles at 9 knots surfaced; 60 miles at 4 knots submerged, 6 miles at 7.3 knots submerged.

Torpedo tubes: six 21in (533mm); 4 forward, 4 aft; torpedoes: 10.
Guns: two 4.7in (120mm) 45-cal; four 13.2mm (2 x 2).
Mines: 20 in central chamber.
Complement: 72.

Right:
Micca returning to Taranto, after having carried out a cargo-ferrying mission to North Africa in 1942.

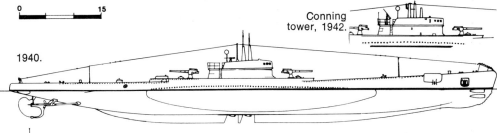

1940.

Conning tower, 1942.

0   15

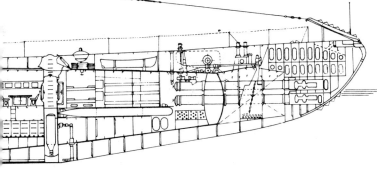

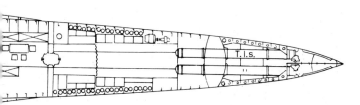

T. l.s.

Long-range torpedo and minelaying boat with partial double hull. Maximum operational depth: 288ft (90m); fuel load: 67 tons. A peculiar feature was the system for laying mines which were contained in a central cylindrical chamber in the lower part of the pressure hull. The mines were stored there, and were released through a watertight hatch in the bottom of the boat. Although experimental and not repeated, she had good seakeeping and was quite manoeuvrable despite her size.

During the war, she laid two minefields off Alexandria (June and August 1940) and was then converted to carry petrol and cargo. In 1941, she was seriously damaged by a submarine torpedo in the Aegean. She re-entered service and resumed transport activity. Between 1941 and 1943 when she was sunk, she carried 2,163 tons of petrol and cargo in 13 missions.

Fate			cause
date:	location:	boat:	(see page 7):
1943	Mediterranean	*Pietro Micca*	s

Calvi Class

Pietro Calvi, Giuseppe Finzi, Enrico Tazzoli.
Builder: O.T.O., La Spezia.
Date: 1932–1935/36.
Normal displacement: 1,550 tons surfaced; 2,060 tons submerged.
Dimensions: 276ft 6in x 25ft 4in x 13ft 0in (84.3m x 7.71m x 5.20m).
Machinery: diesel: 2 Fiat; electric: 2 San Giorgio.
Maximum power: 4,400hp surfaced; 1,800hp submerged.
Maximum speed: 16.8 knots surfaced; 7.4 knots submerged.
Range: 5,600 miles at 14 knots surfaced, 11,400 miles at 8 knots surfaced; 120 miles at 3 knots submerged, 7 miles at 7.4 knots submerged.
Torpedo tubes: eight 21in (533mm); 4 forward, 4 aft; torpedoes: 16.
Guns: two 4.7in (120mm) 45-cal; four 13.2mm (2 x 2).
Mines: *Enrico Tazzoli*: 14, two tubes in stern casing.
Complement: 72.

Long-range boats with complete double hulls, developed from a re-design of the *Balilla* Class. Maximum operational depth: 288ft (90m); fuel load: 75 tons.

The three boats took part in the Spanish Civil War, carrying out a total of five operations. During the first months of the Second World War, they carried out several patrols in the Mediterranean (*Tazzoli*) and Atlantic, departing from and returning to bases in Italy. *Calvi* and *Finzi* were the first Italian boats to pass through the Straits of Gibraltar, and in the autumn of 1940, they were posted permanently to the Atlantic, operating from Bordeaux. *Tazzoli* achieved the best results, sinking 19 merchant ships, totalling 96,533 GRT, in eight patrols.

Calvi was lost in 1942. In 1943, the other two boats were converted to transport materials to the Far East. *Tazzoli* was lost on the first of these missions. *Finzi* was still being refitted at Bordeaux, at the surrender, and was captured by the Germans who re-designated her *U.IT.21* and, without having used her, sank her, probably on 25 August 1944.

Fates

date:	location:	boat:	cause (see page 7):
1942	Altantic	*Pietro Calvi*	n
1943	Altantic	*Enrico Tazzoli*	a
1944	Bordeaux	*Giuseppe Finzi*	c, sb

Calvi returning to Bordeaux from an Atlantic patrol. Note damage to her casing.

Top:
Finzi arriving at Bordeaux from Italy on 30 September 1940.

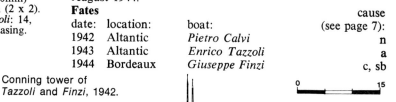

Conning tower of *Tazzoli* and *Finzi*, 1942.

Outboard profile of *Calvi* Class, 1940.

Inboard profile of *Perla* Class.

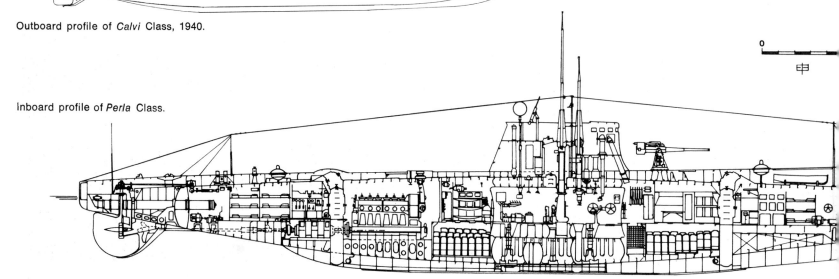

Perla Class

Conning
towers 1942/43.

Perla Class, 1940.

Built by O.T.O.,
La Spezia.

Iride (1940) and
Ambra (1942).

*Perla, Gemma, Berillo,
Diaspro, Turchese, Corallo*:
Builder: C.R.D.A.,
Monfalcone.
Date: 1935–1936/36.
Ambra, Onice, Iride ex-*Iris,
Malachite*.
Builder: O.T.O., La Spezia.
Date: 1935–1936/36.
Normal displacement: 696–
700 tons surfaced; 825–860
tons submerged.
Dimensions: 197ft 6in x 21ft
0in x 15ft 0in/15ft 5in
(60.18m x 6.45m x 4.6m/
4.7m).
Machinery: diesel: 2 Fiat or
C.R.D.A. or Tosi; electric:
2 C.R.D.A. or Marelli.
Maximum power: 1,400hp
surfaced; 800hp submerged.
Maximum speed: 14 knots
surfaced; 7.5 knots submerged.
Range: 2,500 miles at 12
knots surfaced, 5,200 miles at
8 knots surfaced; 7 miles at
7.5 knots submerged, 74 miles
at 4 knots submerged.
Torpedo tubes: six 21in
(533mm); 4 forward, 2 aft;
torpedoes: 12.
Guns: one 3.9in (100mm)
47-cal; two-four single-twin
13.2mm.
Complement: 45.

Short-range boats derived from the *Sirena* Series, but with
a slight increase in displacement and range, and with more
modern equipment. Maximum operational depth: 224ft–
256ft (70m–80m). There were external differences between
the boats built at Monfalcone and La Spezia, especially
in the conning tower profile. In 1940 and 1942, *Iride* and
Ambra were transformed to carry S.L.C. assault craft.
The deck gun was removed and watertight containers (4
on *Iride* and 3 on *Ambra*) were mounted on deck, forward
and aft of the conning tower, which was also modified
and reduced in size. The boats gave good results during the
war and confirmed the wisdom of building the *600* Class.

They took an active part in the Spanish Civil War,
during which, *Iride* and *Onice* were ceded for several
months to the Spanish Nationalist Navy, as *Gonzales
Lopez* and *Aguilar Tablada*. In June 1940, they were all
stationed in the Mediterranean except *Perla* which was in
the Red Sea. She transferred to Bordeaux, with other boats,
circumnavigating Africa, with two replenishment operations
at sea. She returned to Italy in September 1941.

The greatest success against warships by boats of this
Series, was the sinking by *Ambra* (Commander Arillo) and
Dagabur (*Adua* Series) of the British cruiser *Bonaventure*
off Solum on 31 March 1941. *Ambra* also carried out a
successful mission of transporting assault craft in December 1942 to the port of Algiers, which resulted in the
sinking of four ships totalling 20,000 GRT. The most active
boat was *Malachite* with 36 patrols and 29,085 miles logged.

Five of the series were lost to enemy action between
1940 and 1943. *Perla* was captured off Beirut on 9 July
1942, after a surface engagement, at the conclusion of
which, she was boarded by the British corvette *Hyacinth*
which took her in tow. Re-designated *P.712*, she was ceded
to the Greek Navy in 1943 and served until 1947. *Ambra*
was sabotaged on 8 September 1943: the other three boats
emerged from the war unscathed. During the period of
co-belligerency, *Onice* transferred to the United States
where she carried out training activities on the Atlantic
coast.

Fates

date:	location:	boat:	cause (see page 7):
1940	Mediterranean	*Berillo*	n
		Gemma	e–s
		Iride	a
1942	Mediterranean	*Corallo*	n
		Perla	c
1943	Mediterranean	*Malachite*	s
		Ambra	sb
1947	—	*Onice*	r
1948	—	*Diaspro, Turchese*	r

Turchese at Messina in 1938.

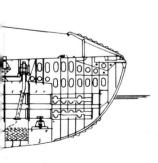

Adua Class

Adua, Axum, Aradam, Alagi (1):
Builder: C.R.D.A., Monfalcone.
Date: 1936–1936/37.
Macallé, Gondar, Neghelli, Ascianghi, Sciré, Durbo, Tembien, Lafolè, Beilul (2):
Builder: O.T.O., La Spezia.
Date: 1937–1938/38.
Dagabur, Dessiè, Uarscieck, Uebi Scebeli (3).
Builder: Tosi, Taranto.
Date: 1936–1937/37.
Normal displacement: 680–698 tons surfaced, 848–866 tons submerged.
Dimensions: 197ft 6in x 21ft 0in x 13ft 0in (60.18m x 6.45m x 4.6m/4.7m).
Machinery: diesel: (1) 2 C.R.D.A., (2) 2 Fiat, (3) 2 Tosi; electric: (1) 2 Fiat, (2) 2 Marelli, (3) 2 Marelli.
Maximum power: 1,400hp surfaced; 800hp submerged.
Maximum speed: 14 knots surfaced; 7.5 knots submerged.
Range: 2,200 miles at 14 knots surfaced, 3,180 miles at 10.5 knots submerged; 7 miles at 7.5 knots submerged, 74 miles at 4 knots submerged.
Torpedo tubes: six 21in (533mm); 4 forward, 2 aft; torpedoes: 12.
Guns: one 3.9in (100mm) 47-cal; two-four single-twin 13.2mm.
Complement: 45–46.

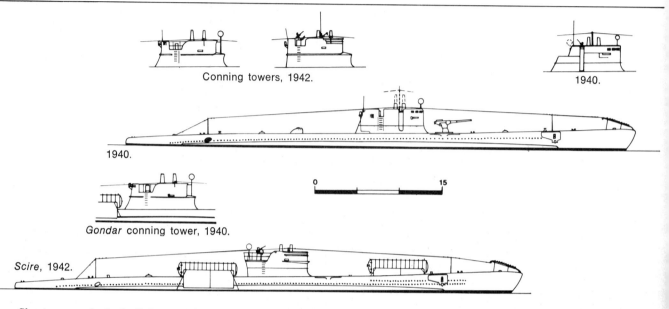

Conning towers, 1942.

1940.

1940.

Gondar conning tower, 1940.

Scire, 1942.

Short-range single hull boats, with midships ballast tanks and blisters, essentially a repetition of the earlier *Perla* Series. It was the most numerous series of the *600* Class and gave good results during the war. Despite the rather low surface speed, they were strong and manoeuvrable. Minor differences in displacement and construction existed between boats built in different yards. Two boats of the same type (ex-*Gondar* I and ex-*Neghelli* I) were sold to Brazil in 1937. Maximum operational depth: 256ft (80m); maximum fuel load: 47 tons.

The early boats of the Series took part in the Spanish Civil War, and all the boats were severely tested during the Second World War. They operated in the Mediterranean with the sole exception of *Macallé*, which was stationed in the Red Sea.

Between 1940 and 1941, *Gondar* and *Sciré* were modified to carry S.L.C. assault craft. The deck gun was removed and watertight containers were fitted on deck, one forward and two, aft of the conning tower. During the war, almost all the conning towers in this Class were modified and made smaller, as can be seen in the photographs and drawings.

The 'Africans'—they were so called after places in the Italian African colonies—achieved a high degree of success against British warships in the Mediterranean (Table 22).

There were many other successes against heavily escorted merchant ships. The most active boat was *Alagi* with 55 patrols and 36,729 miles logged. Of the two boats used to transport assault craft, *Gondar* was lost on her first mission: *Sciré* completed four missions against Gibraltar and one against Alexandria, during which, her S.L.C.s sank or damaged more than 22,000 GRT of merchant shipping (Gibraltar) and seriously damaged the British battleships *Valiant* and *Queen Elizabeth* (Alexandria, 19 December 1941). *Sciré* was lost on 10 August 1942, while attacking the port at Haifa.

Of the seventeen boats of the Series, only *Alagi* survived the war. Thirteen were lost in action between 1940 and 1943: *Aradam* and *Beilul* were lost through other causes at the surrender. *Axum* was lost during the period of co-belligerency.

Fates

date:	location:	boat:	cause (see page 7):
1940	Mediterranean	Durbo, Gondar, Lafolé, Uebi Scebeli	n
1940	Red Sea	Macallé	v–sb
1941	Mediterranean	Adua, Neghelli, Tembien	n
1942	Mediterranean	Dagabur, Dessié, Uarscieck	n
1943	Mediterranean	Ascianghi, Sciré	n
		Aradam	sb–a
		Beilul	c–a
		Axum	v–sb
1947		Alagi	r

Table 22: Major successes of the Adua Class during the Second World War

Boat:	Commander:	Date:	Result:	Type:	Ship:
Neghelli	Ferracuti	19 July 1940	damaged	cruiser	Coventry
Dagabur	Romano	31 March 1941	sank	cruiser	Bonaventure (with Ambra, Commander Arillo)
	Torri	14 December 1941	sank	cruiser	Galatea (with U 557, Commander Paulssen)
Alagi	Puccini	12 August 1942	damaged	cruiser	Kenya
Axum	Ferrini	18 August 1942	sank	cruisers	Cairo and Nigeria

Durbo, with the original conning tower, in 1939.

Alagi during an exercise in 1942. The conning tower modification is different from that carried out in Axum.

Axum, with modified conning tower, in 1941.

Foca Class

Foca, Zoea, Atropo.
Builder: Tosi, Taranto.
Date: 1936–1937/39.
Normal displacement: 1,318–1,333 tons surfaced; 1,647–1,659 tons submerged.
Dimensions: 266ft 9in x 23ft 6in x 12ft 4in (82.8m x 7.16m x 5.31m).
Machinery: diesel: 2 Fiat; electric: 2 Ansaldo.
Maximum power: 2,880hp surfaced; 1,250hp submerged.
Maximum speed: 15.2 knots surfaced; 7.4 knots submerged..
Range: 2,500 miles at 14 knots surfaced, 7,800 miles at 8 knots surfaced; 120 miles at 7 knots submerged.
Torpedo tubes: six 21in (533mm); 4 forward, 2 aft, torpedoes: 6.
Guns: one 3.9in (100mm) 43-cal (*Atropo* and *Zoea* from 1941: one 3.9in (100mm) 47-cal); four 13.2mm (2 x 2).
Mines: two tubes aft, 16 mines; one midships chamber, 20 mines.
Complement: 60–61.

Long-range torpedo and minelaying boats with partial double hull. Maximum operational depth: 288ft (90m); normal fuel load: 63 tons. Derived—with significant improvements—from the *Micca* Class, from which, they adopted the same minelaying system (20 mines in a central chamber). They retained the same number of torpedoes as the *Micca* Class, but their displacement was less. The number of mines was increased and the gun armament was re-adjusted. Mounting the deck gun on a revolving platform on the conning tower, as in the *Brin* Class, was unacceptable: in 1941, *Atropo* and *Zoea* had the gun mounted on deck, forward of the conning tower, the size of which was decreased.

Detail of the stern minelaying arrangement of a *Foca* Class boat.

The *Foca* Class boat *Zoea* at Taranto in 1942.

Atropo at Taranto in April 1941, with modified conning tower and re-positioned deck gun.

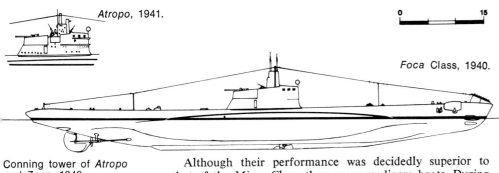

Atropo, 1941.

Foca Class, 1940.

Conning tower of Atropo and Zoea, 1942.

Although their performance was decidedly superior to that of the *Micca* Class, these were mediocre boats. During the war, they were used mainly to carry cargo and fuel to Africa: *Atropo* carried out 23 missions, transporting 10,778 tons; *Zoea,* 21 missions, 1,113 tons. Armed with torpedoes, they also made several 'ambush' patrols. As minelayers, like all the other Italian minelaying boats, their

activity was circumscribed: their most important operation was the laying of offensive minefields along the coast of Palestine by *Foca* and *Zoea* in October 1940, and in Greek waters by *Atropo*. *Zoea* completed her operation, but *Atropo* had to break off because of damage caused by the premature explosion of two mines: *Foca* was lost, probably because of a similar accident.

During the summer of 1942, *Zoea* accidentally sank while moored at Taranto. She was immediately salvaged and re-entered service shortly afterwards. During the period of co-belligerency, *Atropo* and *Zoea* were used for training Allied anti-submarine units, respectively in the Atlantic (Bermuda and Guantanamo, Cuba) and in the eastern Mediterranean (Haifa and Alexandria).

Fates

date:	location:	boat:	cause (see page 7):
1940	Mediterranean	Foca	uc
1947		Atropo, Zoea	r

Argo Class

Argo, Velella.
Builder: C.R.D.A., Monfalcone.
Date: 1931–1937/37.
Normal displacement: 794 tons surfaced; 1,018 tons submerged.
Dimensions: 206ft 9in x 22ft 6in x 10ft 6in (63.15m x 6.93m x 4.46m).
Machinery: diesel: 2 Fiat; electric: 2 C.R.D.A.
Maximum power: 1,500hp surfaced; 800hp submerged.
Maximum speed: 14 knots surfaced; 8 knots submerged.
Range: 5,300 miles at 14 knots surfaced, 10,176 miles at 8.5 knots surfaced; 100 miles at 3 knots submerged, 8 miles at 8 knots submerged.
Torpedo tubes: six 21in (533mm); 4 forward, 2 aft; **torpedoes:** 10.
Guns: one 3.9in (100mm) 47-cal; four 13.2mm (2 x 2).
Complement: 44–46.

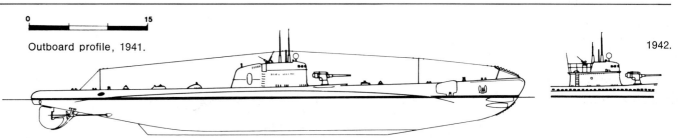

Outboard profile, 1941.

1942.

Medium-displacement boats, with partial double hull, built to a design of Cantieri Riuniti dell'Adriatico, deriving from the *Balilla* Class. The two boats had been ordered by Portugal and laid down in 1931. The contract was subsequently rescinded. The Italian Navy acquired them in 1935, and construction, already well advanced, was resumed.

Velella patrolling the Atlantic on 19 March 1941.

Maximum operational depth: 288ft (90m); fuel load: 60 tons.

The *Argo* Class were among the best of the Italian boats. Their surface speed was not high, but their range was good and they were strong and manoeuvrable. During the war, they were repeated, with slight improvements, as the *Tritone* Class.

Between 1938 and 1939, the two boats were stationed in the Mediterranean and the Red Sea, and returned to Italy before the outbreak of hostilities. Initially employed in the Mediterranean, towards the end of 1940 they were sent to the Atlantic, where they distinguished themselves by sinking or damaging 15,260 GRT of merchant shipping. *Argo* damaged the Canadian destroyer *Saguenay* with a torpedo.

In the second half of 1941, the two boats re-entered the Mediterranean where *Argo* distinguished herself in actions off Bougie in November 1942 and July 1943, during the Allied landing in Sicily. *Velella* was torpedoed by the British submarine *Shakespeare* off Salerno on 7 September 1943. *Argo,* refitting at Monfalcone on 8 September 1943, was sunk by her crew.

Fates

date:	location:	boat:	cause (see page 7):
1943	Mediterranean	Argo	sb
		Velella	s

Marcello Class

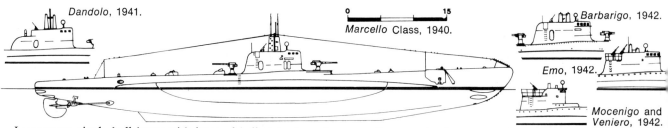

Dandolo, 1941.

Marcello Class, 1940.

Barbarigo, 1942.

Emo, 1942.

Mocenigo and Veniero, 1942.

Mocenigo, Dandolo, Veniero, Provana, Marcello, Nani, Barbarigo, Emo, Morosini:
Builder: C.R.D.A., Monfalcone.
Date: 1937–1939/39.
Cappellini, Faà di Bruno.
Builder: O.T.O., La Spezia.
Date: 1938–1939/39.
Normal displacement: 1,060–1,063 tons surfaced; 1,313–1,317 tons submerged.
Dimensions: 239ft 6in x 22ft 8in x 15ft 6in (73m x 7.19m x 5.1m).
Machinery: diesel: 2 C.R.D.A. or Fiat; electric: 2 C.R.D.A.
Maximum power: 3,600hp surfaced; 1,100hp submerged.
Maximum speed: 17.4 knots surfaced; 8 knots submerged.
Range: 2,500 miles at 17 knots surfaced, 7,500 miles at 9.4 knots surfaced; 8 miles at 8 knots submerged, 120 miles at 3 knots submerged.
Torpedo tubes: eight 21in (533mm); 4 forward, 4 aft; torpedoes: 16.
Guns: two 3.9in (100mm) 47-cal; four 13.2mm (2 x 2).
Complement: 57–58.

Below:
Marcello at the time of her commissioning in 1928.

Right:
Detail of the conning tower of *Barbarigo,* seen leaving Bordeaux for an Atlantic patrol in 1942. Note the reduced height of the periscope sleeves, the 13.2mm twin anti-aircraft guns, and the flags displaying tonnage sunk.

Long-range single hull boats with internal ballast tanks and external blisters, derived directly from the *Glauco* Class. Maximum operational depth: 328ft (100m); normal fuel load: 59 tons.

Cappellini and *Faà di Bruno* were built later, but were essentially identical with the earlier units. The *Marcello* Class were among the best Italian ocean-going boats of the Second World War, quite fast, strong and manoeuvrable. On trials, the fastest was *Provana* with 18.24 knots surfaced, 8.5 knots submerged. In June 1940, the eleven boats of the Class were deployed in the Mediterranean. After only seven days of war, *Provana* was rammed and sunk by the French corvette *La Curieuse,* which was escorting a convoy attacked by the submarine off Oran. *Cappellini* escaped adventurously from the Spanish port of Ceuta where she had sought refuge after an action with British ships.

From August 1940, the Class were sent to the Atlantic. Operating from Bordeaux, mainly against merchant shipping, they achieved a good degree of success: 28 ships, 136,020 GRT sunk; 17 ships, 60,835 GRT damaged. The highest score was by *Barbarigo:* 7 ships, 33,827 GRT sunk; 4 damaged, including a destroyer.

In two strange episodes, off the Brazilian coast (May 1942) and Freetown (October 1942), *Barbarigo* took part in bold attacks against naval formations by night. On both occasions, her commander, Mario Grossi, felt that he had hit and sunk American battleships. In fact, the vessels were smaller ships and none of the torpedoes scored a hit. These incidents were exploited by the wartime press, and arguments dragged on until several years after the war.

During a patrol in the Central Atlantic, *Cappellini* took

an active part in the rescue of survivors from the British liner *Laconia,* which was sunk by the German *U 156* on 12 September 1942.

Four boats were lost in the Atlantic. *Barbarigo* and *Cappellini* were transformed into transport submarines for the Far East in 1943: *Barbarigo* was sunk at the beginning of her first mission; *Cappellini* was captured by the Japanese at Sabang, where she had just arrived from Bordeaux on 10 September 1943. The Japanese ceded her to the German Navy which re-designated her *U. IT. 24* and re-armed her with a 4in (102mm) deck gun. In May 1945, she was incorporated in the Japanese Navy as *I. 503.* Found by the Americans at Kobe, she was scrapped the following year.

From the summer of 1943, several boats were brought back from the Atlantic to the Mediterranean: *Emo, Veniero* and *Mocenigo* were lost between 1942 and 1943. The only boat to survive the war was *Dandolo* (Commander Turcio). On 16 July 1943, she sank the British cruiser *Cleopatra,* and with 39,327 miles logged, established the record for Italian boats in the Mediterranean.

Fates

date:	location:	boat:	cause (see page 7):
1940	Mediterranean	*Provana*	n
	Atlantic	*Faà di Bruno*	n
1941	Atlantic	*Marcello, Nani*	n
1942	Atlantic	*Emo, Morosini*	a
	Mediterranean	*Veniero*	a
1943	Atlantic	*Barbarigo*	a
	Mediterranean	*Mocenigo*	a
	Pacific	*Cappellini*	c–r
1947		*Dandolo*	r

Brin Class

Brin, Galvani, Guglielmotti:
Builder: Tosi, Taranto.
Date: 1936–1938/38.
Archimede, Torricelli.
Builder: Tosi, Taranto.
Date: 1937–1939/39.
Normal displacement: 1,016 tons surfaced; 1,266 tons submerged.
Dimensions: 231ft 4in x 22ft 6in x 13ft 6in (72.4m x 6.68m x 4.54m).
Machinery: diesel: 2 Tosi; electric: 2 Ansaldo.
Maximum power: 3,000hp surfaced; 1,100hp submerged.
Maximum speed: 17.3 knots surfaced; 8 knots submerged.
Range: 9,000 miles at 7.8 knots surfaced, 3,800 miles at 15 knots surfaced; 90 miles at 4 knots submerged, 8 miles at 8 knots submerged.
Torpedo tubes: eight 21in (533mm); 4 forward, 4 aft; torpedoes: 14.
Guns: one 3.9in (100mm) 43-cal (*Brin, Guglielmotti, Archimede* from 1942: one 3.9in (100mm) 47-cal; four 13.2mm (2 x 2).
Complement: 54 .

Long-range partial double hull boats, developed from the *Archimede* Class. Maximum operational depth: 288ft (90m); fuel load: 61 tons.

The *Brin* Class adopted the same arrangement of mounting the deck gun in the conning tower as the *Foca* Class, which made their external appearance very similar to the latter boats. Again, it proved unsatisfactory and, from 1942, was altered. The 3.9in (100mm) 43-cal gun was replaced by the 3.9in (100mm) 47-cal, and this was transferred to the traditional position, forward of the conning tower, the dimensions of which, had been reduced.

Archimede and *Torricelli* were built 'secretly', to replace the boats of the same name which had been ceded to Spain in 1937 (see *Archimede* Class).

These boats represented an improvement on the *Archimede* Class: their hull shapes were more streamlined, and they had higher speed for the same installed power. On the whole, they were good boats, despite their tendency to ship heavy seas over the stern.

From 10 June 1940, all the boats were stationed in the Red Sea except *Brin* which had recently returned to Italy. *Torricelli* and *Calvi* were lost during the first days of the war. *Torricelli*, seriously damaged, was sunk by her own crew after a heavy engagement with British naval forces, during which, a round from her deck gun hit the destroyer *Khartoum* (1,690 tons), causing a fire which led to the loss of the destroyer.

Archimede and *Guglielmotti* carried out occasional patrols in the Red Sea and in the Indian Ocean. In May 1941, with other boats from Italian East Africa, they reached Bordeaux, having been replenished at sea by the German auxiliary cruiser *Atlantis*. After several patrols in the Mediterranean, *Brin* also transferred to Bordeaux. In the Atlantic, the three boats sank or damaged seven merchantmen totalling 53,200 GRT.

In September 1941, *Brin* and *Guglielmotti* returned to the Mediterranean where *Guglielmotti* was torpedoed and sunk by the British submarine *Unbeaten* in March 1942. *Archimede* remained in the Atlantic and was sunk by American aircraft off the coast of Brazil in April 1943. *Brin*, the sole survivor, was stationed at Colombo in Ceylon during the period of co-belligerency, in an anti-submarine training role for British units in the Indian Ocean.

Fates

date:	location:	boat:	cause (see page 7):
1940	Red Sea	*Torricelli*	n
	Indian Ocean	*Galvani*	n
1942	Mediterranean	*Guglielmotti*	s
1943	Mediterranean	*Archimede*	a
1948		*Brin*	r

Brin, 1941.

Brin, 1943.

0 ___ 15

Brin Class, 1940.

Left:
Brin at Cagliari late in 1941 after changes had been made to her conning tower and to her deck-gun layout.

Detail of a *Brin* Class boat, showing the characteristic mounting of the gun on the conning tower – a position that gave unsatisfactory results.

Liuzzi Class

Console Generale Liuzzi, Reginaldo Giuliani, Alpino Bagnolini, Capitano Tarantini.
Builder: Tosi, Taranto.
Date: 1938–1939/40.
Normal displacement: 1,166–1,187 tons surfaced; 1,484–1,510 tons submerged.
Dimensions: 252ft 6in x 23ft 0in x 13ft 9in (76.1m x 6.98m x 4.55m).
Machinery: diesel: 2 Tosi; electric: 2 Ansaldo.
Maximum power: 3,500hp surfaced; 1,500hp submerged.
Maximum speed: 17.5 knots surfaced; 8.4 knots submerged.
Range: 13,000 miles at 8 knots surfaced, 3,200 miles at 17 knots surfaced; 110 miles at 4 knots submerged, 8 miles at 8 knots submerged.
Torpedo tubes: eight 21in (533mm); 4 forward, 4 aft; torpedoes: 12.
Guns: one 3.9in (100mm) 47-cal; four 13.2mm (2 x 2).
Complement: 58.

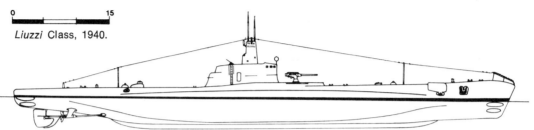

0 ____ 15

Liuzzi Class, 1940.

Bagnolini and *Guiliani*: modified conning tower, 1941.

Long-range partial double hull boats derived from the *Brin* Class, with slight increases in size, displacement, range and surface speed. The hull shape forward, was modified and the deck gun was abolished from the conning tower. Maximum operational depth: 288ft (90m); fuel load: 80 tons. They were good boats, though they retained some of the defects of the *Brin* Class, such as their inability to weather rough seas from the stern. On trials, *Liuzzi* achieved a maximum speed of 17.88 knots surfaced, 8.54 knots submerged. In 1941, *Bagnolini* and *Giuliani* had their conning towers modified and reduced in size. In 1943, they were converted to transport cargo to the Far East.

During the early months of the war, the four boats were deployed in the Mediterranean. On 12 June 1940, *Bagnolini* (Commander Tosoni-Pittoni) sank the British cruiser *Calypso*, south of Guado. *Liuzzi* was sunk by

destroyers on 27 June 1940. The three survivors were transferred to Bordeaux. *Tarantini* was torpedoed by the British submarine *Thunderbolt*, while returning from her first patrol. The other two boats sank or damaged eight merchantmen totalling 48,873 GRT.

From March 1941 to May 1942, *Giuliani* was stationed at the German Submarine School at Gotenhaven (Gdynia) to train Italian commanders in attack techniques against escorted convoys. At the surrender, she was refitting at Singapore before returning to Bordeaux with a valuable cargo. She was captured by the Japanese and ceded to the Germans who re-designated her *U. IT. 23.* In February 1944, she was sunk in the Straits of Malacca by the British submarine *Tally-Ho. Bagnolini* was captured at Bordeaux by the Germans and converted to a transport submarine. Re-designated *U. IT. 22,* she was lost in the southern Atlantic in March 1944, while carrying cargo to the Far East.

Fates

date:	location:	boat:	cause (see page 7):
1940	Mediterranean	*Console Generale Liuzzi*	n
	Atlantic	*Capitano Taranti*	s
1943	Atlantic	*Alpino Bagnolini*	c–a
	Pacific	*Reginaldo Giuliani*	c–s

Far right:
The launching of *Liuzzi* at Taranto on 17 September 1939.

Centre:
Detail of *Bagnolini*'s conning tower after modifications.

Below:
The *Liuzzi* Class *Bagnolini* being attacked by airc.aft in the Atlantic.

Marconi Class

Guglielmo Marconi,
Leonardo da Vinci:
Builder: C.R.D.A.,
Monfalcone.
Date: 1938–1940/40.
Michele Bianchi, Luigi
Torelli, Alessandro Malaspina,
Maggiore Baracca.
Builder: O.T.O., La Spezia.
Date: 1939–1940/40.
Normal displacement: 1,195
tons surfaced; 1,490 tons
submerged.
Dimensions: 251ft 0in x 22ft
4in x 15ft 6in (76.5m x
6.81m x 4.72m).
Machinery: diesel: 2 C.R.D.A.;
electric: 2 Marelli.
Maximum power: 3,600hp
surfaced; 1,500hp submerged.
Maximum speed: 17.8 knots
surfaced; 8.2 knots submerged.
Range: 2,900 miles at 17 knots
surfaced, 10,500 miles at 8
knots surfaced; 110 miles at
3 knots submerged, 8 miles at
8 knots submerged.
Torpedo tubes: eight 21in
(533mm); 4 forward, 4 aft;
torpedoes: 16.
Guns: one 3.9in (100mm)
47-cal; four 13.2mm (2 x 2).
Complement: 57.

Long-range single hull boats, with blisters: derived from the *Marcello* type but with slight increases in displacement and speed, and greatly increased range. One of the 3.9in (100mm) 47-cal deck guns was eliminated. Maximum operational depth: in excess of 288ft (90m); fuel load: 72 tons. These boats, which duplicated the excellent performance of the *Marcello* type, are considered to have been the best Italian ocean-going submarines built before the war.

Between 1941 and 1942, the conning tower was modified in all boats of the Class: size was reduced and the periscope sleeves were lowered. During the summer of 1942, *Da Vinci* was temporarily adapted, on a temporary basis, to carry a *CA* type midget submarine. The transformation entailed the removal of the deck gun, and the installation, forward of the conning tower, of a 'cell' fitted with clamps (shackles) to carry the *CA*, which could be freed while submerged, and could be retrieved by the carrier submarine (known as the 'kangaroo') while awash. Tests showed that the midgets needed improving before they could be considered operational.

Da Vinci re-shipped her deck gun and resumed normal activity in the Atlantic where she was later lost. Early in 1943, *Torelli* was extensively modified to carry cargo to the Far East. Apart from several Mediterranean patrols at the beginning of the war, by *Da Vinci, Marconi* and *Bianchi,* this Class operated in the Atlantic. *Malaspina* was the first boat to reach Bordeaux. She arrived from Naples on 4 September 1940 and scored the first Italian success against merchant shipping in the Atlantic by sinking the tanker *British Fame,* off the Azores.

In the Atlantic, the boats of this Series sank 38 merchant ships (216,227 GRT) and damaged seveni (24,465 GRT). Sixteen ships (116,686 GRT) were sunk by *Da Vinci* alone, six of them (58,973 GRT) during a single patrol under the command of Lieutenant G. F. Priaroggia. *Da Vinci* is also credited with the largest ship sunk by Italian submarines in the Atlantic, the liner *Empress of Canada* (21,517 GRT).

All the boats of the Class were lost in the Atlantic between 1941 and 1943 except *Torelli* which, at the surrender, was about to leave Singapore for Bordeaux with a valuable cargo. She was captured by the Japanese and ceded to the Germans who re-designated her *U. IT. 25.* In May 1945, she returned to the Japanese with the designation *I 504.* Found at Kobe in September 1945, she was scrapped the following year.

Fates

date:	location:	boat:	cause (see page 7):
1941	Atlantic	*Maggiore Baracca,*	
		Alessandro Malaspina	n
		Michele Bianchi	s
		Guglielmo Marconi	uc
1943	Atlantic	*Leonardo da Vinci*	n
1943–1946	Atlantic	*Luigi Torelli*	c–r

Left: *Baracca* at her commissioning in the summer of 1940. Below: *Marconi* at Bordeaux in July 1941. Note that, by this time, the conning tower has been modified and reduced in size.

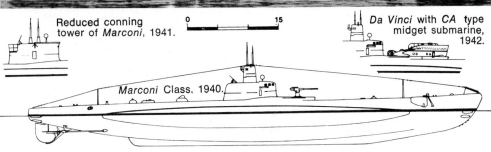

Reduced conning tower of *Marconi,* 1941.

0   15

Marconi Class, 1940.

Da Vinci with *CA* type midget submarine, 1942.

Cagni Class

Ammiraglio Cagni,
Ammiraglio Caracciolo,
Ammiraglio Millo,
Ammiraglio Saint Bon.
Builder: C.R.D.A.,
Monfalcone.
Date: 1939–1941/41.
Normal displacement: 1,708
tons surfaced; 2,190 tons
submerged.
Dimensions: 228ft 0in x 25ft
6in x 17ft 0in (87.9m x 7.76m
x 5.72m).
Machinery: diesel: 2 C.R.D.A.;
electric: 2 C.R.D.A.
Maximum power: 4,370hp
surfaced; 1,800hp submerged.
Maximum speed: 16.5 knots
surfaced; 8.5 knots submerged.
Range: 10.700 miles at 12
knots surfaced, 19,000 miles at
5.7 knots surfaced; 10 miles at
8.5 knots submerged, 107
miles at 3.5 knots submerged.
Torpedo tubes: fourteen 17.7in
(450mm); 8 forward, 6 aft;
torpedoes: 36.
Guns: two 3.9in (100mm)
47-cal; four 13.2mm (2 x 2).
Complement: 78.

Long-range single hull boats with blisters, built to a
C.R.D.A. design, derived from the Bernardis type. They
were the largest boats built in Italy. Maximum operational
depth: 328ft (100m); fuel load: 180 tons. Developed specifically for attacking ocean shipping, they had long range
and a powerful underwater and surface armament. The
adoption of 18in (457mm) torpedoes which were adjudged adequate against merchant ships, allowed the
installation of 14 torpedo tubes and an exceptional torpedo
load (36). Despite their large size, the boats were quite
manoeuvrable, had good seakeeping and were fairly com-
fortable. In the event, only *Cagni* experienced ocean-
going operations; the other three operated and were lost
in the Mediterranean.

The conning tower, according to the design, was to have
been similar to that of the *Marcello* Class, but it was
modified and reduced in size, immediately after delivery
to the navy, or during fitting out. On entering service in
mid 1941, they were used to supply the forces in North
Africa, and on ambush patrols in the Mediterranean.

Cagni and *Saint Bon* completed five transport missions;
Millo, four and *Caracciolo,* one: transporting a total of
approximately 2,370 tons of cargo. The last three mentioned
boats were lost while so engaged, and in the autumn of
1942, *Cagni* was finally sent to operate in the Atlantic

where she made two long patrols. The first of these started
at La Maddalena on 6 October 1942 and finished at
Bordeaux on 20 February 1943, setting a record of 137
days at sea for Italian submarines. Her second patrol of
84 days was made in the area off the Cape of Good Hope
and was interrupted by the surrender, whereupon, she
made for Durban. During these patrols, she sank two
merchant ships (total 9,395 GRT) and seriously damaged
the British armed merchant cruiser *Asturias* (22,445 GRT).

Cagni returned to Italy at the beginning of 1944. During
the period of co-belligerency, she was used to train Allied
and Italian anti-submarine forces, operating out of
Palermo. At the end of the war she was de-commissioned
and subsequently scrapped.

Fates

date:	location:	boat:	cause (see page 7):
1941	Mediterranean	*Ammiraglio Caracciolo*	n
1942	Mediterranean	*Ammiraglio Saint Bon,*	
		Ammiraglio Millo	s
1948		*Ammiraglio Cagni*	r

Cagni moored at Taranto
after her return to Italy in
1944.

Caracciolo returning to
Taranto from a cargo mission
to North Africa in 1941.

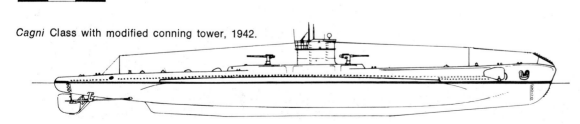

Cagni Class with modified conning tower, 1942.

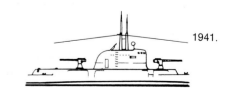

1941.

Acciaio Class

Acciaio, Cobalto, Nichelio, Platino:
Builder: O.T.O., La Spezia.
Date: 1940–1941/42.
Alabastro, Asteria, Avorio, Giada, Granito, Porfido:
Builder: C.R.D.A., Monfalcone.
Date: 1940–1941/42.
Argento, Bronzo, Volframio ex-Stronzio.
Builder: Tosi, Taranto.
Date: 1940–1942/42.
Normal displacement: 715 tons surfaced; 870 tons submerged.
Dimensions: 197ft 0in x 21ft 4in x 14ft 9in (60.18m x 6.44m x 4.78m).
Machinery: diesel: 2 Fiat (*Argento, Bronzo, Volframio* 2 Tosi); electric: 2 C.R.D.A. (*Argento, Bronzo, Volframio* 2 Ansaldo).
Maximum power: 1,400hp surfaced; 800hp submerged; *Argento, Bronzo, Volframio* 1,500hp surfaced; 800hp submerged.
Maximum speed: 14 knots surfaced; 7.3 knots submerged; *Argento, Bronzo, Volframio* 14.5 knots surfaced.
Range: 2,300 miles at 14 knots surfaced, 5,000 miles at 8.5 knots surfaced; 7 miles at 7 knots submerged, 80 miles at 3 knots submerged.
Torpedo tubes: six 21in (533mm), 4 forward, 2 aft; or eight 21in (533mm), 4 forward, 4 aft; torpedoes: 8 or 10.
Guns: one 3.9in (100mm) 47-cal; four 13.2mm (2 x 2).
Complement: 48.

Final development of the successful *600* Class, with improvements to internal equipment and layout. Maximum operational depth: 224–256ft (70–80m); normal fuel load: 41 tons. These boats gave good results despite the poor quality of the materials used in their construction— a handicap common to many Italian boats during the war. The thirteen boats of this Series were extensively active in the Mediterranean and achieved several successes against warships and merchantmen during 1942. All, except *Giada*, *Platino* and *Nichelio*, were lost in action or destroyed at the surrender. *Bronzo* was captured at Syracuse on 2 July 1943, having surfaced near British naval units thinking them to be Italian; her commander was unaware that the base had been occupied by the British. Re-designated *P. 714*, she was ceded in 1944 to the French who renamed her *Narval*. She was scrapped in 1948. *Giada*, having been temporarily re-designated *P.V.2* in 1948, was completely overhauled and put back into service in 1952. She was discarded in 1966. *Platino* was discarded in 1948: *Nichelio* was ceded to the U.S.S.R. (temporary designation *Z.14*) in 1949 as war reparation.

Fates

date:	location:	boat:	cause (see page 7):
1942	Mediterranean	*Alabastro*	a
		Cobalto	n
1943	Mediterranean	*Acciaio*	s
		Argento, Asteria, Avorio	n
		Bronzo	c
		Volframio	sb
1948	—	*Platino*	r
1949	—	*Nichelio*	r
1966	—	*Giada*	r

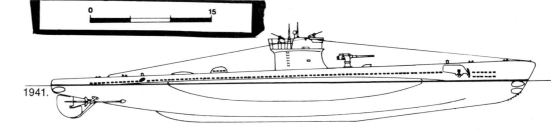

1941.

Giada on patrol in 1942.

Flutto Class

First series (12 units).
Flutto, Gorgo, Nautilo, Marea, Tritone, Vortice:
Builder: C.R.D.A., Monfalcone.
Date: 1941–1942/43.
Grongo, Murena, Sparide:
Builder: O.T.O., La Spezia.
Date: 1942–1943/–.
Cernia, Dentice, Spigola:
Builder: Tosi, Taranto.
Date: 1943–

Second series (24 units).
Alluminio, Antimonio, Fosforo, Manganese, Silicio, Zolfo:
Builder: O.T.O., La Spezia.
Date: 1942– .
Bario, Cadmio, Cromo, Ferro, Iridio, Litio, Oro, Ottone, Piombo, Potassio, Rame, Rutenio, Sodio, Vanadio, Zinco:
Builder: C.R.D.A., Monfalcone.
Date: 1943–
Amianto, Magnesio, Mercurio:
Builder: Tosi, Taranto.

Third series (12 units).
Attinio, Azoto, Bromo, Carbonio, Elio, Molibdeno, Osmio, Osigeno, Plutonio, Radio, Selenio, Tungsteno;
6 units: C.R.D.A., Monfalcone; 3 units: Tosi, Taranto; 3 units: O.T.O., La Spezia. (None of the third series was laid down; construction of the second series was suspended at the surrender):

Normal displacement: 945 tons surfaced, 958 tons surfaced; 1,113 tons submerged, 1,170 tons submerged.
Dimensions: First series: 206ft 9in x 22ft 9in x 16ft 0in (63.15m x 6.98m x 4.87m); Second series: 210ft 0in x 22ft 9in x 16ft 4in (64.19m x 6.98m x 4.93m).
Machinery: diesel: 2 Fiat; electric: 2 C.R.D.A.
Maximum power: 2,400hp surfaced; 800hp submerged.
Maximum speed: 16 knots surfaced; 7 knots submerged.
Range: 5,400 miles at 8 knots surfaced, 2,000 miles at 16 knots surfaced; 80 miles at 4 knots submerged, 7 miles at 7 knots submerged.

Torpedo tubes: six 21in (533mm); 4 forward, 2 aft; torpedoes: 12.
Guns: First series: one 3.9in (100mm) 47-cal; four 13.2mm (2 x 2); Second series: two single 20mm 70-cal or 20mm 65-cal.
Complement: 49.

Tritone on trials in July 1943.

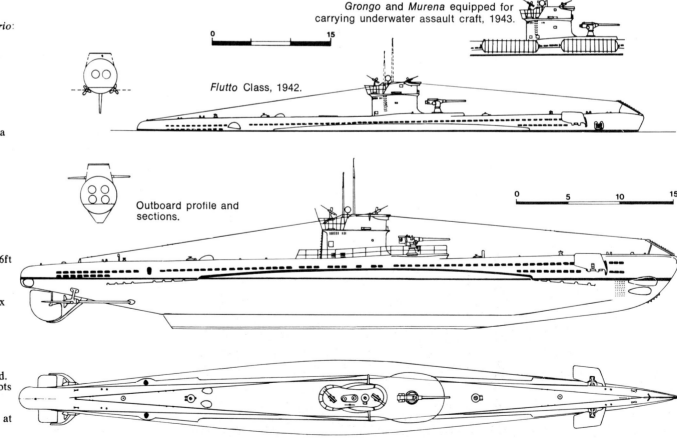

Grongo and *Murena* equipped for carrying underwater assault craft, 1943.

Flutto Class, 1942.

Outboard profile and sections.

Flutto.

Medium-displacement boats with partial double hulls, developed from the *Argo* Class. Maximum operational depth: 400ft (120m); emergency full fuel load: 52 tons; maximum range at economic speed: approximately 13,000 miles.

Dimensions were slightly increased; the conning tower size was reduced, internal arrangements and silent trim mechanisms were improved, hull strength and anti-aircraft armament were increased and crash-dive time was reduced to approximately 30 seconds.

The *Flutto* Class were the best medium-displacement boats in Italy until 1945.

A total of 48 boats had been planned, subdivided into three Series of 12, 24 and 12 boats. The second series had slightly larger dimensions than the first, in order to eliminate certain trim problems: the third series was to have been an exact copy of the second.

The construction programme was to have been completed by the end of 1944, but only eight of the first series (*Flutto, Gorgo, Nautilo, Marea, Tritone, Vortice, Murena* and *Sparide*) entered service before 8 September 1943. The others, and all of the second series were lost while fitting out or building, at the surrender. Only three more boats were launched (*Grongo, Litio* and *Sodio*): none of the

Marea leaving Taranto in 1944.

units of the third series and several of the second were never laid down.

Grongo and *Murena* were equipped (during fitting out) with four cylinders for carrying underwater assault craft. Both boats were captured by the Germans on 8 September 1943 and designated *U.IT.20* and *U.IT.16*; later they were lost.

Only five (*Tritone, Gorgo, Flutto, Marea, Vortice*) boats of the first series were able to take an active part in operations: they were used chiefly in the Mediterranean and three of them were lost in action.

In 1949, *Marea* was ceded to the U.S.S.R. as war reparation. *Vortice* designated *P.V.1* from 1949 to 1952 and overhauled a number of times, remained in service with the Italian Navy until 1967.

Nautilo, captured by the Germans at the surrender, and designated *U.IT.19*, was sunk at Pola (Pula) in 1944; salvaged and rebuilt after the war, she was commissioned in the Yugoslav Navy as *Sava.*

Several boats of the second series, captured while building, were launched by the Germans, but none were completed. *Bario,* launched by the Germans under the designation *U.IT.7,* was damaged during an air attack in 1945. Almost completely rebuilt, she re-entered service in 1961 as *Pietro Calvi.*

Fates

date:	location:	boat:	cause (see page 7):
1943	Mediterranean	*Flutto, Gorgo, Tritone*	n
		Grongo	sb–c b
		Murena, Nautilo	sb–c b
		Sparide	sb b
		Bario	c–b
		Ferro	c sb
		Litio	c b
		Piombo, Potassio, Rame, Sodio, Zinco	c sb
1949	—	*Marea*	r
1967	—	*Vortice*	r

R Class

Romolo, Remo:
Builder: Tosi, Taranto.
Date: 1942–1943/43.
R 3, R 4, R 5, R 6:
Builder: Tosi, Taranto:
Date: 1943–
R 7, R 8, R 9:
Builder: C.R.D.A.,
Monfalcone.
Date: 1943–
R 10, R 11, R 12.
Builder: O.T.O., La Spezia.
Date: 1943–
Normal displacement: 2,210
tons surfaced; 2,606 tons
submerged.
Cargo capacity: 610 tons.
Dimensions: 232ft 0in x
25ft 0in (*R 11, R 12,* 26ft 3in)
x 17ft 6in (70.7m x 7.86m
(*R 11, R 12,* 7.92m) x 5.34m).
Machinery: diesel: 2 Tosi;
electric: 2 Marelli.
Maximum power: 2,600hp
surfaced; 900hp submerged.
Maximum speed: 13 knots
surfaced; 6 knots submerged.
Range: 12,000 miles at 9 knots
surfaced; 110 miles at 3.5
knots submerged.
Torpedo tubes: several units
were to have had two 17.7in
(450mm).
Guns: three single 20mm
70-cal on 'disappearing'
mounts.

Partial double hull transport submarines, with four water-tight holds of a total capacity of 785 cu. yards (600 cu. m). Maximum operational depth: 328ft (100m); maximum fuel load: 200 tons.

Developed for the transportation of cargo to and from the Far East, they could also be employed to carry fuel over medium distances. Only two boats (*Romolo* and *Remo*) were able to enter service before the surrender, and both were lost during their maiden voyages. The construction of the other three boats was never completed. Two of the boats under construction at Taranto (*R 3* and *R 4*) were launched after the war, and were subsequently discarded and scrapped: the other two were dismantled on the ways.

The boats building in the north, were incorporated in the German Navy (*U.IT.1–U.IT.6*) which continued their construction, but none entered service and all were lost between 1944 and 1945. The hull of *R 12* is still (1972) used by the Italian Navy as a floating diesel fuel storage tank at Ancona (GRS. 523).

The *R* Class, although they could not be tested in service, are considered to have been particularly well-conceived.

Fates

date:	location:	boat:	cause (see page 7):
1943	Mediterranean	*Romolo*	a
		Remo	s
		R 7, R 8, R 9	c b
		R 10, R 11, R 12	c sb

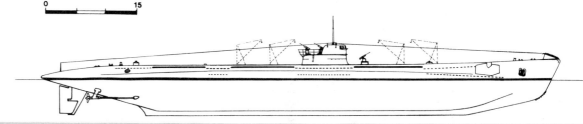

The incomplete hull of *R. 12,* used as a floating diesel oil tank (GRS.523) after the war.

Midget submarines and special craft

During the Second World War, the Italian Navy commissioned numerous midget submarines and used a well-designed 'human torpedo', the S.L.C. (*Siluro a Lenta Corsa* = slow-running torpedo, also known as a 'pig'), with great success.

This was a 21in (533mm) torpedo fitted with an electric motor powered by batteries, with an explosive charge in the detachable head. The weapon was manned by two operators equipped with breathing-gear.

Designed by the naval engineers, Elios Toschi and Teseo Tesei in about 1935, they derived from the weapon known as the 'leech' with which, in November 1918, Paolucci and Rossetti attacked the Austrian battleship *Viribus Unitis* in the port of Pola.

Carried in watertight containers by submarine to the target's vicinity, the S.L.C. passed beneath anti-submarine nets and the head containing the charge was removed and fixed to the target's hull or propellers. The torpedo and two-man crew withdrew and a clockwork mechanism detonated the charge at a pre-determined time.

Between 1941 and 1943, underwater assault craft sank or seriously damaged 50,000 GRT of merchant shipping and 63,000 tons of warships, in daring attacks on Alexandria and Algiers. A major success was achieved during the night of 18/19 December 1941 when three S.L.C., transported by *Sciré* to within a few miles of Alexandria, seriously damaged the British battleships *Valiant* and *Queen Elizabeth* (30,600 tons), a tanker and a destroyer.

The British copied their 'chariots' from the Italian S.L.C., and in co-operation with the British craft, the Italians achieved further success during the period of co-belligerency, seriously damaging the incomplete hull of the aircraft carrier *Aquila* at Genoa, thus preventing its use as a blockship by the retreating Germans.

The principal characteristics of the S.L.C. were as follows. Length: 22ft (6.7m); diameter: 21in (533mm); propulsion gear one 1.1hp electric motor (subsequently 1.6hp); speed: normal 2.3 knots, maximum 4.5 knots; range: 15 miles at 2.3 knots, 4 miles at 4.5 knots; explosive charge: 485lb (220kg), subsequently 551.25lb (250kg) and 661.5lb (300kg); maximum operational depth: 82–100ft (25–30m).

The first two midget submarines built by the Italian Navy after the First World War, entered service in April 1938. They were the *CA. 1* and *CA. 2* (CA = coastal type A) experimental boats which did not give good results as torpedo boats because they were unstable platforms at periscope depth, even in moderate seas.

In 1941, they were transformed to carry frogmen (*gamma* men). Periscope and torpedoes were removed, and arrangements were made for the entry and exit of divers, and the carrying of eight explosive charges. While tests were being made, construction was ordered of two new and improved boats, specially designed to carry frogmen.

The *CA* boats were to have been transported by submarines to attack American and West African Atlantic ports. Carrying, releasing and retrieving tests were carried out at Bordeaux in September 1942, with *CA. 2* and *da Vinci*. The implementation of the Atlantic missions was postponed until the second series of craft would be trained and ready (presumably in December 1943), but the surrender found both craft still being completed at La Spezia and put an end to the plan.

Before Italy entered the war, the design of a new type of 'pocket' submarine, the *CB* (coastal type B) was developed, deriving from the *CA* type, but considerably improved. During the war, 22 *CB* craft were ordered, but only 12 (*CB. 1*–*CB. 12*) were delivered to the Italian Navy between January 1941 and August 1943. *CB. 13*–*CB. 22*, still under

Below:
An S.L.C. ('human' torpedo), known as a 'pig'.
Bottom:
CB8, one of the 12 *CB* coastal type 'pocket' submarines actually delivered to the Italian Navy.

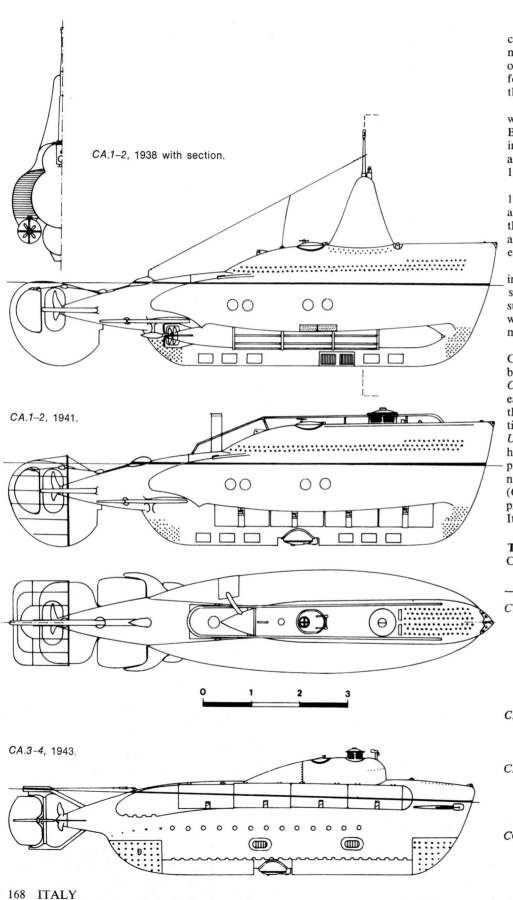

CA.1–2, 1938 with section.

CA.1–2, 1941.

0   1   2   3

CA.3–4, 1943.

construction at the surrender, were completed and commissioned by the Navy of the R.S.I. (Fascist Government of Northern Italy). The complete programme had called for another fifty CBs, but none was laid down because of the surrender.

Designed primarily for an anti-submarine role, the CBs were used instead for offensive missions, mainly in the Black Sea where they had several successes, the most important being the sinking of the Soviet submarines S 32 and Shch 306 by CB. 3 and CB. 2 on 15 and 18 June 1942.

Of the six boats sent to the Black Sea by rail early in 1942, one was lost and five were captured by the Germans at the surrender and ceded to the Rumanian Navy. Of the remainder, one was captured by the Germans at Pola and another five operated with the Italian Navy until the end of the war.

In the spring of 1943, it was decided to build and employ in groups, a new type of midget, replacing the normal short- and medium-range boats in areas where anti-submarine activity was particularly effective. Smaller boats would operate in greater safety and could be produced more quickly and cheaply, and in greater numbers.

Two very similar designs were approved; one by Societa' Caproni (CC = Costiero Caproni = coastal Caproni) and one by Cantieri Riuniti dell'Adriatico of Monfalcone (CM = Costiero Monfalcone = coastal Monfalcone): a prototype of each was ordered. After evaluation trials, it was decided that one of the two types would be chosen for standardization and that the recognition code would be CU (Costiero Unificato = coastal standard). By 8 September 1943, orders had been placed for 16 CM and 8 CC, in addition to the prototypes, but the programme called for a much greater number of boats. Despite rapid and satisfactory progress (CM.1 was launched on 5 September 1943), the surrender prevented any of these units being commissioned in the Italian Navy.

Table 23: Details of Italian midget submarines

Class:	Number built:	Boats:	Date built:
CA	4	CA. 1 torpedo version	1938
		CA. 2 carrier for frogmen version	1941
		CA. 3, CA. 4	1943
CB	12 + 10	CB. 1 – CB. 12	1941–1943
		CB. 13 – CB. 22	
CM	0 + 3	CM. 1 – CM. 3	
CC	3	CC. 1 – CC. 3	

CM.1 on trials.

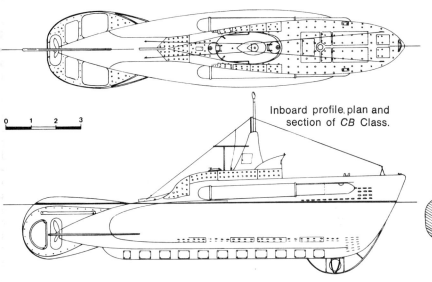

Inboard profile, plan and section of CB Class.

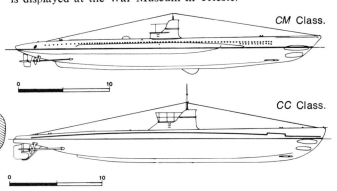

CM Class.

CC Class.

CM. 1 was completed by the Germans as U. IT. 17 and ceded to the Navy of the R.S.I.. She was returned to the Italian Navy in 1945 and was de-commissioned. Only one of the other two CMs had been laid down and none of the CCs were completed. Part of the incomplete hull of CM. 2 is displayed at the War Museum in Trieste.

Displacement (tons): surfaced/ submerged	Dimensions: ft(m)	Machinery (hp): diesel/electric	Speed (knots): surfaced/ submerged	Range (miles at knots): surfaced/ submerged	Armament:	Complement:
13.5/16.4	32ft 9in x 6ft 3in x 5ft 3in (10m x 1.9m x 1.6m)	one 60/one 25	6.5/5	700 at 4/57 at 3	Two 18in(457mm) 'cage' type torpedo launchers	2
12/14		—/one 21	7/6	—/70 at 2	Two torpedoes Eight 220.5lb(100kg) charges Twenty small charges (limpet mines)	3
12.8/14	34ft 1½in x 6ft 3in x 5ft 10½in (10.4m x 1.9m x 1.8m)	—/one 21	7/6	—/70 at 2		3
36/45	49ft 2in x 9ft 10in x 6ft 10in (15m x 3m x 2.10m)	one 90/one 100	7.5/7	1,400 at 5/50 at 3	Two 18in(457mm) external non-watertight torpedo tubes Two torpedoes	4
92/114	107ft 11in x 9ft 2in x 8ft 10in (32.9m x 2.8m x 2.7m)	two 600/two 120	14/6	2,000 at 9/70 at 4	Two 18in(457mm) forward torpedo tubes Two 13.2mm machine-guns in twin 'disappearing' mounts	8
99.5/117	108ft 3in x 8ft 10in x 7ft 2in (33m x 2.7m x 2.18m)	two 700/two 120	16/9	1,200 at 10/70 at 4	Three 18in(457mm) forward torpedo tubes Two 13.2mm machine-guns in twin 'disappearing' mounts	8

Type *CB* midget submarines moored at Sevastopol in the Black Sea, in October 1942.

CA Class.
Midget submarines transportable by railway, designed for torpedo firing (*CA. 1* and *CA. 2*) and later transformed into carriers for frogmen. From the start, *CA. 3* and *CA. 4* were designed for employment as assault craft. All units were lost at the surrender.

CB Class.
Midget submarines transportable by railway, developed by CAP (Caproni Group). Test depth: 180ft(55m). The boats of the second series were completed for the R.S.I.

Fates

date:	location:	boat:	cause (see page 7):
1942	Black Sea	*CB. 5*	b
1943	Black Sea	*CB. 1, CB. 2, CB. 3, CB. 4, CB. 6*	c
	Mediterranean	*CB. 7*	c
1948		*CB. 8, CB. 9, CB. 10, CB. 11, CB. 12*	r

CM Class.
Single hull midget submarines with internal ballast tanks. Maximum operational depth: 232ft(70m). Modified tank engines (P.40) were mounted. None were completed before the surrender.

Fates

date:	location:	boat:	cause (see page 7):
1943	Mediterranean	*CM. 1, CM. 2*	c–r

CC Class.
Single hull midget submarines with internal ballast tanks. Maximum operational depth: 232ft(70m) designed. None entered service: construction suspended at surrender.

Foreign submarines in Italian service

Rismondo, ex-Ostvetnik, after modification refit in 1941.

Bajamonti Class (2 units)
Francesco Rismondo ex-*N 1, Antonio Bajamonti* ex-*N. 2* (see Yugoslavia: *Smeli, Osvetnik, Hrabi*)
Details as in Yugoslav section except: displacement: 665 tons surfaced; 822 tons submerged.
In April 1941, at the time of the occupation of Yugoslavia by Axis forces, Italian troops captured a number of

Yugoslav ships in port. On 17 April, the submarines *Osvetnik, Smeli* and *Hrabi* were found almost intact at Cattaro (Kotor). They were incorporated in the Italian Navy as war booty, and initially designated *N. 1, N. 2* and *N. 3. N. 3* (ex-*Hrabi*), built in Britain between 1926 and 1928, similar to the British *L* Class, was scrapped in 1941 because of her poor state of repair. *N. 1* and *N. 2* were refitted and modernized at Pola, and entered service in the Italian Navy as *Francesco Rismondo* and *Antonio Bajamonti*.

They were short-range partial double hull boats, built at the Ateliers et Chantiers de la Loire of Nantes between 1927 and 1929. In 1941, they were still in good condition, and during their refit, their armament was partially replaced and their conning towers were modified. Despite several good features such as submerged stability and noteworthy diving time (35 seconds), their 'age' and limited operational depth (200ft (60m)) confined them to a training and experimental role. Both boats were lost at the surrender.

Fates

date:	location:	boat:	cause (see page 7):
1943	Mediterranean	*Francesco Rismondo*	c, sb
		Antonio Bajamonti	sb

FR.112 Class (2 units)
FR.112 ex-*Saphir*, *FR.116* ex-*Turquoise*
(see France: *Saphir* Class)
Coastal submarines captured at Bizerte in December 1942. *FR.116* was scuttled there in May 1943, without having been re-commissioned. *FR.112*, transferred to Naples, was stricken on 21 April 1943 and used as a floating battery-charging unit.

FR.117 Class (1 unit)
FR.117 ex-*Circé*
(see France: *600 tonnes* Class)
Ocean-going submarine salvaged at Toulon where she had been scuttled in November 1942. Towed to Genoa, she was undergoing refit at the surrender and was subsequently scrapped by the Germans.

FR.111 Class (four units)
FR.111 ex-*Phoque*, *FR.113* ex-*Requin*, *FR.114* ex-*Espadon*, *FR.115* ex-*Dauphin*
(see France: *Requin* Class)
Details as in French section
Coastal submarines captured at Bizerte in December 1942. Transferred to Italy and put in dock for conversion to transport submarines. Only *FR.111* entered service and she was lost in action. The other three were still in dock at the surrender and were subsequently sunk or scrapped by the Germans.

FR.112, ex-*Saphir*, at Naples in 1943.

Fates

date:	location:	boat:	cause (see page 7):
1943	Mediterranean	*FR.111*	a
		FR.113	sb
		FR.114, FR.115	c

FR.118 (Class 1 unit) *FR.118* ex-*Henri Poincaré*
(see France: *1500 tonne* Class)
The Italian Navy incorporated numerous French naval ships as spoils of war. Among them were ten submarines which had been captured by the Germans at Bizerte and Toulon in November-December 1942 and ceded to Italy.

These ten boats belonged to four classes (*Requin, Saphir, 600 tonne* and *1500 tonne*). Only eight of them received Italian designations, which consisted of the letters *FR* followed by a three-digit number. *Nautilus* of the *Saphir* Class, and *Calypso, 600 tonne* Class, were lost during an air attack on Bizerte in January 1943, while awaiting transfer to Italy.

The *Requin* Class boats (*FR.111, FR.113, FR.114, FR.115*) were converted to transport submarines. All their original armament except the two 13.2mm anti-aircraft guns, was removed. The boats were equipped to carry 50 tons of cargo and 145 tons of fuel. Only *F.111* (ex-*Phoque*) entered service before the surrender, but she was lost in action. The transformation and refit of the other boats were appreciably delayed by the poor condition in which they were captured, and the lack of spare parts. At the surrender they were still in the yards at Pozzuoli, Genoa and Castellamare di Stabia, and were sabotaged or captured by the Germans.

Of the two *Saphir* Class minelaying boats, only *FR.112* (ex-*Saphir*) reached Italy from Bizerte. When the Axis troops in Tunisia surrendered in May 1943, *FR.116* (ex-*Turquoise*), immobilized, was scuttled at Bizerte with the *600 tonne* Class *FR.117* (ex-*Circé*).

Because of her poor condition and lack of replacement parts, *FR.112* was de-commissioned without having been refitted, and was used as a floating battery-charging unit for submarines and corvettes in the harbour at Naples.

At the surrender, the only *1500 tonne* Class boat, *Henri Poincaré*, whose Italian designation probably was to have been *FR.118*, was still refitting at Genoa, where she had been towed from Toulon after her salvage (she had been scuttled by her crew in November 1942 and salvaged by the Italian Navy). On 9 September 1943, she was captured by the Germans who did not continue her refit.

S Class (9 units)
S.1 ex-*U 428*, *S.2* ex-*U 746*, *S.3* ex-*U 747*, *S.4* ex-*U 429*, *S.5* ex-*U 748*, *S.6* ex-*U 430*, *S.7* ex-*U 749*, *S.8* ex-*U 1161*, *S.9* ex-*U 750*
(see Germany: Type VII C and Type VII C 41–42)
In 1943, the Italian Navy received nine submarines (*S 1–S 9*) of the VII C type from the German Navy, to replace the Italian ocean-going boats which had been converted to transport cargo to and from the Far East. At the surrender, they were still training in Germany and were reintegrated in the German Navy with their former numbers. Several sources mention the possibility of a tenth submarine of the same type, *S 10* (ex-*U 1162*) having been scheduled for cession to the Italians, but not delivered because of the surrender.

Japan

Right: *I.59* (later *I.159*).
Below right: *I.29* in 1942.

With the naval treaties of Washington in 1922 and London in 1930, Japan's position as a major naval power was officially recognized. The overall displacement limitations imposed by the treaties established that the Japanese Navy was to be exceeded, in the battleship category, only by the United States and the British Navies, according to the well-known 5–5–3 ratio. Japan was not satisfied with this, however, and proposed a ratio of 10–10–7 which she felt more suited her needs. Britain and America utterly refused to raise the limits or modify the proportions. Japan then began to develop a new strategy of 'attrition', based on the employment of a large underwater fleet.

The Imperial Navy held that in the event of a war with the United States, the Philippines, Borneo and Indonesia should be invaded immediately, and that the fleet should then assume a defensive role while awaiting the reaction of the enemy, who would almost certainly try to liberate the occupied territories.

The Japanese Navy, operating near its own bases, would have the advantage. In addition, American ships would suffer heavy losses to Japanese submarines. During this phase of the anticipated war, Japanese submarines would play a major role and it was essential that they be fully prepared. For this reason, the Japanese delegates to the London Naval Conference of 1930 fought to prevent the underwater arm being internationally prohibited, and to achieve the same amount of overall tonnage for submarines as had been granted to the other two major powers.

Although the 'big three' were each recognized as having the right to commission underwater fleets up to a total of 52,000 tons displacement, Japan was not satisfied and insisted that not less than 78,000 tons be allocated. Until the naval treaties were revoked in 1934, Japan stayed within the prescribed limits.

Between 1925 and 1940, the Japanese Navy developed its submarine forces on the basis of three types of boat: a type of cruiser-submarine (*Junsen*) whose prototype had been inspired by the British *K* Class and the German *U 139* types of the First World War, to be used for reconnaissance and in operations far removed from base; a long-range or Fleet type (*Kaidai*), developed from the preceding type but with slightly increased displacement, for co-operation with surface forces and for patrolling enemy ocean routes; a medium type, originally derived from the French *Schneider-Laubeuf* boats of the early years of the century, intended for home defence.

While the *Junsen* were to have operated mainly individually, replacing cruisers in the reconnaissance role (several were equipped with a floatplane), the *Kaidai* were intended to operate in flotillas, in direct co-operation with the battle squadrons of the Imperial Fleet.

Inevitably, this led to the surface characteristics of these boats being developed to the maximum extent: speed, seakeeping, range and gun armament, and the resultant high displacements and dimensions limited submerged manoeuvrability, and lengthened diving times. The effectiveness of American anti-submarine measures was to prove fatal to these large Japanese boats.

When Japan attacked America in December 1941, the Imperial submarine fleet was far from the goals that had been established, with a total force of only 64 boats, 41 of which were of the cruiser and Fleet types, and two, of the medium type, of recent construction: 21 were obsolete and of little value. Approximately 20 boats of the three principal classes were under construction.

Following the building between 1921 and 1922 of the prototypes *I. 51* and *I. 52* which derived respectively from the British *K* Class squadron boats of 1917 and the German *U 139* type cruiser-submarines, also of 1917, the Japanese concentrated on the building of the *Junsen* type (*I. 1* Class commissioned between 1926 and 1932 and followed by another two boats completed in 1932 and 1935) and the *Kaidai* type (*I. 153* and *I. 156* Classes of 1927) from which all the larger cruiser and Fleet types derived. The normal displacement of the early *Junsen* types was in the order of 2,200 tons surfaced, and reached 3,000 tons submerged. Speed was approximately 20/8 knots with a surface range of 20,000 miles at economical speed.

Armament consisted of one or two 5.5in (140mm) or 5in (127mm) deck guns, six 21in (533mm) torpedo tubes and, in several boats, a catapult and floatplane usually stowed (wings removed) in a cylindrical watertight container, accessible from inside the boat.

The first *Kaidai* were of smaller dimensions and their displacement was in the order of 1,800/2,300 tons. Maximum surface speed was high, approximately 20 knots, with a maximum range in excess of 10,000 miles at 10 knots. Armament normally consisted of a 4.7in (120mm) deck gun and six to eight 21in (533mm) torpedo tubes.

All subsequent classes were developed on the basis of these characteristics, with changes and improvements dictated by experience and technological progress. An interesting aspect of the evolution of the large Japanese boats, was the alternation of the various classes of cruiser and Fleet submarines, derived one from another without any apparent logical connection. On balance, however, the Japanese did nothing more than improve the two original designs, adapting them to their planned roles: the dimensions and armament varied but the same basic construction characteristics were always retained.

By 1941, the most recent Fleet submarines were virtually identical, in dimensions, speed and range, with the latest cruiser-submarines, to the point where the boats could be considered as belonging to a single type, differing only in their armament.

After the building of several medium-displacement boats (*RO. 57, 60* and *29* Classes), no other boats of this type were laid down until 1933.

With a normal displacement of 940/1,200 tons, a speed of 19/8.2 knots, a surface range of 8,000 miles at 12 knots and a torpedo armament of four 21in (533mm) torpedo tubes, the two *RO. 33* boats which were commissioned between 1935 and 1937, were 'guinea-pigs' for the building of approximately forty similar boats (*RO. 35* and *RO. 100* Classes) after the war had started. Thanks to their small size and good submerged manoeuvrability, they rendered the Japanese valuable service in areas near Japanese bases.

In December 1941, the only four Japanese minelaying boats were still in service. They were of the *I. 121* Class, built between 1924 and 1928, and inspired by the German *U 122* Type of 1917. (The Japanese had obtained the German *U 125* immediately after the First World War and had commissioned her as *O. 1*). These boats were anything but successful, mainly because of their longitudinal instability while submerged; a very serious defect, especially in minelayers.

During the mid thirties, the Japanese built two prototypes of midget submarines, and later built numerous craft of this kind. Originally, it had been intended that they be carried, with their two-man crew, aboard large surface ships, which would launch them during naval engagements, to confuse the enemy and inflict losses. In 1941, however, it was decided to use them to attack naval bases: five of them took part in the attack on Pearl Harbor but all were lost without achieving success.

The great victory of carrier-borne aircraft against the US Pacific Fleet at Hawaii, completely obscured the lack of success of the Japanese submarines, 27 of which took part in the operation without result.

After Pearl Harbor, Japanese Submarine Command reported: 'We have ascertained that it is very difficult for submarines to attack warships and to block a well guarded harbour. We are of the opinion that the main targets of submarines should be merchant ships and not warships.' This assessment was not heeded by the Japanese high command.

Of particular importance from the point of view of technical achievement, were the large submarine-aircraft carriers of the *I. 13* and *I. 400* Classes. The *I. 13* Class were cruiser-submarines whose design had been modified during construction. The *I. 400* Class were designed, from the outset, as submarine-carriers, with a normal displacement of 5,223/6,560 tons, an overall length of 400ft (120m), a complement of three bomber-type floatplanes and an extremely long range. They were the largest submarines in the world at that time. With their aircraft, they were to have attacked the west coast of the United States, and the locks of the Panama Canal, but they never did so and almost all of them were captured intact at the end of the war.

The medium-displacement boats built during the war, were the equivalent of the Royal Navy's *U* and *V* Classes, but they were produced in lesser numbers and their mode of employment achieved decidedly inferior results.

Another technically very interesting type built during the war, was the high submerged speed boat. As early as 1937 to 1938, the Japanese had built in the greatest secrecy, a small experimental boat, capable of a high underwater speed, using an electric motor of great power, high-capacity batteries and a hull shape offering minimum resistance when submerged. Eventually, only a single high-performance screw was used. The principal characteristics of the prototype, code-named *N. 71* and scrapped in 1940, were:

Normal displacement: 213/240 tons.
Dimensions: 140ft 5in × 10ft 10in × 10ft 4in (42.8m × 3.3m × 3.15m).
Machinery: one diesel; one electric.
Power: 1,200/1,800hp.
Speed: 14/23–25 knots.
Range: 3,830 miles at 12.5 knots/33 miles at 7 knots.
Complement: 11.
Maximum operational depth: 256ft (80m).
Armament: three 18in (457mm) forward torpedo tubes.

This boat was not completely successful despite her submerged bursts of speed in the order of 25 knots, because her small size and hull shape had an adverse effect on surface manoeuvrability, seakeeping and safety. However, she contributed significantly to the development of the *I. 201* and *Ha. 201* Classes, built at the end of the war. Comparable, respectively, to the German Type XXI (ocean-going) and Type XXIII (coastal) boats, the Japanese elektro-boote were also prefabricated, and had many features in common with the

German boats, although developed independently. The first of the *I. 201* Class was laid down several weeks before the German prototype of the *X* type. Neither *I. 201* nor *Ha. 201* were ready until the final months of the war, by which time, the enemy's superiority allowed no freedom of action and the boats were unable to prove their undoubtedly noteworthy capabilities.

During the war, 126 new submarines were built in Japan. One hundred of these belonged to the Classes previously mentioned: the remainder were specially designed as transport submarines for the isolated garrisons in the Pacific atolls, and bases besieged by the Americans. These were boats which could be simply and quickly built, in which everything had been reduced to essentials. Capacity varied between 60 and 400 tons of cargo and/or fuel, depending on the type.

The Japanese Army designed and built approximately twenty small submarines with a cargo capacity of 40 tons. The Imperial Navy built several hundred midget submarines, all derived from the 1938 *A* type, and a large number of underwater Kaiten-type assault craft for suicide attacks. They derived from standard torpedoes and were to be used during the final phase of the war.

Once hostilities had begun, the Japanese Navy, like others before them, discovered numerous technical shortcomings in its boats and deficiencies in the training of their crews.

Despite their large size, habitability had been almost ignored in Japanese boats. Interior space had been utilized almost exclusively for equipment and was inadequate for the crew, especially during long patrols. During the early months of the war, it was noted that Japanese submariners tired very quickly, and their general standard of performance was inferior to that of American and European crews.

The slow diving speed and poor manoeuvrability of the large boats were aggravated by another bad feature: the large size of the hull was easy to locate by sonar and very vulnerable to depth-charge patterns. The conning tower bulk reflected excellent echoes on radar screens which could locate them at great distances when surfaced.

At the beginning of the war, Japanese instrumentation was inadequate: radar, firing computers and sonar were lacking. The Japanese did have, however, excellent night binoculars which gave them a great advantage over the Americans in night sightings. From June 1944, nationally manufactured radar and sonar were installed, but they arrived too late and never reached the sophistication of American equipment. The Japanese suffered many losses because of the inferiority of their long-range search equipment. As the American equipment and tactics were refined with such items as airborne radar, sono-buoys, escort carriers and hunter-killer groups, the Japanese boats were subjected to ever increasing losses, while achieving fewer successes, despite the exceptional determination of their crews and the excellent performance of their torpedoes, which were clearly superior to the American weapons.

From the outset, Japanese boats were equipped with Type 95 21in (533mm) oxygen-propelled, wakeless torpedoes capable of a run of 21,880 yards (20,000m) at the exceptional speed of 50 knots, or 40,478 yards (37,000m) at 36 knots, compared to the 15,316 yards (14,000m) at 28 knots and 6,126 yards (5,600m) at 45 knots for the American weapons. The Type 95 was the submarine version of the famous 24in (610mm) Type 93 (long lance) carried aboard destroyers and light cruisers, which produced excellent results in the night actions during the Guadalcanal campaign, and elsewhere.

Development of Japanese submarines, 1918–1945.

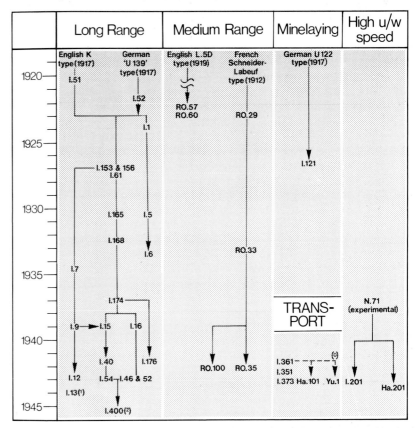

For deck armament, the Japanese at first used mainly the 5.5in (140mm) 50-cal and 3in (76mm) 40-cal guns, with maximum ranges respectively, of 19,155 yards (17,500m) and 15,972 yards (14,600m), as well as the 4.7in (120mm) weapon. Subsequently, they adopted the excellent 4in (102mm) 65-cal gun, with a high rate of fire and with a maximum range of 23,302 yards (21,300m).

The 4in (102mm) could also be used against aircraft, but the three earlier guns were of little use in this role because of their limited elevation, low rate of fire and difficult ammunition handling. Anti-aircraft weapons ranged from the initial 13.1mm to the famous 25mm, installed in twin or triple mounts, in almost all boats built or modernized during the war.

The shortcomings in crew training stemmed from the fact that all pre-war training had been conducted in home waters, with little thought given to the more difficult conditions in tropical and arctic seas, and when, later, Japanese boats had to operate in these areas, their crews were completely unacclimatized.

During the war, the colouring of Japanese boats changed from the very dark grey of the pre-war period, to the light blue-grey of the final years. There is no evidence that camouflage was adopted except in extremely rare cases.

From the end of the First World War until 1945, the Japanese Navy made two successive name changes, either total or partial, of its submarines. The first, in about 1926, saw the change from a general progressive numbering (e.g.: *No. 59*, *No. 72*, etc.) to numbering by Type (e.g.: *I. 21*, *RO. 60*, etc.). The second change occurred on 20 May 1942: in many of the *I* Class which had been built up to that time, the number *I* was inserted ahead of the original number (e.g.: *I. 21* = *I. 121*, *I. 74* = *I. 174*, etc.). Furthermore, during the war, many boats were assigned designations which had belonged to boats, now lost.

From the time of Pearl Harbor until the Battle of Midway in June 1942, the 27 Japanese boats at sea in the Hawaiian Islands achieved no appreciable results, with the sole exception of *I. 6*. On 11 January 1942, she torpedoed the American aircraft carrier *Saratoga*, putting her out of action for several months and preventing her participation in the battles of the Coral Sea and Midway.

For the latter operation, Admiral Yamamoto had planned the deployment of a large number of boats, partly in the usual reconnaissance role and partly in ambush near American bases. Thanks to the decoding of Japanese communications, the American ships left their bases before the arrival of the Japanese boats, which were unable to intervene effectively. The only success achieved was by *I. 168* which sank the carrier *Yorktown* (already seriously damaged by Japanese aircraft) and an accompanying destroyer, on 4 June 1942.

During the period between the Battle of Midway and the American invasion of Guadalcanal in August 1942, the Japanese boats were concentrated in the Indian Ocean and in areas off Australia, New Guinea and Samoa. In this short time, a few boats sank numerous Allied merchant ships or auxiliaries.

During the subsequent Solomons campaign, Japanese boats took part in ever increasing numbers: in January 1943, there were 38 boats in the area, to attack warships and to replenish the garrison at Guadalcanal, which was very difficult to accomplish with surface ships.

Within a few months, twenty of these boats had been lost during transport missions. For these, the boats had been completely disarmed to provide cargo space, and this seriously affected the morale of the crews. The boats not employed on such missions, registered some important successes against warships, such as that of 14 September 1942 when an American convoy, bound for Guadalcanal from Espiritu Santo and escorted by the carriers *Wasp* and *Hornet* and by the battleship *North Carolina* were attacked by a group of submarines. *Wasp* and a destroyer were sunk, *North Carolina* was seriously damaged. Once again, the Japanese boats attacked only the warships, leaving the convoy to proceed undisturbed, with precious reinforcements for Guadalcanal.

During the next phase of the Solomons campaign, Japanese boats continued to operate only against warships, sinking a destroyer in the battle for Santa Cruz on 26 October, and the light cruiser *Juneau* on 12 November 1942.

After a relatively static period in underwater operations during the spring of 1944, the remaining 25 operational ocean-going boats were taken under the command of the Sixth Fleet (Vice-Admiral Takagi) in anticipation of the American advance towards the Marianas group of islands. Takagi moved his headquarters to the island of Saipan, in the Marianas, and set up a base for the boats, from which to operate against the enemy in those waters. The improvised base lacked the necessary equipment for the repair and adequate maintenance of the boats, so that their operational effectiveness decreased.

Thirteen boats, practically the entire operational submarine fleet, took part in the battle of Leyte Gulf in October 1944. At that time, apart from about twenty older boats, suitable only for training, only 32 fully operational boats remained in the Imperial Navy. Several of these were used as transports, four were operational in the Indian Ocean and 13, recently built, were still undergoing training.

The boats scheduled for the Philippines left their bases after much delay and their action was ineffective: *I. 56* damaged an American escort carrier, but during the action, three Japanese boats were lost. After this, the Japanese boats were very depleted in numbers and could do very little against enemy warships. Their most important action before the end of the war, was the sinking of the heavy cruiser *Indianapolis* by *I. 58* on 29 July 1945. *Indianapolis* had carried several parts of the atomic bombs, soon to be dropped on Hiroshima and Nagasaki, from San Francisco to the island of Tinian, in the Marianas.

During the final months of the war, Japanese boats were chiefly employed in operations of little importance to the naval war: replenishing garrisons on islands which had been by-passed by the American forces, and the transporting and support of kaiten, the Imperial Navy's equivalent of the kamikaze. These were piloted torpedoes carried by surface craft or by ocean-going submarines, mounted in cradles on deck. The kaiten pilots sacrificed themselves by guiding the weapon to explode against the target.

The first sortie of boats carrying kaiten took place on 20 November 1944 and others followed until the end of the war. The early attacks against warships had limited success, and not until April 1945 were the kaiten launched against merchantmen. Using *I. 36* and *I. 47* as 'parents', the kaiten achieved several successes and within a short time, all the remaining ocean-going boats were used for this kind of mission. In the last months, several auxiliary or merchant ships and several small warships were sunk.

At the end of the war, about fifty submarines were captured by the Americans in Japanese bases. They were mostly old boats used for training, or recently built boats, still completing. They were either scrapped or sunk off the coast of Japan. Considerable interest was roused in American naval circles by the high-speed underwater boats, and the large aircraft-carrier submarines, one example of which, was brought to the United States and subsequently sunk off the American coast in 1946.

During the war, Japanese boats sank 184 Allied merchantmen totalling 907,000 GRT, and numerous warships including two aircraft carriers, two cruisers and some ten destroyers and escort vessels. Several submarines and minor and auxiliary vessels were also sunk. Losses totalled 129 boats, 70 of which were sunk by surface ships, 18 by aircraft, 19 by submarines and 22 lost to various causes, air attack in port, accidents or unknown. Losses and new boats commissioned were mutually compensating throughout the war: 126 boats entered service between December 1941 and August 1945.

At the end of 1942, the number of boats with which Japan had begun the war (64) remained unchanged, despite the fact that 20 new units had been launched. In 1943, 37 new boats entered service, and the total available at the end of that year reached a peak of 77. From then on, the submarine force began to decline because of the greatly increased effectiveness of Allied anti-submarine measures. At the end of 1944, Japanese boats had been reduced to 57, despite the 39 new boats which entered service during that year. In 1945, another 30 boats were completed before the war ended, but because of heavy losses, the total was virtually unchanged until the surrender on 15 August, at which time, about 50 boats remained; most of these, however, were of little combat value.

If one compares the relatively low number of operational boats with the results achieved, it will be seen that the results were far from slight, even though they were less than the Japanese Navy had expected. Results might have been better had more effort been

After surrendering in 1945, *I.203* lies moored alongside (from left to right) *Ha.203*, *Ha.204* and *Ha.106*.

I. 21 (later, *I. 121*), one of the four Japanese minelaying submarines.

devoted to attacking the enemy's long supply lines, as the Japanese Submarine Command and the Germans had advised.

The interruption, even temporary, of those lines of communication, would have had serious repercussions on the conduct of American operations. Not only did the Japanese not attack American traffic in the Pacific nor British traffic in the Indian Ocean, but they never bothered those convoys bound from the United States to Soviet Far

Eastern ports, which supported the U.S.S.R. against Japan's ally, Germany. Frequent German reminders did nothing to change Japan's attitude which was dictated by political motives, as Japan was not at war with Russia.

Not until the final months of the war did the Japanese Navy begin to attack enemy shipping with some success, especially with the kaiten, but by then it was too late and the outcome of the war was already decided. The poor strategic use (which had harmful influences on design) of submarines by Japan is the reason why their results were so limited and inferior to the American boats, whose priority was the destruction of merchant shipping.

Chogei, a submarine depot ship designed to operate with the fleet.

KD1 (Kaidai) Type

I. 51 ex-*No. 44.*
Builder: Kure Dockyard.
Date: 1919–1924.
Normal displacement: 1,500 tons surfaced; 2,430 tons submerged.
Dimensions: 300ft 0in x 29ft 0in x 15ft 0in (91.4m x 8.8m x 4.6m).
Machinery: diesel: 2; electric: 2.
Maximum power: 5,200hp surfaced; 2,000hp submerged.
Maximum speed: 20 knots surfaced; 10 knots submerged.
Range: 20,000 miles at 10 knots surfaced; 100 miles at 4 knots submerged.
Torpedo tubes: eight 21in (533mm); 6 forward, 2 aft; torpedoes: 24.
Guns: one 4.7in (120mm) 50-cal.
Complement: 60.

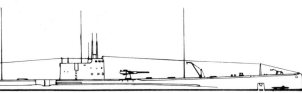

The prototype of the Japanese Fleet submarines, this vessel was based on British lines. Originally, she had four diesels and four shafts, and a 3in (76mm) gun in addition to the 4.7in (120mm), but these were removed between the wars. In her latter days, this large boat was used for training and was taken out of service in 1941. She had been ordered in the 1919 Programme. Maximum service depth: 200ft (60m).

Fates			cause
date:	location:	boat:	(see page 7):
1941		*I. 51*	r

KD 2 (Kaidai) Type

I. 152 ex-*I. 52,* ex-*No. 51.*
Builder: Kure Dockyard.
Date: 1920–1925.
Normal displacement: 1,500 tons surfaced; 2,500 tons submerged.
Dimensions: 330ft 9in x 25ft 0in x 16ft 3in (100.8m x 7.6m x 5.1m).
Machinery: diesel: 2; electric 2.
Maximum power: 6,800hp surfaced; 2,000hp submerged.
Maximum speed: 22 knots surfaced; 100 miles at 4 knots submerged.
Torpedo tubes: eight 21in (533mm); 6 forward, 2 aft; torpedoes: 16.
Guns: one 4.7in (120mm) 50-cal; one 3in (76mm) 40-cal.
Complement: 60.

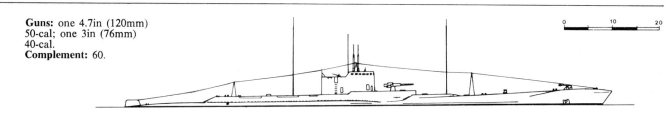

This design was inspired by, and largely based on, the German First World War U-Cruisers of the *U 139* type. Like the slightly smaller but longer-ranged and more powerfully armed (more torpedoes) *I. 51*, she was used in a long series of trials to establish the role of the *Kaidai* type of large submarine. After 1940 she was used for training and in 1942 she was declared obsolete. She was scrapped before the end of the war. Unlike *I. 51*, however, she remained long enough in service to be renumbered with a '100' number instead of her two-figure designation. Maximum service depth: 195ft (59m).

Fates			cause
date:	location:	boat:	(see page 7):
1942		*I. 152*	r

L.3 Type

RO. 57 ex-*No. 46, RO. 58* ex-*No. .47, RO. 59* ex-*No. 57.*
Builder: Mitsubishi, Kobe.
Date: 1921–1923.
Normal displacement: 897 tons surfaced; 1,195 tons submerged.
Dimensions: 250ft 0in x 23ft 6in x 13ft 0in (76.2m x 7.38m x 3.7m).
Machinery: diesel: 2; electric: 2.
Maximum power: 2,400hp surfaced; 1,600hp submerged.
Maximum speed: 17 knots surfaced; 8 knots submerged.
Range: 5,500 miles at 10 knots surfaced; 80 miles at 4 knots submerged.

This design of medium submarine was ultimately based on the British *L* Class. Ordered under the 1921 Programme. Service depth: 195ft (59m). Capable of a patrol lasting twenty days. In 1941, all three became training submarines. They were hulked early in 1945 and were surrendered in this condition to the Americans.

Fates

date:	location:	boat:	cause (see page 7):
	Japan	RO. 57, RO. 58, RO. 59	x

Torpedo tubes: four 21in (533mm) forward; torpedoes: 10.
Guns: one 3in (76mm) 40-cal high angle; one machine-gun.
Complement: 60.

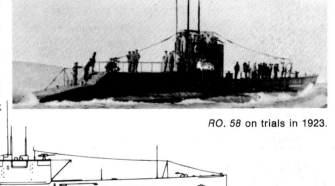

RO. 58 on trials in 1923.

KT (Kai-Toku-Chu) Type

RO. 29 ex-*No. 68, RO. 30* ex-*No. 69, RO. 31* ex-*No. 70, RO. 32* ex-*No. 71.*
Builder: Kawasaki, Kobe.
Date: 1922–1927.
Normal displacement: 665 tons surfaced; 1,000 tons submerged.
Dimensions: 243ft 6in x 20ft 0in x 12ft 3in (79.2m x 6.1m x 3.7m).

Machinery: diesel: 2 Fiat; electric: 2.
Maximum power: 1,200hp surfaced; 1,200hp submerged.
Maximum speed: 13 knots surfaced; 8 knots submerged.
Range: 6,000 miles at 10 knots surfaced; 85 miles at 4 knots submerged.
Torpedo tubes: four 21in (533mm) forward; torpedoes: 8.
Guns: one 4.7in (120mm) 50-cal; one machine-gun.
Complement: 43.

Having already used British, German and (in some earlier classes) American designs, the Japanese did not ignore the French. This Class was developed from the *Schneider-Laubeuf* type. Maximum operational depth: 195ft (59m). The slow speed of these boats, as well as their age, relegated them to training before the war: indeed, *RO. 29* had already been discarded in 1936. The others were hulked during the war and were surrendered in that condition to the Americans.

Fates

date:	location:	boat:	cause (see page 7):
1945	Japan	RO. 30, RO. 31, RO. 32	x

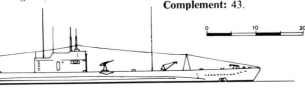

L.4 Type

RO. 60 ex-No. 59, RO. 61 ex-No. 72, RO. 62 ex-No. 73, RO. 63 ex-No. 84, RO. 64, RO. 65, RO. 66, RO. 67, RO. 68.
Builder: Mitsubishi, Kobe.
Date: 1922–1926.
Normal displacement: 990 tons surfaced; 1,322 tons submerged.
Dimensions: 250ft 0in x 24ft 3in x 12ft 3in (76.2m x 7.38m x 3.7m).
Machinery: diesel: 2; electric: 2.

Maximum power: 2,400hp surfaced; 1,600hp submerged.
Maximum speed: 16 knots surfaced; 8 knots submerged.
Range: 5,500 miles at 10 knots surfaced; 80 miles at 4 knots submerged.
Torpedo tubes: six 21in (533mm) forward; torpedoes: 10.
Guns: one 3in (76mm) 40-cal; one machine-gun.
Complement: 60.

RO. 63.

A further development of the *L. 3* type, and thus, of the British *L* Class design, but with a stronger torpedo armament, and with the gun in a different position from its immediate predecessors. Maximum operational depth: 195ft (59m). Used operationally early in the war, but the only success achieved was the sinking of the American seaplane tender *Casco* by *RO.61* on 31 August 1942. From 1943, the survivors were employed in training.

Fates

date:	location:	boat:	cause (see page 7):
1941	Pacific	RO. 60, RO. 66	v
1942	Pacific	RO. 61, RO. 65	b
1945	Pacific	RO. 64	m
	Japan	RO. 62, RO. 63, RO. 67, RO. 68	x

KRS (Kirai-Sen) Type

I. 121 ex-I. 21, ex-No. 48, I. 122 ex-I. 22, ex-No. 49, I. 123 ex-I. 23, ex-No. 50, I. 124 ex-I. 24.
Builder: Kawasaki, Kobe.
Date: 1919–1927.
Normal displacement: 1,383 tons surfaced; 1,768 tons submerged.
Dimensions: 279ft 6in x 24ft 6in x 14ft 6in (85.2m x 7.5m x 4.3m).
Machinery: diesel: 2; electric 2.

Maximum power: 2,400hp surfaced; 1,100hp submerged.
Maximum speed: 14.5 knots surfaced; 7 knots submerged.
Range: 10,500 miles at 8 knots surfaced; 40 miles at 4.5 knots submerged.
Torpedo tubes: four 21in (533mm) forward; torpedoes: 12.
Guns: one 5.5in (140mm) 50-cal.
Mines: 42.
Complement: 75.

I. 23 (later I. 123).

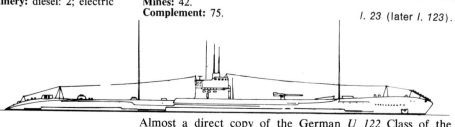

Almost a direct copy of the German *U 122* Class of the First World War, this was the only minelaying class in the Japanese Navy. They were not a great success. In 1940 they were all converted to carry aviation spirit, as re-fuellers for seaplanes. *I. 122* and *I. 121*, the two survivors of the Class were relegated to training in 1943, but had by then, sunk five Allied ships of 20,009 GRT.

Fates

date:	location:	boat:	cause (see page 7):
1942	Pacific	I. 123, I. 124	n
1945	Pacific	I. 122	s
		I. 121	x

Junsen Type

Class I. 1, Variant J. 1
(4 units).
I. 1 ex-*N. 74, I. 2* ex-*N. 75,
I. 3* ex-*N. 76, I. 4*:
Builder: Kawasaki, Kobe.
Date: 1923–1926/32.

Class I. 5, Variant J. 1M
(1 unit).
I. 5:
Builder: Kawasaki, Kobe.
Date: 1929–1932.

Class I. 6, Variant J. 2
(1 unit).
I. 6:
Builder: Kawasaki, Kobe.
Date: 1932–1935.

Class I. 7, Variant J. 3
(2 units).
I. 7:
Builder: Kure Dockyard.
Date: 1934–1937.
I. 8.
Builder: Kawasaki, Kobe.
Date: 1935–1938.

Normal displacement:
J. 1: 2,135 tons surfaced;
2,791 tons submerged.
J. 1M: 2,243 tons surfaced;
2,921 tons submerged.
J. 2: 2,243 tons surfaced;
3,061 tons submerged.
J. 3: 2,525 tons surfaced;
3,538 tons submerged.
Dimensions:
J. 1: 320ft 0in x 30ft 3in x
16ft 6in (97.5m x 9.23m x
4.94m).
J. 1M: 320ft 0in x 30ft 3in x
16ft 6in (97.5m x 9.06m x
4.94m).
J. 2: 323ft 0in x 29ft 9in x
17ft 6in (98.5m x 9.06m x
5.31m).
J. 3: 358ft 6in x 29ft 9in x
17ft 3in (109.3m x 9.10m x
5.26m).
Machinery: diesel: 2; electric:
2.
Maximum power:
J. 1 and *J. 1M*: 6,000hp
surfaced; 2,600hp submerged.
J. 2: 8,000hp surfaced;
2,600hp submerged.
J. 3: 11,200hp surfaced;
2,800hp submerged.
Maximum speed:
J. 1 and *J. 1M*: 18 knots
surfaced; 8 knots submerged.
J. 2: 20 knots surfaced;
7.5 knots submerged.
J. 3: 23 knots surfaced;
8 knots submerged.

Range:
J. 1 and *J. 1M*: 24,400 miles
at 10 knots surfaced; 60 miles
at 3 knots submerged.
J. 2: 20,000 miles at 10 knots
surfaced; 60 miles at 3 knots
submerged.
J. 3: 14,000 miles at 16 knots
surfaced; 60 miles at 3 knots
submerged.
Torpedo tubes:
J. 1 and *J. 1M*: six 21in
(533mm); 4 forward, 2 aft;
torpedoes: 20.
J. 2: six 21in (533mm);
4 forward, 2 aft; torpedoes:
17.
J. 3: six 21in (533mm)
forward; torpedoes: 21.
Guns:
J. 1 and *J. 1M*: two 5.5in.
(140mm) 50-cal.
J. 2: one 5in (127mm) 40-cal;
one 13.1mm; one floatplane;
one catapult.
J. 3: one 5.5in (140mm)
50-cal; two single 13.1mm
(1943: one replaced by two
25mm in twin mount); one
floatplane; one catapult.
Complement: *J. 1*: 92; *J. 1M*:
93; *J. 2*: 97; *J. 3*: 100.

I. 1 in 1926.

Double hull cruiser-type submarines derived from the German *U* type cruiser-submarines of 1917, from the prototypes *I. 51* and *I. 52* (later *I. 152*), launched respectively in 1921 and 1922.

From the original type (*Junsen 1*) whose prototype was laid down in 1923, three successive series were derived (*J. 1M, J. 2* and *J. 3*) built between 1929 and 1938.

Variant J. 1
Known as the *I. 1* Class, this first version of the *Junsen* type was designed for long-range reconnaissance and for use ahead of surface battle forces: it had a high surface speed, noteworthy for its time. The four boats of the Class were the first Japanese boats to be armed with the 5.5in (140mm) deck gun. Their performance allowed

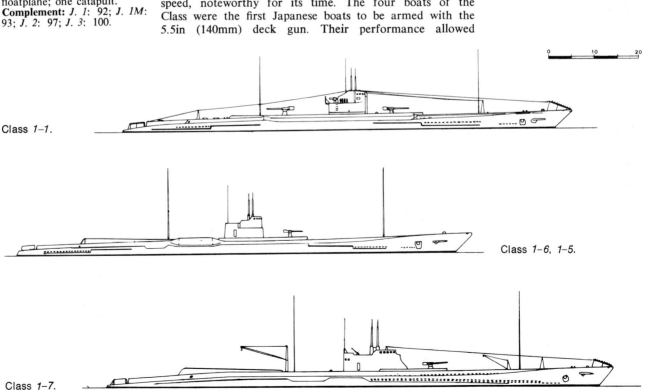

Class *1–1*.

Class *1–6, 1–5*.

Class *1–7*.

patrols of 60 days. Maximum operational depth: approximately 256ft (80m).

Between 1942 and 1943, *I. 1* and *I. 2* were modified to carry a midget submarine: positioned on deck behind the conning tower, its installation necessitated removal of the after deck gun and a reduction in the number of torpedoes carried. Alternatively, a *Daihatsu* type landing craft, 47ft 6in (14m) long, could be carried, or several amphibious armoured vehicles with their associated equipment.

Variant J. IM

I. 5, the only example of this Variant, carried a small dismantled seaplane, stowed in watertight cylindrical containers, one on each side of the conning tower at deck level. One container housed the wings; the other, the

fuselage and floats. The aircraft was launched by a deck-mounted catapult behind the conning tower. *I. 5* was the first Japanese boat equipped with aircraft but, in general, the arrangement proved unsatisfactory. The storage and assembly of the aircraft, a *Watanabe E9 W1* (Slim) seaplane, were too complex and time-consuming, and the catapult, which operated in the opposite direction to that of the boat, was certainly ill-conceived, as it took no advantage of the boat's speed during take off. In 1940, all the aircraft equipment was removed and replaced by a second 5.5in (140mm) deck gun.

Variant J. 2

This Variant was also represented by a single vessel, *I. 6*. Developed from the preceding Variant, she was fitted with a more powerful diesel engine which gave her a higher surface speed, but to the detriment of range. Designed to carry two 5.5in (140mm) guns, she was completed in a similar manner to the earlier Variant. After 1942, her original aircraft appears to have been replaced by a Yokosuka E 14 Y1 (Glen).

Variant J. 3

This differed from the preceding Variants in that, though inspired by the *Junsen* type, it was developed from Variants 3 and 4 of the *Kaidai* type. The two boats of the *I. 7* Class were the largest submarines yet built by the Japanese at the time of their commissioning. The aircraft equipment was similar to that aboard *I. 5* and *I. 6* and, ultimately, was not very effective. At the end of 1944, *I. 8* had her aircraft arrangements removed and replaced by equipment designed to carry four kaiten. Maximum operational depth: 328ft (100m).

In general, the *Junsen* type were mediocre boats. The large hull size gave them excellent surface seakeeping, but greatly limited their submerged manoeuvrability, and their minimum crash-dive time was rather high. Their long-range reconnaissance use was limited and during the war, they operated mainly as normal long-range attack boats. The eight boats of this type sank sixteen Allied merchant and auxiliary ships totalling 87,744 GRT, and seriously damaged another two (12,312 GRT). Their only significant success against warships was by *I. 6* which seriously damaged the American carrier *Saratoga* (33,000 tons) off Hawaii on 11 January 1942. None of the boats emerged from the war unscathed. *I. 1, I. 3* and *I. 4* were lost between late 1942 and early 1943, while replenishing garrisons in the Solomons.

Fates

date:	location:	boat:	cause (see page 7):
1942	Pacific	*I. 3, I .4*	n
1943	Pacific	*I. 1, I. 7*	n
1944	Pacific	*I. 2, I. 5, I. 6*	n
1945	Pacific	*I. 8*	n

Kaidai Type

Class I. 153, Variant KD. 3A
(4 units).
*I. 153 ex-N. 64, ex-I. 53,
I. 155 ex-N. 78, ex-I. 55:*
Builder: Kure Dockyard.
Date: 1924–1927.
I. 154 ex-N. 77, ex-I. 54:
Builder: Sasebo Dockyard.
Date: 1924–1927.
I. 158 ex-I. 58:
Builder: Yokosuka Dockyard.
Date: 1924–1928.

Class I. 156, Variant KD. 3B
(5 units).
I. 156 ex-I. 56, I. 157 ex-I. 57:
Builder: Kure Dockyard.
Date: 1926–1928/1929.
I. 159 ex-I. 59:
Builder: Yokosuka.
Date: 1927–1930.
I. 60, I. 63:
Builder: Sasebo Dockyard.
Date: 1926–1929/30.

Class I. 61, Variant KD. 4
(3 units).
I. 61, I. 162 ex-I. 62:
Builder: Mitsubishi, Kobe.
Date: 1926–1929/30.
I. 64:
Builder: Kure Dockyard.
Date: 1928–1930.

Class I. 165, Variant KD. 5
(3 units).
I. 165 ex-I. 65:
Builder: Kure Dockyard.
Date: 1929–1932.
I. 166 ex-I. 66:
Builder: Sasebo Dockyard.
Date: 1929–1932.
I. 67:
Builder: Mitsubishi, Kobe.
Date: 1929–1932.

Class I. 168, Variant KD. 6A
(6 units).
I. 168 ex-I. 68:
Builder: Kure Dockyard.
Date: 1931–1934.
I. 169 ex-I. 69, I. 172 ex-I. 72:
Builder: Mitsubishi, Kobe.
Date: 1931–1935/37.
I. 70:
Builder: Sasebo Dockyard.
Date: 1933–1935.
I. 171 ex-I. 71, I. 73:
Builder: Kawasaki, Kobe.
Date: 1933–1935/38.

Class I. 174, Variant KD. 6B
(2 units).
I. 174 ex-I. 74:
Builder: Sasebo Dockyard.
Date: 1934–1938.

I. 175 ex-I. 75:
Builder: Mitsubishi, Kobe.
Date: 1934–1939.

Class I. 176, Variant KD. 7
(10 units).
I. 176–I. 185 ex-I. 76–I. 85.
Builder: Kure Dockyard.
Date: 1939–1942/43.

Normal displacement:
KD. 3A, KD. 3B: 1,800 tons
surfaced; 2,300 tons
submerged.
KD. 4: 1,720 tons surfaced;
2,300 tons submerged.
KD. 5: 1,705 tons surfaced;
2,330 tons submerged.
KD. 6A: 1,785 tons surfaced;
2,440 tons submerged.
KD. 6B: 1,810 tons surfaced;
2,564 tons submerged.
KD. 7: 1,833 tons surfaced;
2,602 tons submerged.
Dimensions:
KD. 3A: 330ft 0in x 26ft 0in x
15ft 9in (100.6m x 7.9m x
4.83m).
KD. 3B: 331ft 4in x 26ft 0in
x 16ft 0in (101m x 7.9m x
4.9m).
KD. 4: 320ft 6in x 25ft 6in x
15ft 9in (97.7m x 7.8m x
4.8m).
KD. 5: 320ft 6in x 26ft 9in x
15ft 6in (97.7m x 8.2m x
4.7m).
KD. 6A: 343ft 6in x 27ft 0in
x 15ft 0in (104.7m x 8.2m x
4.5m).
KD. 6B: 344ft 6in x 27ft 0in x
15ft 0in (105m x 8.2m x
4.6m).
KD. 7: 346ft 0in x 27ft 0in x
15ft 0in (105m x 8.2m x
4.6m).
Machinery: diesel: 2; electric:
2.
Maximum power:
*KD. 3A, KD. 3B, KD. 4,
KD. 5:* 6,800hp surfaced;
1,800hp submerged.
KD. 6A, KD. 6B: 9,000hp
surfaced; 1,800hp submerged.
KD. 7: 8,000hp surfaced;
1,800hp submerged.
Maximum speed:
*KD. 3A, KD. 3B, KD. 4,
KD. 5:* 20 knots surfaced;
8 knots submerged.
KD. 6A, KD. 6B, KD. 7:
23 knots surfaced; 8 knots
submerged.
Range:
KD. 3A, KD. 3B: 10,000
miles at 10 knots surfaced;

90 miles at 3 knots submerged.
KD. 4, KD. 5: 10,800 miles
at 10 knots surfaced; 60 miles
at 3 knots submerged.
KD. 6A: 14,000 miles at
10 knots surfaced; 65 miles at
3 knots submerged.
KD. 6B: 10,000 miles at 16
knots surfaced; 65 miles at 3
knots submerged.
KD. 7: 8,000 miles at 16
knots surfaced; 50 miles at
5 knots submerged.
Torpedo tubes:
KD. 3A, KD. 3B: eight 21in
(533mm); 6 forward, 2 aft;
torpedoes: 16.
KD. 4: six 21in (533mm);
4 forward, 2 aft; torpedoes:
14.
KD. 5, KD. 6A: six 21in
(533mm); 4 forward, 2 aft;
torpedoes: 14.
KD. 6B: six 21in (533mm);
4 forward, 2 aft; torpedoes:
14.
KD. 7: six 21in (533mm)
forward; torpedoes: 12.
Guns:
KD. 3A, KD. 3B: one 4.7in
(120mm) 40-cal.
KD. 4: one 4.7in (120mm)
40-cal.
KD. 5: one 3.9in (100mm)
68-cal; one 12mm.
KD. 6A: one 3.9in (100mm)
68-cal; one 13.2mm.
KD. 6B: one 4.7in (120mm)
40-cal; two single 13.1mm.
KD. 7: one 4.7in (120mm)
40-cal; two 25mm (2 x 1).
Complement:
KD. 3A, KD. 3B, KD. 4: 79.
KD. 5, KD. 6A, KD. 6B:
82–84.
KD. 7: 88.

*I. 65 (later I. 165), first boat
of its type.*

Long-range or Fleet submarines, developed from the *Kaidai
1* and *2* types (prototypes *I. 51* and *I. 52*), in turn, derived
respectively from the large British *K* Class and German
U 139 types of the First World War.

These were double hull boats with a lower displacement
than that of the cruiser types, and were scheduled for
combined action with surface forces. They had good
range and a maximum surface speed of the order of 20
knots, which was deemed sufficient for operating with
battleships. Between 1924 and 1939, the basic *Kaidai* type
was developed in seven successive variants, excluding the
two prototypes (*KD.1* and *KD.2*) which, when the war
started, were operationally valueless, having entered
service more than fifteen years earlier.

Variants KD.3A and KD.3B
These two variants consisted of nine boats, which differed
from each other mainly in the shape of their hull extremities and conning towers. They derived from the Variants
KD.1 and *KD.2,* and had strengthened structural members,
which led to a reduction in speed and underwater range.
Maximum operational depth: 200ft (60m).

Variant KD.4
The first of the three boats in this Class was commissioned
in 1929, before all the units of the preceding variant had
been completed. They were slightly shorter than the preceding boats and had two fewer torpedo tubes and spare
torpedoes, but had a slightly increased range. Maximum
operational depth: 200ft (60m).

Variant KD.5
Ordered under the 1927–1931 Programme, the three boats
of this variant were almost identical with the previous one,
except for greater structural strength which allowed a
maximum operational depth of 246ft (75m), and the
mounting of a 4in (102mm) 68-cal deck gun in place of the
4.7in (120mm) 40-cal weapon. From December 1944, *I.165*
was used for training, but in April 1945, she was converted
to a carrier for two kaiten. The deck gun had to be
removed.

From top to bottom: The submarine-cruiser *I.157 (ex-1.57)* completed in 1929; the boats of the *I.61* class were similar to the *I.57* class, and were renumbered in May 1942. The exception was *I.61*, as she was lost accidentally shortly before 1941; *I.73*, seen here on 24th April 1939 in Ariake Bay; *I.72*. Note the auxiliary rudder on the stern, common to many large Japanese submarines, to improve underwater handling.

Kaidai type *I.68* (later *I.168*) at speed.

Variant *KD.6A*

Ordered in 1931, this variant, consisting of six boats, was essentially a repeat of the earlier variant, except that displacement was slightly increased, and more powerful diesels were installed, with a consequent increase of maximum surface speed to 23 knots. *I.171, I.172* and *I.173* were armed with a 4.7in (120mm) 50-cal gun: the remaining units had 4in (102mm) 68-cal guns like those in Variant *KD.5.* After 1942, *I.171* was converted to a cargo submarine: the deck gun was removed and the number of spare torpedoes reduced. In addition to several tons of cargo, *I.171* could carry a *Daihatsu* type landing craft. Storage capacity gave this Variant a patrol endurance of 45 days.

Variant *KD.6B*

Ordered in 1934, the two boats of this variant were similar to the preceding one, despite a slight increase in displacement and structural strength, which increased maximum operational depth to 278ft (85m). Surface range was slightly decreased. In 1943, *I.174* was converted to a cargo submarine.

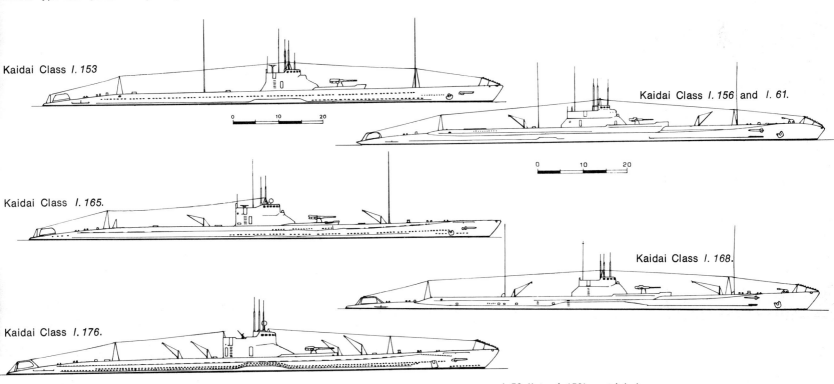

Kaidai Class *I. 153*

Kaidai Class *I. 156* and *I. 61.*

Kaidai Class *I. 165.*

Kaidai Class *I. 168.*

Kaidai Class *I. 176.*

I. 53 (later *I. 153*) on trials in 1927.

Table 24: Major successes of Kaidai Class submarines, 1941 to 1945

Boat:	Commander:	Date:	Result:	Type:	Ship:	GRT:
I. 168	Tanabe	7 June 1942	sank	carrier	*Yorktown*	19,000
			sank	destroyer	*Hamman*	—
I. 176	Tanabe	20 October 1942	sank	cruiser	*Chester*	9,200
I. 175	Tabata	24 November 1943	sank	escort carrier	*Liscome Bay*	6,730

From top to bottom: *I.68* (foreground) and *I.69*, with the
aircraft carrier *Kaga* and a cruiser in Ariake Bay, March
1936; *I.54*, *I.53* and *I.55*, three boats of the *Kaidai* type, in
1938; *I.176* in 1942. Bow detail of *I.75* (later *I.175*), in dry
dock at Kobe after fitting out. Note the microphones of the
hydrophone system arranged in a semi-circular pattern, the
completely retracted diving planes, and the caps of the
starboard torpedo tubes.

Variant *KD.7*

With ten boats completed between 1942 and 1943, this
was the most numerous of the *Kaidai* type. Ordered in
1939, the building of the boats was delayed in favour of
others, which were building at the same time and were
thought to be more urgently needed.

The design was developed from the preceding variant
with slight changes: less installed power, less surface range,
and torpedo armament concentrated exclusively forward.
Originally, this variant was to have been armed with only
two 25mm twin mounts, but during construction, one of
the mounts was replaced by a 4.7in (120mm) gun. After
1942, *I.176*, *I.178* and *I.181* were converted to transport
submarines, capable also of carrying a *Daihatsu* type
landing craft when the 4.7in (120mm) gun had been
removed. The 1942 Programme called for another ten
boats, but these were subsequently cancelled.

Like all the large Japanese ocean-going boats, the *Kaidai*
had good surface characteristics; speed, range, seakeeping
and armament, but their submerged characteristics and
habitability were rather mediocre. During the war, they
operated extensively and are credited with some of the
greatest successes achieved in the Pacific against American
warships between 1941 and 1945.

The 33 boats of the *Kaidai* type sank 38 merchant and
auxiliary ships totalling 146,948 GRT and seriously damaged
another eleven ships totalling 57,382 GRT. In addition,
they sank or damaged numerous minor warships including
a submarine and a Landing Ship Tank. Two boats, *I. 63* and
I. 67 were lost to accidents in 1940: eight surrendered at
the end of the war (of which, *I. 153, I. 154* and *I. 155* had
been de-commissioned): *I. 61* was payed off in 1942
because of damage sustained in a collision. The remainder
were sunk during the war. *I. 70*, sunk off Pearl Harbor by
aircraft from the carrier *Enterprise* on 10 December 1941,
was the first Japanese boat lost during the war.

Fates

date:	location:	boat:	cause (see page 7):
1941	Pacific	*I. 70*	a
1942	Pacific	*I. 60, I. 172*	n
		I. 64, I. 73	s
		I. 61	v–r
1943	Pacific	*I. 178, I. 182*	n
		I. 168	s
		I. 179	v
1944	Pacific	*I. 175, I. 176, I. 177, I. 180, I. 181, I.185*	n
		I. 166, I. 183	s
		I. 171, I. 174	uc
		I. 169	b
		I. 184	a
1945	Pacific	*I. 165*	a
		I. 153, I. 154, I. 155, I. 156, I. 157, I. 158, I. 159, I 162	x

Kaichu Type

Class RO. 33, Variant K. 5 (2 units).
RO. 33:
Builder: Kure Dockyard.
Date: 1933–1935.
RO. 34:
Builder: Mitsubishi, Kobe.
Date: 1934–1937.

Class RO. 35, Variant K. 6 (18 units).
RO. 35, RO. 36, RO. 37, RO, 38, RO, 40, RO. 41, RO. 43, RO. 45, RO. 46, RO. 48:
Builder: Mitsubishi, Kobe.
Date: 1941–1943/44.
RO. 39, RO. 40, RO. 41, RO. 42:
Builder: Sasebo Dockyard.
Date: 1941–1943/43.
RO. 44, RO, 47, RO, 49, RO. 50, RO. 55, RO, 56 ex-RO. 75:
Builder: Tamano.
Date: 1942–1943/44.
Units of the same series cancelled in 1943:
RO. 51–RO. 54, RO. 70–RO. 74, RO. 76–RO. 99, RO. 200–RO. 227.

Normal displacement:
K. 5: 940 tons surfaced; 1,200 tons submerged.
K. 6: 1,115 tons surfaced; 1,447 tons submerged.
Dimensions:
K. 5: 239ft 6in x 22ft 0in x 10ft 6in (73m x 6.7m x 3.25m).
K. 6: 264ft 0in x 23ft 0in x 13ft 3in (80.5m x 7m x 4.07m).

Machinery: diesel: 2; electric: 2.
Maximum power:
K .5: 2,900hp surfaced; 1,200hp submerged.
K. 6: 4,200hp surfaced; 1,200hp submerged.
Maximum speed:
K. 5: 19 knots surfaced; 8.2 knots submerged.
K. 6: 19.8 knots surfaced; 8 knots submerged.
Range:
K. 5: 8,000 miles at 2 knots surfaced; 90 miles at 3 knots submerged.
K. 6: 5,000 miles at 16 knots surfaced; 45 miles at 5 knots submerged.
Torpedo tubes:
K. 5: four 21in (533mm) forward; torpedoes: 10.
K. 6: four 21in (533mm) forward; torpedoes: 8.
Guns: one 3.25in (80mm) 40-cal; two 25mm (2 x 1).
Complement: *K.* 5 42; *K.* 6 54.

RO. 46 in 1944.

Class *RO.33*, Variant K.5.

Class *RO.35*, Variant K.6.

Double hull medium-displacement submarines, developed from the *Kai-toku-chu* type, *RO.29* Class of 1923, in turn, inspired by the *Schneider-Laubeuf* type of 1912. Between 1935 and 1944, twenty boats of this type were built in two variants.

Variant K. 5
Directly derived from the *RO. 29* Class, but with more powerful diesels, greater speed, range and armament. Maximum operational depth: 246ft (75m). The two boats of this Variant were the first modern medium-displacement submarines built in Japan after a lapse of about eleven years.

Variant K. 6
Developed from the preceding variant, they were slightly larger, stronger and faster, but had a lesser surface range. The original design did not specify a deck gun, but during construction, the same armament as *K. 6* was adopted. Ordered under the 1940 Programme, the eighteen boats of this variant were the last medium-displacement conventional boats built by the Japanese Navy. The building of 61 boats under the same programme, and of nine ordered in 1942 and not yet designated, was cancelled in 1943.

The boats of this type were fair medium-displacement submarines with good speed and armament, and storage capacity gave a patrol endurance of 40 days. Submerged

RO.33 on completion in 1935.

handling was decidedly superior to that of the large submarines.

The cancellation of numerous boats in 1943, was caused by the scarcity of steel plates, and by the need to use the available materials for building cargo submarines and boats with a high submerged speed.

Despite their performance, the boats achieved very limited results because they were used to defend bases instead of attacking enemy shipping. The most significant successes were achieved by *RO. 41* and *RO. 50* which sank a destroyer and a Landing Ship Tank, respectively. *RO.50* surrendered at Sasebo in August 1945: all the other boats were lost during the war.

Fates

date:	location:	boat:	cause (see page 7):
1942	Pacific	RO.33	n
1943	Pacific	RO.34, RO.35	n
		RO.38	uc
1944	Pacific	RO.36, RO.37, RO.39, RO.40, RO.42, RO.44, RO.47	n
		RO.45	a
		RO.48	uc
1945	Pacific	RO.41, RO.49, RO.55, RO.56	n
		RO.43	a
		RO.46	s
		RO.50	x

Type A

Class I. 9, Variant A. 1
(3 units).
I. 9:
Builder: Kure Dockyard.
Date: 1938–1941.
I. 10, I. 11:
Builder: Kawasaki, Kobe.
Date: 1938–1941/42.

Class I. 12, Variant A. 2
(1 unit).
I. 12:
Builder: Kawasaki, Kobe.
Date: 1942–1944.
Units of the same class ordered under the 1942 Programme and subsequently cancelled: *I. 700, I. 701*.
Normal displacement:
A. 1: 2,919 tons surfaced; 4,150 tons submerged.
A. 2: 2,934 tons surfaced; 4,172 tons submerged.
Dimensions: 372ft 9in x 31ft 4in x 17ft 6in (113.7m x 9.55m x 5.3m).
Machinery: diesel: 2; electric: 2.
Maximum power:
A. 1: 12,400hp surfaced; 2,400hp submerged.
A. 2: 4,700hp surfaced; 1,200hp submerged.
Maximum speed:
A. 1: 23.5 knots surfaced; 8 knots submerged.
A. 2: 17.7 knots surfaced; 6.2 knots submerged.
Range:
A. 1: 16,000 miles at 16 knots surfaced; 60 miles at 3 knots submerged.
A. 2: 22,000 miles at 16 knots surfaced; 75 miles at 3 knots submerged.
Torpedo tubes: six 21in (533mm) forward; torpedoes: 18.

Guns: one 5.5in (140mm) 50-cal; four 25mm (2 x 2); one catapult; one floatplane.
Complement: 114.

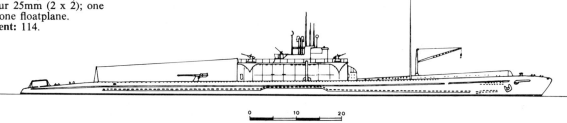

Double hull cruiser-type submarines, derived from the *Junsen 3* type (Class *I. 7*) of 1934, with improved aircraft equipment. Maximum operational depth: 328ft (100m). The four Type *A* boats were built between 1938 and 1944 in two successive variants.

Variant *A. 1*
The catapult was installed on deck, forward of the conning tower, and the hangar was also forward of, and integrated with the conning tower. The seaplane was stowed with wings folded, and was accessible from inside the pressure hull. The preparation, take-off, retrieval and stowage of the aircraft were much speedier and safer. Storage capacity gave duration for ocean patrols of more than 90 days. Communications apparatus was noteworthy. The boats were equipped to operate as command units of submarine groups, in accordance with current doctrine on the employment of submarine flotillas. Three boats of this variant were ordered under the 1939 Programme. The other two boats of the 1942 Programme were subsequently cancelled.

Variant *A. 2*
This variant, of which only a single example was built, was ordered under the 1941 Supplementary Programme. She was very similar to the preceding variant, differing only in the installation of a diesel engine whose power had been halved. Maximum surface speed was considerably reduced but range was increased, reaching 22,000 miles at 16 knots.

The evaluation, already made, of all the large Japanese submarines is also applicable to these boats; excellent surface characteristics, inadequate submerged performance.

During the war, almost all of the boats of this type were lost. The *A. 2* boats were extensively employed and sank twenty merchant and auxiliary ships totalling 103,657 GRT, and damaged another three ships totalling 23,373 GRT. The only major success against warships was the damaging of the Australian light cruiser *Hobart* (6,890 tons) by *I. 11* (Commander Nanaji) on 20 April 1943.

Fates

date:	location:	boat:	cause (see page 7)
1943	Pacific	I. 9	n
1944	Pacific	I. 10	n
		I. 11	uc
1945	Pacific	I. 12	uc

Type A Modified

Class I. 13 (AM).
I. 13, I. 14:
Builder: Kawasaki, Kobe.
Date: 1942–1944/45.
I. 15 (2nd), *I. 1* (2nd).
Builder: Kawasaki, Kobe.
Date: 1944–   /
Normal displacement: 3,603 tons surfaced; 4,762 tons submerged.
Dimensions: 372ft 9in x 38ft 6in x 19ft 4in (113.7m x 11.7m x 5.89m).
Machinery: diesel: 2; electric: 2.
Maximum power: 4,400hp surfaced; 600hp submerged.
Maximum speed: 16.7 knots surfaced; 5.5 knots submerged.
Range: 21,000 miles at 16 knots surfaced; 60 miles at 3 knots submerged.
Torpedo tubes: six 21in (533mm) forward; torpedoes: 12.
Guns: one 5.5in (140mm) 50-cal; five 25mm (1 x 1, 2 x 2); one catapult; two floatplane bombers.
Complement: 118.

Aircraft-carrier submarines developed from the *A. 2* type cruiser submarines. Maximum operational depth: 328ft (100m). This type were to have been a new variant of the *A* type, but were modified during construction: it having been decided to build true underwater aircraft carriers, equipped with floatplane bombers, to be used together with the *Sen-toku* type boats (*I. 400* Class), to attack important targets along the American seaboard.

The original small hangar was replaced by a larger one, also cylindrical in shape, located to the right of the conning tower which was offset to the left. The hangar, accessible from inside the hull, could carry two seaplanes with wings folded. They were launched by a bow catapult, and were recovered by two collapsible cranes on the bow fore-deck. The aircraft were Aichi M 6 A1 (Seiran), which could carry two 550lb (250kg) bombs, or a torpedo or 1,764lb (800kg) bomb, at a maximum speed of 292 miles (470km) per hour.

At their commissioning, they were equipped with radar, and with a primitive type of schnorkel which gave unsatisfactory results.

Of the four boats ordered under the 1942 Programme (Modified), only *I. 13* and *I. 14* entered service. *I. 15* (2nd) and *I. 1* (2nd) were not completed: work was suspended in March 1945 (when they were in an advanced state) to utilize the labour force and limited materials available, for the building of assault craft and high-speed submarines. Another three in the same programme were never laid down and were cancelled in 1943.

The building of the carrier submarines was desired by Admiral Yamamoto, Commander-in-Chief of the Japanese Fleet, but his death in 1943 and the changes in the strategic situation, removed the possibility of their employment for the planned long-range missions. Of the two completed, *I. 13* was lost in July 1945 during a normal patrol and *I. 14* was captured by the Allies at the end of the war, together with the incomplete hulls of *I. 1* (2nd) and *I. 15* (2nd).

Fates

date:	location:	boat:	cause (see page 7):
1945	Pacific	*I. 13*	a
		I. 14, *I. 1* (2nd), *I. 15* (2nd)	x

I.14 in 1945, following her capture by the Americans.

Type B

Class I. 15, Variant B. 1
(20 units).
I. 15, I. 26, I. 30, I. 37:
Builder: Kure Dockyard.
Date: 1939–1940/42.
I. 17, I. 23, I. 29, I. 31, I. 36:
Builder: Yokosuka Dockyard.
Date: 1939–1940/42.
I. 19, I. 25, I. 28, I. 33, I. 35:
Builder: Mitsubishi, Kobe.
Date: 1939–1940/42.
I. 21:
Builder: Kawasaki, Kobe.
Date: 1939–1940.
I. 27, I. 32, I. 34, I. 38, I. 39:
Builder: Sasebo Dockyard.
Date: 1940–1942/43.

Class I. 40, Variant B. 2
(6 units).
I. 40, I. 41, I. 42:
Builder: Kure Dockyard.
Date: 1941–1943/44.
I. 43, I. 44, I. 45:
Builder: Sasebo Dockyard.
Date: 1941–1944/44.
I. 44:
Builder: Yokosuka Dockyard.
Date: 1941–1944.

Class I. 54, Variant B. 3
(3 units).
I. 54, I. 56, I. 58:
Builder: Yokosuka Dockyard.
Date: 1942–1944/44.
Units of the same class
cancelled in 1943:
I. 62, I. 64, I. 65, I. 66.

Normal displacement:
B. 1: 2,589 tons surfaced;
3,654 tons submerged.
B. 2: 2,624 tons surfaced;
3,700 tons submerged.
B. 3: 2,607 tons surfaced;
3,688 tons submerged.
Dimensions:
B. 1: 356ft 6in x 30ft 6in x
16ft 9in (108.7m x 9.3m x
5.14m).
B. 2, B. 3: 356ft 6in x 30ft 6in
x 17ft 0in (108.7m x 9.3m x
5.20m).
Machinery: diesel: 2; electric:
2.
Maximum power:
B. 1: 12,400hp surfaced;
2,000hp submerged.
B. 2: 11,000hp surfaced;
2,000hp submerged.
B. 3: 4,700hp surfaced;
1,200hp submerged.

Maximum speed:
B. 1, B. 2: 23.6 knots
surfaced; 8 knots submerged.
B. 3: 17.7 knots surfaced;
6.5 knots submerged.
Range:
B. 1, B. 2: 14,000 miles at
16 knots surfaced; 96 miles at
3 knots submerged.
B. 3: 21,000 miles at 16
knots surfaced; 105 miles at
3 knots submerged.
Torpedo tubes: six 21in
(533mm) forward; torpedoes:
17; *B. 3:* 19.
Guns: one 5.5in (140mm)
50-cal; two 25mm (2 x 1); one
catapult; one floatplane.
Complement: 101.

I. 15 in 1940.

Type B, Class 1–15.

Class 1–5 with reduced diesel power (1945).

Double hull ocean-going submarines, derived from the *Kaidai 6B* type (*I. 174* Class) and from the *A. 1* type cruisers (*I. 9* Class).

With these boats, the two types of large Japanese submarines (cruiser type and Fleet type) began to merge. The Type *B*, in fact, integrated operational requirements and armament which, until that time, had been kept apart. Submerged performance was slightly improved over the preceding types. Maximum operational depth: 328ft (100m). Between 1939 and 1944, 29 boats of the Type *B* were developed from the original design, in three successive variants.

Variant *B. 1*
With twenty boats ordered under the 1939 Programme and completed between 1940 and 1943, this was the most numerous variant. The design was developed from that of the *I. 174* and *I. 9* Classes, and called for a displacement falling between that of these two Classes. The superstructure was more streamlined than in earlier boats, to improve submerged performance. The hangar, which could accommodate a Yokosuka E14 Y 1 reconnaissance floatplane (Glen), was located at the base and forward of the conning tower, amidships and aligned with the catapult.

Only in *I. 17* were the hangar and catapult fitted aft of the conning tower.

Surface armament was to have consisted of two 25mm anti-aircraft twin mounts, but in fact, one 25mm twin mount was fitted on the conning tower and a 5.5in (140mm) 50-cal deck gun, abaft the conning tower (forward in *I. 17*).

During the war, the aircraft equipment was removed from several boats and replaced by a second 5.5in (140mm) 50-cal deck gun. At the end of 1944, *I. 36* and *I. 37* were modified to carry four kaiten: in conjunction with this, the deck gun, hangar and catapult were removed and another 25mm twin mount was installed. *I. 36* underwent a further modification which allowed her to carry six kaiten.

Variant *B. 2*
Directly derived from the preceding Variant, with increased displacement and with slightly less powerful motors.
In addition to the six boats built under the 1941 Programme, eight were scheduled in the 1942 Programme, but their construction was cancelled with the programme itself. Another, modified and reduced, programme was substituted. During the war, this Variant underwent the

Table 25: Major successes of Type B submarines during the Second World War.

Boat:	Commander:	Date:	Result:	Type:	Ship:	GRT:
I.26	Yokota	31 August 1942	damaged	carrier	*Saratoga*	33,000
I.15	Ishikawa	15 September 1942	damaged	battleship	*North Carolina*	35,000
I.19	Narahara	19 September 1942	sank	carrier	*Wasp*	14,700
I.26	Yokota	13 October 1942	sank	cruiser	*Juneau*	6,000
I.56	Morinaga	25 October 1944	damaged	escort carrier	*Santee*	12,000
I.41	Kondo	3 November 1944	damaged	cruiser	*Reno*	6,000
I.58	Hashimoto	30 July 1945	sank	carrier	*Indianapolis*	9,950

same modifications as the *B. 1* type. Early in 1945, *I. 44* was modified to carry four kaiten: the deck gun and aircraft equipment were removed.

Variant *B. 3*

A further development of type *B* with the same dimensions as the preceding variants, but with diesels of considerably reduced power, which decreased maximum surface speed from 23 knots to 17 knots, but increased range from 14,000 miles to 16,000 miles at 16 knots. Storage capacity allowed patrols of approximately 90 days; submerged range was also slightly increased. From their commissioning, the boats were fitted with Type 22 radar, atop the seaplane hangar.

During the summer of 1944, *I. 56* and *I. 58* were transformed, like the boats of the preceding variants, to carry four kaiten. In March 1945, they were subjected to further modifications to enable them to carry six kaiten. The three boats commissioned, had been ordered under the 1941 Programme: another four boats, ordered at the same time, were cancelled in 1943, and 14 boats ordered under the 1942 Programme (Modified) were also cancelled. This programme also called for the building of a new variant of the *B* type, consisting of 18 boats, but they were never laid down and were cancelled in 1943. They were to have been the same size as the preceding variants, with a normal surface displacement of approximately 2,800 tons, a diesel powerful enough to give a maximum speed of approximately 22 knots, and two extra torpedo tubes.

This type, although by no means immune to the serious shortcomings of the large Japanese submarines, were adequate boats and were widely employed. They achieved good results against auxiliary and merchant shipping (sinking 56 ships (372,730 GRT) and damaging 14 (91,612 GRT)) and against American warships in the Pacific. In addition to the successes listed in Table 25, they sank three destroyers, one submarine and other minor American vessels. All 29 Type *B* boats were lost except *I. 36* and *I. 58* which surrendered to the Americans in August 1945.

Fates

date:	location:	boat:	cause (see page 7):
1942	Pacific	*I. 15*	n
		I. 30	m
		I. 23	uc
		I. 28	s
1943	Pacific	*I. 31, I. 25, I. 35, I. 39, I. 40*	n
		I. 17	n–a
		I. 34	s
		I. 19, I. 21	a
1944	Pacific	*I. 27, I. 32, I. 37, I. 38, I. 45*	n
		I. 29, I. 42, I. 43	s
		I. 26	uc
		I. 33	v
		I. 41	a
1945	Pacific	*I. 44*	a
		I. 56	n–a
		I. 36, I. 58	x

Left, top to bottom: *I.58* of the *B* type, fitted with bow catapult and hangar; *I.26* a the time of her commissioning (note the rangefinder and the 25mm twin mount on the conning tower); *I.54*, first boat of the Variant *B.3* (note the Type 22 radar on the hangar roof); and the launching of *I.17* at Yokosuka on 19 July 1939.

Type C

Class I. 16, Variant C. 1
(5 units).
I. 16, I. 22:
Builder: Kawasaki, Kobe.
Date: 1937–1940/41.
I. 18, I. 24:
Builder: Sasebo Dockyard.
Date: 1937–1940/41.
I. 20:
Builder: Mitsubishi, Kobe.
Date: 1937–1941.

Class I. 46, Variant C. 2
(3 units).
I. 46, I. 48:
Builder: Sasebo Dockyard.
Date: 1942–1944/44.
Units of the same class
construction of which was
cancelled in 1943:
I. 49, I. 50, I. 51.

Class I. 52, Variant C. 3
(3 units).
I. 52, I. 55:
Builder: Kure Dockyard.
Date: 1942–1944/44.
Units of the same class
cancelled in 1943:
I. 57, I. 58, I. 59.
Builder: Kure Dockyard.

Normal displacement:
C. 1: 2,554 tons surfaced;
2,561 tons submerged.
C. 2: 2,557 tons surfaced;
3,564 tons submerged.
C. 3: 2,564 tons surfaced;
3,644 tons submerged.
Dimensions:
C. 1, C. 2: 358ft 6in x
30ft 0in x 17ft 6in (109.3m x
9.1m x 5.3m).
C. 3: 356ft 6in x 30ft 6in x
16ft 9in (108.7m x 9.3m x
5.1m).
Machinery: diesel: 2; electric:
2.
Maximum power:
C. 1, C. 2: 12,400hp surfaced;
2,000hp submerged.
C. 3: 4,700hp surfaced;
1,200hp submerged.
Maximum speed:
C. 1, C. 2: 23.6 knots
surfaced; 8 knots submerged.
C. 3: 17.7 knots surfaced;
6.5 knots submerged.
Range:
C. 1, C. 2: 14,000 miles at
16 knots surfaced; 60 miles at
3 knots submerged.
C. 3: 21,000 miles at 16 knots

surfaced; 105 miles at 3 knots
submerged.
Torpedo tubes:
C. 1, C. 2: eight 21in (533mm)
forward; torpedoes: 20.
C. 3: six 21in (533mm)
forward; torpedoes: 19.

Guns:
C. 1, C. 2: one 5.5in (140mm)
50-cal; four 25mm (2 x 2).
C. 3: two 5.5in (140mm)
50-cal; four 25mm (2 x 1,
1 x 2).
Complement: 101.

Double hull ocean-going attack submarines, developed
from the *Kaidai 6* type, with increased dimensions, displacement and armament, and improved underwater performance. Maximum operational depth: 328ft (100m).
Between 1937 and 1944, eleven Type *C* boats, in three
successive variants, were commissioned.

Variant C. 1

Ordered under the 1937 Programme, the first five boats
were developed specifically for long-range attacks against
warships. Compared to the earlier boats from which they
derived, they were more manoeuvrable underwater, and
had a heavy torpedo armament concentrated in the bow.
Storage capacity gave them an endurance of 90 days, and
they were equipped to carry a midget submarine (Type *A*)
in cradles, on deck, forward of the conning tower, which
was streamlined and considerably smaller than in earlier
boats.

Early in 1943, *I. 16* underwent a refit during which, the
5.5in (140mm) gun was removed and the number of torpedoes was reduced. At the same time, she was equipped
to carry a *Daihatsu* landing craft and many tons of cargo
for the besieged garrisons in the Pacific islands. Other
boats probably underwent similar transformations during
the war.

Variant C. 2

The design of this variant was very similar to that of its
predecessor, but the capability of carrying midget submarines was excluded. Three boats, ordered under the 1941
Programme, were completed. Another three (*I. 49–I. 51*)
of the same programme, and a further four, of the 1942
Programme, were never laid down and were cancelled in

1943 when the Japanese Navy decided to reduce the number
of large submarines because of their heavy losses.

At the end of 1944, *I. 47* and *I. 48* were modified to
carry four kaiten: these were increased to six in March
1945, and a Type 22 air search radar was installed.

Variant C. 3

Developed from the preceding boats, this variant differed
mainly in the reduction of the number of torpedo tubes,
the installation of a second 5.5in (140mm) deck gun, and
appreciable reduction of installed power which lowered
maximum surface speed considerably, but increased range
at economical speed. The installation of less powerful
diesels, common to the last variants of the *A*, *B* and *C*
type boats, was brought about because the Japanese
experienced difficulty in manufacturing high-powered
diesels in wartime.

Early in 1945, *I. 53* was modified to carry four, subsequently six kaiten. Only three of the five boats ordered
under the 1941 Supplementary Programme were completed.
The other two, and 15 included in the 1942 Programme,
were cancelled in 1943 and it was decided to forego the
building of another 25 boats of a successive version of
the Type *C*, authorized under the 1942 Programme
(Modified). This variant, designated *C. 4*, was to have had
a normal surface displacement of 2,750 tons, the same
dimensions as the *C. 3*, a maximum surface speed of 20.5
knots, and an armament similar to that fitted in the boats
of the *C. 1* and *C. 2* Variants.

The eleven Type *C* attack boats, were among the best
submarines built by the Japanese Navy. Despite their large
size, which considerably limited their underwater performance, they were reliable and quite strong. During the
war, they sank 16 merchant and auxiliary ships totalling
80,660 GRT, and damaged another seven totalling 46,072
GRT. The greatest success against warships was achieved
by *I. 20* (Comander Yamada). She carried the midget
submarine which, on 30 May 1942, penetrated the base at
Diego Suarez and damaged the British battleship *Ramillies*
(29,150 tons). All the Type *C* boats were lost during the
war, except *I. 47* and *I. 48* which were captured by the
Americans in August 1945.

I. 16 on trials in 1940.

Fates

date:	location:	boat:	cause (see page 7):
1942	Pacific	*I. 22*	uc
1943	Pacific	*I. 20*	uc
		I. 18, I. 24	n
1944	Pacific	*I. 52*	a
		I. 16, I. 46, I. 54	n
1945	Pacific	*I. 48*	n
		I. 47, I. 53	x

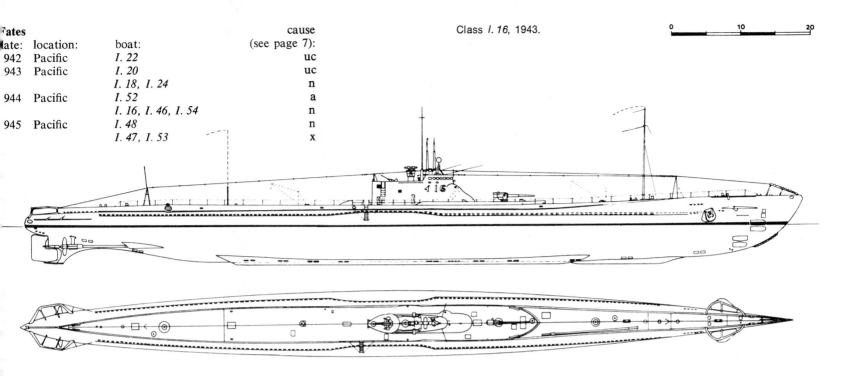

Kaisho Type

RO. 100, RO. 103, RO. 106, RO. 107:
Builder: Kure Dockyard.
Date: 1941–1942/44.
RO. 101, RO. 102, RO. 104, RO. 105, RO. 108, RO. 109, RO. 110, RO. 111, RO. 112, RO. 113, RO. 114, RO. 115, RO. 116, RO. 117, RO. 118.
Builder: Kawasaki, Kobe.
Date: 1941–1942/44.
Normal displacement: 601 tons surfaced; 728 tons submerged.
Dimensions: 199ft 9in x 20ft 6in x 11ft 6in (60.9m x 6m x 3.51m).
Machinery: diesel: 2; electric:
Maximum power: 1,000hp surfaced; 760hp submerged.
Maximum speed: 14.2 knots surfaced; 8 knots submerged.
Range: 3,500 miles at 12 knots surfaced; 60 miles at 3 knots submerged.
Torpedo tubes: four 21in (533mm) forward; torpedoes: 1.
Guns: two 25mm (2 x 1) or 3in (76mm) 40-cal.
Complement: 38.

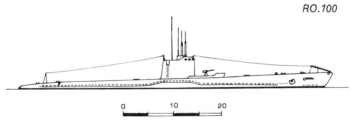

RO.100

Double hull coastal submarines. Maximum operational depth: 246ft (75m). Ordered under the 1940 and 1941 Programmes, they were designed for coastal employment in home waters, and for the defense of naval bases. In their building, account was taken of the experience gained with the medium-displacement *Kaishu* type boats, from which they were developed, though their dimensions were considerably reduced. Originally, it had been planned to arm them with a 25mm anti-aircraft cannon in a twin mounting, but in many boats, this was subsequently replaced by a 3in (76mm) 40-cal deck gun. Because they were to be employed only in the vicinity of bases, their range was limited and storage capacity restricted their duration to 21 days.

Another series of nine boats was planned under the 1942 Programme, but was later cancelled. These small boats were good submarines, possessing adequate submerged manoeuvrability, a fairly fast crash-dive time and, thanks to their small size, were less liable to detection by radar and sonar.

The results achieved by the eighteen *Kaishu* boats, all of which were lost during the war, could have been much greater had they been employed in restricted waters and at focal points against merchant shipping, instead of against large naval formations, in attacks which led to the loss of the boats.

Between 1942 and 1945, they sank six merchant ships (34,680 GRT) and damaged a total of 14,074 GRT. They also hit several warships including a destroyer and a Landing Ship Tank.

Fates

date:	location:	boat:	cause (see page 7):
1943	Pacific	RO.100	a
		RO.101	n–a
		RO.103	m
		RO.102, RO.107	n
1944	Pacific	RO.104, RO.105, RO.106, RO.108, RO.110, RO.111, RO.114, RO.116, RO.117	n
1945	Pacific	RO.109, RO.115	n
		RO.112, RO.113	s

Sen-Toku Type

Class I. 400 (Sto).
I. 400, I. 401, I. 402, I. 403:
Builder: Kure Dockyard.
Date: 1943–1944/–.
I. 401, I. 402:
Builder: Sasebo Dockyard.
Date: 1943–1944/45.
I. 405:
Builder: Kawasaki, Kobe.
Date: 1944–   /–.
Units of the same class
cancelled in 1945: *I. 403,
I. 406–I. 417*.
Normal displacement: 5,223
tons surfaced; 6,560 tons
submerged.
Dimensions: 400ft 3in x
39ft 4in x 23ft 0in (122m x
12m x 7.02m).
Machinery: diesel: 4; electric:
2.
Maximum power: 7,700hp
surfaced; 2,400hp submerged.
Maximum speed: 18.7 knots
surfaced; 6.5 knots submerged.
Range: 37,500 miles at 14
knots surfaced; 60 miles at 3
knots submerged.
Torpedo tubes: eight 21in
(533mm) forward; torpedoes:
20.
Guns: one 5.5in (140mm)
50-cal; ten 25mm (3 x 3,
1 x 1); one catapult; three
floatplane bombers.
Complement: 100.

Large double hull aircraft-carrying submarines. The pressure hull was formed by two cylinders side by side, giving a horizontal 'figure 8' configuration. Maximum operational depth: 328ft (100m).

Initially combining the various features of the large *A, B* and *C* type boats, it was decided that these submarines were to perform all the major tasks normally assigned to those types: control of groups of operational boats, attack and long-range reconnaissance. They were provided, therefore, with a good torpedo armament (eight tubes, 20 torpedoes), and an aircraft catapult.

The original design called for only two aircraft, but later, it was decided to enlarge the boats so as to accommodate three aircraft. Displacement was increased by about 700 tons, and the hangar length was increased to 115ft (34m). To achieve sufficient width at the waterline—ensuring the degree of stability indispensable to flight operations—the pressure hull was formed by two intersecting cylinders, as shown in the midsection drawing.

Storage capacity was sufficient for patrols exceeding 90 days, which was truly exceptional: 37,500 miles at 14 knots, or more than 30,000 miles at 16 knots. Stores for the Aichi M 6 A 1 (Seiran) type aircraft, in addition to fuel, included: four torpedoes, three 1,764lb (800kg) bombs and twelve 500lb (250kg) bombs. The *I. 400* boats were equipped with radar and with a rudimentary and quite

ineffective schnorkel, at the time of their commissioning.

The machinery, which was the only example of its typ to be installed in Japanese boats, consisted of four diese coupled in pairs to two propeller shafts, each of whic was powered by one electric motor, when submerged.

When they were commissioned, these were the larges boats ever built. They had many advanced technica features, but also, they had all the shortcomings of larg Japanese (and foreign) submarines previously built.

Like the *I. 13* boats, designed for the same purpose, th *I. 400* boats were unable to be usefully employed. Afte the death of Yamamoto, their building proceeded slowly and the three boats completed between 1944 and 194 (*I. 400, I. 401* and *I. 402*) remained inactive until the were captured at the end of the war. During the fina months, *I. 402* was converted to a fuel supply boat, bu was never employed as such.

I. 404 was suspended in March 1945 when she was almos complete. She was destroyed during an air attack in Jul 1945. *I. 405* was also suspended, before she had bee launched, and *I. 403* was cancelled together with twelv units also planned under the 1942 Programme (Modified).

Fates

date:	location:	boat:		caus (see page 7)
1945	Pacific	*I. 404*		
		I. 400, I. 401, I. 402		

Inboard profile Class *I–400*

Outboard profile, plan and section
of Class *I. 400*, 1945.

Below: *I.400*, *I.401* and *I.402*, the only three completed boats of the *I.400* Class. Right: *I.402*. Below right: *I.400*, *I.401* and *I.402* after the surrender in August 1945.

Sen-Taka Type

Class I. 201 (ST)
I. 201, I. 202, I. 203:
Builder: Kure Dockyard.
Date: 1943–1945/45.
I. 204, I. 205, I. 206, I. 207, I. 208:
Builder: Kure Dockyard.
Date: 1944–   /.
Units of the same class ordered but not laid down:
I. 209–I. 223.
Normal displacement: 1,291 tons surfaced; 1,450 tons submerged.

Dimensions: 259ft 0in x 19ft 0in x 18ft 0in (79m x 5.8m x 5.46m).
Machinery: diesel: 2; electric: 2.
Maximum power: 2,750hp surfaced; 5,000hp submerged.
Maximum speed: 15.8 knots surfaced; 19 knots submerged.

Range: 5,800 miles at 14 knots surfaced; 135 miles at 3 knots submerged, 17 miles at 19 knots submerged.
Torpedo tubes: four 21in (533mm) forward; torpedoes: 10.
Guns: two single 25mm.
Complement: 31.

High submerged-speed ocean-going submarines. Maximum operational depth: 360ft (110m).

After the heavy submarine losses of the first two years of war, the Japanese became convinced that boats operating mainly submerged at high speed would best counter the increasingly effective American anti-submarine measures. Pre-war experiments with the small *N. 71* were resumed, and led to the design of the *Sen-Taka* type boats, 24 of which were ordered under the 1943–1944 Programme.

They were similar, in size and performance, to the German Type XXI boats which the German Navy had commissioned for the same purpose. Despite the contact maintained between the two navies, however, there appears to have been no effective co-operation with regard to this particular type of boat. Prefabrication of entire hull sections was adopted, and construction time was ten months per boat. The hull and conning tower were streamlined, and the anti-aircraft weapons were on 'disappearing' mounts. The electric motors were almost twice as powerful as the diesels, and the high battery capacity allowed a burst speed of 19 knots for 55 minutes, and an economical speed of 3 knots for approximately 45 hours.

The *I. 201* boats were fitted with a schnorkel, and could undertake patrols in excess of 25 days duration.

Of the eight boats laid down, only *I. 201, I. 202, I. 203* and *I. 204* were commissioned before the end of the war, too late for action, however. The first three were captured by the Americans in August 1945, while they were still working up. *I. 204,* almost completed, was destroyed on 22 June 1945, during an attack on Kure. *I. 205* and *I. 206,* launched respectively in February and March 1945, were captured incomplete at the end of the war. *I. 207* and *I. 208* were suspended in March 1945 and the material on the ways was scrapped to make room for the building of kaiten. None of the boats of the *I. 209* Series were laid down, and the construction of another 76 boats, authorized in the 1944–1945 Programme, was never begun.

Although their general characteristics were inferior to those of the German Type XXI boats, these Elektro-boote were about the best and the most interesting Japanese submarine designs. They were not used in action and so were unable to prove their worth, but their excellent underwater performance, particularly the high burst speed, would have been a serious danger to the Americans, whose anti-submarine measures had been developed to oppose much less sophisticated boats.

The Sen-Taka boats, like the German Type XXI boats, came too late. Japanese industry was no longer able to produce them rapidly in sufficient quantity, and the strategic situation no longer permitted their effective use.

Fates

date:	location:	boat:	cause (see page 7):
1945	Pacific	*I. 204*	b
		I. 201, I. 202, I. 203, I. 205, I. 206	x

Sen-Taka-Sho Type

Class Ha. 201 (STS)
(9 units + 29).
Ha. 201, Ha. 202, Ha. 203, Ha. 204, Ha. 205, Ha. 207, Ha. 208, Ha. 209, Ha. 210:
Builder: Sasebo Dockyard.
Date: 1945–1945/45.
Ha. 206, Ha. 211, Ha. 212, Ha. 220, Ha. 222, Ha. 233, Ha. 234, Ha. 235, Ha. 246:
Builder: Kawasaki, Tanagawa.
Date: 1945– /.
Ha. 213, Ha. 214, Ha. 224, Ha. 225, Ha. 226, Ha. 227, Ha. 237, Ha. 238:
Builder: Mitsubishi, Kobe.
Date: 1945– /.
Ha. 215, Ha. 216, Ha. 217, Ha. 218, Ha. 219, Ha. 228, Ha. 229, Ha. 230, Ha. 231, Ha. 232:
Builder: Sasebo Dockyard.
Date: 1945– /.
Ha. 221, Ha. 223:
Builder: Kawasaki, Kobe.
Date: 1945– /.

Units of the same class ordered but not laid down:
Ha. 239, Ha. 240, Ha. 250–Ha. 253, Ha. 263–Ha. 266, Ha. 276–Ha. 279:
Builder: Mitsubishi, Kobe.
Ha. 241–Ha. 245, Ha. 254–Ha. 258, Ha. 267–Ha. 271:
Builder: Sasebo Dockyard.
Ha. 247–Ha. 249, Ha. 259–Ha. 262, Ha. 272–Ha. 275:
Builder: Kawasaki, Tanagawa.

Normal displacement: 377 tons surfaced; 440 tons submerged.
Dimensions: 174ft 0in x 13ft 0in x 11ft 3in (53m x 4m x 3.44m).
Machinery: diesel: 1; electric: 1.
Maximum power: 400hp surfaced; 1,250hp submerged.

Maximum speed: 10.5 knots surfaced; 13 knots submerged.
Range: 3,000 miles at 10 knots surfaced; 100 miles at 2 knots submerged.
Torpedo tubes: two 21in (533mm) forward; torpedoes: 14.
Guns: one 7.7mm.
Complement: 22.

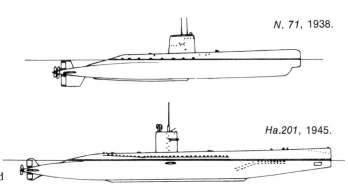

N. 71, 1938.

Ha.201, 1945.

High submerged-speed coastal submarines. Maximum operational depth: 328ft (100m).

In the 1943–1944 Programme, the Japanese decided to build 80 small coastal boats of high submerged performance, whose design derived directly from that of the experimental submarine N. 71 of 1938. The performance and dimensions of these small boats was comparable to those of the German Type XXIII boats. They were intended for the defence of bases and Japanese home waters. The design also showed the influence of the studies that had been made in connection with the building of the ocean-going *I. 201* Class Elektro-boote, and called for

simple, rapidly built boats with prefabricated hulls, completely welded, fitted with a single screw, and with streamlined hulls for submerged speed.

Of small size, very manoeuvrable, and with a burst speed of about 13 knots, the *Ha. 201* boats were to be the coastal equivalent of the *I. 201* type, in the same way that the German XXIII types were the counterparts of the larger XXI boats. Equipped with radar and schnorkel, they could undertake patrols of up to 15 days duration.

The plan called for the building of about 13 boats per month, with a construction time of approximately two months per boat. The first, *Ha. 201,* was laid down at Kure on 1 March 1945 and was completed on 31 May. Subsequent lack of materials caused by the frequent American bombing of Japanese shipyards and production centres, delayed the programme considerably. Of the 80 boats initially planned, to which, another ten were added in 1945, only 38 were begun. Of these, only nine (*Ha. 201–Ha. 205* and *Ha. 207–Ha. 210*) were completed before the end of the war, but none had time to see any action: all were captured by the Americans in August 1945, while they were still working up. Of the remaining 29 laid down, *Ha. 206, Ha. 212–Ha. 215, Ha. 217–Ha. 219, Ha. 218* and *Ha. 219* had already been launched, and were fitting out when they were captured by the Americans at the end of the war. All of them, and all the remaining boats on the ways, were subsequently scrapped.

The same remarks made about the preceding Class, apply to these boats, though their 'emergency construction', based on maximum speed and economy of building, might lead one to believe that they could not be relied on for any prolonged use.

Fates

date:	boat:	cause (see page 7):
1945	*Ha. 201–Ha. 211, Ha. 212–Ha. 215, Ha. 217–Ha. 219, Ha. 211, Ha. 228, Ha. 229*	x

Transport submarines

Cargo submarines (52 units+2, of which, 26 belonged to the Japanese Army). Late in 1942, the need to supply the garrisons left isolated in the Pacific atolls and islands after the American advance, became imperative. The navy had originally used old boats or standard operational boats for this purpose, and now began to build submarines specially designed for the task.

D.1 Type

I. 361, I. 363:
Builder: Kure Dockyard.
Date: 1942–1943/44.
I. 362, I. 364, I. 366, I. 367, I. 370, I. 371:
Builder: Mitsubishi, Kobe.
Date: 1942–1943/44.
I. 365, I. 368, I. 369, I. 372.
Builder: Yokosuka Dockyard.
Date: 1943–1944.
Normal displacement: 1,779 tons surfaced; 2,215 tons submerged.
Dimensions: 241ft 0in x 29ft 3in x 15ft 6in (73.5m x 8.9m x 4.7m).
Machinery: diesel: 2; electric: 2.
Maximum power: 1,850hp surfaced; 1,200hp submerged.

Maximum speed: 13 knots surfaced; 16.5 knots submerged.
Range: 15,000 miles at 10 knots surfaced; 120 miles at 3 knots submerged.

Guns: one 5.5in (140mm); two 25mm; two 42ft 6in (1.3m) landing craft; 82 tons cargo or 110 troops.
Complement: 75.

Ordered under the Modified 1942 Programme. The hulls were a simple design adopted for simple and rapid construction. Originally, it had been intended to fit these boats with two 21in (533mm) torpedo tubes, forward, but the first trials of I. 361 showed that the boat handled poorly, especially in rough conditions, and it was not worth keeping the tubes. The bow was lengthened approximately 6ft (1.8m) from the original design. In addition to the Daihatsu landing craft which were stowed on deck and which could withstand up to 200ft (60m) of depth, the boats carried four rubber dinghies and two electric cranes (mounted on the sides of the conning tower) to handle the cargo, 20 tons of which were stowed on deck. Maximum service depth: 246ft (75m).

Late in 1944 and early in 1945, eight of these boats were converted as kaiten carriers. The 5.5in (140mm) gun was removed, and they could transport and launch five kaiten apiece. Another 92 submarines of this Class were planned, but shortage of steel and the urgency of the anti-submarine escort construction programme stopped the placing of orders. At the end of the war, the five survivors were surrendered to the Americans, but one was lost to a mine soon afterwards.

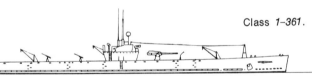
Class I-361.

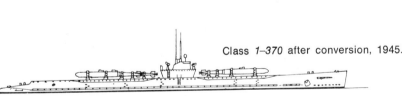
Class I-370 after conversion, 1945.

Fates

date:	location:	boat:	cause (see page 7):
1944	Pacific	I. 364, I. 365	s
1945	Pacific	I. 361, I. 368	a
		I. 362, I. 370	m
		I. 371	s
		I. 372	b
		I. 363, I. 366, I. 367, I. 369	x

D.2 Type

I. 373:
Builder: Yokosuka Dockyard.
Date: 1944–1945.
I. 374:
Builder: Yokosuka Dockyard, laid down but not completed.
Date: 1944.
Boats ordered but not laid down: I. 375, I. 378.
Normal displacement: 1,926 tons surfaced; 2,240 tons submerged.
Dimensions: 242ft 9in x 29ft 3in x 16ft 6in (74m x 8.9m x 5.05m).

Machinery: diesel: 2; electric: 2.
Maximum power: 1,750hp surfaced; 1,200hp submerged.
Maximum speed: 13 knots surfaced; 6.5 knots submerged.
Range: 15,000 miles at 10 knots surfaced; 120 miles at 3 knots submerged.
Guns: one 5.5in (140mm); seven 25mm (1 x 3, 2 x 2) some sources say two 25mm (1 x 2); one 42ft 6in (13m) landing craft; 110 tons cargo; 150 tons petrol.
Complement: 100.

Enlarged and improved versions of the D. 1 type. Maximum depth was greater—328ft (100m)—but endurance (30 days) and range were less, because of the greater cargo capacity. I. 374 was scrapped half complete on the stocks because of the greater urgency of other programmes. I. 373 is believed to have been converted to a kaiten carrier after her completion, but was lost off Shangai in the final days of the war. Another 36 were planned but never ordered, in addition to I. 375–I. 378 which were ordered but never laid down.

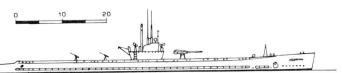

Fates

date:	location:	boat:	cause (see page 7):
1945	China Sea	I. 373	s

Yu.1013, one of the small Army cargo boats, in dry dock.

Sh (Sen-Ho) Type

I. 351, I. 352:
Builder: Kure Dockyard.
Date: 1944–1945.
Ordered from the same yard but not laid down: *I. 353*.
Normal displacement: 3,512 tons surfaced; 4,920 tons submerged.
Dimensions: 363ft 9in x 33ft 4in x 20ft 0in (111m x 10.1m x 6.1m).
Machinery: diesel: 2; electric: 2.
Maximum power: 3,700hp surfaced; 1,200hp submerged.
Maximum speed: 15.75 knots surfaced; 6.3 knots submerged.
Range: 13,000 miles at 14 knots surfaced; 100 miles at 3 knots submerged.
Torpedo tubes: four 21in (533mm) forward; torpedoes: 4.

Guns: four 3in (76mm) trench mortars (2 x 2); seven 25mm (1 x 3, 2 x 2); 390 tons cargo including 365 tons petrol; 11 tons fresh water; 60 550lb (250kg) bombs (or 30 550lb (250kg) bombs and 15 aircraft torpedoes).
Complement: 90.

These, the largest of the Japanese transport submarines, were ordered before the others (under the 1941 Additional Programme), and for a different purpose. They were intended to act as advanced bases for seaplanes and flying boats. The original armament was to have been one 5.5in (140mm) gun and four 25mm, but construction of the boats was so long delayed that no deck guns were available and the unusual armament of mortars was substituted, though the anti-aircraft cannon were reinforced. These boats had an endurance of 60 days, and their service depth was 315ft (96m). Other programmes took precedence over them. *I. 352* was bombed when ninety per cent complete, and the 'improved *I. 351*' type planned under the 1942 Programme was never even ordered.

Fates

date:	location:	boat:	cause (see page 7):
1945	Pacific	*I. 351*	s
	Japan	*I. 352*	b

Ss (Sen-Yu-Sho) Type

Ha. 101, Ha. 104, Ha. 106, Ha. 107, Ha. 108, Ha. 110:
Builder: Kawasaki, Tanagawa.
Date: 1944–1945.
Ha. 102, Ha. 103, Ha. 105, Ha. 109, Ha. 111, Ha. 112:
Builder: Mitsubishi, Kobe.
Never ordered: *Ha. 113–Ha. 200*.
Normal displacement: 429 tons surfaced; 493 tons submerged.
Dimensions: 146ft 0in x 20ft 0in x 13ft 6in (44.5m x 6.1m x 4.04m).
Machinery: diesel: 1; electric: 1.

Maximum power: 400hp surfaced; 150hp submerged.
Maximum speed: 10 knots surfaced; 5 knots submerged.
Range: 3,000 miles at 10 knots surfaced; 46 miles at 2.3 knots submerged.
Guns: one 25mm; 600 tons cargo.
Complement: 22.

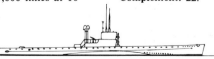

Small and simple submarines designed solely for supply missions. Their construction made extensive use of pre-fabrication and welding and some were completed in as little as five months. Other submarine programmes were cut back, and finally cancelled, but the construction of these boats continued as an emergency measure, though the following 88 boats of the Class were cancelled in May 1944. Maximum depth was 300ft (95m) and endurance was 15 days. All—including the nearly complete *Ha. 111* and *Ha. 112*—were surrendered to the Americans at the end of the war, and were scuttled or scrapped shortly afterwards.

Fates

date:	location:	boat:	cause (see page 7):
1945	Japan	*Ha. 101 – Ha. 112*	x

Yu Class

YU CLASS (12 units).
*Yu. 1, Yu. 2, Yu. 3, Yu. 4,
Yu. 5, Yu. 6, Yu. 7, Yu. 8,
Yu. 9, Yu. 10, Yu. 11, Yu. 12*:
Builder: Kasado Iron Works,
Hitachi Shipbuilding Co.,
Kudamatsu.
Date: 1943–1945.
Normal displacement: 273
tons surfaced; 370 tons
submerged.
Dimensions: 134ft 0in x 12ft
9in x 9ft 6in (40.9m x 3.9m x
2.9m).

Machinery: diesel: 1; electric:
1.
Maximum power: 400hp
surfaced; 75hp submerged.
Maximum speed: 10 knots
surfaced; 5 knots submerged.

Range: 1,500 miles at 8 knots
surfaced; 32 miles at 4 knots
submerged.
Guns: one 37mm; 40 tons
cargo.
Complement: –

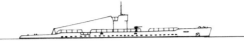

There was little love lost between the Japanese Army and
Navy, so it is not surprising that the former decided to

design and build its own submarines for supplying its
island garrisons, nor that the navy should refuse assistance
in this project. So far as the navy (or the historian) is
concerned, this could only prove an unnecessary diversion
of scarce shipbuilding materials.

The construction of this Class was kept as simple as
possible. Apart from the two surrendered to the Americans,
their fate is unknown.

Fates

date:	location:	boat:	cause (see page 7):
1945	Japan	*Yu. 10, Yu. 12*	x

Yu.1001 Class

*Yu. 1001, Yu. 1002, Yu. 1003,
Yu. 1004, Yu. 1005, Yu. 1006,
Yu. 1007, Yu. 1008, Yu. 1009,
Yu. 1010, Yu. 1011, Yu. 1012,
Yu. 1013, Yu. 1014*.
Builder: Chosen Machine Co.,
Korea.
Date: 1944–1945.

Normal displacement: 392 tons
surfaced; approx 500 tons
submerged.
Dimensions: 160ft 9in x
16ft 6in x 8ft 4in (49m x
5m x 2.6m).
Machinery: diesel: 2; electric: 2.
Maximum power: 700hp

surfaced; 150hp submerged.
Maximum speed: 12 knots
surfaced; 5 knots submerged.
Range: 1,500 miles at 8 knots
surfaced; 32 miles at 4 knots
submerged.
Armament: none; 40 tons
cargo.

The first boats of this Class were laid down for the army
in 1945, by the Ando Iron Works, Tokyo: further details
are unknown.

Foreign submarines in Japanese service

RO.500 ex-U 511, shortly after
arrival at Penang on 16 July
1943.

During the war, the Japanese Navy commissioned several
German and Italian boats, ceded by the Germans or captured at the time of the Italian and German surrender.

The two boats of the *RO. 500 Class* (*RO. 500* ex-*U 511*,
and *RO. 501*, ex-*U 1224*) were German-built boats of the
IX C type. The first was brought to Japan by a German
crew in July 1943, and ceded to the Japanese Navy as a
model for future construction. The second was accepted
at Kiel in February 1944 by a Japanese crew which had
been brought to Europe in the submarine *I. 8* (61 days

from Penang to Brest). She was lost in the Atlantic en
route to Japan, in May 1944. For details of these boats,
see page 70.

The two Italian boats, *I. 503* (*Marcello* Class) and *I. 504*
(*Marconi* Class) were captured at Sabang and Singapore
in September 1943. These were ocean-going boats, converted to carry high value materials to and from the Far
East, and had just arrived from Europe. The two boats
were ceded to the Germans (as *U.IT.24* and *U.IT.25*),
but were not used. At the German surrender, they were
recaptured by the Japanese who handed them over to the
Americans at the end of the war. (See pages 158 and 161).

The other German-built boats (*I. 501*, ex-*U 181*; *I. 502*,
ex-*U 862*; *I. 505*, ex-*U. 219*; *I. 506*, ex-*U 195*) belonging
to the *I. 501* and *I. 505* Classes, were also captured in the
Far East, where they were stationed temporarily at the
time of the German surrender. They were not used by the
Japanese and were surrendered to the Americans at the
end of the war. (See pages 70 and 74 for details of these
boats.)

Fates

date:	location:	boat:	cause (see page 7):
1944	Atlantic	*RO. 501*	n
1945	Pacific	*RO. 500, I. 501, I. 502, I. 503, I. 504 I. 506*	x
1945	Indian Ocean	*I. 505*	x

Midget submarines and human torpedoes

The first two prototype midget submarines (*N. 1, N. 2*) were built at Kure Dockyard in about 1936. The boats had electric motors, torpedo-shaped hulls and lacked a conning tower. Subsequently, another two prototypes were built (*Ha. 1, Ha. 2*), modified and fitted with a conning tower. They formed the test bed for the numerous midgets (*Ha. 3–Ha. 44, Ha. 46–Ha. 61*) of the *A* type, built between 1938 and 1942.

Designed to be carried by surface vessels and by large ocean-going boats, it was intended that they be used in the open sea during encounters between battle squadrons.

Later, came the idea of using midgets to attack major warships in their anchorages. Five Type *A* were used at Pearl Harbor, but without success. Others were employed against Sydney and Diego Suarez where they damaged the British battleship *Ramillies*. Most of the Type *A*, however, were used for coastal defence.

During the war, three successive versions, *Types B, C* and *D*, were developed from the Type *A*, with improved characteristics and fitted with a diesel for surface propulsion and for battery charging.

A total of 126 of these last three types were built.

Table 26: Principal characteristics of Japanese 'Pocket' submarines and underwater assault craft.

Type: (year built) no. units	Normal displacement submerged (tons):	Dimensions:	Machinery type (hp):	Speed (knots): surfaced/ submerged	Range (miles at knots): surfaced/ submerged	Armament:	Complement:
A (Ko-Hyoteki) (1938–1942) 62	46	78ft 6in x 6ft 0in x 6ft 0in (23.9m x 1.8m x 1.8m)	1 electric 600	23/19	— 80 at 2 55 at 19	Two 18in(457mm) torpedoes	2
B (Ko-Hyoteki) (1943) 1	50	80ft 0in x 6ft 0in x 6ft 0in (24.9m x 1.8m x 1.8m)	1 Diesel 40 1 electric 600	6.5/18.5	350 at 6 120 at 4	Two 18in(457mm) torpedoes	3
C (Ko-Hyoteki) (1943–1944) 15	50	80ft 0in x 6ft 0in x 6ft 0in (24.9m x 1.8m x 1.8m)	1–4 Diesels — 1 electric 600	6.5/18.5	350 at 6 120 at 4	Two 18in(457mm) torpedoes	—
D (Koryu) (1945) 110	59.3	86ft 0in x 6ft 6in x 6ft 6in (26.2m x 2.9m x 2.9m)	1 Diesel 150 1 electric 500	8/16	1,000 at 8 320 at 16	Two 18in(457mm) torpedoes	5
Kairyu (1945) 207	19.3	55ft 6in x 4ft 6in x 4ft 6in (17.2m x 1.3m x 1.3m)	1 Diesel 100 1 electric 100	7.5/10	450 at 5 36 at 3	Two 18in(457mm) torpedoes or one 1,323lb(600kg) explosive charge	2
Kaiten 1 (1944)	8.3	38ft 4in x 3ft 3in x 3ft 3in (14.75m x 1m x 1m)	1 torpedo motor 550	—/30	— 12.5 at 30 45 at 12	3,417lb(1,550kg) of explosives	1
Kaiten 2 (1945)	13.4	54ft 0in x 4ft 6in x 4ft 6in (16.5m x 1.35m x 1.35m)	1 hydrogen peroxide 1,500	—/40	— 13.7 at 40 48 at 20	3,417lb(1,550kg) of explosives	—
Kaiten 4 (1945)	13.2	54ft 0in x 4ft 6in x 4ft 6in (16.5m x 1.35m x 1.35m)	1 torpedo motor 1,500–1,800	—/40	— 14.6 at 40 50 at 20	3,969lb(1,800kg) of explosives	—

Several were lost without having achieved any worthwhile results, but the majority were captured in their bases at the end of the war. Massive use of them had been planned, together with similar types of vessel, for the last-ditch defence of Japanese territory.

Similar to the preceding boats, but of smaller dimensions, were the numerous boats of the *Kairyu* type, built in 1945. These could also be used in suicide attacks, with a 1,323lb (600kg) warhead replacing the torpedoes.

In addition to the midgets which were normally armed with torpedoes and carried crews of two, three or five men, the Imperial Navy designed and built numerous assault craft for suicide attacks, during the last year of the war. These were the kaiten (literally, 'turned towards heaven'), tiny submarines built around the motors of the Type 93 oxygen torpedoes. They were operated by one man and were fitted with a large explosive charge in the head, whose weight was 3,307–3,969lb (1,500–1,800kg).

The concept of using torpedoes guided to the target by an operator who voluntarily sacrificed himself, had been considered for some time in Japanese naval circles. They had followed with admiration and interest, the successes achieved by the Italians in two World Wars, though the Italian methods in no way called for the voluntary sacrifice of the pilots.

From the time of the operations in the Solomon Islands, Japanese officers had studied the possibility of converting the Type 93 torpedo to a guided assault craft, and had suggested its use in the open sea, convinced that results would be decidedly better than those achieved with midgets at the beginning of the war.

The first model of the kaiten (Type *1*) was ready early in 1944, and in October of that year, when the exploits of the kamikaze became widespread, the first volunteers for the kaiten were accepted.

There was no difficulty in recruiting among the submariners. Kaiten pilots were trained in the Bay of Tokumaya, in the Inland Sea. Their life, psychological preparation and the moving investiture and farewell to friends, before their one and only mission, were identical with those already practised by the kamikaze.

The kaiten were normally carried to the target area by ocean-going boats, or by surface vessels (the cruiser *Kitakami*, etc.). Surface vessels lowered them to the sea on slides. Submarines, which carried three to six kaiten on deck, used a more complex technique, but one which gave better results than those achieved by the surface craft.

The pilot of the kaiten normally remained inside the parent vessel until a target presented itself. He then transferred to his craft through a watertight tunnel from inside the submarine. During the approach to the target, the pilot remained in contact with the submarine commander who provided final bearings and attack instructions. At about 8,300 yards (7,000m) from the target, the kaiten's engine was started and she pulled away from the parent submarine.

During the run, the pilot could correct his heading by observation through a small periscope. Steering a collision course, the pilot when within 550 yards (500m) of the target, submerged the torpedo to a depth of 13ft (4m) and locked the controls. The explosion of the charge against the target's hull was sufficient to sink a medium-size ship, and the destructive effect was decidedly greater than those of the kamikaze.

The first operational employment of the kaiten took place in November 1944 and they were used with increasing frequency until the last days of the war, using almost all the surviving ocean-going boats as carriers. Overall results were rather limited, probably because of lack of training and the difficulties in manoeuvring the kaiten.

From mid 1944 until August 1945, several hundreds of kaiten of various types were built, but only about fifty of them were used in action. At the end of the war, a large number of them were found.

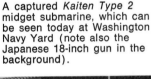

A captured *Kaiten Type 2* midget submarine, which can be seen today at Washington Navy Yard (note also the Japanese 18-inch gun in the background).

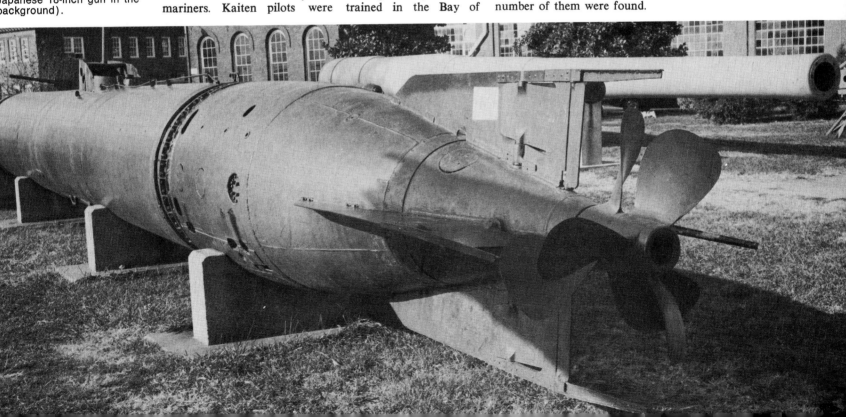

N--therland-

O. 25 being launched at Schiedam on 1 May 1940.

Although Holland possessed the world's third largest colonial empire in 1939, her naval power was small for the heavy commitments attendant on this position. The Dutch Navy, second only to the Royal Navy in age and fighting tradition, and the power of which had been vital to the conquest and retention of her numerous colonies, had diminished appreciably since the days of De Ruyter, when it represented the most worthy opponent of the British Fleet.

By the twentieth century, the Royal Netherlands Navy was a second-rate navy, though not in the quality of its ships and men.

When the Germans invaded the hitherto neutral Low Countries in May 1940, a limited programme to strengthen the fleet was in an advanced stage, but completion was prevented by the German occupation. Several of the new ships, already being fitted out, were towed to Britain where they were subsequently completed: others, and all those still building, were sabotaged and abandoned. The construction of several of these was continued by the Germans, or was resumed by the Dutch after the war.

The commissioned boats stationed in home waters, made their way to Britain and continued to operate for the rest of the war, attached to the Royal Navy. Those stationed in the East Indies (the colonial navy was virtually a separate force)—the majority of the boats—defended Dutch interests in those territories until they were overrun by the Japanese in December 1941. Many of them were lost during the early months of the war in a futile attempt to oppose the Japanese: the remaining boats withdrew to Australia to continue the fight alongside British and American boats.

In May 1940, the Dutch submarine fleet totalled 27 boats commissioned or fitting out: another three were under construction. Eleven were old boats of limited effectiveness: the others, all built in Holland, were excellent submarines, which had entered service between 1932 and 1939.

Originally, all submarines designed for employment in home waters were designated by the prefix O (Onderzeeboot) followed by a figure in arabic numerals (O.8, O.11, etc.). Boats scheduled for the East Indies had the prefix K (Kolonien) followed by a roman numeral (K.VII, K.XI, etc,).

The main difference between the two types of boats were in size and range, which were markedly superior in the 'colonial' boats, in order to meet the requirements of their theatre of operations. This difference was abandoned in 1937: henceforward, new Dutch boats were designated only by the letter O and were considered suitable for employment in European or colonial waters.

In 1940, the oldest Dutch boat in service was O. 8: she was an ex-British 'Holland' type boat which had been commissioned in the Dutch Navy after the First World War. She was captured by the Germans at Den Helder, incorporated in their navy and used for training until 1945.

Next came K.VII, a medium-displacement submarine whose armament included an external twin-tube traversing mount. This arrange-

Development of Dutch submarines, 1922–1939.

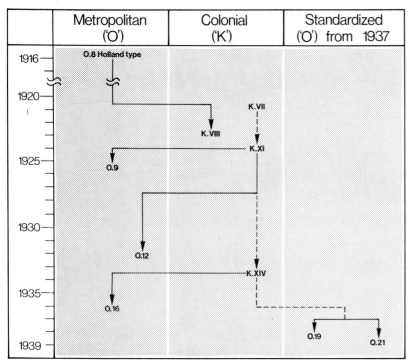

	Metropolitan ('O')	Colonial ('K')	Standardized ('O') from 1937
1916	O.8 Holland type		
1920		K.VII	
		K.VIII	
1925	O.9	K.XI	
1930	O.12		
1935	O.16	K.XIV	
1939			O.19 O.21

O. 23, alongside a depot ship, with a British U Class boat in 1942.

developed from the preceding class, was the first submarine in which the size, speed and range characteristics of the colonial boats were merged with the handling and armament characteristics of boats designed for European waters.

The most modern boats in the Dutch Navy in 1940 were those of the O.19 and O.21 Classes. The former were minelayers with ocean-going characteristics and a notable torpedo armament: the O.21 boats were a copy of the O.19 type, without the minelaying apparatus, and smaller in size.

The O.19 and O.21 Classes were fitted with a rudimentary experimental apparatus which allowed use of the diesel engines while submerged at periscope depth, by means of a tube which provided the necessary air for the diesels, and allowed expulsion of exhaust gases. The schnorkel developed by the Germans during the war, was developed from this device.

The Dutch submarines were strong safe boats and they had good seakeeping qualities: speed, range and armament were also good, especially in the more recently built boats. They showed the usual high quality of Dutch warship design and construction, and the originality of thought which made them well suited to their assigned tasks. The adoption of the Bofors 40mm is symptomatic of this.

When the Germans invaded Holland, of the 27 commissioned boats, 12 were stationed in Dutch waters and 15 (all the K boats plus O.16, O.19 and O.20), in the East Indies. Most of the 12 boats at Dutch bases made their way to Britain and immediately began operating with the Royal Navy. Several boats were sent to the Mediterranean, where O.21 sank the German U 95 in November 1941. In 1940, O.11 and O.22 were lost in the North Sea.

In December 1941, the Dutch boats in the East Indies began operations against the Japanese. From 1942 to 1945, eight boats were lost: most in action, though several were scuttled when the base at Soerabaya was abandoned in March 1942. During that year, several boats were transferred from Europe to the Pacific.

The results achieved by the few Dutch boats in the Pacific and in the Indian Ocean, were remarkable: in addition to numerous Japanese merchant ships and auxiliary vessels, they sank several warships. The most important successes were achieved by K.XIV (Van Hoof) which seriously damaged the Japanese light cruiser Tsugaru (4,400 tons) on 21 June 1944, and by O.19 (Van Hoof) which damaged the Japanese heavy cruiser Nachi (13,000 tons) on 22 April 1945.

The impossibility of obtaining replacements for engines and various items of equipment, forced the Dutch to de-commission several boats in Britain and Australia in 1943, in order to use their parts.

To utilize the excellently trained crews which thus became available, the Royal Navy ceded four boats between 1943 and 1945: one S Class; two T Class and one U Class.

Despite the limited number of available boats and the serious technical and logistic difficulties involved in maintaining them in a fully operational state, the Dutch submarine fleet achieved excellent results in all theatres during the war, proving the good quality of its boats and, above all, of its men, worthy heirs to the great traditions of Tromp and De Ruyter. At the end of the war, the Dutch Navy was left with only eleven boats, to which was soon added O.27, which had been completed by the Germans, and which was found still afloat in 1945. Of the four boats ceded by Great Britain, two were immediately returned: the other two (T Class) remained in service until 1963–66. The last Dutch-built boats that had participated in the Second World War, were paid off in 1958.

ment was characteristic of many Dutch boats and was very similar to those in French boats.

The K.VIII Class of 1923, were developed from the 'Holland' type but had two torpedo tubes less. The three boats of the K.XI Class were slightly larger than the preceding boats and, for the first time in the Dutch Navy, adopted 21in (533mm) torpedo tubes.

The subsequent Class O.9, consisted of boats smaller than those of the preceding class, intended for use in home waters. From the K.XI Class, there also derived the O.12 Class of four boats, commissioned in 1932. Widespread use was made of welding in their hull construction, and the deck gun was replaced by two 40mm 56-cal anti-aircraft cannon, mounted on two sponsons forward and aft of the conning tower. This type of armament was a sensible step. In European waters, the greatest source of danger was aircraft: the opportunity to use deck guns against naval targets would be very rare. In any event, the Bofors 40mm guns could also be used for surface fire at close range.

With the five K.XIV Class colonial boats, the Dutch Navy returned to a more classic concept of surface armament: these boats were, in fact, fitted with a 3.4in (88mm) 45-cal gun. The subsequent O.16,

Old submarines

O.8

O. 8 ex-British *H. 6.*
Builder: Canadian Vickers.
Date: 1915–1916.
Normal displacement: 343 tons surfaced; 443 tons usbmerged.
Dimensions: 151ft 6in x 15ft 6in x 12ft 9in (46m x 4.9m x 3.9m).

Machinery: diesel: 2 M.A.N.; electric: 2.
Maximum power: 480hp surfaced; 320hp submerged.
Maximum speed: 11.5 knots surfaced; 8 knots submerged.
Range: 1,350 miles at 8 knots surfaced.

Torpedo tubes: four 18in (457mm) forward.
Guns: one 37mm anti-aircraft.
Complement: 26.

Holland design, similar to the Italian *H* Class (see Italy). An earlier version of the British *H* Class noted in this work. She was wrecked on the Dutch coast in 1916, salved and interned by the Dutch who then purchased her from Britain. After her capture by the Germans in 1940, she was re-designated *UD. 1* and scuttled at Kiel in 1945 after being used for training.

K. VII

K. VII.
Builder: Fijenoord, Rotterdam.
Date: 1920–1922.
Normal displacement: 507 tons surfaced; 639 tons submerged.
Dimensions: 188ft 0in x 16ft 9in x 12ft 6in (54m x 5.1m x 3.8m).
Machinery: diesel: 2 Sulzer; electric: 2.
Maximum power: 1,200hp surfaced; 400hp submerged.
Maximum speed: 13.5 knots

surfaced; 8 knots submerged.
Range: 3,500 miles at 13 knots surfaced; 13 miles at 8 knots submerged.
Torpedo tubes: six 17.7in (450mm); 2 forward, 2 aft,

The oldest of the colonial submarines still in service in 1940, and also the last of the British-designed Hay-Denny single hull saddle-tank type, developed (but not built) by the famous British firm of Denny just before the First World War. When that war broke out, the design team

2 external traversing amidships.
Guns: one 3in (76mm); one 12.7mm machine-gun.
Complement: 31.

was transferred to Holland, and the Dutch subsequently built several *K. VII* was small for her intended purpose when built, and became obsolete some time before 1939. Maximum service depth was 132ft (40m).

The traversing external torpedo-tube mount was in the casing forward of the conning tower. In 1942, she was sunk in an air raid on Soerabaya.

Fates			cause
date:	location:	boat:	(see page 7):
1942	East Indies	*K. VII*	b

K. VIII Class

K. VIII, K. IX, K. X.
Builder: De Schelde, Flushing.
Date: 1922–1923.
Normal displacement: 521 tons surfaced; 712 tons submerged.
Dimensions: 210ft 0in x 18ft 4in x 11ft 10in (64m x 5.6m x 3.6m).
Machinery: diesel: 2 M.A.N.; electric: 2.
Maximum power: 1,500hp

surfaced; 630hp submerged.
K. VIII: 1,800hp surfaced; 630hp submerged.
Maximum speed: 15 knots surfaced, 9.5 knots submerged.
Range: 3,500 miles at 11 knots surfaced; 12 miles at 8.5 knots submerged.
Torpedo tubes: four 17.7in (450mm); 2 forward, 2 aft.
Guns: one 3.4in (88mm)

45-cal; one 12.7mm machine-gun.
Complement: 31.

Single hull developments of the Holland type. These medium submarines had a maximum diving depth of 132ft (40m). The first two were paid off after reaching Australia in 1942, but the last was scuttled after being damaged by Japanese depth-charges.

Fates			cause
date:	location:	boat:	(see page 7):
1942	East Indies	*K. X*	sb
	Australia	*K. VIII, K. X*	r

K. XI Class

K. XI, K. XII, K. XIII.
Builder: Fijenoord, Rotterdam.
Date: 1924–1925.
Normal displacement: 611 tons surfaced; 815 tons submerged.
Dimensions: 218ft 9in x 18ft 3in x 12ft 0in (67m x 5.7m x 3.8m).

Machinery: diesel: 2 M.A.N.; electric: 2.
Maximum power: 2,400hp surfaced; 725hp submerged.
Maximum speed: 15 knots surfaced; 8 knots submerged.
Range: 3,500 miles at 12 knots surfaced; 13 miles at 8 knots submerged.

Torpedo tubes: two 21in (533mm) forward, torpedoes: 4; four 17.7in (450mm); 2 forward, 2 aft; torpedoes: 8.
Guns: one 3.4in (88mm) 45-cal; one 12.7mm machine-gun.
Complement: 31.

Another class of medium-displacement submarines for colonial use. Developments of the previous class, slightly enlarged and with a stronger torpedo armament. They were the first Dutch submarines with 21in (533mm) torpedo tubes. Maximum operational depth: 200ft (60m).

K. XII was damaged by an internal explosion in Singapore, but was towed to Soerabaya before being scuttled.

The other two boats reached Australia where they were subsequently paid off.

Fates

date:	location:	boat:	cause (see page 7):
1942	East Indies	*K. XIII*	sb
1944	Australia	*K. XI*	r
1945		*K. XII*	r

O.9 Class

O. 9:
Builder: De Schelde, Flushing.
Date: 1925–1926.
O. 10:
Builder: Netherlands Dock & Shipbuilding Co., Amsterdam.
Date: 1925–1926.
O. 11:
Builder: Fijenoord, Rotterdam.
Date: 1925–1926.

Normal displacement: 483 tons surfaced; 647 tons submerged.
Dimensions: 180ft 0in x 18ft 0in x 11ft 6in (54.5m x 5.7m x 3.5m).
Machinery: diesel: 2 Sulzer; electric: 2.
Maximum power: 900hp surfaced; 610hp submerged.
Maximum speed: 12 knots surfaced; 8 knots submerged.
Range: 3,500 miles at 8 knots

surfaced; 11 miles at 7.5 knots submerged.
Torpedo tubes: two 21in (533mm) forward; torpedoes: 4; three 17.7in (450mm); 2 forward, 1 aft; torpedoes: 6.
Guns: one 3.4in (88mm) 45-cal; one 12.7mm machine-gun.
Complement: 29.

Smaller development of the *K. XI* Class for home service. Maximum service depth 200ft (60m). Less power and speed than their predecessors, and one less torpedo tube aft. *O. 11* fell into German hands in 1940 and was expended as a blockship in 1944. The other two escaped to Britain and were scrapped in 1944, obsolete and worn out.

Fates

date:	location:	boat:	cause (see page 7):
1940	Holland	*O. 11*	c–sb
1944	Britain	*O. 9, O. 10*	r

O.12 Class

O. 12, O. 13, O. 14:
Builder: De Schelde, Flushing.
Date: 1930–1931/32.
O. 15:
Builder: Fijenoord, Rotterdam.
Date: 1931–32.
Normal displacement: 546 tons surfaced; 704 tons submerged.
Dimensions: 198ft 3in x 18ft 6in x 11ft 9in (60.2m x 5.8m x 3.8m).
Machinery: diesel: 2; electric: 2; *O. 15*: Sulzer, M.A.N.
Maximum power: 1,800hp surfaced; 600hp submerged.
Maximum speed: 15 knots surfaced; 8 knots submerged.
Range: 3,500 miles at 10 knots surfaced; 12 miles at 8 knots submerged.
Torpedo tubes: five 21in (533mm); 4 forward, 2 aft.
Guns: two 40mm 56-cal.
Complement: 31.

Slightly reduced developments of the *K. XI* Class. As a result of tank testing, the form of the hull was greatly improved for underwater performance. This Class introduced the extremely sensible armament of 40mm Bofors guns, of a special design on disappearing mounts housed in watertight tubes. These tubes were in forward and aft extensions of the conning tower. The hull was strengthened, as were all hatches, to give a greater diving depth than their predecessors.

One boat was captured by the Germans in 1940, another was mined in the same year, a third was scrapped in Britain but the fourth, which had also escaped to Britain, survived the war.

Fates

date:	location:	boat:	cause (see page 7):
1940	Holland	*O. 12*	c–sb
	North Sea	*O. 13*	m
1943	Britain	*O. 14*	r

O. 12 and *O. 13* at a Dutch base, some time before 1940.

K. XIV Class

K. XIV, K. XV, K. XVI:
Builder: Rotterdam Dry Dock.
Date: 1932–1933.
K. XVII, K. XVIII.
Builder: Fijenoord, Rotterdam.
Date: 1932–1933.
Normal displacement: 771 tons surfaced; 1,000 tons submerged;
K. XVII, K. XVIII: 782 tons surfaced; 1,024 tons submerged.
Dimensions: 242ft 6in x 25ft 0in x 12ft 9in (74m x 6.2m x 4m).
Machinery: diesel: 2 M.A.N.; electric: 2.

Maximum power: 3,200hp surfaced; 1,000hp submerged.
Maximum speed: 17 knots surfaced; 9 knots submerged.
Range: 3,500 miles at 11 knots surfaced; 26 miles at 8.5 knots submerged.
Torpedo tubes: eight 21in (533mm); 4 forward, 2 aft, 2 external amidships;

torpedoes: 14.
Guns: one 3.4in (88mm) 45-cal; two 40mm on 'disappearing' mounts.
Complement: 38.

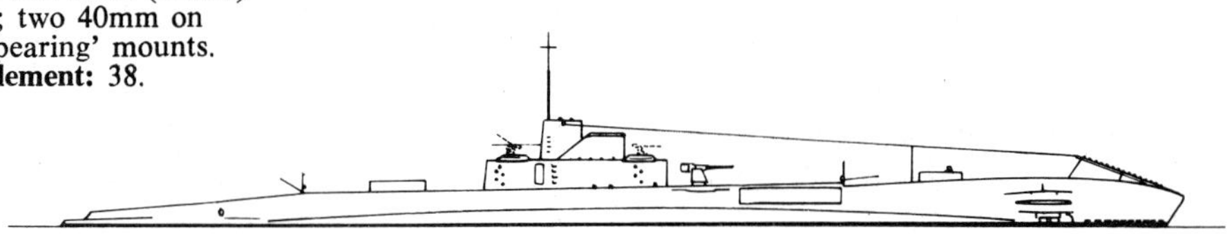

A development of the previous class, but larger, and retaining a deck gun to suit them for their colonial role. Maximum service depth: 264ft (81m).

Three boats were lost operating against the Japanese: the other two were scrapped in the East Indies after the war.

Fates

date:	location:	boat:	cause (see page 7):
1941	East Indies	K. XVI	s
		K. XVII	cs
1942	East Indies	K. XVIII	sb
1946	East Indies	K. XIV, K. XV	r

O.16

O. 16.
Builder: De Schelde, Flushing.
Date: 1935–1936.
Normal displacement: 896 tons surfaced; 1,170 tons submerged.
Dimensions: 254ft 3in x 21ft 9in x 13ft 3in (77m x 6.5m x 4m).

Machinery: diesel: 2 M.A.N.; electric: 2.
Maximum power: 3,200hp surfaced; 1,000hp submerged.
Maximum speed: 18 knots

surfaced; 9 knots submerged.
Torpedo tubes: eight 21in (533mm); 4 forward, 2 aft, 2 external amidships; torpedoes: 14.
Guns: one 3.4in (88mm) 45-cal; two 40mm Bofors on 'disappearing' mounts.
Complement: 38.

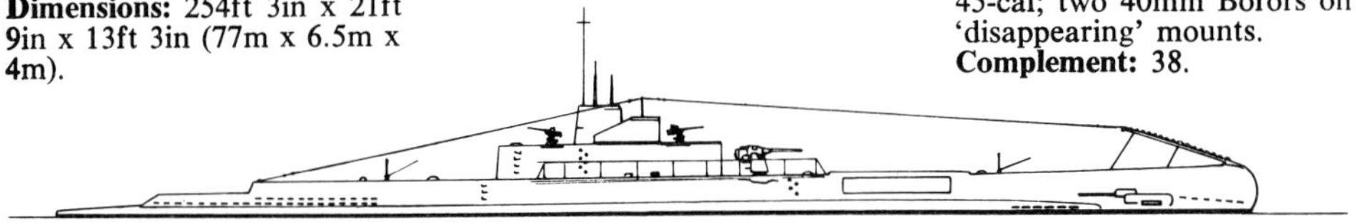

Slightly larger than the K. XIV Class though intended for use in European waters, this boat marked the merging of the two lines of Dutch submarines development. Otherwise, very similar to her immediate predecessors.

Fate

date:	location:	boat:	cause (see page 7):
1941	East Indies	O. 16	m

O.19 Class

O. 19 ex-K. XIX, O. 20 ex-K. XX.
Builder: Wilton-Fijenoord, Schiedam.
Date: 1938–1939 .
Normal displacement: 998 tons surfaced; 1,536 tons submerged.
Dimensions: 264ft 9in x 24ft

3in x 12ft 9in (81m x 7.5m x 4m).
Machinery: diesel: 2; electric: 2.
Maximum power: 5,000hp surfaced; 1,000hp submerged.
Maximum speed: 19.25 knots surfaced; 9 knots submerged.
Torpedo tubes: eight 21in

(533mm); 4 forward, 2 aft, 2 external amidships; torpedoes: 14.
Guns: one 3.4in (88mm) 45-cal; two 40mm Bofors on 'disappearing' mounts.
Mines: 40; 20 vertical tubes.
Complement: 55 .

Submarine minelayers developed from the previous boat. Fitted with vertical minelaying tubes in the ballast tanks on either side, amidships. Partial double hull type, and fitted with the first experimental schnorkel. With this Class, the Dutch finally discarded the separate designations of colonial and home waters boats, dropping the original K numbers assigned. Maximum service depth: 330ft (105m).

O. 20 was scuttled after damage caused by depth-charging, and her sister had to be abandoned after being wrecked in the South China Sea.

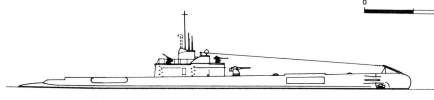

Fates

date:	location:	boat:	cause (see page 7):
1941	East Indies	*O. 20*	n–sb
1945	China Sea	*O. 19*	v

O.21 Class

O. 21, O. 22:
Builder: De Schelde, Flushing.
Date: 1939–1940.
O. 23, O. 24, O. 26, O. 27:
Builder: Rotterdam Dry Dock.
Date: 1939–1940/41.
O. 25.
Builder: Wilton Fijenoord, Schiedam.
Date: 1939–1940/41.
Normal displacement: 881 tons surfaced; 1,186 tons submerged.
Dimensions: 255ft 0in x 21ft 6in x 13ft 0in (77.5m x 6.5m x 4m).
Machinery: diesel: 2 Sulzer; electric: 2.
Maximum power: 5,000hp surfaced; 1,000hp submerged.
Maximum speed: 19.5 knots surfaced; 9 knots submerged.
Torpedo tubes: eight 21in (533mm); 4 forward, 2 aft, 2 amidships external; torpedoes: 14.
Guns: one 3.4in (88mm) 45-cal; two 40mm Bofors in 'disappearing' mounts.
Complement: 55.

Basically similar to the preceding class, except that they were slightly smaller because they did not have to carry mines. Like all the later Dutch boats, they were excellent modern submarines, quite equal to any foreign contemporaries, and superior in their excellent anti-aircraft armament. Their rudimentary schnorkel, however, was not very reliable and was removed from the boats which had escaped to Britain. The Royal Navy showed some interest in the device, but results did not seem to justify further development. Maximum service depth: 330ft (105m).

Five of the Class had been launched by the time the Germans invaded. Of these, four managed to reach Britain, either under their own power, or towed. *O. 25,* which was fitting out, had to be scuttled, but the Germans salved her and commissioned her as their *UD. 3* in 1942. The other

two were launched and completed by the Germans in 1944 as *UD. 4* and *UD. 5.* The last of these survived the war and was re-acquired by the Dutch. The other two were scuttled at Kiel at the end of the war. Of the boats that escaped to Britain, three survived the war.

Fates

date:	location:	boat:	cause (see page 7):
1940	Holland	*O. 26, O. 25*	c–sb
		O. 27	c–r
	North Sea	*O. 22*	n
1949		*O. 23*	r
1956		*O. 24*	r
1958		*O. 21*	r
1958?		*O. 27*	r

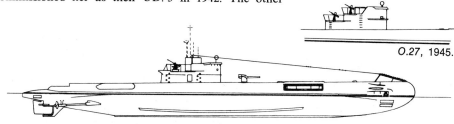

O.27, 1945.

O. 21 alongside a British *T* Class boat. Note the opening for the traversing torpedo mount forward of the conning tower.

O. 27 after her return to Holland in 1945. Note the German style conning tower, and the absence of the traversing torpedo tubes amidships.

Foreign submarines in Dutch service

Dolfijn, ex-British *P. 47*, returning from a patrol.

Tijgerhaai, ex-British *Tarn*.

British *S* Class (1 unit)
Zeehond ex-*Sturgeon*; see Great Britain
Served in European waters after her transfer in 1943. Returned to the Royal Navy in 1945.

British *T* Class (2 units)
Zwaardvisch ex-*Talent, Tijgerhaai* ex-*Tarn*; see Great Britain
Transferred on completion in 1943 and 1945 respectively. Both served in the Far East where *Zwaardvisch* sank the German *U 168* in the Java Sea on 6 October 1944. Remained in Dutch service until scrapped in 1963 and 1966, respectively.

British *U* Class (1 unit)
Dolfijn ex-*P.47;* see Great Britain
Transferred on completion in 1942. Served in European waters. Remained in Dutch service until scrapped in 1947.

U.S.A.

United States Navy submarine *Torsk (SS.423)* in 1945.

The first practical submarine results were achieved in the United States, with the experiments of Bushnell and Fulton. The development of the internal combustion engine and the electric motor enabled Holland and Lake to build their first submarines, and at the end of the First World War, the United States had an underwater fleet which was far from negligible.

During the Second World War, though not at first reaching the standards of operational technique of the German Navy, the United States easily achieved second place among the submarine fleets of the major navies.

While the Germans soon realised that the submarine was a strategic weapon to be used against merchant shipping, the Americans regarded it as an auxiliary craft, designed to attack major warships.

Lieutenant Chester W. Nimitz wrote prophetically in 1912: "The steady development of the torpedo together with the gradual improvement in the size, motive power and speed of submarine craft of the near future will result in a most dangerous offensive weapon, and one which will have a large part in deciding fleet actions."

Even Nimitz, future Commander-in-Chief in the Pacific, was not fully aware of the potential value of the submarine against merchant shipping, but neither was anyone else. The lessons of the First World War were not heeded: like Japan, the United States continued to regard the submarine as a type of boat to be used against battleships.

During the international negotiations for the limitation of naval armaments, the United States never favoured limitation, let alone abolition, of underwater craft, but sought always to limit their employment. On 11 November 1929, shortly before the London Naval Conference of 1930, President Hoover declared: ". . . for many years I have been convinced that ships which carry foodstuffs should be free of all interference during time of war. I would place ships which carry supplies on the same level as hospital ships. We know that the safety of imports of food and means of sustenance for industrialized countries has become the primary cause for their naval armaments, and conversely for countries which produce foodstuffs economic stability depends largely on keeping open the avenues of exportation of their excess production."

The American point of view was obviously prejudiced and they were forgetting that during the course of the War of Secession, they themselves had employed the blockade against the South, impeding the supply of those goods and products for which Hoover now claimed full freedom of movement.

The Americans undoubtedly believed in the submarine, despite their limited ideas concerning its employment. They considered it mainly as one of the essential links in the chain of protection that was to safeguard the American continent from the approach of hostile fleets from the Atlantic and Pacific Oceans. The cordon sanitaire which the navy intended to stretch around American waters, called for the committal of the underwater fleet to the dual role of patrol and attack, individually or together with the fleet.

This was why the United States, when negotiating internationally, always asked for as much underwater tonnage as possible. At Washington, in 1921, in opposition to the British proposal for abolition, the United States asked for a total of 90,000 tons for submarines. Neither at this meeting, however, nor at those which followed, was it possible to reach agreement on a quantitative limitation. Great Britain alone was interested: the other powers, headed by the United States, wanted large underwater fleets. At Washington, an attempt was made to codify employment of the submarine according to a set of humanitarian rules, but these proved so incongruous and contradictory that every navy ignored them when confronted with the realities of war.

During the inter-war period, the United States Navy considered that the prime targets for submarines should be battleships and aircraft carriers, but, when they entered the war, the Naval Staff's order to submarines was: 'Against Japan, unrestricted submarine warfare'.

Because their bases were few and widely scattered, the Americans concentrated on the design of long-range boats, capable of operating at great distances from base. Essentially all pre-war and wartime built boats answered this requirement: large boats with great range, good habitability and considerable surface speed. American boats were generally greater in size and displacement than European boats, even before the war. Apart from the exceptional *Argonaut, Narwhal* and *Nautilus* which displaced 2,700 tons, the pre-war boats displaced an average of 1,300–1,500 tons compared to the 600–1,000 tons of the boats of other navies.

The American Fleet Submarines (ocean-going submarines) had an average range of 10,000 miles and carried sufficient stores for a maximum of 60 days. With a surface speed of 20 knots, they had an average submerged speed of 9 knots and could remain submerged for a maximum of 48 hours at 2.5 knots.

The large hull and conning tower of American ocean-going boats gave them a rather prolonged crash-dive time. Efforts were made during the war, to lower the conning tower silhouette, but it was unimportant because Japanese opposition was always rather limited. These characteristics would have caused trouble for the Americans, had their boats been required for the kind of operations that the Germans conducted in the Atlantic. Had the need arisen, however, it is certain that the Amercan shipyards would soon have been turning out boats to new and adequate designs. Their production efficiency and resources were such that the United States could rectify deficiencies of this sort, far quicker than any other country. There was, however, no such need.

Armament of boats designed after 1930 varied from six to ten 21in (533mm) torpedo tubes: in addition to the weapons in the tubes there was a reserve of 14–18 torpedoes in the bow and stern torpedo rooms. Surface armament usually consisted of a 3in (76mm) 50-cal or 4in (102mm) 50-cal deck gun and two 12.7mm machine-guns. In the new submarines of the *Gato/Balao* Class, the total number of available torpedoes was raised to 24, and surface armament was increased by the installation of one or two 5in (127mm) guns and 40mm and 20mm anti-aircraft guns.

For a long period after entering the war, the United States boats experienced great difficulties with their torpedoes. A high percentage failed to explode or were lost during the run. The reasons for these failures were the superficiality of testing of warheads and the type of magnetic fuze in use. Peacetime exercises had always been conducted using dummy warheads and with torpedoes adjusted to pass beneath the target without hitting. This was sufficient to test propulsion and gyroscopic equipment, but not the offensive power of the weapon. The type of detonator used by the Americans was dual-action, impact and magnetic. The latter was activated by the variation in the magnatic field registered when the weapon passed near a ship's hull. The tactical practice of the period dictated that torpedoes be so adjusted as to pass ten feet beneath the target's keel. In action, the results were practically nil. During a patrol, *Sargo* launched thirteen torpedoes, none of which exploded. Admiral Lockwood, Commander of Submarines, Pacific, ordered experiments to be carried out with live warheads.

During an action by *Tinosa* against a Japanese oil tanker, 15 torpedoes were launched: two hit and exploded, four were lost and nine, having been thoroughly checked, were launched against the stationary target, which they hit without exploding. All torpedo mechanisms were again examined and the defects were gradually eliminated: the detonator mechanism, for example, was found to be too weak to withstand violent impact.

The introduction of the electric torpedo solved all problems and produced notable results. Its entry into service had been delayed until the final phase of the war, because doubts had been expressed about its low speed of 28 knots compared to the 40–50 knots of other torpedoes. The low speed was not a serious handicap, however, as a good fire-direction computer was available, and the torpedo showed no wake. The electric torpedo together with new tactics, including a modified 'wolf pack' technique, contributed in large measure to the destruction of the Japanese merchant fleet. The total number of torpedoes launched by American boats during the Second World War was in excess of 14,500.

The Atlantic Ocean and European waters saw few patrols by American boats other than training operations near ports and shipyards, and reconnaissance patrols in support of the landings in North Africa. Their true operational theatre was the Pacific Ocean where, at first, singly, and then in groups, the submarines were employed in five types of missions: offensive, to cut supply lines and destroy shipping; photographic reconnaissance of landing beaches and naval installations; rescue of aircrew from sea; offensive, in strategic armed reconnaissance of enemy bases; offensive, ambush.

At first, operations were limited to the area around the Philippine Islands, the waters east of Japan, and the straits between the islands of the Japanese archipelago. Eventually, the entire Pacific area including the China Sea and Southeast Asia was covered by American boats.

Until April 1942, Japanese merchant shipping sailed without escorts. In the following July, the first convoys were formed (six to ten ships, at most) escorted by an old destroyer or minor warship. Not until November 1943, did the Japanese organize convoy and protection systems, and use ships specially built for anti-submarine warfare. To counter these measures, the Americans adopted the 'wolf pack' tactic, but with the added refinement of radar. The American packs never exceeded four to five boats: the average pack was three, but the Japanese never came near to the Allies in terms of anti-submarine equipment and tactics.

The American underwater offensive, particularly when directed against oil tankers, ruined the Japanese war economy and·had a decisive effect on the war in the Pacific.

Apart from the successes against warships (201 vessels sunk, including the battlecruiser *Kongo,* the large carrier *Shinano,* the carriers *Shokaku* and *Unryu*; the cruisers *Kako* and *Maya*, etc.), American submarines sank 1,079 merchant ships of more than 500 tons, totalling 4,649,650 GRT: some 600,000 additional tons were rendered useless. This virtually annihilated the Japanese merchant fleet which, beginning the war with some 6 million GRT, had been reduced to 1.8 million GRT by August 1945 (the majority of these were wooden ships serving in the Inland Sea). Although the Japanese had captured more than 4 million GRT of new construction and shipping at the beginning of hostilities, this did not compensate the losses sustained.

Of the 2,117 Japanese merchant ships totalling more than 8 million GRT, lost during the war, sixty per cent were sunk by submarines, thirty per cent by aircraft and ten per cent by mines or surface craft. The United States lost 52 submarines (3,500 men), 45, in action against the Japanese. On 7 December 1941, there were 112 boats in service in the United States Navy. During the war, 203 new boats were commissioned, 28 of which were lost. The standardization of types, the rationalization of construction methods and the widespread use of prefabricated parts gave a building time of between nine and twelve months, which was more than sufficient to replace losses and exert increasing pressure on the enemy. Losses amounted to 15.8 per cent of total boats in service, which was rather low, compared to other navies.

The American submarine force was well ahead of the German fleet, in their use of radar. Many of the sinkings achieved were the result of intelligent application of this device. It saved many boats from surprise attack and enabled the Americans to continue, until the end of the war, surfaced torpedo-boat attacks of the type that the Germans had long since been forced to abandon. As torpedo-boats, the American submarines were excellent, and they never had to fight in conditions where rapid, deep diving and extreme underwater manoeuvrability were all-important, as did their German and British contemporaries.

Development of United States submarines, 1914–1945.

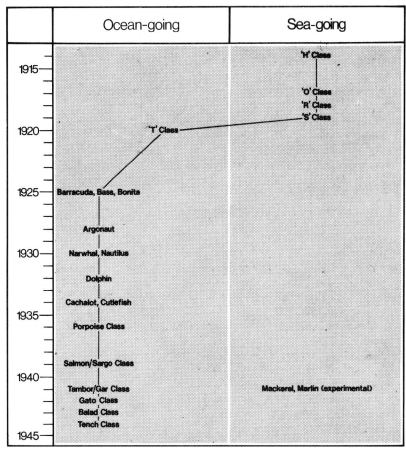

SS.410 *Threadfin* of the *Balao* Series, armed with two 5in (127mm) 25-cal deck guns and two 40mm anti-aircraft cannon.

O Class

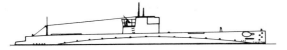

SS.63 *O.2*:
Builder: Bremerton Navy Yard.
Date: 1918.
SS.64 *O.3*, SS.65 *O.4*:
Builder: Quincy, Fore River.
Date: 1917.
SS.67 *O.6*, SS.68 *O.7*, SS.69 *O.8*, SS.70 *O.9*, SS.71 *O.10*.
Builder: Quincy, Fore River.
Date: 1917–1918.
Normal displacement: 521 tons surfaced; 629 tons submerged.
Dimensions: 172ft 3in x 18ft 0in x 14ft 6in (52.3m x 5.4m x 4.0m).
Machinery: diesel: 2 New London Ship & Engine; electric: 2 Electro Dynamic.
Maximum power: 880hp surfaced; 740hp submerged.
Maximum speed: 14 knots surfaced; 10.5 knots submerged.
Range: 5,000 miles at 11 knots surfaced.
Torpedo tubes: four 18in (457mm) forward; torpedoes: 8.
Guns: one 12.7mm machine-gun.
Complement: 32.

These boats were of the saddle-tank type, all built to the Holland design, as enlarged and improved versions of the previous *N* Class. Another six (*O. 11–O. 17*) had been built to Lake's design, but all of these had been scrapped in 1930: *O. 1* was scrapped in 1938, and *O. 5* had been lost in 1925. They had been built for coastal defence and carried only 88 tons of oil fuel. Range, consequently was low: maximum diving depth was 200ft (60m). Originally, they had been armed with a 3in (76mm) gun, but this had been removed from the surviving boats by 1939. They were used for training, and all were scrapped between 1945 and 1946, except *O. 9*, which foundered in 1941.

Fates			cause
date:	location:	boat:	(see page 7):
1941	Atlantic	*O. 9*	v
1945–6		*O. 2, O. 3, O. 4, O. 6, O. 7, O. 8, O. 10*	r

SS.69 training submarine in 1943.
United States Navy submarine *SS.64*.

R Class

SS.78 *R.1*, SS.79 *R.2*, SS.80 *R.3*, SS.81 *R.4*, SS.82 *R.5*, SS.83 *R.6*, SS.84 *R.7*:
Builder: Quincy, Fore River.
Date: 1918–1919.
SS.86 *R.9*, SS.87 *R.10*, SS.88 *R.11*, SS.89 *R.12*, SS.90 *R.13*, SS.91 *R.14*:
Builder: Quincy, Fore River.
Date: 1919.
SS.92 *R.15*, SS.93 *R.16*, SS.94 *R.17*, SS.95 *R.18*, SS.96 *R.19*, SS.97 *R.20*.
Builder: Union Iron Works, San Francisco.
Date: 1917–1918.
Normal displacement: 569 tons surfaced; 680 tons submerged.
Dimensions: 186ft 3in x 18ft 0in x 14ft 6in (56.6m x 5.2m x 4.0m).
Machinery: diesel: 2 New London Ship & Engine; electric: 2 Electro Dynamic.
Maximum power: 1,200hp surfaced; 934hp submerged.
Maximum speed: 13.5 knots surfaced; 10.5 knots submerged.
Range: 3,700 miles at 10 knots surfaced.
Torpedo tubes: four 21in (533mm) forward; torpedoes: 8.
Guns: one 3in (76mm) 50-cal and/or one 12.7mm machine-gun.
Complement: 33.

This was a slightly enlarged version of the *O* Class, armed with 21in (533mm) torpedo tubes. Like the *O* Class, the first group (*R. 1 – R. 20*) were built to a Holland design, the second group (*R. 21 – R. 27*), to the Lake design. The latter had all been scrapped in 1930. *R. 8* was broken up in 1936. Bunkerage was 75 tons of oil: diving depth was 200ft (60m).

R. 3, R. 17 and *R. 19* were lent to the Royal Navy in 1942, as *P. 511, P. 512* and *P. 514. P. 514* was lost in a collision in 1942: the other two were returned to the US Navy in 1944. A flotilla of this Class were stationed in Scotland for anti-submarine duties until November 1942,

when they were returned to the United States. Throughout the remainder of the war, both the American and the British boats were used for training purposes. In 1946, *R. 6* was fitted with a schnorkel as an experiment, the first US submarine so equipped. They were all scrapped between 1945 and 1947 except *R. 19* (see above) and *R. 12*, which foundered in 1943.

Fates

date:	location:	boat:	cause (see page 7):
1942	Atlantic	*R. 19* as *P. 514*	e
1943	Atlantic	*R. 12*	v
1945		*R. 2, R. 14, R. 17*	r
1946		*R. 1, R. 4, R. 5, R. 6, R. 7, R. 9, R. 10, R. 11, R. 13, R. 15, R. 16, R. 18, R. 20*	r
1947		*R. 3*	r

USS R–12 (SS.89).
USS R–13 (SS.90).

S Class

Group 1
SS.105 *S.1*:
Builder: Quincy, Fore River.
Date: 1918.
SS.123 *S.18*, SS.124 *S.19*,
SS.125 *S.20*, SS.126 *S.21*,
SS.127 *S.22*, SS.128 *S.23*,
SS.129 *S.24*, SS.130 *S.25*,
SS.131 *S.26*, SS.132 *S.27*,
SS.133 *S.28*, SS.134 *S.29*:
Builder: Bethlehem Steel,
Quincy.
Date: 1920–1922.
SS.135 *S.30*, SS.136 *S.31*,
SS.137 *S.32*, SS.138 *S.33*,
SS.139 *S.34*, SS.140 *S.35*,
SS.141 *S.36*, SS.142 *S.37*,
SS.143 *S.38*, SS.144 *S.39*,
SS.145 *S.40*, SS.146 *S.41*:
Builder: Bethlehem Steel,
San Francisco.
Date: 1918–1921.

Group 2
SS.116 *S.11*, SS.117 *S.12*,
SS.118 *S.13*:
Builder: Portsmouth Navy
Yard.
Date: 1921.
SS.119 *S.14*, SS.120 *S.15*,
SS.121 *S.16*, SS.122 *S.17*:
Builder: Lake Torpedo Boat,
Bridgeport.
Date: 1919–1920.

Group 3
SS.147 *S.42*, SS.148 *S.43*,
SS.149 *S.44*, SS.150 *S.45*,
SS.151 *S.46*, SS.152 *S.47*:
Builder: Bethlehem Steel,
Quincy.
Date: 1923–1924.

Group 4
SS.153 *S.48*.
Builder: Bethlehem Steel,
Quincy.
Date: 1921.

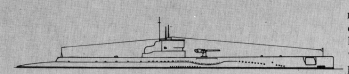

Normal displacement:
Group 1: 854 tons surfaced;
1,062 tons submerged.
Group 2: 876 tons surfaced;
1,092 tons submerged.
Group 3: 906 tons surfaced;
1,126 tons submerged.
Group 4: 903 tons surfaced;
1,230 tons submerged.
Dimensions:
Group 1: 219ft 3in x 20ft 9in x
16ft 0in (66.5m x 6.1m x
4.6m).
Group 2: 231ft 0in x 21ft 9in x
13ft 0in (70.2m x 6.6m x
3.7m).
Group 3: 225ft 3in x 20ft 9in x
16ft 0in (68.4m x 6.1m x 4.6m).
Group 4: 265ft 0in x 21ft 9in x
13ft 6in (81.2m x 6.5m x 3.3m).
Machinery:
Group 1: diesel: 2 New London
Ship & Engine; electric: 2
Electro Dynamic, Ridgeway or
General Electric.
Group 2: diesel: 2 M.A.N. or
Busch-Sulzer; electric: 2
Westinghouse.
Group 3: diesel: 2 New London
Ship & Engine; electric: 2
Electro Dynamic.
Group 4: diesel: 2 Busch-
Sulzer; electric: 2 Ridgeway.
Maximum power:
Group 1: 1,200hp surfaced;

1,500hp submerged.
Group 2: 2,000hp surfaced;
1,200hp submerged.
Group 3: 1,200hp surfaced;
1,500hp submerged.
Group 4: 1,800hp surfaced;
1,500hp submerged.
Maximum speed:
Group 1: 14.5 knots surfaced;
11 knots submerged.
Group 2: 15 knots surfaced;
11 knots submerged.
Group 3: 14.5 knots surfaced;
11 knots submerged.
Group 4: 14.5 knots surfaced;
11 knots submerged.
Range:
Group 1: 5,000 miles at
10 knots surfaced.
Group 2: 5,000 miles at
10 knots surfaced.
Group 3: 5,000 miles at
10 knots surfaced.
Group 4: 8,000 miles at
10 knots surfaced.
Torpedo tubes: four 21in
(533mm) forward; torpedoes:
12.
S.11, S.12, S.13, S.48: five 21in
(533mm) 4 forward, 1 aft;
torpedoes: 14.
Guns: one 4in (102mm)
50-cal; one 12.7mm machine-
gun.
Complement: 42.

This Class was intended to improve on the range, size and number of spare torpedoes carried by its predecessor. A design by Holland and another by Lake were used. The latter was considered inferior and only the prototype (*S. 2*) was built. For the first time, the United States Navy itself produced a submarine design, prepared by the Bureau of Construction and Repair, and the boats in Group 2 in the above Table were built to this design. Bunkerage was: Groups 1 and 3, 168 tons; Group 2, 148 tons; Group 4, 177 tons. Diving depth for all groups was 200ft (60m).

S. 4, S. 5 and *S. 51* were lost between the wars: *S. 2, S. 3 S. 6–S. 10, S. 19, S. 49* and *S. 50* were all scrapped. Between 1942 and 1944, *S. 1, S. 21, S. 22, S. 24, S. 25* and *S. 29* were lent to the Royal Navy. *S. 25* was passed on to the Polish Navy as *Jastrzab* but was lost soon afterwards in a mistaken attack by 'friendly' forces. These boats were used as convoy escorts for a short time but were soon transferred to training duties. They were numbered *P. 551–P. 556* in the Royal Navy.

The boats which remained in American service were also mainly employed for training, but some of them saw service in Philippine and Indonesian waters during the early months of the Pacific war. *S. 44* was still operational on 10 August 1942 when she sank the Japanese heavy cruiser *Kako* off Rabaul. *S. 44* was sunk by the Japanese, but *S. 26, S. 27, S. 28* and *S. 36* were lost to causes other than hostile attack. All the other boats were scrapped or scuttled after the war, but despite having been returned to the US Navy, the gutted hull of *S. 29* was still to be seen in Portsmouth Harbour (England) until very recently.

Fates

date:	location:	boat:	cause (see page 7):
1942	Atlantic	*S. 25* as Polish *Jastrzab*	e
		S. 26	v
	Pacific	*S. 27, S. 28, S. 39*	v
		S. 36	sb
		S. 44	n
		S. 1, S. 21, S. 22, S. 24, S. 29	r
1945–1947		*S. 11–S. 18, S. 20, S. 23, S. 30–S. 35, S. 37, S. 38, S. 40–S. 43, S. 45–S. 48*	r

Barracuda Class

SS.163 ex-V.1 *Barracuda*, SS.164 ex-V.2 *Bass*, SS.165 ex-V.3 *Bonita*.
Builder: Portsmouth Navy Yard.
Date: 1921–1924/26.
Normal displacement: 2,000 tons surfaced; 2,620 tons submerged.
Dimensions: 341ft 6in x 27ft 6in x 14ft 6in (104.2m x 8.2m x 4.4m).
Machinery: diesel: 2 Busch-Sulzer + 2 auxiliary; electric: 2 Elliot.
Maximum power: 6,700hp surfaced; 2,400hp submerged.
Maximum speed: 18 knots surfaced; 8 knots submerged.
Range: 12,000 miles at 11 knots surfaced; 10 miles at 8 knots submerged.
Torpedo tubes: six 21in (533mm); 4 forward, 2 aft; torpedoes: 12.
Guns: one 5in (127mm) 51-cal (*Bass:* one 3in (76mm) 50-cal) replaced in 1943 by two 20mm 70-cal.
Complement: 80.

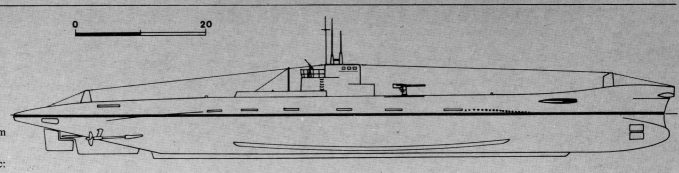

Large displacement submarines developed from the *S* Class (Group 4), designed at the end of the First World War. Until 1931, they were designated *V.1–V.3*. Maximum operational depth: 200ft (60m); normal fuel load: 364 tons.

The *Barracuda* Class were the first Fleet Submarines but, though possessing good range and surface speed, they were generally rather mediocre boats. Their surface propulsion gear consisted of two main diesels and two diesel-generators for cruise speed. In 1940, they were given major refits during which, the electric propulsion machinery was replaced.

During the war they were used mainly for training: their transformation into transport submarines was planned, but the project was abandoned. While on patrol in August 1942, *Bass* was seriously damaged by an engine room fire. All three units were scrapped at the end of the war.

Fates		cause
date:	boat:	(see page 7):
1945	*Barracuda, Bass, Bonita*	f

United States Navy submarine *Bass (SS.164)* which was mainly used for training.

Argonaut

A bow view of USS *Argonaut* (SS.166) taken off the coast of California in July 1942. The minelaying submarine *Argonaut* before her designation was changed to *SM-1* in 1931.

SS.166 ex-V.4. *Argonaut*.
Builder: Portsmouth Navy Yard.
Date: 1925–1928.
Normal displacement: 2,710 tons surfaced; 4,164 tons submerged.
Dimensions: 381ft 0in x 33ft 9in x 15ft 3in (116.1m x 10.3m x 4.7m).
Machinery: diesel: 2 General Motors + 2 auxiliary; electric: 2 Ridgeway.
Maximum power: 6,000hp surfaced; 2,400hp submerged.
Maximum speed: 15 knots surfaced; 8 knots submerged.
Range: 18,000 miles at 8 knots surfaced; 10 miles at 8 knots submerged.
Torpedo tubes: four 21in (533mm) forward; torpedoes: 16.
Guns: two 6in (152mm) 53-cal; two 0.3in machine-guns.

Mines: 60; two minelaying tubes.
Complement: 89.

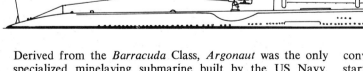

Derived from the *Barracuda* Class, *Argonaut* was the only specialized minelaying submarine built by the US Navy. Originally designated *V.4,* she was renamed *SM.1 Argonaut* on 19 February 1931. Maximum operational depth: 300ft (95m); normal fuel load: 696 tons.

She was a large boat with a long range, but she was not very manoeuvrable and was slow despite the replacing in 1940 of the original main engine which developed only 3,175hp with a maximum speed of approximately 13 knots.

Because of the limited effectiveness of her minelaying equipment, and the considerable space available, she was converted to a transport submarine after the war had started, and was re-classified as *APS 1* on 22 September 1942.

Argonaut's most significant wartime activity was the transporting—with *Nautilus*— of the 2nd Marine Raider Battalion to attack Japanese installations on Makin Island in the Gilberts on 17–19 August 1942.

Fate			cause
date:	location:	boat:	(see page 7):
1943	Pacific	*Argonaut*	n

Narwhal Class

SS.167 ex-V.5 Narwhal:
Builder: Portsmouth Navy Yard.
Date: 1927–1930.
SS.168 ex-V.6 Nautilus.
Builder: Mare Island Navy Yard.
Date: 1927–1930.
Normal displacement: 2,915 tons surfaced; 4,050 tons submerged.
Dimensions: 371ft 0in x 33ft 3in x 15ft 9in (113.1m x 10.3m x 4.7m).
Machinery: diesel: Fairbanks Morse + 2 auxiliary; electric: 2 Westinghouse.
Maximum power: 6,000hp surfaced; 2,540hp submerged.
Maximum speed: 17 knots surfaced; 8 knots submerged.
Range: 18,000 miles at 8 knots surfaced; 10 miles at 8 knots submerged.
Torpedo tubes: six 21in (533mm); 4 forward, 2 aft; torpedoes: 20; from 1942: four external tubes 21in (533mm); 2 forward, 2 aft; torpedoes: 4.
Guns: two 6in (152mm) 53-cal; two .3in machine-guns.
Complement: 90.

Submarines of great displacement, designed for long-range ocean cruising: they were inspired by the German U-cruisers. Maximum operational depth: 328ft (100m); normal fuel load: 732 tons.

Between 1940 and 1941, *Narwhal* and *Nautilus* underwent major modification when the original MAN 5,450hp diesel engine was replaced by a more powerful one. In 1942, four 21in (533mm) torpedo tubes were installed. Despite the modifications, the two boats of the Class were slow and not very manoeuvrable, and their overall results were not good. During the war, they were employed mainly in secondary tasks. *Nautilus* took part, with *Argonaut*, in the raid against Makin Island. Between February 1943 and March 1945, *Narwhal* carried out seven resupply missions to guerilla forces, and landed and picked up agents in the Japanese-occupied Phillipines. Both boats were scrapped at the end of the war.

Fates   cause
date: boat: (see page 7):
1945 *Narwhal, Nautilus*   r

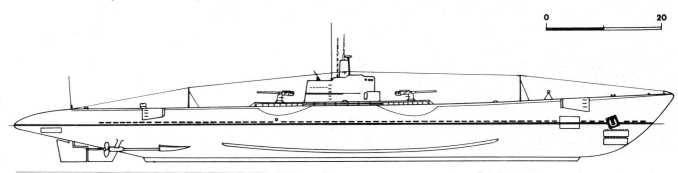

USS Narwhal (SS.167) manoeuvring on the surface.

Dolphin

SS.169 *Dolphin*.
Builder: Portsmouth Navy Yard.
Date: 1930–1932.
Normal displacement: 1,560 tons surfaced; 2,240 tons submerged.
Dimensions: 319ft 3in x 27ft 9in x 13ft 3in (97.2m x 8.5m x 4m).
Machinery: diesel: 2 M.A.N.+ 2 auxiliary; electric: 2.
Maximum power: 3,500hp surfaced; 1,750hp submerged.
Maximum speed: 17 knots surfaced; 8 knots submerged.
Range: 9,000 miles at 10 knots surfaced; 10 miles at 8 knots submerged.
Torpedo tubes: six 21in (533mm); 4 forward, 2 aft; torpedoes: 18.
Guns: one 4in (102mm) 50-cal subsequently replaced by one 3in (76mm) 50-cal; four 0.3in machine-guns.
Complement: 60.

Experimental boat fitted, like the preceding units, with two auxiliary motors to be used as diesel-generators for cruise speed. Normal fuel load: 412 tons; maximum operational depth: 250ft (75m). She was a not very successful attempt to cram most of the features of the preceding pair, into a lightly constructed hull of half the size. She was assigned to training duties after the war had started.

Fate

date: boat: cause (see page 7):
1946 *Dolphin* r

Cachalot Class

SS.170 ex-V.8 *Cachalot*:
Builder: Portsmouth Navy Yard.
Date: 1931–1933.
SS.171 ex-V.9 *Cuttlefish*.
Builder: Electric Boat, Groton.
Date: 1931–1934.
Normal displacement:
Cachalot: 1,170 tons surfaced,
Cuttlefish: 1,210 tons surfaced;
1,650 tons submerged.
Dimensions:
Cachalot: 271ft 9in x 24ft 9in x 13ft 0in (82.8m x 7.5m x 3.9m);
Cuttlefish: 274ft 0in x 24ft 9in x 13ft 0in (83.5m x 7.5m x 3.9m).
Machinery: diesel: 2 General Motors; electric: 2 Electro Dynamic/Westinghouse.
Maximum power: 3,100hp surfaced; 1,600hp submerged.
Maximum speed: 17 knots surfaced; 8 knots submerged.
Range: 9,000 miles at 12 knots surfaced; 10 miles at 8 knots submerged.
Torpedo tubes: six 21in (533mm); 4 forward, 2 aft; torpedoes: 16.
Guns: one 3in (76mm) 40-cal; four 0.3in machine-guns subsequently replaced by two 20mm 70-cal.
Complement: 50.

Medium-displacement experimental submarines in which, for the first time, the US Navy made wide-spread use of electric welding in the construction of hulls. Normal fuel load: 333 tons; maximum operational depth: 250ft (75m).

The welding technique, in which the US Navy was well ahead of her rivals, was used for subsequent construction. In contrast with the preceding classes, the *Cachalot* Class had a conventional type of propulsion gear with only two main propulsion engines connected directly to the propeller shafts. In 1938, the two boats were modernized and the power of the propulsion gear was increased. During the war they were used mainly for training purposes, and they were taken out of service in 1947.

Fates

date:	boat:	cause (see page 7):
1947	*Cachalot, Cuttlefish*	r

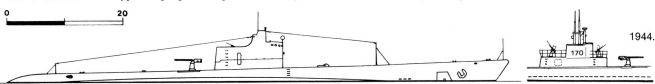

1944.

Left: *Dolphin*.
Right: *Cachalot*.
Below: *Cuttlefish*.

P Class

A broadside view of *Porpoise* taken at Philadelphia Navy Yard in July 1944.

Group 1
SS.172 *Porpoise*, SS.173 *Pike*:
Builder: Portsmouth Navy Yard.
Date: 1933–1935/35.

Group 2
SS.174 *Shark*, SS.175 *Tarpon*:
Builder: Electric Boat, Groton.
Date: 1933–1936/36.

Group 3
SS.176 *Perch*, SS.177 *Pickerel*, SS.178 *Permit* ex-*Pinna*:
Builder: Electric Boat, Groton.
Date: 1935–1936/37.
SS.179 *Plunger*, SS.180 *Pollack*:
Builder: Portsmouth Navy Yard.
Date: 1935–1936/37.
SS.181 *Pompano*.
Builder: Mare Island Navy Yard.
Date: 1936–1937.
Normal displacement:
Group 1: 1,310 tons surfaced; 1,960 tons submerged.
Group 2: 1,315 tons surfaced; 1,968 tons submerged.
Group 3: 1,330 or 1,335 tons surfaced; 2,005 tons submerged.
Dimensions:
Group 1: 301ft 0in x 25ft 0in x 13ft 0in (91.7m x 7.6m x 4m).
Group 2: 298ft 0in x 25ft 0in x 13ft 9in (90.8m x 7.6m x 4.2m).
Group 3: 300ft 6in x 25ft 0in x 13ft 9in (91.6m x 7.6m x 4.2m).
Machinery: diesel: 2 Winton or Fairbanks Morse; electric: 2 General Electric or Elliot.
Maximum power: 4,300hp

surfaced; 2,085–2,336hp submerged.
Maximum speed: 19 knots surfaced; 8 knots submerged.
Range: 10,000 miles at 10 knots surfaced; 42 miles at 5 knots submerged.
Torpedo tubes: six 21in (533mm); 4 forward, 2 aft; torpedoes: 16; *Porpoise, Pike,*

Tarpon, Perch, Permit: two external tubes 21in (533mm); torpedoes: *Perch, Pickerel, Permit:* 18.
Guns: one 3in (76mm) 50-cal; replaced in some boats in 1943 by one 4in (102mm) 50-cal; two 0.5in machine-guns; two 0.3in machine-guns.
Complement: 55.

Pike (SS 173), 1944.

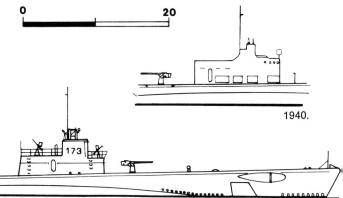

1940.

Double hull ocean-going boats with diesel-electric propulsion. Maximum fuel load: 347–373 tons; maximum operational depth: 250ft (75m).

The *P* Class were the first modern Fleet Submarines of the United States Navy, and from them stemmed all subsequent submarines until 1945. The hull, whose overall length was approximately 300ft (90m), was completely welded. The propulsion system was, for the first time, entirely diesel-electric: the main diesel engines were not connected directly to the propeller shafts, but acted only as generators to power the electric motors. This system was used on all subsequent American submarines, because of simplicity of operation, and greater operational flexibility. A large fuel load carried in the ballast tanks, together with a low specific consumption by the diesel-electric machinery at cruise speed, enabled long ocean patrols to be undertaken. The large size of the boats enabled living conditions to be considerably improved, with spaces devoted exclusively to the recreation of the crew.

The *P* Class possessed good seakeeping qualities, but their large size meant a slow diving time (more than 60 seconds) and their underwater handling was mediocre. Overall, however, they were good boats, strong and well-

armed, and suited to the tasks for which they had been designed.

There were no substantial structural or appearance differences among the three groups of the class, except the arrangement of torpedo tubes, which were external in some boats. During the war, conning-tower layout was modified, and gun armament was improved by increasing the calibre of the deck gun and the number of anti-aircraft weapons.

The *P* Class boats, together with those of the *Salmon/ Sargo* and *T* Classes, were responsible for the first operations against the Japanese in the Pacific, after Pearl Harbor. The ten boats operated uninterruptedly from December 1941 until August 1945, and four were lost during the war: the survivors were broken up some years after the war, with the exception of *Pollack* (SS. 180) which was scrapped in 1947.

Fates

date:	location:	boat:	cause (see page 7):
1942	Pacific	*Shark, Perch*	n
1943	Pacific	*Pickerel, Pompano*	n
1947		*Pollack*	r

Salmon/Sargo Class

Salmon in August 1944.

Group 1
SS.182 *Salmon*, SS.183 *Seal*, SS.184 *Skipjack*:
Builder: Electric Boat, Groton.
Date: 1936–1938/38.
SS.185 *Snapper*, SS.186 *Stingray*:
Builder: Portsmouth Navy Yard.
Date: 1936–1937/38.
SS.187 *Sturgeon*:
Builder: Mare Island Navy Yard.
Date: 1936–1938.

Group 2
SS.188 *Sargo*, SS.189 *Saury*, SS.190 *Spearfish*, SS.194 *Seadragon*, SS.195 *Sealion*:
Builder: Electric Boat, Groton.
Date: 1937–1939/39.
SS.191 *Sculpin*, SS.192 *Sailfish* ex-*Squalus*, SS.196 *Searaven*, SS.197 *Seawolf*:
Builder: Portsmouth Navy Yard.
Date: 1937–1939/39.
SS.193 *Swordfish*.
Builder: Mare Island Navy Yard.
Date: 1937–1939.

Normal displacement:
Group 1: 1,449 tons surfaced; 2,198 tons submerged.
Group 2: 1,450 tons surfaced; 2,350 tons submerged.
Dimensions:
Group 1: 308ft 0in x 26ft 3in x 14ft 3in (93.8m x 7.9m x 4.3m).
Group 2: 310ft 6in x 27ft 0in x 13ft 9in (94.4m x 8.2m x 4m).
Machinery: diesel: 2 H.O.R. or General Motors; electric:

2 Elliot.
Maximum power: 5,500hp surfaced; 3,300hp submerged.
Maximum speed: 20 knots surfaced; 9 knots submerged.
Range: 10,000 miles at 10 knots surfaced; 85 miles at 5 knots submerged.
Torpedo tubes: eight 21in

(533mm); 4 forward, 4 aft; torpedoes: 24.
Guns: one 3in (76mm) 50-cal: subsequently replaced in some boats by one 4in (102mm) 50-cal or 5in (127mm) 25-cal; two 0.5in machine-guns; two 0.3in machine-guns.
Complement: 70.

Sargo (SS 188), 1944.

1940.

Ocean-going boats derived from the *P* Class. Maximum fuel load: 384 tons (Group 1), 428 tons (Group 2); maximum operational depth: 256ft (80m). The number of torpedo tubes was increased to eight: four forward and four aft, and the total number of torpedoes was increased to twenty-four. Unlike the previous Class, these boats had a combination of direct and electric drive from the diesels; they were also faster.

SS.192 *Squalus* sank accidentally during trials off Portsmouth on 23 May 1939. She was salvaged and re-entered service as *Sailfish* on 15 May 1940. The Class began operations in December 1941, and remained in the Pacific until the end of the war. The first merchant ship to be lost by the Japanese was the *Atsutasan Maru*, which was sunk by *Swordfish* off Mainan on 15 December 1941. In April 1942, *Snapper* took part in the evacuation of the beseiged island of Corregidor in the Philippines.

The most important results achieved against warships by boats of this Class were: SS.192 *Sailfish* (Cdr. Ward) sank submarine *I. 4* (2,135 GRT) on 25 December 1942; sank carrier *Chuyo* (16,750 GRT) and damaged carrier *Ryuho*

(13,360 GRT) on 4 December 1943; SS.197 *Seawolf* (Cdr. Warder) damaged light carrier *Naka* (5,850 GRT) on 1 April 1942.

Four boats were lost during the war: one by enemy action, one, as the result of an error by an American ship, and two, scuttled by their crews. The latter were *Sealion* at Cavite in the Philippines where she was repairing at the time of the Japanese occupation, and *Sculpin*, after a protracted action against Japanese units escorting a convoy. *Seal* remained in reserve until 1957: all the other boats were scrapped between 1945 and 1948.

Fates			cause
date:	location:	boat:	(see page 7):
1941	Pacific	*Sealion*	sb
1943	Pacific	*Sculpin*	sb
1944	Pacific	*Seawolf*	e
1945	Pacific	*Swordfish*	n
1945–1948		*Sargo, Saury, Spearfish, Sailfish, Seadragon, Searaven, Salmon, Skipjack, Snapper, Stingray, Sturgeon*	r

T Class

SS.198 *Tambor*, SS.199 *Tautog*, SS.200 *Thresher*, SS.206 *Gar*, SS.207 *Grampus*, SS.208 *Grayback*:
Builder: Electric Boat, Groton.
Date: 1939–1940/41.
SS.201 *Triton*, SS.202 *Trout*, SS.209 *Grayling*, SS.210 *Grenadier*:
Builder: Portsmouth Navy Yard.
Date: 1939–1940/41.
SS.203 *Tuna*, SS.211 *Gudgeon*.
Builder: Mare Island Navy Yard.
Date: 1939–1941/41.
Normal displacement: 1,475 tons surfaced; 2,370 tons submerged.
Dimensions: 307ft 9in x 27ft 3in x 13ft 9in (93.5m x 8.5m x 4.9m).
Machinery: diesel: 2 F.M. or General Motors; electric: 2 General Electric.
Maximum power: 5,400hp surfaced; 2,740hp submerged.
Maximum speed: 20 knots surfaced; 8.75 knots submerged.
Range: 10,000 miles at 10 knots surfaced; 60 miles at 5 knots submerged.
Torpedo tubes: ten 21in (533mm); 6 forward, 4 aft;

torpedoes: 24.
Guns: one 3in (76mm) 50-cal: subsequently replaced by one 5in (127mm) 51-cal; two 0.5in machine-guns; two 0.3in machine-guns: subsequently replaced by two 20mm.
Complement: 80–85.

Ocean-going submarines derived from the *Salmon/Sargo* Class. The number of torpedo tubes was increased to ten, despite a slight decrease in size and displacement. Maximum fuel load: 374–385 tons; maximum operational depth: 288ft (90m). The diesels were all direct-drive.

During the war, the Class underwent several modifications, chiefly to conning-tower layout and surface armament: small sponsons were added forward and aft of the tower, for mounting 20mm and 40mm cannon which replaced the 0.5 calibre weapons. Radar was fitted, and the 3in (76mm) 50-cal deck gun which had been mounted in all boats in 1941, was gradually replaced from 1942, by a 5in (127mm) 51-cal, or 4in (102mm) 50-cal gun.

In December 1941, the twelve boats of the Class were the most modern in the United States Navy, and they began operations immediately, against warships and merchant shipping. *Trout* carried out a food and ammunition supply mission to beseiged Corregidor. *Tautog* sank 26 ships, thereby achieving the highest number of kills in the Second World War.

The most important actions against warships by boats of this Class were: SS.202 *Trout* (Cdr. Ramage) damaged carrier *Tayo* (16,750 GRT) on 28 September 1942; SS.207 *Grampus* (Cdr. Craig) damaged light carrier *Yura* (5,760 GRT) on 18 October 1942; SS.199 *Tautog* (Cdr. Sieglaff) damaged light carrier *Natori* (5,760 GRT) on 9 January 1943.

Seven boats were lost in action between 1943 and 1944. Two were scrapped in 1948: *Tambor*, *Tautog* and *Gar* were converted to training boats in 1946 and were scrapped between 1959 and 1960.

Fates

date:	location:	boat: (see page 7):	cause
1943	Pacific	*Triton, Grampus*	n
		Grenadier	sb
1944	Pacific	*Trout, Grayling, Gudgeon*	uc
		Grayback	n
1948	—	*Thresher, Tuna*	r

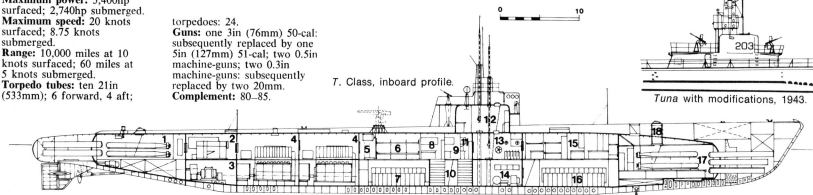

T. Class, inboard profile.

Tuna with modifications, 1943.

1, Stern torpedo room; 2, Machinery control room; 3, Electric motor room; 4, Diesel-dynamo room; 5, Crew showers; 6, Crew space; 7, After battery room; 8, Crew mess; 9, Kitchen (galley); 10, Storeroom; 11, Radio room, 12, Control tower/room; 13, Control room; 14, Pump room; 15, Officer, NCO and crew spaces; 16, Forward battery room; 17, Forward torpedo room; 18, Watertight escape hatch.

Tautog in June 1941, before modification.

M Class

SS.204 *Mackerel*:
Builder: Electric Boat, Groton.
Date: 1939–1941.
SS.205 *Marlin*.
Builder: Portsmouth Navy
Yard.
Date: 1940–1941.
Normal displacement:
Mackerel: 895 tons surfaced;
1,190 tons submerged.
Marlin: 860 tons surfaced;
1,165 tons submerged.
Dimensions:
Mackerel: 239ft. 0in x 21ft 9in
x 12ft 0in (73.9m x 6.7m x
3.4m).
Marlin:
(72.6m x 6.4m x 3.3m).
Machinery:
Mackerel: diesel: 2 E.B.;
electric: 2 Electro Dynamic;
Marlin: diesel: 2 Alco;
electric: 2 General Electric.
Maximum power: 3,360–
3,400hp surfaced; 1,500hp
submerged.

Maximum speed: 16 knots
surfaced; 11 knots submerged.
Torpedo tubes: six 21in
(533mm); 4 forward, 2 aft;
torpedoes: 12.

Guns: one 3in (76mm) 50-cal
(*Marlin* from 1945: one 5in
(127mm) 25-cal); two 0.50
machine-guns (or two 20mm).
Complement: 38.

0   20

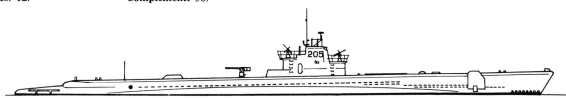

Experimental submarines of medium displacement. Normal fuel load: 116 tons; maximum operational depth: 288ft (90m).

The two *Mackerel* Class boats, built under the 1938 Programme, constituted an attempt, not repeated, to build boats of limited dimensions but having powerful offensive characteristics. The surface propulsion gear was conventional, in that the diesels were connected directly to the propeller shafts. Overall, they were unsuccessful and their range was insufficient for long ocean patrols. During the war they were used mainly for training. In 1945, *Marlin* was modernized and her armament was modified. At the end of the war, the two boats passed into the reserve and were scrapped between 1946 and 1947.

Fates

date:	boat:	cause (see page 7):
1946–1947	*Mackerel, Marlin*	r

Marlin in 1943.

Gato/Balao Class

Gato Series (SS.212–SS.284)
SS.212 *Gato*, SS.213 *Greenling*, SS,124 *Grouper*, SS.215 *Growler*, SS.216 *Grunion*, SS.217 *Guardfish*, SS.218 *Albacore*, SS.219 *Amberjack*, SS.220 *Barb*, SS.221 *Blackfish*, SS.222 *Bluefish*, SS.223 *Bonefish*, SS.224 *Cod*, SS.225 *Cero*, SS.226 *Corvina*, SS.227 *Darter*:
Builder: Electric Boat, Groton.
Date: 1940–1941/43.
SS.228 *Drum*, SS.229 *Flying fish*, SS.230 *Finback*, SS.231 *Haddock*, SS.232 *Halibut*, SS.233 *Herring*, SS.234 *Kingfish*, SS.235 *Shad*, SS.275 *Runner*, SS.276 *Sawfish*, SS.277 *Scamp*, SS.278 *Scorpion*, SS.279 *Snook*, SS.280 *Steelhead*:
Builder: Portsmouth Navy Yard.
Date: 1940–1941/42.
SS.236 *Silversides*, SS.237 *Trigger*, SS.238 *Wahoo*, SS.239 *Whale*, SS.281 *Sunfish*, SS.282 *Tunny*, SS.283 *Tinosa*, SS.284 *Tullibee*:
Builder: Mare Island Navy Yard.
Date: 1940–1941/43.
SS.240 *Angler*, SS.241 *Bashaw*, SS.242 *Bluegill*, SS.243 *Bream*, SS.244 *Cavalla*, SS.245 *Cobia*, SS.246 *Croaker*, SS.247 *Dace*, SS.248 *Dorado*, SS.249 *Flasher*, SS.250 *Flier*, SS.251 *Flounder*, SS.252 *Gabilan*, SS.253 *Gunnel*, SS.254 *Gurnard*, SS.255 *Haddo*, SS.256 *Hake*, SS.257 *Harder*, SS.258 *Hoe*, SS.259 *Jack*, SS.260 *Lapon*, SS.261 *Mingo*, SS.262 *Muskallunge*, SS.263 *Paddle*, SS.264 *Pargo*:
Builder: Electric Boat, Groton.
Date: 1942–1943/44.
SS.265 *Peto*, SS.266 *Pogy*, SS.267 *Pompom*, SS.268 *Puffer*, SS.269 *Rasher*, SS.270 *Raton*, SS.271 *Ray*, SS.272 *Redfin*, SS.273 *Robalo*, SS.274 *Rock*:
Builder: Manitowoc Shipyards.
Date: 1941–1942/43.

Balao Series (SS.285–SS.416).
SS.285 *Balao*, SS.286 *Billfish*, SS.287 *Bowfin*, SS.288 *Cabrilla*, SS.289 *Capelin*, SS.290 *Cisco*, SS.291 *Crevalle*, SS.381 *Sand Lance* (ex-*Ojanco*, ex-*Orca*), SS.382 *Picuda* (ex-*Obispo*), SS.383 *Pampanito*, SS.384 *Parche*, SS.385 *Bang*, SS.386 *Pilotfish*, SS.387

Pintado, SS.388 *Pipefish*, SS.389 *Piranha*, SS.390 *Plaice*, SS.391 *Pomfret*, SS.392 *Sterlet* (ex-*Pudiano*), SS.393 *Queenfish*, SS.394 *Razorback*, SS.395 *Redfish*, SS.396 *Ronquil*, SS.397 *Scabbardfish*, SS.398 *Segundo*, SS.399 *Sea Cat*, SS.400 *Sea Devil*, SS.401 *Sea Dog*, SS.402 *Sea Fox*, SS.403 *Atule*, SS.404 *Spikefish* (ex-*Shiner*), SS.405 *Sea Owl*, SS.406 *Sea Poacher*, SS.407 *Sea Robin*, SS.408 *Sennet*, SS.409 *Piper* (ex-*Awa*), SS.410 *Treadfin* (ex-*Sole*):
Builder: Portsmouth Navy Yard.
Date: 1942–1943/44.
SS.292 *Devilfish*, SS.293 *Dragonet*, SS.294 *Escolar*, SS.295 *Hackleback*, SS.296 *Lancetfish*, SS.297 *Ling*, SS.298 *Lionfish*, SS.299 *Manta*, SS.300 *Moray*, SS.301 *Roncador*, SS.302 *Sabalo*, SS.303 *Sablefish*:
Builder: Cramp Shipyards, Philadelphia.
Date: 1942–1943/45.
SS.304 *Seahorse*, SS.305 *Skate*, SS.306 *Tang*, S.307 *Tilefish*, SS.411 *Spadefish*, SS.412 *Trepang* (ex-*Senorita*), SS.413 *Spot*, SS.414 *Springer*, SS.415 *Stickleback*, SS.416 *Tiru*:
Builder: Mare Island Navy Yard.
Date: 1942–1943/48.
SS.308 *Apogon* (ex-*Abadejo*), SS.309 *Aspro* (ex-*Acedia*), SS.310 *Batfish* (ex-*Acoupa*), SS.311 *Archerfish*, SS.312 *Burrfish* (ex-*Arnillo*):
Builder: Portsmouth Navy Yard.
Date: 1942–1943/43.
SS.313 *Perch*, SS.314 *Shark*, SS.315 *Sealion*, SS.316 *Barbel*, SS.317 *Barbero*, SS.318 *Baya*, SS.319 *Becuna*, SS.320 *Bergall*, SS.321 *Besugo*, SS.322 *Blackfin*, SS.323 *Caiman* (ex-*Blanquillo*), SS.324 *Blenny*, SS.325 *Blower*, SS.326 *Blueback*, SS.327 *Boarfish*, SS.328 *Charr* (ex-*Boccaccio*), SS.329 *Chub* (ex-*Bonaci*), SS.330 *Brill*, SS.331 *Bugara*, SS.332 *Bullhead*, SS.333 *Bumper*:
Builder: Electric Boat, Groton.
Date: 1943–1944/44.
SS.334 *Cabezon*, SS.335 *Dentuda* (ex-*Capidoli*), SS.336 *Capitaine*, SS.337 *Carbonero*, SS.338 *Carp*, SS.339 *Catfish*,

SS.340 *Entemedor* (ex-*Chickwick*), SS.341 *Chivo*, SS.342 *Chopper*, SS.343 *Clamangore*, SS.344 *Cobbler*, SS.345 *Cochino*, SS.346 *Corporal*, SS.347 *Cubera*, SS.348 *Cusk*, SS.349 *Diodon*, SS.350 *Dogfish*, SS.351 *Greenfish* (ex-*Doncella*), SS.352 *Halfbeak* (ex-*Dory*):
Builder: Electric Boat, Groton.
Date: 1943–1944/46.

Units of the same series cancelled in 1944:
SS.353 *Dudong*, SS.354 *Eel*, SS.355 *Espada*, SS.356 *Jawfish* (ex-*Fanegal*), SS.357 *Ono* (ex-*Friar*), SS.358 *Garlopa*, SS.359 *Garrupa*, SS.360 *Goldring*, SS.361 *Golet*, SS.362 *Guavina*, SS.363 *Guitarro*, SS.364 *Hammerhead*, SS.365 *Hardhead*, SS.366 *Hawkbill*, SS.367 *Icefish*, SS.368 *Jallao*, SS.369 *Kete*, SS.370 *Kraken*, SS.371 *Lagarto*, SS.372 *Lamprey*, SS.373 *Lizardfish*, SS.374 *Loggerhead*, SS.375 *Macabi*, SS.376 *Mapiro*, SS.377 *Menhaden*, SS.378 *Mero*, SS.379 *Needlefish*, SS.380 *Nerka*.
Normal displacement:
Gato Series: 1,825 tons surfaced; 2,410 + 2,424 tons submerged;
Balao Series: 1,826 tons surfaced; 2,391 + 2,414 tons submerged.
Dimensions: 311ft 9in x 27ft 3in x 15ft 3in (91.6m x 8.3m x 5.1m).
Machinery: diesel: 4 General Motors or Fairbanks Morse; electric: 4 Elliot or General Electric.
Maximum power: 5,400hp surfaced; 2,740hp submerged.
Maximum speed: 20.25 knots surfaced; 8.75 knots submerged.
Range: 11,800 miles at 10 knots surfaced; 95 miles at 5 knots submerged.
Torpedo tubes: ten 21in (533mm); 6 forward, 4 aft; torpedoes: 24.
Guns: one 3in (76mm) 50-cal, later 4in (102mm) 50-cal or 5in (127mm) 25-cal (see notes); plus two 12.7mm machine-guns.
Mines: capacity for 40 mines in lieu of spare torpedoes.
Complement: 60–80.

Double hull ocean-going submarines developed from the *T* Class. Maximum fuel load: 378–472 tons; maximum operational depth: 300ft (95m) *Gato* Series, 400ft (120m) *Balao* Series.

This Class constituted the standard type of American submarine of the Second World War. From experience gained with the *P, Salmon/Sargo* and, particularly, the *T* Classes, it was decided to build a series of 6 boats (SS.212–SS.217) in the 1940 Programme, to be followed shortly by a series of 67 boats (SS.218–SS.284). All were to be of a new type of Fleet Submarine, derived from and retaining the general size and armament of the *T* Class, but differing in propulsion gear arrangements and in numerous structural and external details. The most noteworthy characteristics were range, habitability, good seakeeping and powerful armament. The hull, entirely welded and of unusual length, was single at its extremities, and double in the centre section: the pressure hull was not cylindrical as in so many submarines, but tapered towards the bow and stern, with areas open to the circulation of water on the upper bow and stern surfaces.

The main fuel tanks and ballast tanks were situated in the centre part of the space between the two hulls. Internal compartmentation was highly developed. The diesel-electric propulsion gear was based on four diesel engines, which powered a like number of electric motors coupled in pairs to the propeller shafts through reduction gears. This system allowed a notable degree of operational flexibility for surface propulsion, thanks to the various combinations that could be obtained, and the notable power available for high speed and cruising, and for charging batteries. The latter were of various types (*Exide, Gould*, etc.) and were made up of 252 elements.

While the last boats of the first series (*Gato*) were still building, a new series of 132 units was ordered in the 1942 War Programme. Named after the first unit of the series, the *Balao* boats were almost the same as the *Gato* boats, but several design changes were introduced to allow more rapid building, using the prefabrication system, and greater structural strength increased the operational depth. There were slight differences in size and displacement among the boats built in various yards, but basically, all the boats of this class entering service between 1941 and 1945, were almost identical.

The Programme called for 205 boats, but only 195 were completed: some were commissioned after the war had ended. The contracts for the last ten were cancelled late in 1944.

During the war, the surface armament of the *Gato/Balao* Class underwent several changes and an overall improvement was effected. The first boats had a 3in (76mm) 50-cal gun and two 12.7mm machine-guns. Later, the calibre of the gun was increased to 4in (102mm) in many boats, and that of the anti-aircraft weapons to 20mm. In contrast with the 12.7mm guns, the 20mm were not positioned on the sides of the conning tower, but on platforms, forward and aft of it. From 1943, many boats were armed with a 5in (127mm) 25-cal gun, specially adapted for use in submarines. At the same time, the first heavy Bofors 40mm 56-cal anti-aircraft guns in single mounts began to replace or complement the Oerlikon 20mm weapons.

All boats of the Class had mountings for deck guns, one forward and one aft of the conning tower. Generally, only one was mounted, located arbitrarily, forward or aft, but it was by no means rare to see boats fitted with two 5in (127mm) 25-cal guns, especially during the later phases of the war. There were generally two anti-aircraft cannon in varying combinations: two 20mm 70-cal; one 20mm 70-cal and one 40mm 56-cal; two 40mm 56-cal.

The surface armament of American boats was superior to that of all other navies. This resulted from the kind of actions conducted in the Pacific, and the particular kind of opposition which American boats had to face. The introduction of heavy anti-aircraft guns necessitated numerous modifications to the conning towers. Initially, the towers were quite small, but as the number and calibre of the weapons increased, the tower size increased considerably, as can be seen from the drawings and photographs. Normally there were two periscopes, of considerable length and size and fitted with protective sleeves: three periscopes were fitted in some boats.

After 1942, the radar antenna was installed abaft the periscopes, mounted on a tapered cylinder, similar to a periscope. The periscope-radar complex also housed the radio antennae (generally of the folding whip type) and two small lookout bridges.

The increased volume of the conning tower appurtenances, led to a notable increase in crash-dive time—which was already, rather high. The US Navy attached

Top: *SS.407 Sea Robin* of the *Balao* Series. Below: *SS.366 Hawkbill*, armed with two 5in (127mm) guns, one 40mm anti-aircraft gun on the forward bridge sponson and one 20mm on the after sponson. She wears the light grey finish adopted in 1943.

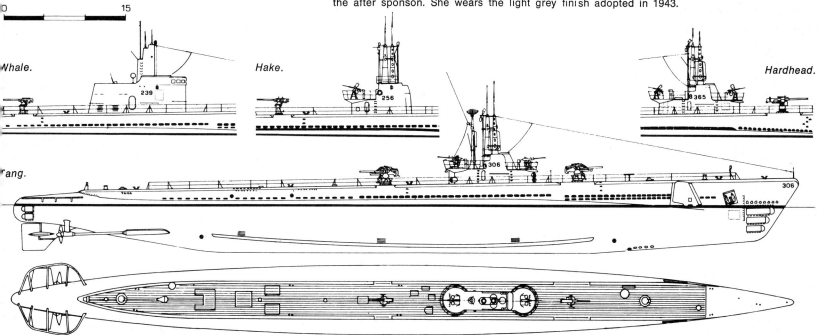

Whale.

Hake.

Hardhead.

Tang.

little importance to this. Minimum dive times of 50–60 seconds, which would have been unacceptable in Atlantic operations, were adequate for the kind of warfare being carried out in the Pacific. The excellent radar outfit usually gave adequate warning of the approach of an enemy.

The only major modification to the underwater armament of the Class, was the partial substitution of electric for conventional torpedoes. The boats' layout enabled a maximum of 40 bottom (moored) mines, magnetic or contact detonated, to be carried in lieu of spare torpedoes; they were laid through the torpedo tubes.

A feature of the Class, was the installation—beginning with the earliest boats—of a small mechanical computer to calculate torpedo launch data. It was particularly useful and accurate, especially after the installation of radar which, with the boat surfaced or awash, enabled target data to be even more precisely ascertained. The acoustic devices—sonar and hydrophones—were sophisticated and effective.

Generally, the *Gato/Balao* Class were successful boats. Fast, strong, well armed and with a high degree of habitability and possessing long range, they met the US Navy's requirements for long offensive cruises in the Pacific, during which, they were self-sufficient, unlike the German boats which often relied on supply ships or submarines.

For some years after the war, and until the commissioning of nuclear attack and missile-launching submarines, the survivors of the Class, together with those of the subsequent *Tench* Class, formed the backbone of the US Navy's submarine fleet. Several boats were put in reserve as soon as the war was over: many others remained in service and were fitted with schnorkels. Subsequently, almost all boats were transformed in accordance with the 'Guppy' Programme (Greater Underwater Propulsive Power) which included the installation of more powerful batteries, the total elimination of surface armament and the streamlining of the conning tower and forward portion of the hull, in order to achieve higher underwater 'burst' speeds. Many boats, in the original, 'Guppy' or semi-'Guppy' (partial transformation versions), were ceded or sold to allied countries. Many of them are still (1972) in service in the American and other navies.

Drum, first boat of this Class, was commissioned on 1 November 1941. She was followed shortly by numerous others: in June 1942, there were already some twenty operational boats and by the end of 1942, approximately 40 of the 73 that had been ordered under the 1940 Programme, had entered service. The first boats of the sub-sequent *Balao* Series, began to enter service during the first months of 1943: several were delivered within nine months from the time they were laid down.

The *Gato/Balao* Class bore the brunt of the Pacific campaign: in fact, they were employed almost exclusively in that theatre. A few boats (*Shad, Herring, Haddo, Gunnel,* etc.) carried out several beach reconnaissance and support missions during the Anglo-American landings in North Africa early in 1943, before being sent to the Pacific. Herring sank the German *U 136* in the Bay of Biscay.

The highest score against Japanese merchant shipping was achieved by *Flasher*: 21 ships sunk, totalling 100,231 GRT. *Rasher, Barb, Tang* and *Silversides* achieved more than 90,000 GRT each. These results appear modest beside those of the best U-boats, but it should be remembered that there were far fewer targets in the Pacific than in the Atlantic.

The average number of patrols by individual American boats was lower than in other navies (the record was held by *Gato,* thirteen patrols), but the vast expanse of the Pacific and the great distance from base to operational area meant that the patrols were of very long duration.

The chief successes achieved by the *Gato/Balao* Class against Japanese naval vessels are listed in Table 26. To these results must be added the sinking of 39 destroyers and numerous escort vessels and submarines. *Flounder* and *Besugo* sank two German submarines in the Pacific in 1944 and 1945 respectively.

The normal function of American boats in the Pacific was the offensive patrolling of enemy sea lanes, and ambush tactics in the numerous islands. They were also frequently employed in laying offensive minefields, landing supplies for Philippine guerrillas, reconnaissance of landing beaches and, during the final phase, coastal bombardment. The rescue of aircrews from the sea, subjected the boats to great risks, as they had to remain in position for long periods in very dangerous areas. A total of 380 airmen were saved by 86 submarines.

From December 1941 until August 1945, 29 submarines of the *Gato/Balao* Class were lost in action or by various other causes. This number is approximately 70 per cent of all the American boats lost during the Second World War.

Two boats were destroyed as 'guinea-pigs' during the atomic tests at Bikini Atoll on 23 July 1946. Some boats were placed in reserve at the end of the war and others remained in service. Subsequently modernized, many of these were ceded to allies. The US Navy still (1972) has 13 used chiefly for training.

Barb (SS.220).

Fates

date:	location:	boat:	cause (see page 7):
1942	Pacific	Grunion	s
1943	Pacific	Amberjack	n
		Corvina	s
		Wahoo	a
		Dorado	e
		Runner	m
		Capelin	uc
		Cisco	a-n
1944	Pacific	Growler, Harder Golet, Shark	n
		Albacore, Flier, Scorpion, Escolar	m
		Darter, Robalo, Tullibee, Tang	v
		Scamp	uc
		Herring	coastal battery
1945	Pacific	Bonefish, Trigger, Lagarto	n
		Snook, Kette	s
		Barbel, Bullhead	a
1946	Pacific	Abadejo, Pilotfish	atomic test

Tench Class

SS.417 *Tench*, SS.418 *Thornback*, SS.419 *Tigrone*, SS.420 *Tirante*, SS.421 *Trutta* (ex-*Tomatate*), SS.422 *Toro*, SS.423 *Torsk*, SS.424 *Quillback* (ex-*Trembler*):
Builder: Portsmouth Navy Yard.
Date: 1944–1944/44.
SS.425 *Trumpetfish*, SS.426 *Tusk*, SS.427 *Turbot*, SS.428 *Ulua*:
Builder: Cramp shipyards, Philadelphia.
Date: 1943–1946/.
SS.435 *Corsair*, SS.436 *Unicorn*, SS.437 *Walrus*:
Builder: Electric Boat, Groton.
Date: 1945–1946/–.
SS.475 *Argonaut*, SS.476 *Runner*, SS.477 *Conger*, SS.478 *Cutlass*, SS.479 *Diablo*, SS.480 *Medregal*, SS.481 *Requin*, SS.482 *Irex*, SS.483 *Sea Leopard*, SS.484 *Odax*, SS.485 *Sirago*, SS.486 *Pomodon*, SS.487 *Remora*, SS.488 *Sarda*, SS.489 *Spinax*,

SS.490 *Volador*:
Builder: Portsmouth Navy Yard.
Date: 1944–1945/48.
SS.516 *Wahoo*:
Builder: Mare Island Navy Yard.
Date: 1944 cancelled 1944.
SS.522 *Amberjack*, SS.523 *Grampus*, SS.524 *Pickerel*, SS.525 *Grenadier*:
Builder: Boston Navy Yard.
Date: 1944–1946/51.
Units of the same series cancelled in 1944:
SS.429 *Unicorn* (II), SS.430 *Vandace*, SS.431 *Walrus*, SS.432 *Whitefish*, SS.433 *Whiting*, SS.434 *Wolfish*, SS.491 *Pompano*, SS.492 *Grayling*, SS.493 *Needlefish*, SS.494 *Sculpin*, SS.526 *Dorado*, SS.527 *Comber*, SS.528 *Sea Panther*, SS.529 *Tiburon*:
Units, to which names had not yet been assigned, cancelled in 1945: SS.438–SS.474, SS.495–SS.515, SS.517–SS.521,

SS.530–SS.562.

Normal displacement: 1,860 tons surfaced; 2,428 + 2,414 tons submerged.
Dimensions: 311ft 9in x 27ft 3in x 15ft 3in (91.6m x 8.3m x 5.1m).
Machinery: diesel: 4 General Motors or Fairbanks Morse; electric: 4 Elliot or General Electric or Westinghouse.
Maximum power: 5,400hp surfaced; 2,740hp submerged.
Maximum speed: 20.25 knots surfaced; 8.75 knots submerged.
Range: 12,000 miles at 10 knots surfaced; 95 miles at — knots submerged.
Torpedo tubes: ten 21in (533mm); 6 forward, 4 aft; torpedoes: 24.
Guns: one or two 5in (127mm) 25-cal; two 40mm or 20mm (see notes).
Mines: capacity for 40 mines in lieu of spare torpedoes.
Complement: 80–90.

Double hull ocean-going submarines derived from the *Gato/Balao* Class. Maximum fuel load: 389–454 tons; maximum operational depth: approximately 400ft (120m). They were virtually copies of the *Gato/Balao* Class, but they were more strongly built and had a better internal layout, which increased their displacement by about 35–40 tons. The notes and technical considerations used to describe the *Gato/Balao* Class are applicable to these boats.

The original Programme was for 146 boats. The building of 110 boats, for which the relative contracts had already been stipulated, was cancelled between 1944 and 1945. Of the remaining 36, only 31 were completed and delivered between October 1944 (*Tench*) and February 1951 (*Grenadier*): the incomplete hulls of five boats were scrapped or otherwise employed. By August 1945, 26 boats had been commissioned, but only about ten completed their training in time to participate in the last operations in the Pacific. None of these boats were lost in action, and after the war, all of them followed the path of the *Gato/Balao* Class. Many were modernized under the 'Guppy' Programme and many are still in service in the US or allied navies.

Torsk in Portsmouth Harbor, N.H., January 1945.

U.S.S.R.

Possession of a large submarine fleet was one of the key points of Soviet naval strategy from the late twenties. Its role was essentially defensive, which strikingly influenced its technical development and, as always when the submarine was confined to defensive operations, compromised its performance. The results achieved by the large fleet of Russian boats during the Second World War were very modest.

The Russian Navy emerged from the revolution of 1917, to which, its ships had contributed decisively, very severely damaged in both size and organization. Although it had been the guns of the cruiser *Aurora* against the Winter Palace at Petrograd that had set the October Revolution in motion, the relationship between the navy and the Lenin Government soon soured and, in 1921, led to the mutiny of the Baltic Fleet. The revolt was crushed, but its logical consequence was a greater mistrust of the navy, which was soon demoted to the 'Naval Force of the Red Army' and its functions were confined to the defence of army operations and coastal defence.

This led to a complete re-structuring of the Russian fleet, in accordance with theories which took into account the decreased importance of battleships and the need of light forces, including submarines, which were to have played an important part in the defensive strategy decided upon.

In 1925, of the large submarine fleet which had participated in the First World War, there remained only a few old boats of the *Bars* and *AG* Classes. The *Bars* were double hull submarines of Russian design, built between 1915 and 1916. The *AG* (AG=Amerikanskij Golland) were single hull boats of the *Holland* type, acquired in the United States in 1916. Several *AG* boats which, because of the chaotic industrial situation of those years had not been completely fitted out, were commissioned between 1925 and 1928.

In 1925, planning began for the development of the new Russian submarine fleet, under the aegis of Peoples' Commissar Frunze. It was decided to design a type of boat derived from previous Russian designs instead of acquiring an example of a modern submarine from abroad and studying its characteristics to obtain knowledge of recent technical developments.

The first design developed by the Submarine Construction Office under B. M. Malunin, one of the foremost Russian naval architects, was inspired by the *Bars* Class boats. Submerged characteristics were considerably improved and the number of torpedo tubes was increased. This was the *Dekabrist* (later, *D*) Class, whose first three boats were laid down in March 1927 at the Baltiskyi yards in Leningrad.

Consisting of six boats, of the full double hull type, commissioned between 1931 and 1932, the *Dekabrist* Class were not very successful and, despite numerous modifications, they were unreliable and unstable when submerged.

During the building of these early boats in 1928, the Russian Navy salvaged the hull of the British submarine *L.55* which had been sunk in the Gulf of Finland by a Bolshevik destroyer on 4 June 1919. She was re-commissioned in 1931 and employed in experiments aimed at

acquiring further knowledge of underwater technology, by comparing Russian and British methods of solving problems.

The experience gained from the *Dekabrist* Class and the tests carried out with *L.55* formed the basis for the design of the next Russian boats, the *Leninets* (later, *L*) Class, 25 boats built between 1933 and 1942 in four successive series. These were a marked improvement on the preceding boats. They had partial double hulls, a displacement of 1,040/1,335 tons, six torpedo tubes and two minelaying tubes and fourteen mines. The presence of mines in the *L* Class and in the previous *D* Class, shows how greatly interested were the Russians in these weapons. They had, in fact, started building the world's first submarine minelayer, *Krab* in 1908, at Nikolayev in the Black Sea. She was not completed until 1915 and her achievement was over-shadowed by German and British developments.

In 1933, the prototypes of two classes of small submarines developed for coastal defence were commissioned. These were the boats of the *Malyutka* (later, *M*) Class, built in prefabricated sections transportable by rail, and the larger boats of the *Shchuka* (*Shch*) Class.

These two Classes, with a combined total of 200 boats, commissioned between 1933 and 1945, would later form the bulk of the Russian submarine fleet. Their designs, progressively improved in successive series, were those which would best suit the roles that had been assigned to the boats. Small, rapid diving and possessing good submerged manoeuvrability, they were particularly well suited to the restricted and shallow waters of the Baltic and the northern shores of the Black Sea.

After the first two classes of medium-range boats, and the prototypes of the small coastal boats, the Russians tried ocean-going boats with the three units of the *Pravda* (later, *P*) Class, built at Leningrad between 1933 and 1937. Performance of the *P* Class was very poor as a result of structural and design weaknesses, and inefficient machinery: they were not repeated. Their lack of success and the limited interest in this type of boat, led to a curtailment of studies relating to ocean-going boats, which were not resumed for many years.

With Stalin's reversal of naval priorities in the late thirties, it was decided to return to the concept of a balanced fleet, including battleships and aircraft carriers as well as light craft and short-range submarines, which had been considered the basis for naval expansion in the preceding decade. This change of policy accompanied the purging of most of the higher echelons from the Russian Navy. On the eve of the war, Russia began to build the 13 boats of the *Katyusha* (*K*) Class, which entered service between 1940 and 1942. These were long-range boats with a good gun armament, eight torpedo tubes and minelaying equipment. They were quite successful: they had a high surface speed (22 knots) and good range (15,000 miles at 9 knots). They were employed in the Arctic, the North Sea and along the Norwegian coast, and remained in service after the war.

The best type of Russian boat, however, was the *Stalinets* (*S*) Class, of fifty medium-displacement boats: the first entered service in 1936 and the last dozen or so were commissioned immediately after the war.

Their design clearly derived from the Turkish submarine *Gür*, built in Spain between 1930 and 1932, to German plans. Basically, they represented the prototype of the German Navy's Type I.A whose design was the basis for the development of the Type IX ocean-going boats. They had good submerged and surface characteristics, were fast, strong and had good range. During the war, they gave a reasonable account of themselves, operating extensively in all areas in which the Russian Navy was committed.

In September 1939, the Russian submarine fleet was the largest in the world, with a strength of approximately 150 boats, the majority of which had been recently built. Small coastal boats, however, represented approximately 75 per cent of the total. From the end of 1939 until the summer of 1941, when Germany attacked Russia, submarine construction was accelerated and when Russia entered the war, her navy had 218 boats deployed in the Baltic, the Black Sea, the Arctic and the Pacific Ocean. The largest concentration was in the Baltic, where many coastal and medium-displacement boats were deployed.

In the Black Sea, coastal boats markedly outnumbered larger submarines: most of the ocean-going and medium-displacement boats were in the Arctic and in the Far East.

At the beginning of the war, the names previously assigned to individual boats (e.g. *Dekabrist, Leninets,* etc.) were abandoned, and all Russian boats assumed new designations consisting of one or more letters, distinctive of the Class, followed by a number (e.g. *S.4, L.3, D.6, Shch 102,* etc.).

Training was generally below the standards of other navies. Building materials were satisfactory, but operational doctrines were inadequate and effectively limited the chances of success from the outset, by imposing defensive tasks on the underwater fleet. That the technological development had been tied to this principle, is shown by the high percentage of small short-range coastal boats. The medium-range and ocean-going boats were built in limited numbers, and then, not until the eve of war, when the Russians had begun to doubt the efficacy of the defensive role that had been assigned to their submarines. Even if the Russians had possessed a greater number of medium- and long-range boats, the nature of their struggle against Germany between 1941 and 1944, gave little scope for the widespread employment of submarines. Nevertheless, an offensive posture from the outset could have caused considerable difficulties to the German Navy, especially in the Baltic and, to a lesser extent, in the Norwegian Sea.

Russian boats in the Arctic and the Black Sea, also represented a threat, though limited and kept in check by effective German anti-submarine measures. There was little technological development of Russian submarines during the war. No new classes were developed, but the existing classes were improved. In particular, the coastal boats progressively increased in size to the extent that in 1944, the boats of the last series of the *M* Class (*M.V*) had a displacement approximately double that of the 1933 prototypes. The medium and ocean-going boats underwent only minor variations in size, and the last series were merely stronger and improved in detail.

The number of new boats commissioned between 1941 and 1945 was relatively low, compared to the enormous efforts which had been made in the years immediately before the war. Altogether, from August 1941 to August 1945, approximately 65 new boats entered service, mostly of the *M, Shch, K* and *S* Classes: they represented a fraction of the number needed to replace the heavy losses sustained. The Russian Navy was the only one to end the war with fewer boats than it had at the start: the number of Estonian and Lithuanian boats captured in 1940, and the British boats ceded in 1944 were insignificant.

When the Germans invaded Russia on 22 June 1941, there were some 35 Russian submarines operating in the Baltic and approximately another fifty were refitting or were obsolete and relegated to training. The major submarine base in the Baltic was at Libau (1st Flotilla) in Latvia, but, as early as 25 June 1941, the base had to be evacuated under pressure from German troops. The boats which could not be moved were scuttled, and the others retired to Riga: when this base was threatened they moved to Reval. The boats of the 2nd Flotilla had had to evacuate their base at Hango in the Gulf of Finland, and were also concentrated at Reval.

In the following August, Reval had to be cleared: all boats unable to move under their own power were scuttled, and the Russian Baltic submarines withdrew to Leningrad and Kronstadt, which were also under siege.

During these operations, many boats were lost to mines which the Germans were laying from every available craft in the shallow waters of the Baltic, or to air and sea forces which were particularly effective in anti-submarine operations.

There were few successes to set against these heavy losses. The first and possibly most important, was obtained by *Shch 307* which sank *U 144* on 9 August 1941. After the withdrawal to Leningrad and Kronstadt, the activity of the Russian Baltic boats decreased significantly.

Towards the end of the summer of 1941, several of the larger displacement boats were employed to supply Kronstadt and the besieged Baltic islands, and three of them were lost while so engaged. At the beginning of winter, when the weather halted operations, 27 Russian boats had been lost in this sector, from a total of approximately 85 that had been available in June. Russian gains amounted to one submarine and four small cargo ships sunk.

In 1942, German pressure increased, and Russian submarine operations were affected. The extensive minefields laid by the Germans, and their complete mastery of the air, greatly decreased the freedom of action of the Russian boats which made only sporadic forays close to their bases, without any significant success.

During 1943 and the early months of 1944, Russian boats rarely gained the open sea. When Finland had been defeated, several boats were sent to operate along the Finnish coast, but although German shipping was weakly escorted, results were modest, probably because of the poor training of the Russian crews.

In 1945, the advancing Russian troops liberated the besieged bases, and German shipping evacuated troops and refugees from Eastern Prussia, giving the Russian boats an opportunity for action. The most important sinkings were of German Transports: *Wilhelm Gustloff*

Development of Soviet submarines, 1930–1945.

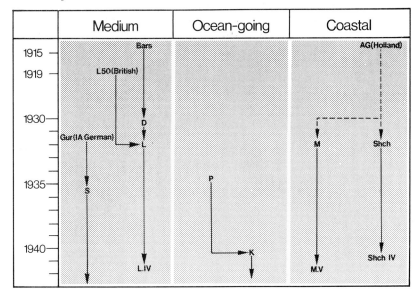

(25,484 GRT) by *S.13*, *Goya* (5,230 GRT) by *L. 3* and *General von Steuben* (14,660 GRT).

In the Black Sea, at the beginning of hostilities, the Germans, using aircraft, quickly mined the entrances to Sebastopol, temporarily blocking in the submarines there. Four boats managed to leave and took station outside the major Rumanian and Bulgarian ports and off the Bosphorous, to intercept German shipping. Thus began the first series of operations in which *Shch 4* was lost off Costanta on 3 July, and the tanker *Peles* was sunk by *Shch 211* on 15 August.

In this sector, where the Germans were much weaker than in the Baltic, and where traffic along the coasts of Romania and Bulgaria offered lucrative targets, results remained modest because the Russians used the wrong tactics.

The fall of Nikolayev, the major submarine base in the Black Sea, worsened the situation considerably, especially as Sebastopol was soon besieged. The coastal submarines were then pulled back to Poti and Batum, ports which lacked adequate facilities for submarines.

In 1942, especially at the beginning of the summer, it was necessary to use several boats for carrying supplies to Sebastopol, thereby reducing the already limited Russian capabilities. Because of the

The Estonian *Kalev*, incorporated in the Russian Navy in 1940, and scuttled at Reval on 18 August 1941 to avoid capture by the Germans.

heavy losses that had been sustained, coastal boats were now confined to the north-western sector of the Black Sea, and the larger boats stayed in the waters of Rumania and the Crimea. From early in 1943, the Russian boats assumed a more offensive posture, which led to the sinking of the Rumanian Transport *Suceava* by *S.33*. Success was still very limited, however, though the adoption of the magnetic fuze for torpedoes improved the situation slightly. Early in 1944, Russian boats intensified their offensive, operating with reconnaissance aircraft based at Odessa and Skadowsk, but losses remained high and only seven targets were hit. Operations in the Black Sea ended when the Russians occupied the Rumanian and Bulgarian coastlines in the autumn of 1944.

A limited number of boats were stationed in the Arctic in June 1941, and these were augmented by several medium-displacement boats from the Far East, and several boats ceded from the Royal Navy. Successes were proportionally higher than in other theatres. From 1942, the Arctic boats based at Murmansk attacked German coastal shipping off the north coast of Norway, forcing the German Navy to provide adequate escorts. *S.101, S.104* and *V. 4* (ex British *Ursula*) sank, respectively, a submarine, an escort vessel and a steamship. Losses were heavy, mainly because of the effective anti-submarine measures encountered.

The few submarines stationed in the Pacific Ocean had no opportunity of action during the brief operations conducted there. Russia declared war on Japan on 8 August 1945, and Japan surrendered unconditionally on 14 August 1945: the American submarines had left little to attack.

Not much is known about the guns mounted in Russian submarines. They were standardized in two calibres: 4in (102mm) 60-cal firing a 39lb (17.4kg) projectile with a maximum range of 22,200 yards (21,300m); and the 45mm rapid-fire anti-aircraft gun. All Russian boats were equipped with light machine-guns and automatic rifles on removable mounts.

Torpedoes were of the 'steam' type, 21in (533mm), with speed and range inferior to those of other navies: 40 knots over a run of 5,470-6,564 yards (5,000–6,000m). Detonators were of the impact type until 1943, when magnetic fuzes were introduced. Mines were of the Type 08, with automatic mooring and fitted with impact fuzes. There is no evidence that Russian boats were equipped with radar or schnorkel during the war.

At the end of the war, the Russian Navy gained possession of numerous modern submarines, some of which had been scuttled in occupied ports. Others had been surrendered and delivered to Russia. These were mainly German boats of the Types XXI, XXIII, VII and IX. A number of them served in the Russian Navy for several years with Russian-built boats that had survived the war.

With experience gained from the Type XXI Elektro-boote during the post-war period, Russia built her first high-speed submarines, beginning thereby, the great qualitative and quantitative development which, in the space of a few years, gave her the largest, and one of the most effective submarine fleets in existence.

D (Dekabrist) Class

D. 1 ex-*Dekabrist*, **D. 2** ex-*Narodovolets*, **D. 3** ex-*Krasnogvardeets*, **D. 4** ex-*Yakobinets*, **D. 5** ex-*Revoljutsioner*, **D. 6** ex-*Spartakovets*.
Date: 1931/32.
Normal displacement: 920 tons surfaced; 1,318 tons submerged.
Dimensions: 284ft 0in x 23ft 6in x 16ft 6in (83.5m x 7m x 4.2m).
Machinery: diesel: 2; electric: 2.
Maximum power: 2,500hp surfaced; 1,250hp submerged.
Maximum speed: 15 knots surfaced; 8.4 knots submerged.
Range: 7,000 miles at 9 knots surfaced; 105 miles at 4 knots submerged.
Torpedo tubes: eight 21in (533mm); 6 forward, 2 aft; torpedoes: 10.
Guns: one 4in (102mm) 45-cal; one-two 45mm.
Mines: 8; two tubes.
Complement: 60.

Medium-displacement double hull submarines, developed from the *B* (*Bars*) Class of 1915–16. Maximum operational depth: approximately 246ft (75m); normal fuel load: 78 tons.

The first three boats of this Class, which marked the start of the re-building of the Russian submarine fleet after the Revolution, were laid down in the Baltiskyi shipyard, Leningrad in March 1927.

Dekabrist began trials in June 1930 and, from her maiden voyage, lacked stability. This defect was partially remedied, but there remained a tendency for the quick-dive tank to open at depth, gravely jeopardizing the safety of the boat.

D. 1 (ex-*Dekabrist*) was lost during an exercise in November 1940, probably as the result of accidental flooding of the negative tank, causing her to dive to a crushing depth. When Germany invaded, the remaining five boats of the Class, all of which had been built at Leningrad, were stationed in the Baltic: because of their limited safety and slow crash-dive time (approximately 150 seconds), they were considered obsolete. Only *D. 2*, which had been seriously damaged by German aircraft on 11 August 1941, during a supply mission in the Baltic, survived the war and was discarded immediately afterwards.

Fates   cause
date: boat: (see page 7)
1940   *D. 1*
1942   *D. 3, D. 6*
1943   *D. 4, D. 5*

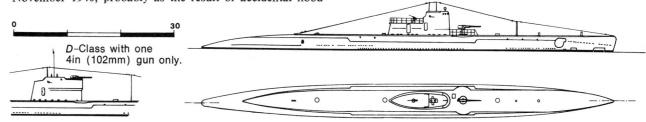

D-Class with one 4in (102mm) gun only.

0 ___ 30

L (Leninet) Class

L. 1 ex-*Leninets*, L. 2, L. 3 ex-*Frunzovest*, L. 4 ex-*Garibaldiets*, L. 5 ex-*Chartist*, L. 6 ex-*Karbonari*, L. 7–L. 25: Unit not completed: L. 25.
Date: 1933/42.
Normal displacement:
L. 1: 1,040 tons surfaced; 1,335 tons submerged.
L. 2, L. 3: 1,200 tons surfaced; 1,550 tons submerged.
Dimensions:
L. 1: 255ft 7in x 23ft 11in x 13ft 9in (77.9m x 7.3m x 4.2m).
L. 2, L. 3: 265ft 9in x 24ft 7in x 15ft 9in (81m x 7.5m x 4.8m).
Machinery: diesel: 2; electric: 2.
Maximum power: 2,600hp surfaced; 1,250hp submerged.
Maximum speed: 14 knots surfaced; 9 knots submerged.
Range: 7,400 miles at 8 knots surfaced; 154 miles at 3 knots submerged.
Torpedo tubes: six 21in (533mm); 4 forward, 2 aft; torpedoes: 12.
Guns: one 3.9in (100mm) 68-cal; one 45mm.
Mines: 14; two tubes.

Medium-displacement partial double hull submarines, derived from the *D* Class, built in three successive series (*L. I–L. III*). Maximum operational depth: 288ft (90m); normal fuel load: 98 tons.

Almost all the major shortcomings of the *Dekabrist* Class were eliminated from these boats. It is not known exactly to which series each boat belonged, but there is reason to believe that *L. 1* to *L. 6* belonged to the first series (*L. I*) and the boats from *L. 7* belonged to the other series. Compared to the *D* Class, the *L* Class boats had slightly increased displacement and range, two fewer torpedo tubes, but a greater number of mines, which were laid through horizontal watertight tubes in the stern.

In June 1941, the boats already commissioned were stationed in the Far East, Baltic and Black Sea. During the summer of 1942, *L. 15* and *L. 16* were transferred to the Arctic, via San Francisco Panama Canal-Halifax. En route, *L. 16* was sunk by mistake off the west coast of America by the Japanese boat *I. 25* on 13 October 1942. *L. 25* which was fitting out at Nikolayev in the Black Sea in 1941, was transferred to Poti to avoid capture, but she does not appear to have been completed before 1944.

The other 24 boats were extensively employed from 1941 to 1945. Their most important success was the sinking of the German steamship *Goya* (5,230 GRT) by *L. 3* in the Baltic on 16 April 1945. Losses totalled six, of which the first was *L. 2* which was mined in the Baltic in August 1941.

Fates

date:	boat:
1941	L. 2
1942	L. 16, L. 24
1943	L. 5
1944	L. 6, L. 23

A boat of the *L. I* Series, in a pre-war photograph.

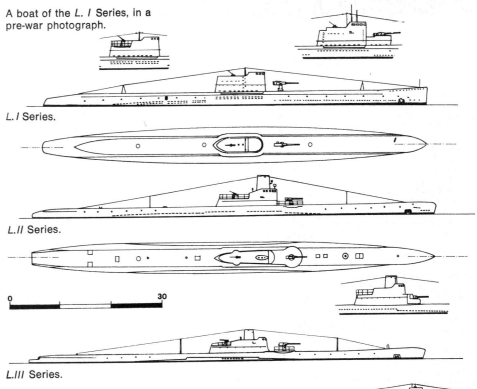

L. I Series.

L.II Series.

0   30

L.III Series.

M (Malyutka) Class

Series M. I–M. II.
*M. 1–M. 13, M. 15, M. 16,
M. 18–M. 28, M. 41, M. 42,
M. 51–M. 63, M. 71–M. 80:*
Date: 1933/37.

Series M. III–M. IV.
*M. 31–M. 36, M. 43 ex-M. 82,
M. 44 ex-M. 84, M 45 ex-
M. 85, M. 46 ex-M. 86, M. 81,
M. 83, M. 89, M. 90, M. 94–
M. 99, M. 101–M. 103, M. 104
ex-Yaroslavski-Komsomolets,
M. 105 ex-Chelyabinskii
Komsomolets, M. 106 ex-
Lenininskii Komsomolets,
M. 107 ex-Novosibirskii
Komsomolets, M. 108,
M. 112–M. 122, M. 171 ex-
M. 87, M. 172 ex-M. 88,
M. 173 ex-M. 91, M. 174 ex-
M. 92, M. 175 ex-M. 93,
M. 176 ex-M. 100:*
Date: 1938/43.

Series M. V.
*M. 200 ex-Mest, M. 201,
M. 204 and others.*
Date: 1943/47.

Normal displacement:
M. I, M. II: 161 tons surfaced;
202 tons submerged.
M. III, M. IV: 206 tons
surfaced; 258 tons submerged.
M. V: 350 tons surfaced;
420 tons submerged.
Dimensions:
M. I, M. II: 123ft 0in x 10ft
2in x 8ft 6in (37.5m x 3.1m x
2.6m).
M. III, M. IV: 146ft 0in x
10ft 10in x 9ft 6in (44.5m x
3.3m x 2.9m).
M. V: 174ft 10½in x 16ft 0in
x 11ft 10in (53.3m x 4.9m x
3.6m).
Machinery: diesel: 2; electric:
2.
Maximum power:
M. I, M. II: 685hp surfaced;
240hp submerged.
M. III, M. IV: 800hp
surfaced; 400hp submerged.
M. V: 1.000hp surfaced;
800hp submerged.

Maximum speed:
M. I, M. II: 13.1 knots
surfaced; 7.4 knots submerged.
M. III, M. IV: 14.1 knots
surfaced; 8.2 knots submerged.
M. V: 15 knots surfaced; 10
knots submerged.
Range:
M. I, M. II: 1,600 miles at
8 knots surfaced; 55 miles at
2 knots submerged.
M. III: 3,440 miles at 9 knots
surfaced; 107 miles at 3
knots submerged.
M. V: 4,000 miles at 8 knots
surfaced.
Torpedo tubes:
M. I–M. IV: two 21in
(533mm) forward; torpedoes: 2.
M. V: four 21in (533mm);
2 forward, 2 aft; torpedoes: 4.
Guns: one 45mm.
Complement: about 18.

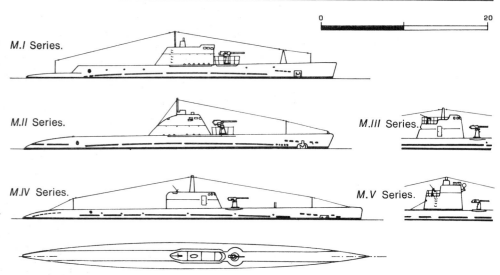

M.I Series.

M.II Series.

M.III Series.

M.IV Series.

M.V Series.

Small single hull coastal submarines, built in sections which could be transported by rail. Maximum operational depth: *M. I–M. IV* 200ft (60m), *M. V* 246ft (75m); normal fuel load: *M. I–M. IV* 5½ tons, *M. V* approximately 20 tons.

The prototype of this large class of small boats, entered service in 1933. It building—inspired by the excellent *Holland* boats (Russian *AG* Class)—was prompted by the need of small boats with good submerged handling, to defend the coastline. Production was concentrated in the Gorki Shipyard on the Volga, whence, the boats were transported in sections by rail to Leningrad, Vladivostok and Nikolayev, for assembly and fitting out.

The first use of welding in Russian submarines was made in the *M* boats. Limited at first, to the superstructure and bow stern casings, the process was later extended to the pressure hull.

The Programme for the *M* boats began in 1933 and did not end until several years after the war. It was divided into five successive series (*M. I–M. V*), with important technical improvements, and with a progressive increase of armament and dimensions (prompted by the inadequate seakeeping of the first two series).

For the Series *I* and *II* boats (Classes *VI* and *VIIbis* according to some Russian sources), the designs specified the building of the hull in four sections: for the Series *III* and *IV* (*XII* Class), in six sections and for the Series *V* (*XV* Class), in seven sections.

It is thought that by 1945, approximately 100 *M* Class boats had been completed. Thirty boats of the *V* Series were completed after the war. The *M* boats were used extensively during the war, chiefly in the Black Sea and in the Baltic, but despite their being quite effective, especially those of the Series *III* and *IV*, only limited results were obtained and losses were heavy (approximately 35 boats between 1941 and 1945).

Fates

date:	boat:
1941	*M. 34, M. 54, M. 58, M. 59, M. 71, M. 72, M. 78, M. 80, M. 81, M. 83, M. 94, M. 98, M. 99, M. 101*
1942	*M. 33, M. 35, M. 60, M. 61, M. 95, M. 97 M. 118, M. 121, M. 175, M. 176*
1943	*M. 31, M. 32, M. 36, M. 51, M. 106, M. 122, M. 172, M. 173, M. 174*
1944	*M. 108*

Two *M* Class coastal boats leaving a Russian base. *M. 115* is in the foreground.

Top: *M.120*, one of the many small coastal boats of the *IV* Series (*M* Class), built during the war.
Centre: *M.35*, one of the first of the *M.IV* Series.
Right: one of the *M* Class boats in the Arctic.

Shch (Shchuka) Class

Shch 101–Shch 141, Shch 201 ex-Sazan, Shch 202 ex-Seld, Shch 203, Shch 204, Shch 205 ex-Nerpa, Shch 206–Shch 209, Shch 210 ex-Krylatka, Shch 211 ex-Kambala, Shch 212, Shch 213 ex-Skumbriya, Shch 214 ex-Evdokia, Shch 215, Shch 216, Shch 301 ex-Shchuka, Shch 302 ex-Okun, Shch 303 ex-Ersh, Shch 304 ex-Komsomolets, Shch 305 ex-Lin, Shch 306 ex-Pinsha, Shch 307 ex-Treska, Shch 308 ex-Semga, Shch 309 ex-Delfin, Shch 310 ex-Beluge, Shch 311 ex-Kumsza, Shch 317–Shch 320, Shch 322–Shch 324, Shch 401–Shch 411:
Date: 1933/42.
Units not completed: *Shch 409–Shch 411, Shch 421–Shch 424* and others.
Normal displacement:
Shch I: 577 tons surfaced; 704 tons submerged.
Shch II, Shch III: 586 tons surfaced; 702 tons submerged.
Shch IV: 587 tons surfaced; 705 tons submerged.
Dimensions:
Shch I: 187ft 0in x 21ft 0in x 12ft 5½in (57m x 6.4m x 3.8m).
Shch II, Shch III: 191ft 11in x 20ft 4in x 13ft 9in (58.5m x 6.2m x 4.2m).
Shch IV: 199ft 6in x 20ft 4in x 14ft 9in (60.8m x 6.2m x 4.5m).
Machinery: diesel; 2; electric **2.**
Maximum power:
Shch I, Shch II, Shch III: 1,370hp surfaced; 800hp submerged.
Shch IV: 1,600hp surfaced; 800hp submerged.
Maximum speed:
Shch I: 11.2 knots surfaced; 8 knots submerged.
Shch II, Shch III: 12.9 knots surfaced; 7 knots submerged.
Shch IV: 13.6 knots surfaced; 8 knots submerged.
Range:
Shch I: 3,250 miles at 8 knots surfaced; 110 miles at 2 knots submerged.
Shch II, Shch III: 6,700 miles at 8 knots surfaced; 100 miles at 2 knots submerged.
Shch IV: 6,140 miles at 7 knots surfaced; 122 miles at 2 knots submerged.
Torpedo tubes: six 21in (533mm); 4 forward, 2 aft;

torpedoes: 10.
Guns:
Shch I: one 45mm.
Shch II, Shch III, Shch IV: two 45mm.
Complement:
Shch I: 35.
Shch II, Shch III, Shch IV: 38.

A *Shch* Type Series III boat at Sevastopol.

Shch IV Series.

Shch I Series.

Shch II Series.

Shch III Series.

Single hull coastal submarines. Maximum operational depth: 288ft (90m); fuel load: *Shch I* 25 tons, *Shch II–Shch IV* 58 tons.

The prototype of this large class of coastal boats was built in 1935, contemporaneously with that of the small *M* Class boats. It too, was inspired by the *Holland* type, but was much larger and had a better performance than the *M* Class.

The *Shchuka* (later abbreviated to *Shch*) Class were comparable in size and characteristics to the small British *U* Class coastal boats, but were far less effective.

Approximately ninety examples were built between 1933 and 1942, divided into four successive series. Characteristics were progressively improved and such initial shortcomings as low speed and limited range were remedied. Armament was increased and dimensions were slightly enlarged. It is not possible to place each boat in her respective series: they differed, as shown in the drawings, even in their exterior appearance.

In general, they had reasonable characteristics and they achieved adequate results during the war. Their most important successes were achieved by *Shch 307* which sank the German *U 144* in the Baltic on 9 August 1941, and by *Shch 211* which sank the tanker *Peles* in the Black Sea on 15 August 1941.

Of the 88 boats built during the war, 32 were lost: the survivors remained in service in the Russian Navy until the mid fifties.

Fates

date:	boat:
1941	*Shch 204, Shch 206, Shch 211, Shch 319, Shch 322, Shch 324, Shch 423*
1942	*Shch 208, Shch 210, Shch 212, Shch 213, Shch 214, Shch 301, Shch 302, Shch 304, Shch 305, Shch 306, Shch 308, Shch 311, Shch 317, Shch 320, Shch 401, Shch 405, Shch 421*
1943	*Shch 203, Shch 207, Shch 323, Shch 406, Shch 408, Shch 422*
1944	*Shch 216, Shch 402*

Shch 201 of the Shch II Series.
S. 56 returning from a patrol.

P (Pravda) Class

P. 1 ex-*Pravda*, P. 2 ex-*Zvezda*, P. 3 ex-*Iskra*.
Date: 1936/37.
Normal displacement: 1,200 tons surfaced; 1,670 tons submerged.
Dimensions: 295ft 3in x 26ft 3in x 10ft 0in (87.6m x 8m x 3.1m).
Machinery: diesel: 2; electric: 2.
Maximum power: 2,700hp surfaced; 1,100hp submerged.
Maximum speed: 18.8 knots surfaced; 7.7 knots submerged.
Range: 5,700 miles at 10 knots surfaced; 105 miles at 4 knots submerged.

Torpedo tubes: six 21in (533mm); 4 forward, 2 aft; torpedoes: 10.
Guns: two 3.9in (100mm) 60-cal; one 45mm.
Complement: 60.

Double hull ocean-going submarines. Maximum operational depth: 246ft (75m); normal fuel load: 93 tons. These boats, built in the Putiloff Yard at Leningrad between 1933 and 1937, were the first Russian attempt to build a long-range attack boat. They were not very successful. A design fault put the propellers too near the surface, and the machinery was subject to frequent breakdowns because of the binding of flexible couplings, despite the installation of special dampers. The boats were not repeated, and their wartime service was limited. All three were lost during the first two years of the war. P. 1 was mined in the Baltic on 17 September 1941.

Fates
date: boat:
1941   *P. 1, P. 2*
1942   *P. 3*

S (Stalinets) Class

*S. 1 ex-Naljm, S. 2–S. 16,
S. 19, S. 31–S. 38, S. 51–S. 58,
S. 101–S. 104:*
Date: 1936/1945.

*S. 17–S. 18, S. 20–S. 24,
S. 26, S. 137, S. 139:*
Date: 1946/48.

Units not completed:
S. 35–S. 38.

Normal displacement: 840 tons
surfaced; 1,070 tons
submerged.
Dimensions: 256ft 0in x 21ft
0in x 13ft 0in (77.8m x 6.4m x
4.4m).
Machinery: diesel: 2; electric: 2.
Maximum power: 4,000hp
surfaced; 1,100hp submerged.
Maximum speed: 19.5 knots
surfaced; 9 knots submerged.
Range: 9,800 miles at 10 knots
surfaced; 148 miles at 3 knots
submerged.
Torpedo tubes: six 21in
(533mm); 4 forward, 2 aft;
torpedoes: 12.
Guns: one 3.9in (100mm)
60-cal; one 45mm.
Complement: 50.

Medium-displacement single hull submarines, with ocean-going characteristics. The large side blisters were inspired by the Turkish submarine *Gür,* built in Spain in 1932, to German designs, from which, the German Navy's Type I. A derived. Maximum operational depth: 328ft (100m); normal fuel load: 105 tons. Minimum crash-dive time: about 30 seconds.

These were the best medium-displacement boats in service in the Russian Navy during the Second World War: fast, strong, well armed, quite manoeuvrable and reliable. Between 1936 and 1945, thirty-three boats were completed; another four (*S. 35–S. 38*) were never completed and another ten were completed after the war (*S. 17, S. 18, S. 20–S. 24, S. 26, S. 137* and *S. 139*).

Compared to the German Type I. A, the Russian *S* boats had a more powerful diesel and were faster (19.5 against 17.7 knots). In several of the early boats, the 4in (102mm) deck gun was located in an enclosed mounting at the base of the conning tower, but as this hindered the

efficient working of the gun, the arrangement was subsequently abandoned.

During the war, the *S* boats were extensively used in all theatres and proved their excellent characteristics: they achieved several of the few successes obtained by Russian submarines. However, offsetting these modest successes were heavy losses—a total of 15 boats were sunk between 1941 and 1945. *S. 2* was lost, probably accidentally, on 3 January 1940. The survivors and those completed in the post-war period, served in the Russian Navy until the mid fifties.

Fates

date:	boat:
1940	*S. 2*
1941	*S. 1, S. 3, S. 5, S. 6, S. 8, S. 10, S. 11, S. 34*
1942	*S. 7, S. 32*
1943	*S. 9, S. 12, S. 55*
1944	*S. 54*
1945	*S. 4*

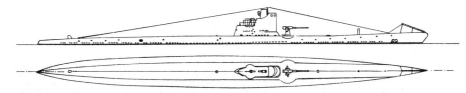

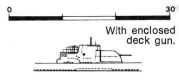

0   30

With enclosed
deck gun.

S. 56 returning from a patrol.

K (Katyusha) Class

K. 1–K. 3, K. 21–K. 24, K. 51–K. 56.
Date: 1940/42.

Normal displacement: 1,480 tons surfaced; 2,095 tons submerged.
Dimensions: 308ft 0in x 23ft 0in x 13ft 0in (97.7m x 7.4m x 4.5m).
Machinery: diesel: 2; electric: 2.
Maximum power: 8,400hp surfaced; 2,400hp submerged.
Maximum speed: 22.5 knots surfaced; 10 knots submerged.
Range: 15,000 miles at 9 knots surfaced; 160 miles at 3 knots submerged.
Torpedo tubes: eight 21in (533mm); 4 forward, 4 aft; torpedoes: 22.
Guns: two 3.9in (100mm) 60-cal; two 45mm.
Mines: 20; two tubes.
Complement: 65.

Double hull ocean-going submarines. Maximum operational depth: approximately 224ft (70m); normal fuel load: 150 tons. The first boat of this Class, *K. 1,* was built at the Marti Yard in Leningrad and was launched on 4 May 1938.

The design of these long-range boats was derived, with considerable improvements, from the preceding *P* Class. Size, displacement, range, maximum surface speed and armament were all considerably increased.

Between 1940 and 1942, thirteen boats were completed, and after the war, another three boats of a modified type were commissioned, probably as the result of reconstructed hulls that had been completed during the war.

In 1941, the few boats already in service, were divided between the Baltic and the Arctic. The latter boats were employed in a manner more in keeping with their ocean-going characteristics, but their success was modest, and five of them were lost.

Fates

date: boat:
1942 *K. 2, K. 23*
1943 *K. 1, K. 3, K. 22*

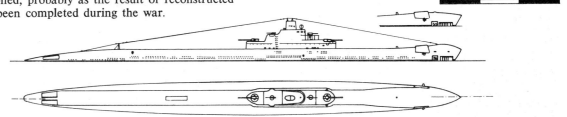

K. 1 leaving an Arctic base for a patrol in Norwegian waters.

Old submarines

In June 1941, eleven submarines whose building dated from before the First World War, were still in service with the Russian Navy.

These were the five remaining boats of the *Bars* Class (the best type built in Russia until the Revolution, and from which, all later types derived); five *A* Class coastal submarines (ex-*AG* Class) of the *Holland* type, acquired during the First World War; and the British *L. 55,* which

had been sunk in the Gulf of Finland by a Boleshevik destroyer on 4 June 1919. She was salvaged in 1928 and re-commissioned in 1931. When the war started, the *Bars* Class boats and *L. 55* were paid off and converted to battery-charging units for submarines.

The five *A* Class boats remained in service, and took part in the Second World War, during which three of them were lost. The two survivors were discarded in 1945.

Table 27: Old submarines in service with the Soviet Navy during the Second World War.

Designation:	Commissioned:	Normal displacement: surfaced/ submerged	Dimensions:	Machinery type: hp	Speed (knots): surfaced/ submerged	Range (miles at knots): surfaced/ submerged	Armament:
B (Bars) Class	1915–1916	664/753	68m x 4.5m x 4.2m	Two diesels 1,370	11.4/9	3,700 at 7 60 at 3	Four 21in(533mm) torpedo tubes
B. 2, ex-*Batrak*, ex-*Volk*				Two electric 840			Six torpedoes
B. 4, ex-*Krasnoarmeyetz*, ex-*Leopard*							Two 3in(76mm) guns
B. 5, ex-*Komissar*, ex-*Pantera*							One 45mm gun
B. 6, ex-*Proletarii*, ex-*Zmeya*							
B. 8, ex-*Kraznoflotez*, ex-*Yaguar*							
Maximum operational depth: 145ft(46m). De-commissioned 1941.							
A (AG) Class	1921–1928	356/453	45.8m x 4.6m x 3.5m	Two diesels 960	12/8	1,500 at 7 80 at 3	Four 18in(457mm) torpedo tubes
A. 1, ex-*N.12*, ex-*Shakhter*, ex-*Trotskii*, ex-*AG.23*				Two electric 480			Four torpedoes
A. 2, ex-*N.13*, ex-*Kommunist*, ex-*AG.26*							One 45mm gun
A. 3, ex-*N.14*, ex-*Marxist*, ex-*Komenev*, ex-*AG.25*							One machine-gun
A. 4, ex-*N.15*, ex-*Politrobotnik*, ex-*AG.26*							
A. 5, ex-*N.16*, ex-*Metallist*, ex-*AG.21*							
L.55 Class	1931		71.6m x 7.2m x 4m	Two diesels 2,200	13.5/8.2	6,000 at 7 100 at 3	Six 21in(533mm) torpedo tubes
L.55, ex-*L.55*		954/1,139		Two electric 1,600			Twelve torpedoes Two 3in(76mm) guns

Below: *B. 6, ex-Proletarii*, one of the *Bars* Class.

Foreign submarines in Russian service

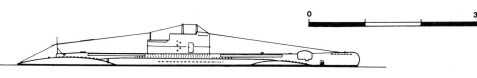

During the war, the Russian Navy captured or were ceded several boats of British and French construction.

Two Estonian submarines (ex-*Kalev* and ex-*Lembit*) built in Britain and two Latvian boats (ex-*Ronis* and ex-*Spidola*) built in France and captured in 1940, after the invasion of those countries by Russia. The Estonian boats were incorporated in the Russian Navy (*Kalev* was scuttled on 28 August 1941 when Reval was abandoned); the Latvian boats were never commissioned and were sunk by the Russians at Libau on 23 June 1941, to prevent their capture by the Germans.

In 1944, the Royal Navy lent an *S* Class (*V. 1*, ex-*Sunfish*) and three *U* Class boats (*V. 2*, ex-*Unbroken*, *V. 3*, ex-*Unison*, and *V. 4*, ex-*Ursula*) to Russia, for employment in the Arctic and the North Sea. *V. 1* (ex-*Sunfish*) was lost in July 1944, through an error in identification by a British bomber: the other three boats served in the Russian fleet until 1949, when they were returned to the Royal Navy, and were broken up. Operating in the Arctic, *V. 4* sank a German merchantman. (For details of these boats see the appropriate national section.)

Right:
The Latvian submarine *Spidola*, seen at her trials in France in 1926. She was incorporated in the Russian Navy in 1940.
Below:
Kalev, still under Estonian colours, alongside her sister *Lembit*, whose stern is just visible to the left.

Brazil

Brazil declared war on Italy and Germany on 22 August 1942 and her naval forces co-operated with the Allies in the defense of shipping against surface raiders and submarines in the South Atlantic.

During the war, the Brazilian Navy had four submarines in commission. They operated predominantly in home waters, and had little contact with enemy ships. The boats were: *Humayta'*, an ocean-going boat built in Italy between 1927 and 1929, and very similar to the *Balilla* Class; *Tamoio* ex *Ascianghi* (I), *Timbira* ex *Gondar* (I) and *Tupi* ex *Neghelli* (I), three coastal boats of the *600* Class, *Adua* Series, acquired from Italy between 1936 and 1937. (See page 154.)

Denmark

Germany invaded neutral Denmark on 9 April 1940. The ships of the Danish Navy were surprised in port and, after an agreement with the Germans, remained under the Danish flag and control. Officially, Denmark was under German 'protection' but, by August 1943, relations between the occupiers and the Danes had deteriorated and, on 29 August 1943, the Germans attempted a coup and the Danish Navy scuttled most of its ships in port. Despite German intervention, a few boats tried to get to Sweden, but most were scuttled including all of the operational submarines and several old boats which, by now, had been reduced to the status of battery-charging boats (*B* Class). All Danish submarines were of domestic design, and all were built at the Royal Dockyard at Copenhagen. Several of the scuttled boats were raised by the Germans, but none of them could be used before the war ended.

C Class

Bellona, Flora, Rota.
Builder: Royal Dockyard, Copenhagen.
Date: 1902–1922.
Normal displacement: 301 tons surfaced; 370 tons submerged.
Dimensions: 155ft 9in x 14ft 6in x 9ft 6in (47m x 5.4m x 2.7m).
Machinery: diesel: 2 Burmeister and Wain; electric: 2.

Maximum power: 900hp surfaced; 640hp submerged.
Maximum speed: 14 knots surfaced; 8 knots submerged.
Torpedo tubes: four 18in (457mm); 3 forward, 1 aft; *Rota*: 1 external deck tube.
Guns: one 57mm (6-pdr).
Complement: 24.

The Danish *Bellona*.

Rota was *C. 1*, *Bellona C. 2* and *Flora, C. 3*. Danish Admiralty designs.

Fates

date:	location:	boat:	cause (see page 7):
1943	Denmark	*Bellona, Flora, Rota*	sb

D Class

Daphne, Dryaden.
Builder: Royal Dockyard, Copenhagen.
Date: 1926–1927.
Normal displacement: 308 tons surfaced; 381 tons submerged.
Dimensions: 160ft 9in x 16ft 0in x 8ft 4in (49.1m x 5.2m x 2.5m).
Machinery: diesel: 2 Burmeister and Wain; electric: 2.
Maximum power: 900hp surfaced; 400hp submerged.

Maximum speed: 13 knots surfaced; 7 knots submerged.
Torpedo tubes: six 18in (457mm).
Guns: one 3in (76mm); one 20mm.
Complement: 25.

Numbered *DI–2*. Danish Admiralty design.

Fates				cause
date:	location:	*Daphne, Dryaden*		sb
1943	Denmark	boat:		(see page 7):

H Class

Havmanden, Havfruen, Havkalen, Havhesten.
Builder: Royal Dockyard, Copenhagen.
Date: 1937–1939, *H. 5* cancelled in 1940.
Normal displacement: 335 tons surfaced; 407 tons submerged.
Dimensions: 155ft 9in x 14ft 6in x 9ft 4in (47.5m x 4.7m x 2.8m).
Machinery: diesel: 2 Burmeister and Wain; electric: 2.
Maximum power: 1,200hp surfaced; 450hp submerged.
Maximum speed: 15 knots surfaced; 7 knots submerged.
Torpedo tubes: five 18in (457mm); 3 forward, 2 aft.
Guns: two 40mm; two 8mm.
Complement: 20.

Like all other Danish submarines, they were painted green. Designed by the Danes. Numbered *H1–4*.

Fates			cause
date:	location:	boat:	(see page 7):
1943	Denmark	*Havmanden, Havfruen, Havkalen, Havhesten*	sb

The Danish *Havmanden*.

Estonia

When Russia invaded Estonia in September 1939, they captured the two Estonian submarines *Kalev* and *Lembit,* built in Britain between 1935 and 1936, and incorporated them in their navy. *Kalev* was scuttled in August 1941: *Lembit* survived the war unscathed.

Kalev Class

Kalev, Lembit.
Builder: Vickers, Barrow.
Date: 1935–1936.
Normal displacement: 600 tons surfaced; 820 tons submerged.
Dimensions: 190ft 0in x 24ft 6in x 11ft 6in (57.9m x 7.5m x 3.5m).
Machinery: diesel: 2 Vickers; electric: 2.
Maximum power: 1,200hp surfaced; 450hp submerged.

Maximum speed: 13.5 knots surfaced; 8.5 knots submerged.
Range: 2,000 miles at 10 knots surfaced.
Torpedo tubes: four 21in (533mm) forward.
Guns: one 40mm.
Mines: 20.

These two minelaying submarines are interesting because they were the only British-built submarines for foreign customers during the inter-war period, which were not directly derived from a type already in service with the Royal Navy. Indeed, the Class was quite unlike any other British-built boat. Their minelaying system, vertical tubes in the saddle tanks, was a Vickers design, developed from German prototypes (and which had, in its turn, influenced the French design for the boats of the *Rubis* type). There were other differences from conventional British design. The boats seem to have been quite efficient.

Fates			cause
date:	location:	boat:	(see page 7):
1939	Estonia	*Kalev, Lembit*	c
1941	—	*Kalev*	sb

Finland

Russian aggression against Finland in 1939, and the 'Winter War' which followed, were ended by a peace treaty in March 1940. On 25 June 1941, Finland declared war on Russia and, in December, on Great Britain (who had already declared war on Finland). On 19 September 1944, she concluded an armistice with the Allies and, on 3 March 1945, formally declared war on Germany.

In 1940, the Finnish Navy had five submarines, of which four were capable of laying mines, an important activity in the Baltic, where they operated. At the end of the war, they were all still in service, but they were scrapped in accordance with the terms of the peace treaty.

Saukko

Saukko.
Builder: Hietalahden Laivatelakka, Helsinki.
Date: 1929–1930.
Normal displacement: 100 tons surfaced; 136 tons submerged.
Dimensions: 106ft 6in x 13ft 6in x 10ft 6in (32.4m x 4m x 3.2m).
Machinery: diesel: 1 Germania: electric: 1.

Maximum power: 170hp surfaced; 120hp submerged.
Maximum speed: 9 knots surfaced; 5 knots submerged.
Range: 375 miles at 9 knots surfaced; 45 miles at 4 knots submerged.
Torpedo tubes: two 18in (457mm); torpedoes: 2.
Guns: one 20mm.
Mines: 9.
Complement: 13.

An interesting small coastal boat, built to German designs. She could be dismantled into two sections for transporting to Lake Ladoga, then, on Finland's eastern boundary. This small minelayer survived the war.

Vessikko

Vessikko.
Builder: Chrichton-Vulkan, Abo.
Date: 1933.
Normal displacement: 250 tons surfaced; 300 tons submerged.
Dimensions: 134ft 2in x 13ft 0in x 12ft 1in (41m x 4m x 3.8m).
Machinery: diesel: 2 Mannheim; electric: 2.
Maximum power: 700hp surfaced; 360hp submerged.
Maximum speed: 13 knots surfaced; 7 knots submerged.
Range: 1,500 miles at 13 knots surfaced; 50 miles at 5 knots submerged.

Torpedo tubes: three 21in (533mm) forward; torpedoes: 6.
Guns: one 20mm.

A German design, built at a time when Germany was still forbidden to build or design submarines on her own territory. This coastal boat was a direct descendant of the German UB II Type, of the First World War, and was the prototype for the Type II boats, Germany was soon to build in numbers. She was built as a speculation and was not taken over by the Finnish Navy until 1936. Service depth: 300ft (91m); Fuel load: 9 tons.

Vetehinen Class

Vetehinen, Vesihiisi, Iko-Turso.
Builder: Chrichton-Vulkan, Abo.
Date: 1930–1931.
Normal displacement: 500 tons surfaced; 715 tons submerged.
Dimensions: 208ft 4in x 20ft 6in x 12ft 9in (63m x 6.1m x 3.9m).
Machinery: diesel: 2 Atlas; electric: 2.
Maximum power: 1,160hp surfaced; 600hp submerged.
Maximum speed: 15 knots surfaced; 9 knots submerged.
Range: 1,500 miles at 10 knots surfaced; 75 miles at 5 knots submerged.
Torpedo tubes: four 21in (533mm).
Guns: one 3in (76mm).
Mines: 20.
Complement: 27.

Like the other Finnish boats, these medium-range torpedo and minelaying submarines were the products of German designers and Finnish shipyards. They were developed from the First World War UB. III Type and were ancestors of the famous Type VII, the chief German protagonist in the Battle of the Atlantic. Thus, Finland, though never building her own designs, has a vitally important niche in the history of submarine development. All three *Vetehinen* Class boats survived the war. Diving limit: 240ft (74m); fuel load: 20 tons.

The Finnish *Vetehinen*.

Greece

On 28 October 1940, Italy attacked Greece. When the country was invaded by Axis forces in April of the following year, the surviving ships of the Greek Fleet escaped to British-controlled Mediterranean ports and continued to operate under the orders of the government in exile, until the end of the war.

In October 1940, the Greek Navy had six submarines: two of the *Katsonis* Class and four of the *Nereus* Class, all of French construction. *Proteus* was sunk by an Italian torpedo-boat in December 1940. The other boats came under the operational control of the Royal Navy in April 1941, and continued operations from Malta and Alexandria, obtaining good results against Italian and German shipping in the Adriatic, Aegean and Central Mediterranean. Three boats were lost between 1942 and 1943: the two survivors were discarded in 1945.

During the war, the Royal Navy ceded three boats which operated with success in the Mediterranean: an Italian *600* Class and two British *V* Class boats.

Katsonis Class

Katsonis:
Builder: Chantiers de la Gironde.
Date: 1927.

Papanicolis.
Builder: Ateliers et Chantiers de la Loire.
Date: 1927.

Normal displacement: 605 tons surfaced; 778 tons submerged.
Dimensions: 213ft 3in x 17ft 6in x 11ft 0in (65m x 5.3m x 3.6m).

Machinery: diesel: 2 Schneider-Carels; electric: 2.
Maximum power: 1,300hp surfaced; 1,000hp submerged.
Maximum speed: 12 knots surfaced; 8 knots submerged.
Range: 1,500 miles at 10 knots surfaced; 100 miles at 5 knots submerged.
Torpedo tubes: six 21in (533mm); 2 forward, 2 aft, 2 bow external; torpedoes: 7.
Guns: one 4in (102mm) 40-cal.
Complement: 39.

French-built submarines, derived from the *600 tonnes* Schneider-Laubeuf type. See France. Maximum service depth: 270ft (85m).

Fates

date:	location:	boat:	cause (see page 7):
1943	Mediterranean	*Katsonis*	n
1945	Mediterranean	*Papanicolis*	r

Nereus Class

Nereus, Proteus, Triton:
Builder: Ateliers et Chantiers de la Loire.
Date: 1927–1928.

Glafkos.
Builder: Chantiers Navals Français, Blainville.
Date: 1928.

Normal displacement: 73 tons surfaced; 960 tons submerged.
Dimensions: 226ft 4in x 18ft 8in x 13ft 7in (69m x 5.7m x 4.1m).
Machinery: diesel: 2 Sulzer; electric: 2.
Maximum power: 1,420hp surfaced; 1,200hp submerged.
Maximum speed: 12 knots surfaced; 8 knots submerged.
Range: 1,500 miles at 10 knots surfaced; 100 miles at 5 knots submerged.
Torpedo tubes: eight 21in (533mm); 6 forward, 2 aft; torpedoes: 10.
Guns: one 4in (102mm) 40-cal; one 40mm.
Complement: 41.

French-built, similar to the *630 tonnes* Simonot type. See France.
Maximum diving depth: 270ft (85m); fuel load: 105 tons.

Fates

date:	location:	boat:	cause (see page 7):
1940	Mediterranean	*Proteus*	n
1942	Mediterranean	*Glafkos*	b
1942	Mediterranean	*Triton*	n
1945		*Nereus*	r

Foreign submarines in Greek service

Transferred British submarines
V Class (2 units)
Pipinos ex-*Veldt*, *Delfin* ex-*Vengeful*; see Great Britain.
Transferred in 1944 and 1945 respectively. Neither was returned to the Royal Navy until 1957. Both were scrapped in 1958.
Ex-Italian *600* Class (1 unit)
Matrozos ex-British *P. 712*, ex-captured Italian *Perla*; see Italy.
Captured by the British in 1942, and transferred to Greece in 1943. Discarded in 1954.

The Italian *Perla* at Beirut after her capture in July 1942. She was ceded to the Greek Navy and renamed *Matrozos*.

Latvia

When the Russians occupied Latvia in September 1939, they captured the two small submarines belonging to that country: *Ronis* and *Spidola,* built in France between 1925 and 1926. They were incorporated in the Russian Navy and were later scuttled without ever having been employed.

Ronis Class

Ronis:
Builder: Ateliers et Chantiers de la Loire, Nantes.
Date: 1926.

Spidola.
Builder: Normand, Le Havre.
Date: 1926.
Normal displacement: 390 tons surfaced; 514 tons submerged.
Dimensions: 180ft 6in x 15ft 0in x 10ft 0in (55m x 4.5m x 3m).
Machinery: diesel: 2 Sulzer; electric: 2.
Maximum power: 1,300hp surfaced; 700hp submerged.
Maximum speed: 14 knots surfaced; 9.25 knots submerged.
Range: 1,600 miles at 14 knots surfaced; 85 miles at 9 knots submerged.
Torpedo tubes: six 18in (457mm); 2 forward, 4 in external twin traversing mounts forward and aft.
Guns: one 3in (76mm); three machine-guns.
Complement: 34.

Fates

date:	location:	boat:	cause (see page 7):
1939	Latvia	*Ronis, Spidola*	c
1941	Baltic	*Ronis, Spidola*	sb

Norway

In April 1940, when the Germans invaded, the Norwegian Navy had nine submarines: three old boats of the *A* Class (*A.2, A.3* and *A.4*) built in Germany between 1911 and 1914, and six of the *B* Class (*B.1, B.2, B.3, B.4, B.5* and *B.6*) of the 'Holland' type, built in Norway between 1923 and 1930.

The Norwegian boats attempted, in vain, to oppose the Germans, and were then scuttled in port, where they were captured. Only *B.1* managed to reach Britain, but she could not be used because of her advanced state of disrepair.

The Germans salvaged several of the scuttled boats and recommissioned three: *UC. 1* ex-*B.5, UC. 2* ex-*B.6* and *UC. 3* ex-*A.3*. These were later lost or discarded before 1945. The first two were used for training, the third was hardly ever used.

During the war, the Royal Navy ceded three boats and these operated with success in the North Sea, under the operational control of the Royal Navy and under the orders of the Norwegian government in exile. *Urred* was lost in February 1943.

A Class

A. 2, A. 3, A. 4.
Builder: Krupp, Germaniawerft.
Date: 1914.
Normal displacement: 250 tons surfaced; 340 tons submerged.
Dimensions: 150ft 10in x 16ft 5in x 9ft 6in (46m x 5m x 2.9m).
Machinery: diesel: 2 Krupp; electric: 2.
Maximum power: 700hp surfaced; 380hp submerged.
Maximum speed: 14 knots surfaced; 9 knots submerged.
Torpedo tubes: three 18in (457mm); 1 forward, 2 aft; torpedoes: 4.
Complement: 15.

The oldest submarines in service, at the beginning of the war, and were totally obsolete. Germania-Krupp type, built in Germany.

Fates

date:	location:	boat:	cause (see page 7):
1940	Norway	*A. 2, A. 3, A. 4*	sb

B Class

B. 1, B. 2, B. 3, B. 4, B. 5, B. 6.
Builder: Naval Dockyard, Horten.
Date: 1915–1923/30.
Normal displacement: 420 tons surfaced; 545 tons submerged.
Dimensions: 167ft 3in x 17ft 6in x 11ft 6in (51m x 5.3m x 3.5m).

Machinery: diesel: 2 Sulzer; electric: 2.
Maximum power: 900hp surfaced; 700hp submerged.
Maximum speed: 14.75 knots surfaced; 11 knots submerged.
Torpedo tubes: four 18in (457mm) forward.
Guns: one 3in (76mm).
Complement: 23.

'Holland' type, single hull coastal submarines, built in Norway to an American design. Successful in their day, but obsolete by 1940 .

Fates

date:	location:	boat:	cause (see page 7):
1940	Norway	B. 2, B. 3, B. 4, B. 5, B. 6	sb
1942	Norway	UC. 1 ex-B. 5	r
1945	Norway	UC. 2 ex-B. 6	r

A Norwegian B Class boat, scuttled in May 1940.

Foreign submarines in Norwegian service

U Class (2 units)
Urred ex-*P. 41, Ula* ex-*Varne*, ex-*P. 66*; see Great Britain. Transferred in 1941 and 1943 on completion. *Urred* was not named until 1943, the year she was lost. *Ula* remained in the Royal Norwegian Navy until she was scrapped in 1965.

Fates

date:	location:	boat:	cause (see page 7):
1943	North Sea	Urred	uc
1965		Ula	r

V Class (1 unit)
Utsira ex-*Variance*; see Great Britain. Transferred on completion in 1944. Served with the Royal Norwegian Navy until sent to Germany for breaking up in 1965.

Fate

date:	location:	boat:	cause (see page 7):
1965	Germany	Utsira	r

Poland

On 1 September 1939, the Polish Navy had five submarines belonging to the *Wilk* and *Orzel* Classes: respectively of French and Dutch construction, these boats, intended for use in the Baltic, were all fitted with minelaying equipment. An order had been placed in France for two more boats, but subsequent events prevented their building.

After the Polish defeat, *Orzel* and *Wilk* escaped from the Baltic and made their way to Britain in October: *Rija, Zbik* and *Sep* sought refuge in Sweden where they were interned until 1945.

Operating from bases in Britain, *Orzel* and *Wilk* continued the fight against Germany, under the control of the Royal Navy. *Orzel*, which distinguished herself attacking German shipping during the landings in Norway, was lost in June 1940.

During the war, Great Britain ceded several boats to the Polish Navy, which operated under orders from the government in exile in London: Jastrzab ex-*P.551*, ex-*S.25*, an old boat of the American *S. 1* Class, ceded to the Royal Navy in 1941, and then ceded by them to Poland in the same year; *Sokol* ex-*Urchin*, ex-*P.39* and *Dzik* ex-*P.52*, both British *U* Class, ceded respectively in 1940 and 1943. *Jastrzab* was lost in a collision in the Arctic in May 1942: the other two boats operated with particular success in the Mediterranean and the North Sea and were returned to Great Britain after the war.

Wilk Class

Rijs:
Builder: Ateliers et Chantiers de la Loire, Nantes.
Date: 1929.
Zbik:
Builder: Chantiers Navals Français, Blainville.
Date: 1930.
Wilk.
Builder: Normand, Le Havre.
Date: 1929.
Normal displacement: 980 tons surfaced; 1,250 tons submerged.
Dimensions: 246ft 0in x 18ft 0in x 13ft 0in (79m x 5.4m x 5m).

Machinery: diesel: 2 Vickers-Normand; electric: 2.
Maximum power: 1,800hp surfaced; 1,200hp submerged.
Maximum speed: 14 knots surfaced; 9 knots submerged.
Range: 3,500 miles at 10 knots surfaced; 100 miles at 5 knots submerged.
Torpedo tubes: six 22in (550mm); 2 forward, 4 external traversing; torpedoes: 10.
Wilk: 21in (533mm).
Guns: one 3.9in (100mm); one 40mm.
Mines: 38 in vertical tubes.

French-built Normand-Fenaux type minelaying submarines. *Rijs* and *Zbik* were interned in Sweden throughout the war. *Wilk* escaped to Britain and served under British control for the rest of the war. All three boats returned to Poland and were scrapped in 1957. Diving limit: 264ft (80m).

Zbik, one of the Polish boats interned in Sweden until 1945.

Orzel Class

Orzel, Semp.
Builder: Rotterdam Dry Dock Co.
Date: 1936–1939.
Normal displacement: 1,092 tons surfaced; 1,450 tons submerged.
Dimensions: 275ft 6in x 22ft 0in x 13ft 0in (84m x 6.7m x 4.8m).
Machinery: diesel: 2 Sulzer; electric: 2.

Maximum power: 4,740hp surfaced; 1,000hp submerged.
Maximum speed: 19 knots surfaced; 9 knots submerged.
Torpedo tubes: eight 21in (533mm); 4 forward, 4 external traversing.
Guns: one 4in (102mm) 40-cal; one 40mm.
Mines: 40.
Complement: 56.

Dutch-built minelaying submarines. *Semp* reached Sweden in 1939 and was interned throughout the war. She remained in service in Poland for some time after the war. *Orzel* made an epic voyage to Britain in 1939, and was lost in 1940.

Orzel in 1939.

Fate date:	location:	boat:	cause (see page 7):
1940	North Sea	*Orzel*	uc

Rumania

Rumania declared war on Russia on 22 June 1941. Her naval forces operated with those of the Axis in the Black Sea until 23 August 1944, the date of the Rumanian armistice with the Allies.

The Rumanian *Delfinul*.

During the war, the Rumanian Navy had three submarines commissioned, *Delfinul. Marsouinul* and *Requinul* as well as several ex-Italian midgets, *CB* types, ceded by the Germans after their capture in September 1943. According to several sources, the three boats mentioned above, were still in service at the end of the war.

Delfinul

Marsouinul

Delfinul.
Builder: Quarnaro.
Date: 1926–1931.
Normal displacement: 650 tons surfaced; 900 tons submerged.
Dimensions: 225ft 0in x 19ft 6in x 12ft 0in (68.6m x 5.9m x 3.7m).
Machinery: diesel: 2 Sulzer; electric: 2 .
Maximum power: 1,840hp surfaced.
Maximum speed: 14 knots surfaced; 9 knots submerged.
Torpedo tubes: six 21in (533mm); 4 forward, 2 aft.
Guns: one 4in (102mm) 35-cal.

Italian-built, medium-displacement submarine. Probably survived the war. Although completed in 1931, she was not taken over by the Rumanians until 1936.

Marsouinul (S. 1).
Builder: Galatz Shipbuilding Yard.
Date: 1942.
Normal displacement: 620 tons surfaced.
Dimensions: 216ft 6in x 18ft 4in x 12ft 0in (66m x 5.6m x 3.7m).
Machinery: diesel: 2; electric: 2.
Maximum power: 1,840hp surfaced.
Maximum speed: 16 knots surfaced; 9 knots submerged.
Torpedo tubes: six 21in (533mm).
Guns: one 4in (102mm).

Medium-displacement submarine, built in Rumania to a foreign design. Sources differ as to whether she was Dutch or German. Probably survived the war.

Requinul

Requinul (S. 2).
Builder: Galatz Shipbuilding Yard.
Date: 1942.
Normal displacement: 585 tons surfaced.
Dimensions: 190ft 3in x 16ft 9in x ? (58m x 5.1m x ?).
Machinery: diesel: 2; electric: 2.
Maximum power: 1,840hp surfaced.
Maximum speed: 17 knots surfaced; 9 knots submerged.
Torpedo tubes: four 21in (533mm).
Mines: 40.

Like *Marsouinul,* built to Dutch or German designs. Mine-laying submarine. Probably survived the war.

The Rumanian *Requinul* in dry dock.

Yugoslavia

When Axis troops invaded Yugoslavia in April 1941, almost all of that nation's fleet was captured in port and subsequently incorporated in the Italian Navy. Only a few ships managed to scuttle themselves or reach a British base. Among the latter was *Nebojsa* which passed into control by the Royal Navy and operated in the Mediterranean until the end of the war.

The other three boats of the Yugoslav submarine fleet, *Hrabri,* sister of *Nebojsa, Smeli* and *Osvetnik* were captured by the Italians at Cattaro (Kotor), but only the latter two were put into service, renamed *Bajamonti* and *Rismondo:* later, they were lost. *Hrabri,* antiquated and worn out, was scrapped in 1941.

Hrabri Class

Hrabri, Nebojsa.
Builder: Armstrong, Newcastle.
Date: 1927–1928.
Normal displacement: 975 tons surfaced; 1,164 tons submerged.
Dimensions: 235ft 0in x 23ft 6in x 13ft 2in (72m x 7.3m x 4m).
Machinery: diesel: 2 Vickers; electric: 2.
Maximum power: 2,400hp surfaced; 1,600hp submerged.
Maximum speed: 15.5 knots surfaced; 10 knots submerged.
Torpedo tubes: six 21in (533mm); 4 forward, 2 aft.
Guns: two 4in (102mm).
Complement: 46.

Armstrong-designed developments of the British *L* Class (See Great Britain). They were built, using material left over from wartime contracts that had been cancelled, and followed the later members of the British *L* Classes in having two 4in (102mm) guns (*L. 50* type, none of which, survived the inter-war period).

Fates			cause
date:	location:	boat:	(see page 7):
1941	Mediterranean	*Hrabri*	c
1946	Mediterranean	*Nebojsa*	r

Smeli Class

Smeli, Osvetnik.
Builder: Ateliers et Chantiers de la Loire, Nantes.
Date: 1927–1929.
Normal displacement: 630 tons surfaced; 809 tons submerged.
Dimensions: 227ft 0in x 18ft 0in x 14ft 0in (66.5m x 5.4m x 3.8m).
Machinery: diesel: 2 M.A.N.; electric: 2 Compagnie Générale Electrique.
Maximum power: 1,480hp surfaced; 1,100hp submerged.
Maximum speed: 14.5 knots surfaced; 9 knots submerged.
Torpedo tubes: six 22in (550mm); 4 forward, 2 aft.
Guns: one 3.9in (100mm) 40-cal; one 13.2mm.
Complement: 45.

French Simonot design. They had three periscopes, and an excellent diving time of 35 seconds. Maximum depth: 200ft (60m); fuel load: 25 tons. See Italy for their 1941 refit.

Fates

date:	location:	boat:	cause (see page 7):
1941	Yugoslavia	*Smeli, Osvetnik*	c
1943	Italy	*Bajamonti*	sb
		Rismondo	c–b

The three Yugoslav boats (from the left, they are *Osvetnik*, *Smeli* and *Hrabri*) captured by the Italians in April 1941.

Neutral navies

A few of the smaller navies which were not involved in the war, owned small numbers of submarines. All except Spain and Sweden, obtained submarines from Britain, America, Germany, France, Holland, Japan or Italy. Even Spain had built most of her submarines to foreign designs. Most of the submarines listed below were sisters or near sisters of boats in service in the navies of the countries that built them.

Table 28: Submarines in service with neutral navies during the Second World War

Country:	Number in Class:	Built:	Type:	Year of commissioning:	Country:	Number in Class:	Built:	Type:	Year of commissioning:
Argentina	3	Italy	*Mameli* type	1932	Sweden	3	Sweden	*Najad* Class (sea-going type)	1942
Chile	3	Britain	*Oberon* type	1929		3	Sweden	*Delfinen* Class (sea-going type)	1935
	6	U.S.A.	*H* Class (originally built for Britain, but delivered to Chile)	1917		3	Sweden	*Draken* Class (sea-going type)	1926–30
						1	Sweden	Minelayer	1925
Peru	4	U.S.A.	*Elco* design	1928		3	Sweden	*Bävern* Class (sea-going type)	1922
Portugal	3	Britain	Vickers design	1935		9	Sweden	*V* Class (coastal)	1942–5
Siam (Thailand)	4	Japan		1937		2	Sweden	*Hajen* Class (coastal)	1918
					Turkey	2	Britain	British *S* Class type (see page 110)	1942
Spain	3	Spain	Spanish Admiralty design	1944–5					
	5	Spain	American *Elco* design (one other lost during Civil War)	1929		3	Germany	Germania type (1 lost 1942)	1939
						1	Spain	German design, Dutch equipment	1932
	1	Spain	American *Elco* type (one other lost during Civil War and one scrapped)	1916		1	Italy	Bernadis type	1931
						2	Netherlands	German design	1927

Index

SUBMARINES
OF WORLD WAR TWO

Submarines of World War Two describes all the classes of submarine deployed by the combatant nations during the war – from midgets to large U-cruisers – and includes also projected and experimental designs. For each class of submarine, the principal technical characteristics are presented: construction, displacement, dimensions, speed, range, operational depth, fuel load, armament and complement, together with a brief history of wartime operations and the fate of each member of the class.

Over 400 illustrations enable the reader to compare the appearance and characteristics of all the submarine classes that took part in the Second World War. Also included is a brief outline of the evolution of the submarine and submarine warfare – including the interplay of wartime experience, design improvement and tactical innovation – placing the subject in its true historical perspective.

In one extensively illustrated volume, here are comprehensive details of the 2,500 submarines of all nations in service or on the stocks between 1939 and 1945.

Cover photograph: a crowded tower on a surfaced
Type VII U-boat, 1941 (AKG London)

£20.00 PRINTED IN GREAT BRITAIN

ISBN 1-85409-532-3

9 781854 095329